Howard Cosell speaks out on:

The National Football League:

"Some things about the NFL never change. It's still a monopoly."

Boxing:

"If it can't be cleaned up and regulated, then it shouldn't be permitted."

Sports and Sex:

"If you're going to make millions of dollars in sports and be the role model for America's youth, you'd better conform to the 'hero standard' or pay the consequences."

"... devilishly interesting—even fascinating."

— *The Blade* (Toledo, OH)

"Cosell's latest critique of the American sports machine is amusing, thought-provoking and worth reading."

— *The Trenton Times*

Howard Cosell speaks out on:

Sports in College:

"Many of our college athletes [are] illiterates parading as college students."

Women in the Locker Room:

"New England Patriots owner Victor Kiam made a total fool of himself with his flip reaction to some of his players harassing and abusing reporter Lisa Olson in the locker room. Cincinnati Bengals coach Sam Wyche came off as a total idiot when he banned female reporters."

"Howard's best book."

—Karl Malden

"... a feisty performance...."

— *Vancouver Province*

Howard Cosell speaks out on:

The Pete Rose Scandal:

"There's little doubt that Pete Rose was a factor in the death of Bart Giamatti."

Money and Baseball:

"Where is the sanity in sports? Here is [Darryl Strawberry], a player with great potential, but at this stage of his career, to pay him money worthy of the greats of the game is ridiculous. With today's sports salaries being what they are, maybe Ted Williams, Joe DiMaggio, Willie Mays, Hank Aaron or Mickey Mantle *would* be deserving of this kind of remuneration, but a Canseco or a Strawberry at $5 million? Preposterous!"

WHAT'S WRONG WITH SPORTS

HOWARD COSELL
WITH SHELBY WHITFIELD

POCKET BOOKS

New York   London   Toronto   Sydney   Tokyo   Singapore

POCKET BOOKS, a division of Simon & Schuster Inc.
1230 Avenue of the Americas, New York, NY 10020

Copyright © 1991 by Howard Cosell and Shelby Whitfield

ISBN: 0-671-76919-7

First Pocket Books printing May 1992

10 9 8 7 6 5 4 3 2 1

POCKET and colophon are registered trademarks of
Simon & Schuster Inc.

Cover art by Roger Sandler/Black Star

Printed in the U.S.A.

For my beloved Emmy, my bride of 46½ years, the greatest person of my life, my daughters Jill and Hilary, and my five grandchildren—Justin, Jared, Caitlen, Colin, and Payton. Also for the memory of Bart Giamatti, former baseball commissioner, Larry Fleischer, NBAPA ex-executive director, and Elton Rule, ex-ABC president, three giants of their professions who left legacies of which we can all be proud.

CONTENTS

	Foreword by Al Davis	xi
One	Addicted to Jocks	1
Two	Clubbed Fingers and Unholy Alliances	7
Three	Greatest Loss	21
Four	Athletic Corruption and Bogus Education	31
Five	Hypocrites and Hucksters	42
Six	Agents and Propositions	61
Seven	From Campanis to the Greek to Kiam to Wyche	91
Eight	Gaming Cancer Runs Amok	126
Nine	Alvin Pete Purged; "Too Tall" Anointed	162
Ten	Duly Adjudicated Illegal Monopoly	177
Eleven	Scabs and Court Fights	185
Twelve	Millionaires in Short Pants	218
Thirteen	Community Rape; Franchise Chess Revisited	230

Contents

Fourteen	Limburger Smells Better	245
Fifteen	Winfield Cleansed; Dowd and Fay Botch Boss's Execution	269
Sixteen	Two Shocks on Christmas Day	297
Seventeen	Sex, Lies, and Videotape	311
Eighteen	Cocaine, Steroids, and Bible Belt Urine	327
Nineteen	Footprints Cast in Stone	346
Twenty	No One's Lived a Better Life	357
Twenty-one	My Lost Treasure	365
	Index	367

FOREWORD

by Al Davis

So Howard Cosell has written another book! When I
initially heard the news, I had to wonder why he was writing
again. He certainly didn't need the money. Howard made
millions during his career, and he invested wisely.

Besides, Howard had already written three books, two of
which were major best-sellers. His last book, *I Never Played
the Game,* was on *The New York Times* list for twenty-three
weeks, and as is usual with Cosell, it created a storm of
controversy. Another Cosell book would be likely to ruffle
many more feathers, and at seventy-three years of age, does
Howard really want that?

The answer, I suspect, is that not only does Howard want
it, he needs it. The Cosellian ego cries out for a forum from
which he can express his views about what had happened in
sports in the six years since his last book.

It is clear to me that Howard still has the fire that I have
always admired so much. His critics will claim that he's a
bitter old man; some will say that his time has passed.
Absurd! Rubbish! Howard remains as sharp as a tack; his
mind is the same as it has always been—a steel trap.
Howard hasn't changed one iota.

Howard Cosell long ago admitted to being arrogant,
pompous, obnoxious, vain, cruel, verbose, and a show-off.

In our association of almost twenty years, I have found him to be all those things. But I have also found him to be inordinately intelligent, humane, understanding, warm, and caring, too!

My wife, Carol, suffered a massive heart attack in 1979 and lapsed into a coma. Doctors gave her little chance to live, and expecting the worst, I moved into the hospital with her. During those trying months when Carol made a miraculous recovery, Howard was always available when I needed him for support. His comments, as well as those of others, on such televised events as "Monday Night Football," resulted in thousands of cards, letters, and prayers for Carol. This personal concern, this generosity of spirit—this is the Howard Cosell, the person, I know.

In many ways Cosell is a paradox of a man, a fact that serves to make sense of the *TV Guide* poll conducted at the height of Howard's career, which found him to be the most liked, and at the same time the most disliked, sportscaster in America.

Perhaps the fire that burns brightest in Howard's makeup is his penchant for championing the cause of the underdog. Historically, if he was not supporting a young Muhammad Ali in his fight against the military draft, it was Curt Flood against baseball's reserve clause, the AFL against the NFL, the ABA against the NBA, or the USFL against the NFL.

In many cases his stances have been unpopular and have prompted hate mail, death threats, and vendettas undertaken by certain media representatives. Yet Howard has never wavered from his convictions, and his family has been incredibly supportive. His main strength for so much of his life came from Emmy, his feisty friend, companion, and loving wife of forty-six years.

Emmy's iron constitution and determination are best demonstrated by an incident that took place in May of 1988. She was suffering from lung cancer and had lost thirty pounds, going from 120 down to 90. One day after her surgery—which had been touch and go—I visited her at Mt. Sinai Hospital in New York City, walking into her room with great concern.

The first thing Emmy said after opening her eyes and looking at me was "When in the hell are you going to get a quarterback!"

When Emmy died recently, Howard lost his best friend, his greatest fan, and his only true boss. She was a wonderful and remarkable woman, and all of us will miss her. And, God help us, who will keep Howard in line?

History will reflect that Howard Cosell was easily the dominant sportscaster of all time, and certainly the most famous. Howard, along with others, made TV's "Monday Night Football" an institution, and everyone knows that it's not the same without him. I vividly remember an article by Tony Kornheiser of *The Washington Post* when Howard left "Monday Night Football." Kornheiser wrote, "Love him or hate him, crave him or curse him, Howard Cosell did more to popularize sports on television than anyone else. *Sports Illustrated*'s Frank Deford says of Cosell, 'He *is* sports in our time.'"

Perhaps the most impressive quote from Kornheiser's article came from Dick Enberg, the highly respected NBC sportscaster, who said, "Howard opened a door that fifteen or twenty years ago was well locked. Then you took the company line. If you thought a call was wrong, you didn't say so. You said, 'Well, the umpire was closer to it than I was.' You didn't criticize the calls, the players, or the organization. Howard was the first to be critical and journalistic."

Enberg continued, "Now, after you unlock that door, there's a long, long hallway to walk. Howard's at the end of it—the rest of us don't walk that far. I'm not a critical broadcaster. I'm grateful that I can say critical things, and all of us should be thankful to Howard for that. It's a discredit to our profession that we haven't given him his due respect. I wish my colleagues would say, 'He was a giant.'"

Over the past twenty years, Howard has agreed with me on many issues, but there have also been many times when we disagreed, and many times when he has been critical of me, both in private and in public. The best example was my decision to move the Raiders from Oakland to Los Angeles. As a lawyer, Howard felt strongly that I had solid legal grounds to move the franchise, but I wish I had a dollar for every time that he stated that I was morally wrong to move the club, that I had a moral obligation to stay in Oakland. He chastised me then and no doubt will chastise me again. Fan support and fan loyalty are important to a football club, and the fans in Oakland were supportive and loyal, but that alone could not make me competitive, and I had good and valid reasons for moving. Certainly the overwhelming victories in court by the Raiders were testimony to that.

Cosell could have been a Raider if he were just a little tougher. Like the Raiders, who have won three Super Bowl championships and possess the best team won-loss record in the history of pro sports over the last three decades, Howard is a winner. He would have looked good in silver and black, and the skull-and-crossbones patch is an ideal insignia for the Cosell personality. Our team mottos are "Commitment to Excellence" and "Pride and Poise." Howard is certainly long in those departments.

I told Howard when he started this project, "Just write, Howie baby, just write. The readers will win!"

CHAPTER ONE

Addicted to Jocks

There is a harsh truth in America today. Sports have become a great emotional outlet and escape for the country. To millions, involvement in the sports world is a fantasylike experience in which the average American can forget his everyday troubles. Sports have become a necessity in the lives of the American people, and the ramifications of this need threaten to invade every avenue of American life.

It's no simple matter. Sport as we know it today involves labor law, sociology, and politics. The industry, amateur and professional, has become so greedy and massive that it has lost perspective and suffered a decline in values.

I share this feeling with Prof. Gary Fox, a knowledgeable and respected teacher at Miami University of Ohio. Professor Fox has dedicated much of his professional life to sport and its role in society. Another consequential American who shares these views is Russell Baker, the nation's leading essayist and satirist. These men view the industry from afar and with proper focus.

To begin with, look at the monies involved, monies that are paid to satisfy the public's apparently insatiable appetite for sports. As out of hand as it may seem already, there are signs that we may be seeing only the beginning of this phenomenon.

Examples. In basketball, the average player's salary in the NBA is now $1 million per season; Patrick Ewing of the New York Knicks was the first professional athlete to command a salary of $4 million per season, and the following year, John "Hot Rod" Williams of the Cleveland Cavaliers, not a superstar, inked a shocking $26.5-million contract that called for a mind-boggling $9 million in the first season. The deal made Williams the highest-paid player in professional team sports, and his contract stipulates that should he be traded in the first year of the deal his salary will jump to $12 million. A merchandising genius named David Stern, the commissioner of the NBA, has managed to secure for the organization almost a billion dollars a year for rights to carry the NBA games on television and cable. The commissioner was rewarded with a five-year, $27.5-million contract, which included a $15-million bonus, making him the highest-paid commissioner in the history of sports.

And the new National Football League television package calls for $3.2 billion, the richest sports television contract of all time. The NFL players didn't wait long to claim some of that money. San Francisco 49er quarterback Joe Montana signed a $13-million contract that rewarded the two-time Super Bowl MVP with a salary of $4.5 million in 1990, making him the highest-paid player in NFL history.

In the National Hockey League—a largely regional sport that does not have a national TV contract—Los Angeles Kings center Wayne Gretzky, arguably the best player of all time, has a contract that calls for $4 million in compensation for one season.

In baseball, when Peter Ueberroth was commissioner, he negotiated a $1.5-billion package for TV and cable rights; the average player's salary in baseball is in excess of $650,000 a year, and within three months following the 1989 season, clubs paid players almost $22 million in signing bonuses; in addition, the $3-million-per-season player became a reality, and the $2-million-per-year player became almost commonplace.

In boxing, where the monies paid have always been staggering, the Leonard-Duran "fight" in Las Vegas produced over $7 million for the punchless Duran, and over $15 million for the punched-out Leonard. After that fiasco,

Bob "Honest Bob" Arum—"the Apostle of Apartheid"—said that he would promote more Duran fights. Obviously, as long as the public embraces "seniors boxing," it will continue, and the bucks will roll in.

Imagine Foreman pitted against Cooney for millions of dollars, or Tyson against anyone for millions! One can go on and on. P.T. Barnum was right: there's a sucker born every minute, and with the gullible boxing public apparently ever ready to buy it, and with the advent of pay-TV, boxing purses may be headed for the stratosphere.

In another unsettling development, it is now urged that athletes be paid for performing while in college. Even the righteous *New York Times* has joined in this chorus.

And it's not only in the area of money that I see cause for alarm. In football, players have routinely played while using painkillers and steroids, or even while suffering from broken bones. Lives are literally at stake, but the public doesn't seem to care.

Racism in sports, despite many denials, remains open and obvious.

Drugs and drug use also are rampant in all areas. Drug-related deaths are no longer unusual in sports. Restricted drug testing is accepted now, but one need only look at Lawrence Taylor of the New Jersey Giants to know that the effectiveness of this testing is suspect. Taylor has written openly in his own book about how he beat drug-testing procedures by the substitution of somebody else's urine—clean urine—for his own. Yet the public, with the explicit aid of the Giants management, continues to exalt Taylor as a hero.

As a matter of plain fact, today there is no business organization in America more powerful than the National Football League, as demonstrated by the strength of its congressional lobby, and by the help given it by the judiciary in recent favorable decisions.

Unfortunately, it can also be argued that no single business organization in America is less concerned with the public's interest than the National Football League. As cities vie for franchises and new stadiums are built at considerable public expense, team owners and operators continue to be ready to move wherever the money is.

3

What about the new international football league? Is this really a device for the extension of the National Football League monopoly (which was found to be illegal)? Or is there a real public demand all over the world for professional football?

What about the proposed new baseball league, eagerly embraced by the players' union and touted by promoters, some of whom are associated with the ownership of casinos and racetracks? Is there a need for this, or is it merely a bargaining ploy, something pursued by publicity seekers? Talk of a new league may have been initiated to prod major league baseball into expansion, something the National League has done by adding two new teams at a ridiculous expansion fee of $95 million per club.

It's estimated that sport in America—amateur, college, and professional combined—is a $50-billion-a-year business. That gross revenue is up from $47.2 billion in 1988. Sonny Reizner, director of gaming for the new Rio Hotel in Las Vegas and one of the country's leading authorities on the subject, estimates that between $41 billion and $51 billion is wagered, both legally and illegally, each year on sports in America. It's incredible that about as much is wagered on sports as is spent by the sports industry itself. Despite all denials, the National Football League is one organization that has encouraged and protected the gambling industry. I'll address this in detail later in the book.

While all of these issues are troublesome enough, perhaps the most sickening issue in sports today is the increasing corruption in college athletics, and the impact that it has on our educational systems.

There are many other issues that need to be discussed as well, such as the commercialization of sports, strikes, scab teams, union-busting, AIDS in sports, and so on. Who is there to deal with all of these matters, with the question of what is happening to American education because of the distorted emphasis on sports?

And in addition to the issues, there are so many personalities to be dealt with—Pete Rose, Pete Rozelle, Bart Giamatti, Fay Vincent, Lawrence Taylor, Billy Martin, Donald Trump, John McEnroe, and George Steinbrenner, to name just a few.

In the midst of this confusion, there are the unholy alliances that continue more strongly now than ever before, and that have a deleterious effect on sports in general. Examples are the alliances between the print media and the sports operators, between print and the broadcast networks, and print and the ever-growing cable outlets.

In an age when a majority of people get their news from television rather than print, in sports—in an apparent contradiction—print has a grip on television presentations as never before. Newspapers and networks work closely together on such things as rankings, polls, and broadcast listings. It is as though they work in concert on the sports promotions and productions. Television producers and announcers are most responsive to critics and sportswriters than ever before. Broadcasters should be totally independent of the print medium and should in no way be subservient to any sports publication. These problems are particularly apparent with regard to *USA Today*. Witness, too, the emergence of the competing sports daily, *The National,* sparked by Mexican money.

And then there's the question of whether or not many of the people who represent sports in print are even qualified by way of background, education, and experience to deal with matters involving labor law, medicine, sociology, or politics, and all of the complex, interrelated matters that govern the conduct of sports in this country today.

Maybe above all, there is the question of whether or not the sports broadcast industry, structured the way it is now, will ever allow these issues to be discussed openly and truthfully. Certainly there are people qualified to delve into some of these areas, to deal with questions and key personalities, but would they not risk forfeiting their livelihood if they tried to do so?

All of these matters bear upon why I have decided to write still another book, unfettered as I fortunately am by ties to the various leagues and clubs, operators, networks, or anybody else.

I have carefully chosen as my colleague in writing this book Shelby Whitfield, the director and executive producer of ABC Radio Sports. Shelby's office is just a few feet down the hall from mine. He has been a sports broadcaster for more than twenty-five years, was the TV-radio broadcaster for the old Washington Senators, and was a respected broadcast journalist for the Associated Press for seven years before joining ABC. He knows the broadcast industry, and by working with me on a daily basis, he is intimately familiar with my views. He has written his own forthright and successful book, *Kiss It Goodbye,* the story of the Senators under Bob Short and Ted Williams.

There are no secrets about this book or about my ideas. It is being written with the knowledge of Cap Cities/ABC executives Aaron Daniels, the former president of the ABC Radio Networks (who retired in 1990 and was succeeded by Bob Callahan), and Bob Benson, vice president for ABC Radio News. They, like other ABC executives, don't agree with all my views, but to their credit, they respect my right to express them.

The time has come, the walrus said, to speak of many things. And while I do not pretend that I have a monopoly on brains and talent, nor do I pretend to be the world's only honest man, I believe that after a lifetime of work in sports I have earned the right to review important current events in sports from my point of view.

And based upon the impressive commercial success of my former books, *Cosell by Cosell, Like It Is,* and *I Never Played the Game,* I have every reason to believe that the American public will read this book as readily as they have the others.

Keep in mind that it is primarily an overview, presenting my opinions on the issues and personalities since my last book was published six years ago.

So here we go again. I am still not playing the games. And as Jim Brown said in his challenging book, *Out of Bounds,* I have chosen my adversaries not because of their weakness, but because of their power.

<u>CHAPTER</u> TWO

Clubbed Fingers and Unholy Alliances

At ten minutes before ten o'clock on the night of August 31, 1989, the ring of the telephone awakened Emmy and me from a sound sleep. As is normally the case, we had retired to bed at eight P.M.

I shook the sleep from my head and answered, "Hello?"

"Hello, Howard. This is Sam Donaldson. How are you?"

"Emmy and I were asleep, Sam. What's up?"

Sam went on to explain that he was going on the air live in ten minutes with "Prime Time Live" and requested that I give him some questions to ask one of his guests, New York Yankees owner George Steinbrenner, who would be interviewed live from one of his ships at his Tampa shipyard.

Donaldson said he wanted pertinent questions about Pete Rose and Bart Giamatti, about the possible sale of the Yankees, and about George's worsening relationship with the fans; he wanted a whole array of information.

I was dumbfounded!

"Sam, I can't believe this," I replied. "I haven't talked to you for a year and a half. I'm never invited on any of the ABC news shows anymore, but you are calling me for questions." I gave Sam a quick brush-off, but no questions.

There was a time when I was frequently invited to appear on ABC shows such as "Nightline" and "This Week with

David Brinkley" to discuss timely sports issues. Then, with no explanation, those invitations ceased. In the meantime, the other network news programs continue to deluge me with requests to discuss major sports stories. Apparently someone at my old television home has decided I am persona non grata.

Unable to get back to sleep after Sam's call, I turned on the TV set to see how Donaldson was going to handle Steinbrenner.

It was a totally disjointed show, of which Cher was the star. She wore a horrible little nonoutfit. She was almost nude.

When Donaldson got to Steinbrenner, George was at his best and Sam couldn't really get anywhere with him. Frankly I don't know why Sam had him on the program.

At one point, George said, "Sam, what are you talking to me for? Why don't you show Cher again?"

The live audience roared its approval.

The whole interview with Steinbrenner was pathetic. Here was Sam Donaldson, a nationally respected and highly paid reporter, supposedly fearless, having made his reputation by hollering at and abusing presidents, and he was totally unprepared for an interview ten minutes before airtime on a live, nationally televised news program. Lacking the depth and the knowledge to handle the interview was one thing, but being totally unprepared was another. The incident points out the shoddiness and increasing lack of professionalism in broadcast journalism.

Another excellent example of the current sorry state of the industry, and the need for proper reportage of sports, occurred on the night of Pearl Harbor Day, December 7, 1989. As a favor to the Friars Club, of which I am a long-term member who has been honored with roasts by both the New York and Hollywood clubs, I agreed to take part in a special boxing program.

The club had a fight-night party, with the closed-circuit telecast of the Leonard-Duran "fight" piped into its Manhattan premises. A record crowd of nearly five hundred filled the three levels of the club to watch the contest on TV screens.

It was a sophisticated gathering that included many

celebrities. Among them were actors Anthony Quinn, Robert Wagner, Raul Julia, and Charles Durning, comedians Pat Cooper and Robert Klein, and the ex–world middleweight champ Rocky Graziano, who six months later suffered a stroke and died.

Before the telecast started, I manned the club's public address system, simulating a fight pre-scene broadcast as if I were at ringside for ABC Sports: "Live from the spanking new, incredible Mirage Hotel in Las Vegas, Nevada, Steve Wynn's greatest wonder, this is Howard Cosell reporting."

After I finished the usual introductions, the place went crazy with applause.

I said, "I want you to listen to me carefully, because these are the only words of truth, unfettered, that you will hear tonight. After my words, you will get a night of promotion from the boxing fraternity." I reminded them that I was the best-qualified person in America to tell them what they were about to see.

"Nobody knows these men, nobody, as I do." And I went through the fact that I had called the first Leonard-Duran fight, broadcast June 20, 1980, from Olympic Stadium in Montreal, Canada. Then I explained that some five months later, in the New Orleans Superdome, I called their second fight.

I also reminded them that I introduced Ray Leonard to the whole world at the Montreal Summer Olympics of 1976. I recounted that Roone Arledge, executive producer of ABC Sports, had called me and said that he needed a star for the games. (It turned out, of course, that the games produced three stars—Nadia Comaneci, Bruce Jenner, and Sugar Ray Leonard. Ironically, all three were to encounter disarray in their private lives in the decade just concluded.) Sugar Ray fit the bill, with his Ali shuffle and his flashing personality. With him at the time was Thomas "Sarge" Johnson, the man who created Leonard as a fighter, and a man who died tragically in a plane crash near Warsaw. Sarge Johnson never received credit, but it was he who really created Sugar Ray Leonard.

So I went through all of that, and the crowd at the Friars loved it. They applauded, and Durning, with whom I had made a TV movie, ran over to hug me.

Then I said, "What you are about to see should not have been licensed. These men shouldn't be permitted to fight. It is a creation of promoter Bob Arum, 'Honest Bob' Arum, a graduate of the Harvard School of Law, more dangerous by far than Don King, because he is a brilliant man intellectually, and King is not. King is a good promoter, that's all."

Then I told the Friars crowd that the fight would be broadcast with an accompanying commentary by a bastion of "journalists": Marvin Hagler, almost too absurd to mention; Gil Clancy, a member of the boxing fraternity and an apologist for boxing, a man whose conflicts of interest (as boxing trainer, manager, matchmaker, and commentator) are notorious; and Tim Ryan and Al Bernstein, two commentators of little significance. I warned this crowd not to expect this foursome to tell it like it is.

Furthermore, I warned them to expect a pitiful fight because both men were finished. Moreover, I explained that the fact that Leonard couldn't put away Thomas Hearns when he was helpless in the fifth round of their June 1989 match was proof positive that Sugar Ray could no longer punch. The crowd received a perfect briefing, one they couldn't get anywhere else in the world.

Then we sat back and watched the miserable spectacle. Leonard was a shell of his former self; better moves have been seen in aerobics classes. Duran was a disgrace, pitiful, but still Leonard couldn't finish him. Roberto's best efforts were a couple of head butts. It was obvious that neither of these men could fight anymore. As a result, the fight was a total joke.

And Messrs. Hagler, Clancy, Ryan, and Bernstein did not tell it like it was. The promoters would never permit them to report accurately that both fighters had badly eroded skills and should not have been in the ring.

After the sordid affair, I was a hero with the crowd at the Friars. They were talking about it for days. I had told it like it was before it even happened. And my point is, sports commentators have an obligation to report events accurately. The poor suckers across the country who plunked down their thirty bucks to watch this fight on pay-TV didn't get anything close to accuracy from the so-called announcers.

Another example and further documentation that the

reportage of sports-related matters in this country is at an absolute nadir occurred on September 5, 1989. In one of the most astounding cases of irresponsible journalism encountered in my lifetime, the New York *Daily News* printed a story that defied belief.

A full front-page headline and photo of Bart Giamatti screamed the "news" that the late baseball commissioner, who had died of a heart attack four days earlier, had been warned of his impending death by a physician. The cover page teased a full-page story by columnist Mike Lupica in the sports section.

The main thrust of the story was that a senior attending surgeon at Memorial Sloan-Kettering Hospital in Manhattan, Dr. William G. Cahan, had seen Giamatti on television attending a Mets game on the afternoon of August 20. Dr. Cahan, from watching a closeup of a hand on the TV screen, concluded that Commissioner Giamatti had a condition known as clubbing of the fingers. The fingertips expand and deflect the nails, causing them to curve up from the sides and the front. It was the opinion of Dr. Cahan that the clubbing condition was an indication that Giamatti was seriously ill and had little time to live.

Dr. Cahan dispatched a letter of warning to Dr. Bobby Brown, president of the American League, and asked that Brown pass it on to Giamatti. Instead, Brown discussed it with Bart on August 31, ironically enough, one day before the commissioner died of the heart attack.

The amazing part of the story was that Bart Giamatti did not have clubbing of the fingers. Dr. Cahan's mistaken diagnosis was based on having seen the hand of the person sitting behind Giamatti, a baseball security person who had accompanied the commissioner to the game.

The *Daily News* and Mike Lupica, now a columnist for *The National,* had proceeded with their blockbuster front-page story without first checking with anyone to see if Giamatti did indeed have clubbed fingers.

To further discredit that story, certain medical authorities disputed the printed facts, claiming that clubbing of the fingers is not related to heart attacks. One of those was Dr. Leonard Stone, a noted cardiologist and associate clinical professor of medicine at Mt. Sinai Hospital and Medical

Center in New York, who said that even if Giamatti had clubbing, it would not have been a manifestation of a condition causing a heart attack. Dr. Stone said clubbing of the fingers could be a symptom of any number of disorders —including congenital heart diseases—that would *not,* according to Stone, cause an attack: a variety of chronic lung diseases such as emphysema and lung cancer, and certain inflammatory bowel diseases. Or it could be merely an inherited, congenital condition. It would not have related to Giamatti's condition, as it had nothing to do with cardiovascular distress. The man whose fingers Dr. Cahan did see on TV, Bill Carbone, says that his condition is inherited, and that his doctor tells him he is in no medical danger.

It's interesting how Mike Lupica got the bogus clubbed-fingers story. Writer Gay Talese tried to give it to columnist Pete Hamill, who told Talese that he wasn't interested but suggested that he talk to Lupica. Little Mike, who has writing ability, bought the story hook, line, and sinker.

To compound the journalistic felony, both the *Daily News* and Mike Lupica failed to give a proper retraction or correction to the story. The erroneous story caused considerable grief and distress to the late commissioner's family, but according to current commissioner Fay Vincent, who was appalled by the article, neither Lupica nor a representative of the *Daily News* ever apologized to Giamatti's widow, Toni, or to any other family member.

I find this story beyond belief and one that leaves an indelible mark against journalism as a whole. The *Daily News* will claim that writer Talese, a friend of Dr. Cahan's, is a very reliable writer, but that doesn't excuse someone from checking the facts. The fact remains that the *Daily News,* the paper with the largest circulation in the greatest city in the world, printed, in front-page fashion, a story that was erroneous. It's a classic example of a sportswriter lacking the proper qualifications to delve into matters related to sports other than scores and locker room talk. But what's totally mind-boggling about this piece was the fact that one of the basic rules of journalism, checking simple facts, was ignored.

So there you have three glaring examples—the Sam Donaldson incident, the reportage of the Leonard-Duran fight, and the Giamatti clubbed-fingers story—of the lack of true journalism in connection with sports in our country today.

The hard fact is that sports and sports-related issues have long been treated with little serious regard by both the electronic and print media.

For many years, I have been vocal about the lack of professionalism in sportswriting. Unfortunately there is no reason to change this opinion. Indeed, I see reason to reiterate it. The petulance, the hysteria, the rage, and the vitriol that permeate too much of sportswriting and sports sections in this country are shameful indications of just how absent objectivity and professionalism are. Sports pages to this day remain a testament to jealousy, public infighting among supposed colleagues, bitterness, and protection of turf. Only in the Toy Department of Life, the sports section, is this tolerated in America.

In essence, a treasured privilege is being abused, a trust is being misused, and responsibilities are being shirked. The sports media in this country is too often derelict in its duty, the First Amendment is being manipulated, and the American people suffer.

But America seems to have a double standard when it comes to journalism. The kind of reporting the public expects and demands from newsmen and newswomen, whether in print or network news broadcasts, is too often absent in sports. It's sad, but the public seems willing to accept this.

Educated in the simplistic and erroneous view that sports is just a lot of fun and games, the public is encouraged to believe that sports reporters have a less serious job than their news counterparts, that wins, losses, and the results of polls are all sports reporters need to supply. This is not true. The public should have the truth about many complicated issues in sports today.

And while an adversarial relationship between the reporter and the subject is the foundation on which newspeople operate—and the foundation upon which freedom of the press operates—in sports, this adversarial quality is sorely lacking. Instead, reporters too often are the buddies, the mouthpieces, for the sports owners and operators they are covering; too often they function as worshiping handmaidens of the athletes they interview.

And still too many reporters accept favors in the form of lodging, travel, tickets, meals, drinks, and other gratuities from clubs, leagues, and operators. It is a field rife with conflict of interest, with favoritism, and with ties to local teams by local reporters.

Scandals that can't be ignored are reported, then quickly forgotten. Too often they are treated like aberrations. Surely it does not take a genius to detect a pattern in the increasing number of scandals and unpleasant incidents in sports.

The plain hard truth is that there are few voices left in sports in America willing to buck the powerful establishment and speak the truth. It does not have to be this way and it should not be this way.

Let me make clear at this point, however, that there are always individual exceptions to the rule—reporters who stretch beyond the prevailing standards of mediocrity, who do honor to their profession, and who have not forgotten that to be a journalist in America is a privilege, a trust, and a responsibility.

Few sportswriters ask the hard questions. A rare and delightful exception is David Kindred, a former columnist for *The Washington Post* and *The Atlanta Constitution,* now a columnist and associate editor for *The National.*

Kindred, one of the brilliant sportswriters in the country, who lost out in a bid to become editor in chief of *The Atlanta Constitution* and in what I considered a gamble accepted a job with *The National,* admitted in a conversation with me, "Our value system in journalism has gone so astray that we can make a hero out of a little lowlife like Pete Rose. I am not absolving myself here, because like others, I glorified Rose, godded him up, as a player. I always disliked him as a person, but as a player, I thought he was inspiring. Where was the media during all the years the Rose scandal was festering? A lot of media people had to know the guy was gambling, everyone knew he was a big horse player."

Kindred continued, "In the sports world, we overglorify the personalities and don't subject them to the normal moral code."

One person who more than anyone else may have recognized this country's problem with sports journalism was the late commissioner of baseball, A. Bartlett Giamatti.

He recognized that the media was paying increased attention to sports. Newspapers were devoting more column inches to sports than in the past; they were hiring extra reporters to give double and triple coverage to local teams. Both print and broadcast media were hyping the reporters they call experts, meant to provide the inside view on the business of sports, or critiques of television sports coverage and television sports broadcasters. He knew full well that while the number of reporters and the volume of coverage were on the increase, it unfortunately did not follow that the same held true for quality.

Bart Giamatti came to baseball from academia; he was the president of Yale University. He was a man of intellect, depth, honesty, and passion, and he tried to keep sports— and the people who write about it on a daily basis—honest as well.

In April of 1988, when Bart was president of the National League, he delivered a powerful speech to the American Society of Newspaper Editors in Washington, D.C. I read Dr. Giamatti's speech and found it to be written with wit, eloquence, and style. But I am not sure that his audience, mostly men, wished to be held up to such scrutiny, especially by someone who found them to be so terribly wanting. Here is an excerpt of Dr. Giamatti's address:

> My concern, which is very real, springs from an impression rather than from data. It is the very strong impression that editors generally ignore the sports section in the sense . . . that the same set of editorial standards—for accuracy, for competence, for imposing standards of all kinds for rewriting and editing— are simply not applied consistently or rigorously to the sports sections as they are applied to all other sections of the paper.

Dr. Giamatti then cites the coverage of the labor dispute between the Players Association and the baseball owners regarding the conspiracy not to sign free agents. Dr. Giamatti faults newspaper editors and sportswriters for not using the word "alleged" prior to the words "conspiracy" and "collusion" in many of the stories filed, until such time as the arbitrator or judge had ruled on the case, and collusion or conspiracy was proven.

Again, from Dr. Giamatti's speech:

Do you really think that if it was said by a union that owners or CEOs who'd compete in any other industry had "colluded," that you would have left out the word "alleged" before there was a definitive ruling? . . . Of course not. Not if it was unproven. Why is this story different? Because it is baseball, or sports, and therefore not serious? It is a matter of law and due process. Is that serious? Why aren't sports—as a business—as serious as crime or computers or anything else?

Let us say there is a strike in baseball, as there was, alas, in football. Who will cover it? Why, the beat writers and the columnists. Do you have any idea how completely unfit your fine sportswriters are to cover a labor story? . . . If all the schoolteachers in your city go on strike, should the paper send the part-time or the full-time education writer?

. . . then why are the sportswriters covering the financial or legal or labor issues of this major set of major industries that make up professional (and some "amateur") sports? . . . It is because this is sports, the Toy Department. The rest of the newspaper is serious; this is play. The rest of the newspaper is school; this is recess.

. . . at least in my opinion, the sports section is worth the same standards of editing and rewriting care because there ought to be one set of editorial standards and quality of rewrite in a paper . . . in fact, I think how a culture chooses to take its leisure is fully as important or serious an index to that culture's overall health as how it goes about its work.

Dr. Giamatti said much more, including the fact that he believed some of the best writing—in terms of logic, clarity, and strength—occurs on America's sports pages, rendering all the more disturbing the lack of standards, or the double standard, that operates in American newspapers today. Dr. Giamatti appealed to the professional pride of newspaper editors, asking them not to take sports for granted.

Like Dr. Giamatti, I have sounded this theme for years. Every day in every newspaper, America tolerates on its sports pages what it would never tolerate on the front page or on the business page.

Dr. Giamatti, who spent most of his life as an educator, was a man of enormous integrity. The way the New York *Daily News* and Mike Lupica handled the clubbed-fingers story would undoubtedly have been enough to make Bart Giamatti roll over in his casket.

But this is not to say that newspapers are alone in deserving blame for shoddy standards.

On television, I have witnessed the slow dissolution and disappearance of any attempt at real journalism, and the elevation of announcers who are shills for organized professional sports, and of ex-jocks, many of whom cannot even speak grammatically correct English. These people are given huge salaries and free rein on the airwaves.

Television is content to think of sports in terms of events, to make money from its partnerships with the leagues and operators. As a result, TV does little more than mention in passing any stories of corruption, of scandal, of injustice, discrimination, monopoly, and violations of the public interest.

No one even attempts in-depth sports shows like my old "Sportsbeat" program on ABC. The networks say they have no place for it, and the local stations dare not spoil their relationships with their hometown teams and area promoters.

In truth, the marketplace of ideas in the sports world has shrunk from the equivalent of a first-rate department store to a limited-items discount store, where only secondhand, shoddy merchandise is purveyed.

In a *Sports Illustrated* article in May of 1989 entitled "Yearning for Howard" and subtitled "Without Cosell Sportscasting is E-Z Listening," the author, Franz Lidz, wrote:

At least Cosell said something. The current network guys—Bob Costas, Al Michaels, and Brent Musburger —never say anything. What's worse, they don't stand for anything.

So what did Cosell stand for? I called him up and asked. It didn't take long for him to start telling it like it is. "I stood for the Constitution, in the case of the U.S. versus Muhammad Ali," he said. "I stood for the 5th and 14th Amendments. I stood for minority causes I believed in. I stood for journalism. Sportscasters today aren't concerned with issues and causes. Can you see any of those other guys putting their careers on the line for an Ali? Okay, maybe for Ali McGraw.

"It's ridiculous! What happened to the so-called talent hired to cover the games? What are they getting their millions for?"

To be cheerleaders, that's what. To assure us that everything's all right. To make us feel at home on the range by never saying a discouraging word. After all, the networks have shelled out millions to show this stuff, so why cheapen it? ABC's Al Michaels has said, "We can't reach the point where we're treating sports the same as a war story or a domestic crisis. It should never reach that point."

Well, this is going to make Michaels unhappy, but like it or not, sportscasters are journalists. They are not just covering games, they're reporting news events. By telling it like they think we hope it is, they're degrading the whole field.

NBC's Marv Albert feels it more prudent to enhance your likability than to worry about journalism. "Television is an exposure business," Albert says. "Likability numbers are what market researchers count on their fingers and toes. The higher your numbers the more money you make. The idea is to be likably inoffensive. It doesn't pay to be Cosell anymore."

Little Bob Costas, another NBC sportscaster, feels much the same way. "I'd like to be perceived as an entertaining sportscaster," he told Lidz. "I don't have the heart to nail people."

18

Lidz's conclusion was that Costas brought that same critical vigor to the baseball "Game of the Week," on which controversy meant questioning an umpire's call, then quickly adding, "But these guys do a great job, they really do."

"TV sports people don't break stories, and they don't bruise them either," continued Lidz. "They hardly touch them. The way they tap-danced around the Pete Rose allegations, you would've thought they would have studied under Bojangles Robinson. The Al Campanis affair? Ted Koppel broke that on 'Nightline.' Who exposed Jimmy the Greek? Not the group at CBS, who worked with him for twelve years on 'NFL Today.' It was a local news crew from WRC-TV in Washington, D.C."

And who had to confirm what I've publicly been saying on radio for years—that the NFL's drug-testing practices are questionable, and that there's racial discrimination in connection with that testing? It was a consumer affairs reporter for another Washington, D.C., TV station, WJLA, Roberta Bascom, who broke her version of the story during Super Bowl week of 1990.

All in all, the Franz Lidz piece in *Sports Illustrated* did an excellent job of briefly summing up the smelly situation that exists in TV sports reporting today.

It is indeed strange that Terry O'Neil, the zealously ambitious and viciously vindictive executive producer of NBC Sports, claims to be a paragon of journalistic practices and ethics. Astonishingly enough, the quotes from his star announcers, not Abbott and Costello but Albert and Costas, speak eloquently of O'Neil's journalistic fiber and credibility.

It's even worse at CBS Television Sports. Nothing has changed there since I wrote my last book. Neal Pilson is still head of the sports division, and his philosophy continues to be "The public doesn't want sports journalism."

What an insult to the American public.

And what an astonishing remark to be made by the head of a network sports division. First of all, it simply isn't true. This reporter's career is proof of that. The career of Roone Arledge, a giant among broadcast executives, the former head of ABC Sports and current president of ABC News, is further proof of its inaccuracy. But the falsity of Pilson's assertion isn't even the fundamental issue here—the first and paramount obligation of Pilson's division is to report sports-connected news, even if a portion of the public isn't interested, and to deny this responsibility is patently laughable.

Yet this almost unbelievable position is taken by a man of intelligence, one who is Madison Avenue slick, and a graduate of the highly respected Hamilton College and the Yale School of Law.

Perhaps Neal Pilson was best summed up by Bart Giamatti, who was, as noted, an ex-president of Yale. He said, "Pilson is a personable guy. I like him. I have to do business with him. We have a very lucrative business relationship. But I keep thinking that he's an embarrassment to the Yale School of Law."

Pilson's attitude, unfortunately, is not an anomaly. There are many more examples of unholy alliances between the media and sports operators, and I will address them later in the book.

CHAPTER THREE

Greatest Loss

Sports in general and baseball in particular were deprived of a great leader when Bart Giamatti was snatched away by a heart attack. The man was a rare gem.

Bart recognized the unholy alliances in sports and the evils of racism, gambling, drugs, and the dilution of education by big-time college athletics. He recognized that there had been too much compromise and commercialism in sports.

Giamatti made an impact on baseball during his two-year tenure as National League president, but it's a shame he never got the chance to prove himself as a great commissioner.

I think Bart Giamatti would have handled a lot of things differently from Fay Vincent. Bart was a warmer and more compassionate man than Vincent, and I think there's a good chance that Giamatti would have canceled the 1989 World Series after the earthquake. He surely would have handled the George Steinbrenner case with more professionalism, and he would most certainly not have meddled in the affairs of the National League involving the dispute between the umpires and NL president Bill White. White was so wounded by the lack of support by Fay Vincent that he threatened resignation.

Ironically, the two things in baseball for which Bart Giamatti will be most remembered both dealt with Pete Rose, a man whose values are totally different from those of the late commissioner. While National League president, Giamatti suspended Rose for thirty days for misconduct on the field, and later, when commissioner, he banned Rose for life for his gambling on baseball games. It's ironic that Rose played a role in Bart's tragic ending.

There's little doubt that Pete Rose was a factor in the death of Bart Giamatti.

David Kindred, the sportswriter, who was interviewing me on the sun deck of my summer home in the Hamptons at the time of Bart's death, agreed with me on that point.

It was September 1, 1989. The beautiful day in Westhampton turned into one of the saddest days of my life when the word came that Giamatti had suffered a fatal heart attack some two hours earlier.

Kindred stated to me, "They can say or write what they want, but as far as I'm concerned, I believe that Pete Rose was the principal cause of Bart Giamatti's death."

We agreed that the five-month-long Pete Rose ordeal, the long drawn-out investigation, the worrisome legal hassles, and the subsequent lifetime ban of Rose, had surely contributed to Giamatti's condition. No, it wasn't homicide, but Rose's belligerent, arrogant, persistent denial in the face of massive evidence of guilt, his sneaky legal maneuvering and stonewalling, had made it a difficult and stressful tenure as commissioner of baseball for Dr. Giamatti.

Perhaps thinking that any indication of dismay would be viewed as a sign of weakness, Dr. Giamatti consistently refused to acknowledge that the Rose case was taking a toll on his health.

Two weeks before his death, he gave the Associated Press statements that dismissed as frivolous the suggestion that he had been overly stressed by the Rose matter: "While it's a serious matter, it doesn't take most of my time. Most of my time is spent on other things. The way it's been played, and there's no reason it shouldn't have been played this way, would make you think that I have been sitting here worrying about Rose. But that hasn't been the case for months."

His denial aside, friends and others close to Giamatti felt that the Rose case did indeed precipitate his fatal attack.

One of those, Ed Erickson, who was Giamatti's driver for eight years when Bart was president of Yale, said, "The problem is he takes everything to heart. The Pete Rose matter—he wouldn't let it roll off his back. It was too much pressure for him."

One of Bart's closest friends, and the man who succeeded him as commissioner, Fay Vincent, was unsure what effect, if any, the Pete Rose affair had on the health of Giamatti. "Obviously it's a medical question," Vincent said. "I don't know if it had any effect or not."

It's something that can be debated forever, but I will always believe that Pete Rose contributed to the death of Commissioner Giamatti. In October of 1989, on the TV program "Inside Edition" produced by Av Westin, I told narrator Bill O'Reilly, "In the lifetime suspension, Pete Rose got what he deserved. They [the sportswriters] don't say this, but in my view, and I say it, Pete Rose contributed vitally to the death of one of the greatest men I've ever known, and I think one of the greatest men in human society, A. Bartlett Giamatti.

"I think Rose exacerbated his condition, at least in part, and led to Giamatti's heart attack. I know certain baseball people feel the same way."

However, I would be less than candid if I failed to point out that my close friend contributed to his own death by his self-proclaimed primary vice—chain cigarette smoking. On occasion, he had tried to stop, but he couldn't do it. He was severely addicted to nicotine and smoked at least three packs of Carltons per day. On a stressful day—and there were plenty of those the last five months of his life—it was not unusual for Bart to smoke up to four and a half packs.

Furthermore, his health was not helped by his failure to exercise, and his lack of physical conditioning was apparent when he would become winded after walking short distances. He was also overweight, a condition he occasionally tried to control by dieting. Maybe from stress more than anything else, he did lose twenty pounds during the Pete Rose ordeal.

During his days at Yale, Zackey's Deli was Bart's favorite hangout. He would regularly spend his Sunday mornings at Zackey's, eating, drinking coffee, smoking, and talking, not necessarily in that order. He was a regular guy who never refused to meet and talk with anyone who came into the deli.

Bart's gray Vandyke beard made him look older than his age, and he had dark circles around his eyes. His normally rumpled attire made him look more like the educator he was for most of his life than a league president or baseball commissioner.

On the day of Bart's death, he and his deputy commissioner, Fay Vincent, chartered a small plane and flew to their vacation homes in Cape Cod. Fay chartered the same plane they always used, a King Air twin-engine with the same pilot who usually flew them to the Cape.

Vincent says, "There was nothing unusual about the flight. I would always drop Bart off at Martha's Vineyard, where Toni would meet him, and I would proceed onto the Cape proper where my place was."

On Bart's last day, Toni met him at the airport and they drove to the Martha's Vineyard shopping district, where they were to shop for a wedding gift for the daughter of Bud Selig, the owner of the Milwaukee Brewers.

After a large meal, they ran from shop to shop, looking for the gift, and Bart complained to Toni, "I'm getting tired and we're going to have to go home." Toni willingly acquiesced.

While riding in the car, he complained of a pain under his left arm and said he wasn't feeling well.

Toni said, "Bart, those are symptoms of a heart attack. Do you think you're having a heart attack?"

"No," he responded, but he grew increasingly weak, and when he got home, he went right to the bedroom to lie down. Toni brought him a glass of ginger ale, but found he had passed out.

After brief attempts to revive him failed, Bart's son, Marcus, a twenty-eight-year-old actor, called the police, who dispatched a rescue squad.

The Edgartown unit arrived at the Giamatti summer cottage on Oakdale Drive at three P.M. The officers were unable to get Giamatti to respond.

A short time later, emergency medical technician David Bell arrived and relieved the police. He quickly determined that Giamatti had suffered a massive heart attack and began performing CPR.

He worked on Bart on the floor of the bedroom, then in the ambulance during the fifteen-minute ride to the Martha's Vineyard hospital, and then in the hospital's emergency room.

Bell said:

> When I arrived, I found the victim in full cardiac arrest, and his heart had stopped. I got a pulse once or twice, but he never regained consciousness.
>
> His family was emotionally distraught. They said he was fifty-one, so considering his age, I kept trying. We worked on him for over an hour and a half. His age was the factor there, not who he was. Had he been ninety-eight, we probably wouldn't have tried so long, because you know after a half hour he's not going to come back.
>
> I didn't know the man I was working on was the commissioner of baseball until after it was all over. I had no idea who he was. I just did my job instinctively. I don't think it would've made a difference to me if I had known who he was. Maybe it was better that I didn't. I don't know.

Bart Giamatti was gone. An autopsy showed that he suffered from heart disease and had had a prior heart attack several years ago, although he may not have known it.

Dr. William Zane, a medical examiner for Barnstable County, Massachusetts, said, "Giamatti died as a result of restrictive coronary heart disease. The manner of death was natural."

One could speculate forever about how much the Rose ordeal or the excessive smoking may have shortened the commissioner's life, but there seems little doubt that some preventive medical care might have extended his life, perhaps for many years.

Bart did not see a doctor on a regular basis, and apparently neither he nor Fay Vincent realized that the commissioner was in bad health. Furthermore, Fay couldn't remember the last time Bart had even visited a doctor.

As surprising as it may seem, Bart was not required to take a physical when he was named to succeed Peter Ueberroth as commissioner. Bud Selig, the head of the search committee, now says the committee was shortsighted in that regard.

The current commissioner, Vincent, had to satisfy the search committee and all the owners that he was in acceptable health before he was named to succeed Giamatti.

By this point, you must have gotten an impression of how much I admired Bart Giamatti. His death was a severe blow to me.

Our friendship first developed when I was teaching at Yale, when Bart was president of that great school. The relationship became even closer when he entered baseball and became president of the National League in 1986. I became a confidant and trusted adviser to Bart, even more so after he became baseball commissioner in 1989. Rarely did a week pass without our conversing, frequently more than once a week.

Perhaps my assessment of Bart was best summed up on the morning of the day of his death when David Kindred asked me what kind of job I thought Bart was doing and what type of job I thought he would do in the future.

My response, which Kindred recorded on tape, was: "I think Bart Giamatti is the best thing that ever happened to sports in America. No, wait. That's not fair. That's overstating it. Just say I think Giamatti is a terrific man. A dead-honest man. An extraordinarily brilliant man. I think he showed unbelievable patience in the Pete Rose case."

In retrospect, maybe I didn't originally overstate my praise of Bart.

Upon his death, everyone came out of the woodwork extolling the man, and that's the way it should have been. From ex-commissioners to owners to players to media types, the praise was virtually unanimous.

The memorial service held at Carnegie Hall in his honor was a thing of beauty. The famed old building was packed with people from all walks of life. I'll never forget the Yale Glee Club's rendition of "Amazing Grace," Bart's favorite hymn. The eulogies and readings by Fay Vincent, Bud Selig, sportscaster Joe Garagiola, and most of all, by Bart's beloved son, Marcus, were inspirational beyond belief. Dry eyes were the exception. The entire service was a fitting tribute to the memory of a great American.

After the stirring service, one of the first people who came to me, crying unashamedly, was Bill Bartholomay, chairman of the board of the Atlanta Braves. Like many of us, he was overwhelmed by the brilliance of the eulogy given by Marcus Giamatti. Marcus had the inflective nuances of his father's voice, and as an actor, he knew how to use it to best effect. He admitted that his father had helped him to learn various vocal techniques. But more importantly, he talked about how he had learned patience from his father, about how his father taught him all the values from which he now lives, and about how important education was. It was a remarkable tribute to his father.

Bart Giamatti was a mortal man, and like all of us, he had good thoughts and bad thoughts about people. Many of the good thoughts have been eulogized since his passing, but some of his critical thoughts have never been disclosed.

Some of his harshest words were reserved for his predecessors in the commissioner's office.

Of Bowie Kuhn, Bart said, "What in the world is Bowie up to? Why do I see him on the 'MacNeil-Lehrer Report'? He's on every show all over the place. What is the man trying to do? He doesn't say a thing, nothing definite about anything. Not definite in support of me or anything else. Say what you want about Ueberroth, he's definite."

However, Bart was deeply frustrated by some of the problems he thought Peter Ueberroth left behind, foremost being the Pete Rose investigation. And Bart blamed Peter for the collusion cases brought against the owners by the Players Association. He knew, and I advised him in advance, that the owners had no chance of winning against charges that they colluded to keep from signing free-agent players.

Bart said, "It's Ueberroth's fault. He created those problems and ran out and left them."

He also blamed Peter for the problems associated with the $1.1-billion television contract with CBS. The money was great, but Congress was in an uproar over the reduced number of regular-season network games on television. Later, in 1989, Bart's successor had to negotiate some additional telecasts of regular-season games to appease the irate Congress.

It was almost as if Ueberroth saw these problems coming down the track, jumped out of the way, and let them run into Giamatti.

There's no doubt that Bart will be best remembered for the Pete Rose case. As much as I admired his handling of that delicate and important matter, I would much prefer to see his legacy become a nationwide understanding of his learned views about the problems of college athletics in this country. His philosophy on the matter was the subject of a number of my radio programs and syndicated columns over the past few years.

In December of 1986 I had the following Q & A session with Bart:

Q: Dr. Giamatti, in your view, are big-time college sports bad for our schools?

A: Yes, very bad, insofar as they commercialize undergraduates for the purpose of producing revenue. There is an appropriate relationship between academics and athletics. Athletics can be an extension of the best values we have and the best a university has to offer its students. But that's not the way it is today. Commercialism has ruined college sports.

Q: What about the argument that big-time college sports revenue supports the minor sports on campus, thus making fencing or field hockey available to students who desire such sports?

A: I'm not sure that's really the case to begin with, Howard. But the idea that a school would justify abuses and corruption in football or basketball in order to provide fencing is an appalling argument both morally and legally. If a university offers sports, it must decide to treat every single sport equally. There can be no distinction between "major" sports, such as football, and "minor" sports, such as lacrosse. Those distinctions instigate part of the trouble. That's like saying that Yale has a physics department so its revenue can support the philosophy department.

Q: Is there an analogy here?

A: Absolutely, there's a very strong analogy between academic departments that bring in revenue and intercollegiate sports. Howard, people just don't understand that the real big-time, the real big money that comes into research universities, is not from sports but from the federal research money, and that is the money that supports the schools, not sports revenue.

Q: Would you elaborate?

A: Certainly. Let's say a school gets one million dollars from the Defense Department for research. That one million goes to support the real costs of doing the research, the light for the rooms, the heat, the air-conditioning—the basics. Then you get what's called indirect recovery money to support the research, and that's sixty-five percent to seventy-two percent above the million. The kind of money I'm talking about swamps the big-time college sports money. And all the big-time schools get this research money, ever since the Manhattan Project. And it's that money which is necessary for a university's sustenance; it's that money which builds the library or new laboratories.

Q: Have you ever seen a lab or library built by sports revenues?

A: No! Expanded athletic facilities, perhaps, but no academic facilities. Universities do not need sports revenues to support anything. That's the justification given to the kids and the alumni, and it's the justification for the commercialization of the athletes. It simply isn't true.

Q: Do you sense a growing skepticism on the part of the public regarding big-time college sports?

A: Yes, absolutely.

Q: What do you envision happening over the next few years?

A: Increasing scandals and an increasing NCAA policy

of containment, which won't work. You can't contain an oil spill. Ultimately I see the federal government deciding that the only way out of the morass is a federal inquiry and a federal commission. That would be unfortunate, since the only people less capable of governing college sports than the current group doing it would be a federal agency.

Q: We'd be coming full circle?

A: Yes, in a manner of speaking. President Teddy Roosevelt ordered a federal inquiry into college sports around 1905. The NCAA grew out of that investigation. I envision a repeat of that cycle, not quite a century later.

Q: Any additional points you'd like to make, Dr. Giamatti?

A: Yes, Howard. About five or six years ago research by private corporations came to our campuses. At that time the academic community went through intense soul-searching, drew up policy papers, and got together to formulate ways to protect students and faculty from interference by the private sector. Such interference as might occur from a big chemical company, for instance, could be very detrimental to academic freedom and the university's autonomy. But with the proper guidelines it has worked out very well so far. It has never occurred to a living soul to protect the universities and the students from TV and from the commercialization of both the students and the university. No one at any university would permit graduate students, postdoctoral students, or faculty to be interfered with that way, or commercialized that way. But we have allowed TV, which is part of the private sector in effect, to destroy our undergraduates and harm the universities. To me, that is the true scandal of big-time college sports and the American educational system.

Bart Giamatti didn't waste much time with grandiose philosophical generalizations. When it came to college athletics, he told it like it was.

CHAPTER FOUR

Athletic Corruption and Bogus Education

As much as Bart loved baseball and sports in general, he, in his wisdom, recognized the inherent threat that the corruption of college sports by big-time money interests represents to the ideals of our country. The undermining of the American educational system by college athletics going "big-time" is among the most pertinent problems in our country today, and it's for that reason that I will devote the next few chapters to this issue.

Dr. Giamatti was not alone in holding this view. Another who shares this feeling is a great American named John Brademas. "I rejected the presidency of the University of Miami of Florida [back in 1980] because the top priority was to make the school number one in the country in football and basketball," said Brademas, now the president emeritus of New York University, the largest private university in the world.

Dr. Brademas is one of the most distinguished educators in the country. Before coming to New York, he served as a Democratic congressman from Indiana for twenty-two years, the last four as majority whip in the House of Representatives. He served with distinction on the Subcommittee for Education and Labor and is the author of much of the education legislation on the country's law books today.

He is a graduate of Harvard and was a Rhodes scholar at Oxford.

For the chairman of the board of the University of Miami to offer Dr. Brademas that type of a mandate was to insult the man's intelligence, integrity, and credibility. It serves as an example of the undermining of values of this country.

"Oh, no, I wouldn't take your job for anything in the world. It is not the purpose of a college or university to excel in football or basketball. Our priorities don't coincide," Dr. Brademas told the Florida school.

A man named Edward Foote did accept the Miami presidency in 1981, and shortly thereafter he reached half of the school's mandated goal. The "football factory," with a sparkling array of "student-athletes," achieved the national championship on three occasions in the eighties—1983, 1987, and 1989.

Foote, a Yale graduate, was for eleven years associated with another fine academic institution, Washington University of St. Louis. A former newspaper reporter in the nation's capital during the sixties with *The Washington Star* and later, *The Washington Daily News,* both now defunct, Foote was special adviser to the chancellor and board of trustees at Washington University before going to Florida.

Under Foote, Miami football prospered. There were quarterback greats—Jim Kelly, Bernie Kosar, Vinny Testaverde, and Steve Walsh, all now in the NFL—and enough wins for the school to proclaim itself the "team of the eighties."

The school's basketball program has been less successful. Miami brought in a big-time coach, Bill Foster from Clemson, but results have been disappointing. Foster resigned after a poor 1989 season, and Miami hired Leonard Hamilton of Oklahoma State as his successor.

The Hurricanes thought they had a ticket to the Final Four when they won the bidding war—the "auction"—for a great "student-athlete," 7'1" Tito Horford of the Dominican Republic.

Tito originally enrolled at LSU, but left before ever playing a game. Later, he was denied admission to several schools, but Miami saw fit to admit the basketball giant.

Dr. Foote and the school's football coach at the time,

Jimmy Johnson, both told me that Horford was "entitled to an education," which raises multiple questions as to standards of admission, courses to be taken, and of course, the athlete's ability to cope on a college level.

Horford proved to be less than a dominant player and lacked a strong supporting cast. He averaged fourteen points per game in two seasons at Miami; then he dropped out of school for the NBA draft. The Milwaukee Bucks drafted him, but in spite of great size and promise, he has failed to make an impact in the pros.

Even though Miami is lagging far behind in its goal of achieving the national championship in basketball, one is safe in assuming that the school is still seeking a player with whom the 'Canes can strike it rich.

You may not be surprised that I'm not too popular at the University of Miami. When I appeared in Washington before Sen. Howard Metzenbaum's Subcommittee on Antitrust, Monopolies and Business Rights of the Senate Judiciary Committee—which was investigating the corruption and lack of ethics in big-time college sports—along with North Carolina coach Dean Smith, sportswriter John Underwood of *Sports Illustrated,* and President Foote, I was not easy on Miami.

I chided Dr. Foote for having a football program that represented everything bad in college athletics. The Miami football program, under the questionable ethics of Jimmy Johnson—who got the Oklahoma State program on NCAA probation before moving to Miami—had proved to be a great pipeline for players to the NFL, but represented little of what a college football program should be about.

Foote was to tell me later, "Why don't you lay off us, you're killing us."

Dean Smith came in for lighter treatment. I said, "I am delighted that you have Dean Smith here, Senator, because Dean Smith is now famous for losing the big ones gracefully."

Unfortunately, at the time of my appearance before Senator Metzenbaum's committee, I was unaware of the bizarre mandate that Miami had offered Dr. Brademas.

Fortunately for college athletics, Dr. Brademas rejected Miami's offer to help glorify that school's athletic program and opted instead to work for the greater good of college sports in general. He has been a principal figure in the creation of the UAA—the University Athletic Association. Some of the greatest universities in the entire world make up the league: the University of Chicago, Washington University of St. Louis, Case Western Reserve, Brandeis, Emory, Carnegie-Mellon, Johns Hopkins, the University of Rochester, and NYU.

The formation of this sports conference in 1985 was one of the great moves to take place in sports in my lifetime, because it puts sport in its proper place.

Schools in the UAA do not grant athletic scholarships or financial aid based on athletic ability. Athletes receive money only if they qualify for grants-in-aid from the government, or from the university based solely on academic criteria or financial need. The only exception is Johns Hopkins, which awards athletic grants-in-aid to its Division I lacrosse players. All nine schools are dedicated to the principle that the president or chancellor of the university is the person responsible for the control of the athletics.

As Dr. Brademas says, "There's a place for sports in university life. We believe in athletics at NYU. We support a sports program. But we believe first and foremost that the fundamental purpose of a center of learning is the academic thrust of a university. The UAA is our attempt to keep our priorities straight, while still offering sports. We play Division III basketball. There is no commercialization."

This is not the first time in recent years that academic-minded schools have banded together to form a conference. In 1983, the Colonial League was formed, a Division I-AA consortium of Bucknell, Colgate, Davidson, Holy Cross, Lafayette, and Lehigh. Now known as the Patriot League, current members include five of the six originals (excluding Davidson), plus Army and Fordham. But there's a special quality to the UAA that lies deep within the histories of some schools that have joined, for many of these schools were once powers in at least one major sport.

Take the University of Chicago. Once its football teams were known as the "Monsters of the Midway." They won six Big Ten football championships and then won Big Ten basketball championships too. Pictures of Amos Alonzo

Stagg filled the trophy room. Jay Berwanger was the first recipient of the Heisman Trophy in 1935. But the glory didn't last. The university had other priorities. Football declined, the university dropped out of the Big Ten, then dropped football in 1939. It was eventually reinstated, and the Maroons played in the Midwest Conference, which they left at the end of 1986.

Carnegie-Mellon, formerly Carnegie Tech, once was a big-time football power, too, with a great history of postseason play, and was the alma mater of the great running back Merlyn Condit, who went on to play in the NFL.

Washington University played Division I football and was coached successively by Weeb Ewbank and Jimmy Conzelman, later great pro coaches who are in the NFL Hall of Fame.

As for NYU, once it was big-time in both football and basketball. In the late twenties, because of the scandals and corruption occurring even then, the Carnegie Foundation did a study on big-time sports and concluded they were inimical to academia, and so NYU began a long, slow process of deemphasizing football. But it produced winning teams in the thirties, and the rivalry between NYU and Fordham, led by the "Seven Blocks of Granite," among them Vincent T. Lombardi, drew constant national attention. I was a student at NYU and then at NYU's law school from 1935 until 1940 (I received my BA in three years), and I remember fondly the years of exciting competition. But the times and the tenor of the university changed. And with the changes came the end of football.

But I went back to NYU four years ago, at the university's invitation, to watch its new basketball team play. Rocked by scandals in the fifties and sixties, NYU had dropped its basketball program in the seventies and had just brought it back. It gave me a great deal of pleasure to watch the Violets play.

It is probably very clear that I'm pleased that NYU has joined the UAA, because intramural and interschool athletic competition, if it's done the right way, should be an integral part of the college experience for young men and women. The UAA faces an uphill climb in many ways. The travel distances between the schools in some cases are more than a thousand miles. The schools do not necessarily compete in common sports: only five field football teams; a year after the formation of the league, Emory started a basketball team; Johns Hopkins is continuing to play Division I lacrosse.

But there are enough schools, enough teams, and enough sports to make the conference feasible. It's the correct thing, the way college sports should be played in this country. If every school operated this way, I would not be forced to call for serious reform or the abolition of big-time college sports.

No doubt it will be difficult to reform college athletics on a national level, and I think part of the problem is rooted in the values of American society. As a nation, we love sports, and we especially love the money-making side of sports. Because of this, any efforts at reform must involve the university boards of trustees, and where public universities are concerned, the state legislatures and governors as well. These individuals and governing units will have to show more vigorous leadership and insist that the academic purpose of the school must come first.

As it stands today, big-time universities have turned their sports departments lock, stock, and barrel over to the special interests. Some schools even have athletic departments that are incorporated businesses that function almost totally outside the control of the university. The University of Michigan is a prime example. The university president retains a kind of overseer position, generally staying away from the department until a crisis erupts, a scandal emerges, a coach must be fired, or an athletic director dismissed. University presidents who would never dream of abdicating their responsibilities in handling the academic side of their schools do so when it comes to sports and do it almost automatically.

American universities operate in a totally schizophrenic manner when it comes to athletics and academics, promoting one set of standards for academics and another entirely for sports. If universities would apply the standards to sports that are applied to academics, some of the problems inherent in the commercialization of big-time sports would be solved. If university presidents would wrest back the power and demonstrate the control over athletic departments that they wield elsewhere, college sports would be much improved.

Don't get the impression that I think there's anything wrong with winning. I do not. Competitiveness and a winning spirit are two important ideals that contribute to the greatness of this country. I admire those coaches who go for the win instead of the tie.

What I abhor is the coach or athletic director who seeks to win at any cost. Competitive drive and winning philosophies do not in any way justify cheating.

Winning in college athletics, or at any level of athletics for that matter, is not the most important thing. Vince Lombardi was erroneously credited with having a philosophy that called for winning at all costs. He was a man of immense integrity. Winning, and above all, playing at your best level, were important to him, but that did not compromise his standards of honesty and fair play.

Let me be abundantly clear about one point. Not all college coaches and athletic directors subscribe to the win-at-all-costs theory. Unfortunately, the pressure of winning from alumni, especially the wealthy contributors to the athletic program, seems to squeeze this group into a smaller and smaller minority.

There are honest and clean coaches, men such as Bob Knight of Indiana, Digger Phelps of Notre Dame, and Mike Krzyzewski of Duke, who are concerned with academic standards. But even the most honest coaches have the problem of policing overzealous, wealthy alumni, who, in many cases, place winning above the rules. And for every clean college coach, there are scores of coaches who are masters of bending and breaking the regulations. Unfortunately, there are scores of coaches who brag about their "clean" programs while their schools are maintaining different academic standards for athletes. Moreover, these same coaches choose to close their eyes to the system that exploits the athlete for top dollars from stadium tickets and concessions and massive dollars from television and radio rights.

Then there's the basic question of how badly the schools want a clean program. The National Collegiate Athletic Association (NCAA) regulates big-time college sports in this country, and I have always had a very low opinion of the

NCAA when it comes to enforcing rules. After all, these regulations are not law, even though some states are now passing self-serving legislation to support certain NCAA rules. For example, the State of Texas in 1990 fined agent Johnny Rogers $10,000 for making illegal contact with University of Houston quarterback Andre Ware, who still had college eligibility remaining. On the other side of the ledger, the State of Nebraska, also in 1990, passed legislation that requires the NCAA to adhere to all phases of due process before taking any action against the University of Nebraska football program.

California and Louisiana are other states that have passed laws making it illegal for an agent to make contact with a college athlete who still has eligibility remaining. The State of Texas has gone a step further by passing legislation making it a crime for anyone to offer high school athletes any inducement to attend a certain college. This statute makes the offense a third-degree felony, punishable by two to ten years in prison and a fine of up to $5,000.

David Berst, head of the NCAA Enforcement Division, has mixed feelings about the legislation. He hopes it will be a deterrent to cheaters, but at the same time fears it will make it more difficult for the NCAA to successfully effect cases against the violators. He fears that in the face of possible prosecution by the states, people will be more reluctant to admit indiscretions to the NCAA investigators.

The NCAA Enforcement Division is already a toothless tiger. The big problem encountered by the NCAA in its effort to police schools and enforce rules is the lack of subpoena power. The organization, headquartered at Overland Park, Kansas, outside Kansas City (it moved from Shawnee Mission, Kansas, in 1990), has no power to subpoena evidence or witnesses in its investigations.

Then there's the question of manpower. The group has twenty-nine people (only fifteen of whom go into the field) in its enforcement division, which is charged with controlling 292 schools in Division I basketball and 106 schools in Division I football. It's an impossible task!

The schools themselves are the ones that make the NCAA rules, yet the coaches and athletic directors, not the school chancellors and presidents, control and dominate the

NCAA conventions, where regulations are revised and enacted. If the schools really wanted the rules enforced, they would have more than twenty-nine people trying to do it. It's my feeling that the NCAA has long outlived its usefulness—if indeed it ever had any usefulness—and it is slowly becoming obsolete.

Oh, it won't die out completely. The organization was once very powerful, and it is hard for the men of the NCAA to realize that their power is diminishing. (In fact, maybe they won't realize it until it is no longer there.) They won't give up without a struggle. In the process, they'll talk ideals, they'll talk student-athletes, they'll talk academics, and they'll talk about protecting the innocent college kids from the corrupt and venal agents. But it's just talk. What they really want to protect is their own power, money, and status. What they can't recognize, of course, is that the power has waned, the glory days are over, and that all that's left are the bare bones, the skeleton of a carnivore that once ruled college sports.

And the fact that Walter Byars has been succeeded by Richard Schultz as NCAA executive director is not likely to change things one iota. It's tweedledee as opposed to tweedledum.

When the NCAA convened in Dallas in 1987, the membership, as usual, was dominated by the sports establishment. The convention soundly repudiated the college and university presidents' report and recommendations for cleaning up big-time college sports.

Chancellor Ira Michael Heyman of Cal-Berkeley, a former law professor who addressed the convention, said, "At too many places we have created a world where athletic concerns dominate educational concerns . . . many of us have become callous to corruption."

He cited the bribing of high school athletes, the altering of high school transcripts, the admission of functional illiterates to colleges and universities, and the physical and emotional abuse of athletes by coaches as some of the key problems faced by the NCAA and the schools. The presidents' committee suggested cutting back football scholarships by five per school.

The NCAA swiftly answered the report, ignoring the

football cutback request and even reinstating two basketball scholarships, bringing the number back to fifteen per school. It did this in defiance of unprecedented scandals, corruption, and even death in the big-time college sports arena.

Four years later, again in Dallas, the NCAA held what it called a "reform convention." It enacted a few cutbacks, but, believe me, it won't slow down the college sports monster.

And the question is: Does the public care?

Why is the public willing to accept a double standard for college athletes? The public attitude seems to promote a belief that athletes are dumb—white or black, they are just dumb jocks. So what does it matter if they are literate? Or competent in mathematics? What does it matter if they go to school unprepared? After all, they are not going to school to be educated. They are going to school to perform on fourth-and-long, or to sink foul shots under pressure during the last thirty seconds of a game. They are enrolled to help fill the stadium, the arena, to get the school on TV. And when they are finished playing college ball, they'll go to the pros and make millions, and what will it really matter if they're never able to read a newspaper or to balance a checkbook? High-priced agents will do it all for them, no doubt. What's the big deal here, a few thousand kids who can't read or multiply?

As a society, how can we tolerate this? What kind of callousness, what kind of decadence, permits a culture to allow its children to graduate from school and still be functionally illiterate? That permits a class of people—athletes—to be overtly used as a means of entertainment for the public?

Why must many of our college athletes be illiterates parading as college students?

I point to the classic case of Kevin Ross, the basketball star at Creighton, who left stardom at the university to attend a second-grade class at a Chicago school so that he could learn to read. Ross had filed an exploitation suit against Creighton, and the case is unsettled as of this writing.

Then there's the sad case of Dexter Manley, the Washington Redskins defensive lineman who went through Oklahoma State University as a "student-athlete," but who had to enroll in the Lab School of Washington, a workshop for people with reading disabilities, before he could learn to read. I presented the achievement award to Dexter at an impressive dinner held at the Washington Shoreham Hotel.

It was a moving moment for Dexter, but his life would be shattered later the same week when he was suspended from the NFL as a three-time loser in a battle with cocaine. I'll expand on Dexter's case in the chapter on drugs.

The cases of Kevin Ross and Dexter Manley are an indictment of our educational system, and in particular, our college athletic systems. Some college jocks are granted bachelor's degrees when they can hardly read and write. Dexter Manley attended Oklahoma State for four years, but when he went into the NFL, he couldn't read the word "cat." Some receive diplomas, but they can't tell Einstein from Eisenhower, or Isaac Newton from a Fig Newton.

Naturally there are the exceptions. Much is made of the rare Rhodes scholar athletes: Bill Bradley, the basketball great from Princeton; Pete Dawkins, the football star from Army; and Tom McMillen, the basketball standout from Maryland. All three parlayed their academic brilliance with athletic celebrity to enter the political arena.

But that threesome is the rare exception. And when the TV and radio announcers brag about the high-grade-point athletes and academic all-Americans, it gives the public a distorted impression. For every honor student in big-time college athletics, there are dozens whose reading ability is restricted to the level of "See Spot run."

CHAPTER FIVE

Hypocrites and Hucksters

In the midst of the Watergate scandal, which brought Richard Nixon's administration tumbling down, Bob Knight was quoted as saying, "When they get to the bottom of Watergate, they will find a basketball coach."

The academic scandals on campuses across the country represent only one part of the overall problem in college athletics today. The actual recruitment of high school athletes is an even bigger source of concern. Recruiting is a process whereby the coach attempts to sell the teenage athlete on himself, his staff, his school, and sometimes his conference. Assistant coaches do much of the recruiting, head coaches spend their time on the "blue-chip" prospects, and sometimes the alumni are involved, with or without the approval of the coaches. Normally, the slicker the salesman, the more successful the recruitment. But just as car sales-people have different approaches, so do recruiters. Some are high-pressure, some are low-key. Most drive expensive cars. Most wear expensive clothes. Some wear expensive jewelry. Recruiters study the backgrounds of the kids and their families and adopt an approach accordingly.

If a family is interested in academics, the coach and his staff emphasize academics. If the kid and his family are interested in exposure for the pros, the recruiter emphasizes how many of his players have made the pros and how much media exposure his school receives. Many recruit through family members, girlfriends, and other friends. The good ones are equally adept at recruiting in a country-club atmosphere or at the breakfast table of a ghetto family. All college athletic recruiters are salesmen and all are hypocrites.

One of the best, basketball coach Dale Brown of Louisiana State University, admits it. John Feinstein, the former writer for *The Washington Post* and now features writer for *The National* and the author of a number of excellent books on basketball, was allowed to make some recruiting visits with Brown. On my ABC radio program "Speaking of Everything," Feinstein recounted the following:

> Brown admitted in this recruit's home, "You know, Chris, I'm sitting here telling you what a good guy I am, and why you should come play for me, and how I care about people, and how I care about my players. If I was everything I'm telling you I am, I'd be off working for Mother Teresa. I wouldn't be sitting here recruiting you. And let's face it. Recruiting is nothing but hypocrisy." This is Dale Brown talking still, while he's recruiting: "And I'm sitting in your home in New Jersey tonight, telling your parents how easy it is to fly from Newark to New Orleans and to come to nearby Baton Rouge to see you play. Tomorrow afternoon, I will be back in Baton Rouge, and I will be telling young men down there why they should stay close to home."

At least Dale Brown was honest enough to look the recruit in the eye and say, "I'm a hypocrite. That's why I'm here."

Even the coaches with the good reputations, the Bob Knights, the Dean Smiths, the Mike Krzyzewskis, are all salesmen, and in some ways, they're all hypocrites, too.

For the less honorable of the breed, the outlaw coaches—and there are scores of those—it's open season on recruits. Or better yet, open season on NCAA regulations. It's illegal according to the NCAA for student-athletes to receive more than tuition, room, and board. They used to receive $15 per month laundry money, but that was stopped. So, it's not surprising that cars and cash are the two leading inducements offered to recruits. Most coaches keep their hands clean and stay clear of these sins, conveniently looking the other way while the "boosters" of the school arrange for the gifts. Frequently, these gratuities are channeled through the athlete's family. At many big-time programs, players with no visible means of support drive fancy cars, flash cash, and wear expensive clothes and jewelry. Many players, both during recruitment and afterward, receive creative and exotic inducements. It's expensive, but recruiters frequently offer houses or apartments to family members, and a wealthy group of supporters wouldn't think of providing a house or apartment without luxurious furnishings.

Among other illegalities, there are jobs for family members and air travel for the player, girlfriends, and other friends and family. There are game tickets that can be sold for profit, many times at inflated prices, to alumni. In the old days, it was fashionable for alumni and supporters to stuff money into the players' sneakers in the locker room. Now, the great players command trust funds and real estate deals. There are cases of schools paving roads to players' homes, promising the ownership of racehorses, and providing telephone credit cards, and sadly enough, some unscrupulous alumni have provided drugs to players.

It is not unusual for the supporters of big-time college teams to provide slush funds for "taking care of" players. In most cases, the coaches know it is going on, but they "don't want to know about it."

And one time-tested and effective recruiting inducement for athletes is sex. Many pretty girls, recruited by the coaches, have gotten very friendly with the recruits and influenced their decisions.

All the recruiting violations I have listed are documented, and they point up what a sorry business it is. It stinks to high heaven! How dare the educators of our country allow this corrupt system to exist!

The coaches should be ashamed of their profession; many of them, however, are only concerned with their own great deals. It's not unusual for college football or basketball coaching jobs to approach $1 million per season in compensation. Just as there seems to be no limit to the extent school backers will go to procure a great player, there also seems to be no limit for landing a great coach.

The basic salary can be several hundred thousand dollars. In addition, many coaches get new homes in the deal, substantial life insurance policies, revenue from radio/TV shows, club memberships, real estate deals, annuities, revenue from summer camps, shoe and athletic-equipment endorsements, and speaking fees. When a big-time coach can put together that type of deal, he can make a million easily and quickly.

John Thompson receives a salary of over $300,000 at Georgetown University, and he has a Nike shoe deal for $200,000 per season. That's before anything else. No wonder he can turn down a $6-million offer from the Denver Nuggets.

Many coaches have numerous incentive and bonus clauses in their contracts. There are high payoffs for conference titles, bowl bids, reaching the final sixteen, final eight, or Final Four, winning the national title, or being selected coach of the year. Other coaches have attendance clauses that pay handsomely; if game attendance reaches a certain figure, a coach receives a cash bonus.

And these "educator"-coaches are, for the most part, given carte blanche to break their contracts and jump schools if a better offer comes along. Some have negotiated clauses or windows in their contracts that permit them to bail out legally for a higher bidder, but more simply jump or break their contracts with the institutions of higher learning. It's almost unbelievable that schools and organizations which permit coaches to renege on their contracts will insist that student-athletes comply with the rules. Again, it's a blatant case of hypocrisy and exploitation.

In another questionable procedure, the coaches who receive better offers frequently use the offers to squeeze the school and backers for a better deal. A prime example is Michigan State University football coach George Perles. The former Pittsburgh Steeler assistant was set to become the head coach of the Pittsburgh franchise of the USFL, but jilted that organization to take the head job at his alma mater, MSU. That might have been excusable, but when Perles threatened to become head coach of the Green Bay Packers, he pressured Michigan State for a much better financial arrangement and contract. And later, when Perles threatened to become head coach of the New York Jets, he insisted that Michigan State add to his duties the job of athletic director. Only after State said yes, over the objection of its president, who was outvoted, did Perles agree to stay at the university.

Again, I point to John Thompson, the highly respected basketball coach at Georgetown University. Many years ago, he was able to renegotiate a sweetheart deal at Georgetown after the University of Oklahoma tried to lure him away with a lucrative package. One can go on and on with these examples.

One former charismatic millionaire coach is Jim Valvano, until recently the basketball coach at North Carolina State University, having jumped from Iona College. By coaching his Wolfpack team to an upset victory in the NCAA basketball championship tournament at Albuquerque, New Mexico, he changed his life forever. After a not-so-impressive 17-10 record in the regular season of the Atlantic Coast Conference, his club won three games in the ACC Tournament, including victories over North Carolina with Michael Jordan and Sam Perkins, and Virginia with Ralph Samson, to make it into the NCAA Tournament. There they won six games, upsetting the Phi Slamma Jamma Houston team in the championship game.

Valvano took much heat in 1989 when Peter Golenbock wrote his forceful, controversial, and much-maligned book *Personal Fouls,* exposing many ills in Valvano's program. The book, whose publication Valvano and his supporters tried to prevent, and which they later tried to discredit, prompted several investigations. One, by the State of North Carolina, led to Valvano's being stripped of his athletic directorship. Another, by the NCAA, led to his program's being placed on probation for rules violations.

Before Golenbock's book, Valvano had besmirched himself by the recruitment and support of Chris Washburn, a druggie and a petty thief, and a discredit to society as a whole. Washburn belonged in a correctional facility or a rehabilitation center, not in an institution of higher learning.

Valvano, a flashy, show-business type, attracts trouble, much of it his own making. One of his more famous indiscretions was using his own N.C. State gym as the set for one of his new-car commercials.

Some feel Valvano is a fun-loving kid who never grew up. He has the image of a real character, a stand-up comedian. But he rakes in the millions, and they loved him at basketball-mad N.C. State.

One place that didn't appreciate Valvano was nearby Duke, an archrival in the ACC. Duke is a great academic school and is considered to have a class coach and one of the classiest basketball programs in the country. Yet the behavior of its student body at home games is deplorable. In 1990, after N.C. State was found guilty of permitting its players to reap substantial profits from the sale of tennis shoes, the Duke fans greeted the introduction of State players by throwing dozens and dozens of sneakers onto the floor.

In other seasons, Duke fans have thrown other items onto the floor, such as the time an opposing player facing a sex charge was showered with hundreds of condoms upon his introduction.

I got a firsthand look at the Duke mania when I went down to the Durham, North Carolina, school for a seminar. I was the leadoff speaker at a sports seminar organized by John Wiestart, professor of law at Duke, and coauthor of a classic textbook on sports and the law. There was a huge audience—and I led off with the famous Duke battle cry used at Blue Devil games: "If you can't go to college, go to State. If you can't go to State, go to jail."

The Duke students roared, just as they did at the Duke basketball game where I first heard the chant. And remember, the Duke program is one of the showcase basketball programs in the country.

Nevada–Las Vegas basketball coach Jerry Tarkanian has spent a lifetime fighting the NCAA in the courts—and trying, without much success, to convince the public that he's not an outlaw coach. He won the NCAA championship in the '89–90 season and then was hit with probation because of rules violations committed years ago.

Like Tarkanian, Dana Kirk was a winning coach, at Memphis State University, but he wound up going to jail for income tax evasion, and additionally he was the subject of a gambling investigation. Furthermore, the government accused Kirk of charging youngsters at his basketball camp $1 per Coke for soda he got free under a government grant.

Kentucky Wildcat coach Eddie Sutton resigned under pressure after the NCAA charged his program with numerous violations, the most notorious of which was sending $1,000 in cash by air freight to the family of player Chris Mills in California. That move went astray when the package tore open and an Emery air-freight employee discovered the money. Emery leaked the information to the press, leading to an investigation, which was bad news for Kentucky.

Many coaches considered Kentucky to have some type of immunity from NCAA punishment, some apparent favored status. At the height of the investigation into the mess at Kentucky, UNLV coach Jerry Tarkanian said, "The NCAA will get so mad at Kentucky that it will slap Cleveland State with two more years of probation."

Actually the NCAA was tough on the Wildcats. It considered the death penalty (suspension of the program) before settling on three years' probation. The Wildcats were barred from postseason play for two seasons, were kept off television for one season, were restricted to three new scholarships for two seasons, and had to return NCAA tournament proceeds from participation in the '88 championships. Despite the probation, coach Rick Pitino, who had jumped from Providence College to the New York Knicks, jumped to Lexington to take on the Wildcat rebuilding project.

Eddie Sutton sat out a season and landed on his feet as head coach at Oklahoma State. Another recycling job. Amazing.

Larry Brown, perhaps the most notorious job-jumping coach, now heading up the San Antonio Spurs, had great success as head coach at UCLA and later Kansas, before leaving a step ahead of the NCAA, which handed down probation rulings because of violations committed during his tenure.

As sportswriter John Feinstein said on my radio program, "Larry is a very good basketball coach. I don't think any of us need to debate that. But he has to at least admit he has done some things wrong. Larry sits on television and says, 'I've never done anything wrong.' He's two for two in getting programs placed on probation. And I think if Larry were to sit down with you, Howard, he'd say, 'I care about my players. I care about my program. I care about college basketball.' At that moment he would; five minutes later though, he would care about something else."

Then there's the sad case of Charles "Lefty" Driesell, the former basketball coach at Maryland. This snake-oil-selling, slick-talking huckster is a disgrace to the sport and education as a whole. A great player, Len Bias, had to die of cocaine intoxication before Driesell's corrupt program at Maryland was unmasked.

After the death of Bias on June 19, 1986, it took more than four months for Driesell to bow out as head coach. His departure came not just in the wake of Bias's death, but following, as well, indictments of two other players for cocaine possession, and an additional academic scandal and failure involving several members of the basketball team. A resignation that should have been immediate was wrung out of him like a confession. I can't overuse the word—it was a disgrace.

I blasted him daily on my ABC radio shows, and finally, at the urging of my good friend, the late renowned attorney Edward Bennett Williams, I agreed to talk with Driesell, a client of Williams's, on the phone.

Lefty said, "You're killing me, Howard, with your commentaries. You don't understand me. I'm an educator." I told Lefty that I understood him very well, that I felt he was a disgrace to his profession, and that no school should allow him to set foot on its campus. I don't think Lefty was too happy with our telephone chat.

After his resignation as head coach, Driesell stayed at Maryland for a year as associate athletic director and doubled as a telecaster for ACC games. Then, astoundingly enough, he became basketball coach at James Madison

University, where the misinformed and unenlightened now hail his program as a great success.

At Maryland, a confused chancellor, John Slaughter, had to shoulder the blame of putting up with Driesell's shoddy regime. Then he compounded his errors by bringing in Bob Wade, a Baltimore inner-city high school coach, who quickly established a losing tradition and got the school in trouble for NCAA rule violations before being fired.

Maryland was placed on NCAA probation, much to the chagrin of its new coach, Gary Williams, who left Ohio State to return to his troubled alma mater.

Maybe the shoddiest big-time college basketball reign of all time was turned in by Tates Locke of Clemson in the seventies. In five years, this pill-popping, hard-drinking, coed-chasing former head coach of Army and Miami of Ohio turned the Tigers from a loser into a winner in the rugged Atlantic Coast Conference—but he amassed an amazing record of cheating and rule-breaking that landed the school on three years of probation before he resigned in disgrace. This was a coach who once had a solid reputation and who gave the legendary Bob Knight an assistant coaching job under him at Army. Locke made a partial confession to his many coaching sins, and a full confession to the sins of Clemson supporters, in his revealing book, *Caught in the Net.*

A wealthy ex-Clemson football player, B. C. Inabinet, an industrialist from Columbia, South Carolina, supplied Tiger basketball stars with cash, new cars, clothes, and other goodies. Good old B.C., with deep pockets and a heart as big as his huge frame, flew recruits—and their friends and relatives—all over the southeastern part of the country in his private plane. But he wasn't too discreet, as he would openly complain that Tates couldn't win enough games with the players he bought.

Bad apples seem to always float back to the surface of the barrel in the coaching business. After leaving Clemson, Locke became an assistant and later head coach with the old Buffalo Braves in the NBA; was a head coach at Jacksonville University for three years before getting fired; was an assistant under Tark the Shark at UNLV; and later was an assistant under Bob Knight at Indiana, before becoming head coach at Indiana State in 1989. Despite Locke's sordid record and admission of horrendous cheating practices at Clemson, Knight remained loyal to his old friend at Army. Undoubtedly that's why he hired him as an assistant at IU and then helped him get the head job at Indiana State. Knight, the best and most volatile coach in America, is loyal to a fault.

The player who was most candid about his deal with Clemson while Locke was there was Wayne "Tree" Rollins, former Atlanta Hawks star and now a member of the Detroit Pistons. Rollins placed the worth of his illegal package to attend Clemson at about $60,000, a figure he said was very accurate. In Locke's book, Tree claims he got, mostly from B. C. Inabinet, "about $14,000 per season. That's counting the money I was being paid for my Monte Carlo, the clothing, gas money, and pocket money."

It's no surprise that Tates Locke feels there are many "supporters" like B. C. Inabinet across the country, at many upstanding schools, offering the same kind of package deals to kids with exceptional athletic ability.

Rollins claims that other players received more than he received. He became close to the recruitment of a Rocky Mount, North Carolina, sharpshooting guard named Phil Ford, who went on to be an all-American at North Carolina and later played in the NBA. According to Tree, toward the end of the recruitment, when Phil had just about picked North Carolina over Clemson, he asked Phil why he wasn't coming to "our place." Rollins said, "I told him about the deal Clemson was giving me. You know what he told me? He said, 'I got a better deal at Carolina.'"

Rollins says he knows that in the seventies, David Thompson got close to $90,000 at N.C. State. He said that Thompson, who was an all-American at N.C. State and later an NBA star (he scored seventy-three points in one game for the Denver Nuggets) before developing drug problems, was getting close to $30,000 per season in college, and that Wolfpack supporters had paved a road to his house. State got a one-year probation from the NCAA for its indiscretions in the recruiting of Thompson. Norm Sloan, then the coach at N.C. State, won the national championship with Thompson, and I've had recruiters tell me that the year's probation was worth it.

But Rollins himself was widely recruited by dozens of schools. He recalls his visit to Kentucky. "They just happened to drive past a Thoroughbred horse farm. How ironic. The assistant coach I was with points to one of the horses and says, 'Tree, if you'll come here, someday you'll get one of them.'" Rollins feels sure that the cheating in recruitment was widespread in the Atlantic Coast Conference. He quotes John Lucas, the all-American from Maryland, who has spent fifteen years in the NBA, less the several times he has been out for cocaine rehabilitation, as saying Maryland had "the greatest alumni in the league. We were the best-taken-care-of team in the ACC."

There seems little doubt that the most highly recruited high school basketball player of all time was Moses Malone of Petersburg, Virginia. Well over 150 schools came after Moses, who seemed a safe bet to lead some college to the Final Four.

A book could be written about the deals offered Moses and his family. Houses, cars, cash, you name it. It was sickening.

He visited a record twenty campuses, which led the NCAA to enact a regulation restricting to five the number of campuses a recruit can visit.

It was quite a circus for Moses. Within a three-month period, he was in more Learjets than most Forbes 500 CEOs will fly in a career.

The University of New Mexico kept an assistant coach, John Whisenant, in Petersburg for thirty consecutive days. It was Whisenant who said that all college recruiters cheat. "It's just like speeding. Everyone does it at one time or another. Just a few get caught."

Moses saw it all. There was a new Cadillac left at the front door of his ghetto home. He could have had a Rolls-Royce for the asking.

Religion even entered into the recruitment of Malone. The Reverend Oral Roberts, who wanted Malone for his Tulsa-based university so badly he could taste it, flew his

Learjet to visit Moses. During one visit Oral placed his hands on Moses's mother, Mary, and prayed for the healing of her arthritis. Mary told Shelby Whitfield, "I think it helped. At least I felt better. Reverend Roberts was a nice man."

When Dick Vitale, the ranting and raving basketball analyst who was the head coach at the University of Detroit at the time, sent a note to Mary Malone, who was sick, he wrote, "We are praying for your recovery." The prospect of getting a Moses Malone will make a college basketball coach pray a lot and give him visions of the Promised Land—the Final Four.

Lefty Driesell had his prayers answered. After helping Moses's mom get a better job, and helping Moses make arrangements to buy a new car, Lefty thought he had his man. Ultimately he did, but not before Moses decided the new Plymouth Duster was not fitting for a student-athlete of his magnitude and held out for a better car.

Norm Ellenberger, the head coach of the University of New Mexico, after learning that he had lost out in the "Malone marathon," said, "What's the big deal? Let Driesell get the kid a bigger car. Hell, I'll get him a fucking Sherman tank if he wants one."

Later, Ellenberger's school was hit with a heavy NCAA penalty for cheating. But who do you think was the top assistant coach of the nationally ranked UTEP Miners and the man who took over the club when head coach Don Haskins lost his voice and missed a number of games in 1990? Right, Norman Ellenberger. And in the '90–91 season, Ellenberger left UTEP to become an assistant coach under Bob Knight at Indiana. It's unbelievable! Does college basketball rehabilitate? Or does it just recycle?

Malone did get his fancy car, a new Chrysler Imperial, but after receiving several hundred dollars' worth of dental care from Maryland sources (yes, also a violation of NCAA rules), and after impregnating a Maryland coed who helped recruit him (the same girl who previously dated another Maryland star), he jumped to the pros, signing with the Utah Stars of the ABA before ever playing a game for Maryland.

Moses was the first player to jump directly from high school to the pros, and he became an all-star in his rookie year in the ABA. Now a standout performer for the Atlanta Hawks, he is a twelve-time NBA all-star selection who is arguably the best offensive rebounder of all time, and a cinch for the Pro Basketball Hall of Fame.

In 1990, there were published reports that University of Illinois basketball recruits were offered $75,000 to $85,000 to play for the Fighting Illini. That may sound substantial, but given inflation and the seemingly limitless escalation of sports salaries, it doesn't compare too favorably with some of the offers that have been uncovered from the seventies. To put it into perspective, the average salary in the NBA in 1980 was $180,000, and as mentioned earlier, the average salary was $1 million in 1990. Using this rate of escalation, it would stand to reason that the price of the "pros" playing in college gyms has also escalated.

The earlier-mentioned Kentucky probation is not the harshest NCAA basketball probation of all time. Clemson's three-year sentence in the seventies was a tough one, but Southwestern Louisiana received the harshest, a death penalty of two years in the seventies. David Berst of the NCAA confirms the Ragin' Cajun basketball penalty as the toughest.

Southeastern Louisiana State started a five-year probation in 1989, and because of violations, it voluntarily dropped its men's basketball programs. But Berst says the terms of the Southeastern Louisiana penalty were not as tough as SWL's.

The offers to basketball players are usually greater than to football players, since it requires far fewer basketball players to turn a program around. That doesn't mean, however, that there isn't plenty of corruption to go around for the footballers as well.

Marcus Dupree was perhaps the most recruited high school football player in the history of the game. Oklahoma won the sweepstakes for Marcus, and he showed flashes of brilliance before encountering personal problems and a personality conflict with Barry Switzer, his coach. Switzer ran Dupree off, and the latter signed with the United States

Football League. After having a good season with the New Orleans Breakers in 1984, Marcus suffered injuries and fizzled out without making a major impact in pro ball. He attempted a comeback with the LA Rams in 1990.

Barry Switzer had a football dynasty at the University of Oklahoma, which toward the end featured a wide array of scandal. Just for starters, there were guns, rapes, robberies, shootings, and drugs. Brian Bosworth, the all-America linebacker at OU, who received a mint to sign with the Seattle Seahawks, where injuries and attitude kept him from making it big as a pro, was ridiculed for his kiss-and-tell book about his years at Oklahoma. But after the revelations proved correct and Barry Switzer was forced to resign, Boz's whistle-blowing looked pretty accurate.

Switzer, a likable, fun-loving coach, with some questionable scruples, is the subject of one of the funniest bumper stickers to come out of sports. Barry had a much-publicized affair with the wife of one of his assistant coaches. The coach, defensive coordinator and assistant head coach Larry Lacewell, didn't appreciate Barry's behavior, so he resigned and took a job as the head coach at Arkansas State. He's now the defensive coordinator at the U of Tennessee.

The bumper stickers that popped up all over Oklahoma may have been a little embarrassing for the Lacewells and the Switzers. They read: BARRY'S GOT IT IN FOR LARRY.

Switzer didn't discuss this in his entertaining best-selling book, *Bootlegger's Boy,* but he did refute personal charges of drug use, gambling, and game-fixing.

Coaching sex scandals are not confined to the Big Eight. Former NFL player Maxie Baughan was fired as head coach of Cornell of the Ivy League for having an affair with the estranged wife of one of his assistant coaches.

And years ago, Sonny Randle, another ex-NFL player and a married man, had a publicized affair with a coed at the University of Virginia where he was the head football coach.

And folks, these are the educator-coaches who are setting examples for the student-athletes at the universities of our country.

The harshest football penalty in the history of the NCAA was the death penalty handed Southern Methodist University in 1987. The SMU penalties were for the usual infractions—cash and cars, primarily—but these were flagrant and repeated abuses.

The Mustangs, a school with a great football heritage in the Southwest Conference, fielded no team in 1987 and 1988, and numerous restrictions are expected to keep the program down for years. SMU took some horrible beatings when they fielded a predominantly freshman team in 1989, but did manage wins over the University of Connecticut and North Texas State.

Only Arkansas and Rice avoided probation in the SWC in the eighties. Throughout the state of Texas, cheating was rampant, as the University of Houston, the University of Texas, Texas A&M, Texas Christian, Texas Tech, Baylor, and SMU were each caught and convicted.

The SMU case shocked the nation. For a school that had turned out all-American greats such as Doak Walker, Kyle Rote, and Eric Dickerson, having no football was a traumatic experience for its alumni.

The already sleazy story took on a more shocking aspect when it was discovered that the governor of Texas, Bill Clements, was aware of the illegal payments to SMU students! Governor Clements apologized and three years later, in 1990, finished out his reign as the state's highest official.

One of the many things that disturbed me about the SMU situation was the fact that the NCAA allowed the affected players to enroll at other schools and play football. These are players who willfully took illegal payments and broke NCAA rules, and they should not have been able to go play football at any big-time school in the country. Yet most of them scattered to big-time programs and were rewarded with scholarships.

SMU was rightfully penalized for misdeeds, and therefore, so should the individual players have been penalized. We don't tolerate corruption elsewhere. Why do we tolerate it in sports?

There was a tendency for much of the country to blame the entire state of Texas for what happened at SMU. This attitude was not correct. Texas deserved no such censure, because Texas is not alone in its shame. Look at the football scandals throughout the Southeast during the past decade. The University of Florida has been rife with scandal.

Granted, Texas is football crazy. Funerals and weddings are scheduled so that they won't conflict with high school football games, where crowds often exceed thirty thousand.

Football is a religion in Texas. No one knows that better than I, from my years with "Monday Night Football." During one game in Dallas, I made the idle but truthful observation that Robert Newhouse was a journeyman player, that he was no Calvin Hill. Both Tex Schramm and Gil Brandt, respectively the Cowboys president and the head of player personnel, agreed with me. The football fans of Texas did not. The hysteria that ensued over this one observation was shocking to me and to Emmy. The mail I received, the phone calls, the petitions to have me removed from the broadcast, the death threats, told me more than I ever wanted to know about how seriously Texas takes its football.

Another example of Texas's football mania concerns the famous play in the 1954 Cotton Bowl game between Alabama and Rice. When Tommy Lewis came off the Crimson Tide bench to tackle the Owls running back Dickie Moegle (he has since changed the spelling of his name to Maegle), who was headed for a touchdown, there was hell to pay. The game officials awarded a touchdown to Rice, but later, Lewis was to receive so much hate mail, including death threats from irate Texans.

So, while I deplore the rabid fan mentality found in Texas, the state deserves a great deal of credit for the steps it took under Gov. Mark White, Governor Clements's predecessor, to clean up high school football, where so many of the problems begin. The "no-pass, no-play" academic law passed by the state legislature was a great stride in the proper direction. If you don't pass your courses, you don't play high school ball. It's a controversial law, but the state stuck with it, and there isn't a state in the nation that wouldn't profit from passing the same kind of law.

But Texas has a long way to go. For the past thirty years, there have been cases where family heads with outstanding football-playing sons have been promoted to much better jobs expressly to enable the family, and in particular, junior, to move to a new school district.

But those overzealous high school conditions don't mean Texas should be singled out for special criticism for the scandals at SMU, because Texas is just one more state where corruption is countenanced on behalf of winning and on behalf of big-time college sports.

Another example is big-time college football coach Jackie Sherrill, who won a national championship at Pittsburgh before being lured to Texas A&M for megabucks. After charges of cheating, unethical practices, and rules violations, Sherrill was forced to resign as head coach of the Aggies. After sitting out two seasons, Sherrill was named head coach at Mississippi State.

Another head football coach, Danny Ford, brought a national championship to Clemson with some cheating mixed in along the way. In 1982, under Ford, Clemson was found guilty of numerous NCAA rules violations. It's hard to believe, but Ford later lobbied against the construction of a learning center for student-athletes. Perhaps no one should have been surprised when, in 1990, the NCAA opened another investigation of Ford's program and threatened the Tigers with still another probation. In the middle of the latest investigation, Clemson rewarded Ford with a million-dollar buyout and forced him to leave. Later, the NCAA placed the Tigers on probation.

Whoever said crime doesn't pay?

The dishonor roll of schools convicted of cheating and placed on probation by the NCAA in the eighties is as follows:

Adelphi, basketball; Alabama A&M, soccer; Alabama State, football; Alaska-Anchorage, basketball; Alcorn State, basketball; American U, basketball; Arizona State, baseball, gymnastics, wrestling, basketball, football, track; Arkansas State, basketball; Army, football; Auburn, basketball, football twice; Austin Peay, basketball, football twice, tennis, track; Baylor, basketball; Bradley, basketball; Brooklyn College, basketball; Cal–Santa Barbara, basketball; Cal Poly–Pomona, basketball, cross-country, football; Cal Poly–San Luis Obispo, basketball; Cal State–Fresno, basketball; Cal State– Northridge, football; California, football; Central Florida, basketball; Cheyney U, basketball; Clemson, football; Cleveland State, basketball; Colorado, football; East Carolina, basketball, football; East Tennessee State, basketball; Eastern Kentucky, basketball; Eastern Washington, basketball; Elizabeth City State, basketball; Florida, football; Florida State, basketball, football; Georgia, basketball, football twice; Georgia Tech, tennis; Grambling, basketball; Hampton U, tennis; Houston, football; Idaho State, basketball; Illinois, football twice; Iowa, golf, softball, swimming, volleyball; Iowa State, football; Jackson State, football; Kansas, basketball, football; Kansas State, football; Kentucky, basketball twice; Kenyon College, diving, swimming; Loyola-Maryland, basketball; LSU, basketball, football; Marist College, basketball; McNeese State, basketball; Memphis State, football three times, basketball twice; Miami-Florida, football; Middle Tennessee State, basketball; Minnesota, basketball, football; Mississippi, football; Mississippi State, basketball, golf, softball, tennis; Missouri, football; N.C. State, basketball, football; Nebraska, football, softball; New Mexico, basketball; New York Tech, basketball; Northeast Louisiana, basketball; Oklahoma, football twice, track; Oklahoma City U, basketball; Oklahoma State, football three times; Oral Roberts, basketball twice; Oregon, basketball, football; Oregon State, basketball, football; San Diego State, basketball; San Francisco State, basketball; San Jose State, basketball, football; SMU, football three times; South Carolina, basketball; South Florida, basketball; Southeast Missouri State, basketball, track; Southeastern Louisiana, basketball; Southern Cal, football twice; Southern Illinois, basketball twice; Southern Miss, football twice; Southern U, football; St. Louis U, basketball; TCU, basketball, football; Tennessee, football; Tennessee State, football; Tennessee Tech, golf; Texas, football twice; Texas A&M, football; Texas Tech, football; Tulane, basketball; U of Akron, basketball; U of Bridgeport, basketball; U of Cincinnati, basketball twice, football twice; U of New Haven, basketball; U of San Diego, football; U of San Francisco, basketball twice; U of Toledo, track; UCLA, basketball twice, track; UNLV, football; Utah, football; UTEP, cross-country, track; Virginia Tech, basketball, football twice; Wake Forest, basketball; Washington, basketball; West Chester U, wrestling; West Texas State, basketball twice, football, tennis, track; West Virginia, basketball twice; West Virginia Wesleyan, basketball; Western Kentucky, basketball; Western State College, football; Wichita State, basketball, football; and Wisconsin, basketball twice, football twice.

What an unholy mess!

CHAPTER SIX

Agents and Propositions

Sadly, there is still more to tell about the diseased college-athletic system in America.

In February of 1990, Notre Dame officials made a decision that was to generate a public relations uproar, a decision that brings into focus the sad state of big-time college athletics today. This great university, which had developed a well-deserved reputation for leading the nation in academic ideals and integrity, opted for the big TV football dollars, ethics be damned.

The Fighting Irish pulled out of the College Football Association television deal with ABC and ESPN to sell its own home games to NBC for a total of $38 million, a decision that reeked of greed. It was a classic sellout. Notre Dame took the money and ran.

Notre Dame and sixty-five other big-time football schools formed the CFA in 1977 so that they could keep the football revenue and not share it with the other Division I NCAA schools. By signing its own television deal, Notre Dame was doing to its fellow CFA members what the CFA had done to the other NCAA institutions. From an ethical standpoint, it is difficult to defend the Notre Dame decision, but financially, it does appear to be a shrewd one.

This Notre Dame decision, which left the other CFA

schools in shock, was engineered by the Reverend William Beauchamp, a Notre Dame executive vice president, and Fighting Irish athletic director Dick Rosenthal, a former banker. It had the blessings of Notre Dame president the Reverend Edward Molloy. The highly questionable deal must have made past Notre Dame officials cringe, people such as former president the Reverend Theodore Hesburgh, the Reverend Edmond Joyce, former VP in charge of athletics, and former athletic directors Moose Krause and Gene Corrigan.

Following the shocking defection, ABC Sports threatened to sue, and CFA executive director Chuck Neinas had to scramble to keep his organization from falling apart. There was speculation that independent schools such as Miami of Florida, Pitt, and Syracuse might follow Notre Dame's suit, and more seriously, that the entire Southeastern Conference might pull out of the CFA and make an independent deal with CBS.

Dennis Swanson, the president of ABC Sports, after losing out on the Olympics, baseball, the NBA, and the Final Four, needed the CFA package badly to keep a strong presence in the marketplace. Within a couple of days, ABC and ESPN jointly renegotiated with the CFA a reduction from $350 million to $300 million to compensate for the Notre Dame withdrawal. With all of its many TV appearances under the CFA agreement, Notre Dame would have received about $20 million. By going on its own with NBC, the Fighting Irish will receive $38 million, a nice little $18 million boost. The bottom line was that the Notre Dame decision would cost the other CFA schools about $30 million over the length of the five-year contract. The University of Kansas was the first to retaliate by pulling out of a scheduled basketball date at Notre Dame.

There has been plenty of negative fallout from Notre Dame's defection, enough so that the damage may be irreparable. Georgia athletic director Vince Dooley told *Sports Illustrated,* "I wasn't surprised by this, I was shocked. Surprised, shocked, greed and ultimate greed. That's the reaction I'm getting from this."

Another athletic director, Frank Broyles of Arkansas,

said, "To me, Notre Dame has vacated its leadership role. This is greed."

And Penn State football coach Joe Paterno commented, "We got to see Notre Dame go from an academic institute to a banking institute."

The College Football Association received another jolt in 1990 when the federal government questioned the legality of the football agreement between ABC and the CFA. The Federal Trade Commission contended that the contract restrains trade by denying the schools the right to sell their own individual national television packages. The case is not expected to be resolved until well into 1991.

The Notre Dame money grab was a personal disappointment for me, but Notre Dame remains a great university. I have always been appreciative of the value Notre Dame places on education.

I was greatly relieved to hear the Reverend William Beauchamp, on CBS Television in March of 1990, pledge that the great institution would retain its tradition of high admission standards for athletes. In perspective, the Irish football television deal would seem to be an aberration.

In truth, Notre Dame is about as pure as any university can be in today's athletic climate; because of the school's rich sports tradition, going all the way back to Knute Rockne, they can recruit pretty much whomever they want.

As Gerry Faust clearly demonstrated, however, not just anyone can win in football at Notre Dame. At the present time, they have a great football coach in Lou Holtz. This cunning little comedian, who craves Clark candy bars, knows how to win college football games and to lead young men. (It appears that Holtz will have to find another favorite candy bar, as the manufacturer has announced that the Clark bar is being phased out.) He has demonstrated this talent previously at North Carolina State, Arkansas, and Minnesota.

The Fighting Irish are just as fortunate to have Richard "Digger" Phelps leading their basketball program. Digger has made the Final Four just once in twenty years, but he has winning teams and they usually make the NCAA tournament. He has the uncanny knack for getting his team sky-high for the big game.

Digger's an incurable showboat who plays to the television cameras, but he's an educator, and he cares about his players. College sports would be much better off if there were more Digger Phelpses.

Notre Dame does a lot of things right. For example, it doesn't believe in transfer student-athletes, or in recruiting junior-college players. Many schools thrive off transfers, most of whom for one reason or another don't belong in the college program. And the junior colleges have become a feeder system for the illiterates who can't get into a four-year college. Many of the juco players don't even have a legitimate high school diploma.

But the Lou Carneseccas, Jerry Tarkanians, John Chaneys, and Lefty Driesells of the world will take a juco scarecrow in a minute if they think he can post up, block out, shake and bake, or pick and roll. It's enough to turn one's stomach.

There are other practices, established by the NCAA, that I think are incompatible with the educational system. Freshman eligibility is ridiculous; a student needs a year of adjustment, academically and socially, before he is subjected to the pressures of varsity athletics. Coaches such as Joe Paterno know this, yet he feels he must play freshmen to be competitive with the other schools. I admire Joe Paterno as a man and as an educator. His program at Penn State is a fine one, but this practice smacks of hypocrisy.

The same can be said for the practice of redshirting—holding an athlete out of competition for a year and giving him five years to complete school. How absurd. The practice of staying on an extra year in the student body when the primary motive is to play sports is disgraceful.

Don't get the impression that I feel all schools do it wrong. The Ivy League, for example, has the right idea: no spring football; no freshman eligibility; no redshirting; grants-in-aid based on need only; and some admirable admission standards. But the late Bart Giamatti was concerned that even the Ivy League would eventually compromise some of its ideals because of athletics. Bart was afraid that Penn, Cornell, and especially Columbia might lower the admission standards for jocks. Columbia actually did change its admission criteria in the midst of its football team's forty-four-game losing streak, in an effort to enroll some better athletes.

The big-time college football junkies will ridicule my position on Ivy League sports, but let me say this. Ivy League football—Harvard vs. Yale—is as much a part of the college sports scene and tradition as anything coming out of the Big Ten. I enjoy the history and tradition behind the game. I was saddened to learn that Army had been hit by a relatively minor NCAA football probation in the early eighties, but by and large, Army vs. Navy is much healthier and more meaningful than Auburn vs. Alabama or Oklahoma vs. Nebraska. And it's good football to watch, too, high caliber without the patina of professionalism that taints big-time college football. I also truly enjoy the way the cadets and the midshipmen celebrate. When their caps come off in a victory wave, I am proud of the progress that has been made in education.

One thing that big-time college athletes, not military-academy athletes, have to contend with is sports agentry. And that, my friends, means more scandal, more big-time corruption. In America, where traditionally nothing is certain but death and taxes, we now have a new sure thing—college sports scandal.

The problem of tainted agent-player relationships has existed for decades, but incidents of the past few years have served to accentuate it.

In the old days, not many jocks knew what an agent was, and some team managements simply refused to deal with agents. One of the first athletes to use an intermediary in salary negotiations was Jim Ringo of the Green Bay Packers. And what I'm about to reveal is going to destroy one of the great sports stories of all time.

Legend has it that in 1964 Packers head coach and general manager Vince Lombardi called Ringo into his office to talk contract. The great center supposedly told Lombardi that he would have to deal with his representative. At that point, so the story went, Vince excused himself, left the office, and returned in a few minutes to inform Ringo that his agent would have to talk to the Philadelphia Eagles because he had just been traded.

But in 1990, Ringo told me that the story is not true. Jim

said, "I did have a friend [not an agent] tell Lombardi that I wanted a $15,000 raise, from $22,000 to $37,000. Sportswriters had been incorrectly stating that I was one of the highest-paid players in the league. I had just been named All-Pro, played in the Pro Bowl, and I wanted a substantial raise. It was no surprise to me that Vince was outraged at my request for a boost in pay. He arranged a trade which sent me, along with running back Earl Gros, to the Eagles for a number-one draft pick and linebacker Lee Roy Caffey."

Ringo continued, "It was Pat Peppler, then Packers director of player personnel, not Vince Lombardi, who informed me that I had been traded. As a matter of fact, I first revealed the trade to the public through a broadcaster, Ted Pierce, in my then hometown, Easton, Pennsylvania, before the Packers or league office had a chance to announce it."

Why did Ringo not dispute Lombardi's version of how he was informed of the trade? Jim told me, "It was a great story, and who was I at the time to say Vince was wrong? I didn't want to discredit Vince Lombardi. I didn't want to discredit the Packers in any way, because I enjoyed my years in Green Bay."

Ringo, a former Buffalo Bills head coach and a member of the Pro Football Hall of Fame, feels he was the first athlete in pro sports to be fired or traded for having someone act as an agent for him in salary negotiations.

Vince died of cancer in 1970, before agents became commonplace later in the decade. In the eighties, agents proliferated in epidemic proportions.

Some sports agents today are accountants; some are relatives of players. As a lawyer, however, it doesn't make me happy to say that most are lawyers. For while many are legitimate, many are crooks.

In my view, there is no doubt that a player should have representation in dealing with general managers and owners in all professional sports. Most athletes are not properly prepared or equipped to deal with experienced and sophisticated sports executives, many of whom, if permitted, would employ athletes under conditions of relative slavery.

But for every agent who is willing to give an athlete fair representation at a fair price, there is an unscrupulous flesh peddler who is willing to rip off the jock, frequently a jock who has breezed through college without ever really attending classes. Sadly, many of these athletes are no better equipped to select a legitimate agent than they are to deal with the sports management executives. Consequently, all too frequently, it results in the athlete's getting ripped off, and in the process, breaking all sorts of rules.

Many agents recruit college kids with the same kinds of bait the colleges use to recruit high school kids. There are the standard lures such as new cars, cash, clothes, and jewelry, but some agents are more worldly, offering drugs, women, wild parties, and transportation, mostly air, but including stretch limos and Rolls-Royces.

The number-one agent tactic, however, is to loan the player and/or his family substantial sums of money, usually on a cosign basis. Once a player takes money through a signed loan, the agent has him hooked.

A prime example was the Charles Shackleford case. The ex–North Carolina State star, a former member of the New Jersey Nets and one who played in Europe this past season, was another in a long line of Jim Valvano recruits brought to N.C. State to play basketball with little or no regard for his quality as a student or person. Shackleford turned out to be the final nail in Jim Valvano's coffin. Regardless of the outcome of point-shaving charges, the fact that Shackleford illegally accepted $65,000 in loans while in school was enough to topple Valvano's already shaky empire. If Valvano is not recycled in another basketball coaching position—and any school that hires him should receive the death penalty—he'll wind up as a high-paid, jive-talking analyst in some broadcasting booth. Preposterous. (Later, Valvano was hired as a basketball commentator by ABC and ESPN.)

Don't get the impression that all agents are crooks. Many are legitimate and render valuable services to the athlete. But it's a highly competitive, cutthroat business, and like the schools selling their product to the high school kids, it's a sales job all over again—with the agent having to convince the college kid that he's the right person to represent him.

There are famous and wealthy superagents in the sports world. The most prominent is Boston-based attorney Bob

Woolf, who has represented Joe Montana, Larry Bird, Vinny Testaverde, Anthony Carter, Doug Flutie, and Dexter Manley, to name a few.

Equally effective—and unquestionably the most despised by sports management—is Howard Slusher, a tough, cunning lawyer who is more than a match for any general manager.

Slusher plays in my charity golf tournament each January at the Morningside Club in Palm Springs. Our relationship goes way back, and I am amused each time he tells me the story about trying to insert favorable comments about me in a book he was trying to sell. One publisher rejected the comments, claiming favorable comments about Howard Cosell would not be commercial. It seems that some book publishers are afflicted with newspaper mentality.

Without a doubt, Slusher is the toughest agent of our time. He won't hesitate to have a player sit out a season, and a favorite ploy of his is to have clients negotiate—and if necessary, hold out—as a group.

Mark McCormack's International Management Group is the largest of the sports agencies. McCormack's a powerful man in professional sports, and, as his organization promotes many sports events which have his clients as participants, many of his activities smack of conflict of interest. He has more divisions than one can imagine.

Among the heavyweights at IMG are Barry Frank and Ralph Cindrich, the latter being head of football operations, controlling a large group of players.

Other superagents include Leigh Steinberg and the famous Ed Hookstratten, who does not concentrate on athletes.

The best, however, was the late Larry Fleisher. He was the top professional basketball agent and easily the most caring and responsible agent of all time. This was a great man in sports, more responsible than any other for the success of the NBA.

Then there's Art Kaminsky's Athletes and Artists, another big-time outfit. Art started as a hockey agent, but now makes megabucks representing sportscasters. He spent much of his time in the eighties keeping Jim Valvano in million-dollar commitments while Jim's N.C. State basketball program went to hell in a handbasket. Valvano's blind leadership and uncanny ability to assemble a string of outlaws masking as student-athletes is enough to turn one's stomach. It exemplifies all that is wrong with college sports in America.

And what will basketball-crazy N.C. State do about it? Little. First, under coach Norm Sloan, it won the national championship, followed by NCAA probation, and then, under Coach Jim Valvano, it won the national championship, again followed by NCAA probation. N.C. State will expect Valvano's successor, Len Robinson, an N.C. State alum, to win still another national championship. It's sickening.

It's systems like the one at N.C. State that attract the shady sports agent. When kids are on the take from schools and school supporters, it should not be a surprise that the same kids are on the take from unscrupulous agents.

The case that brought sports agents to the attention of America was the trial of agents Norby Walters of New York and Lloyd Bloom of Sherman Oaks, California. In a landmark action, the federal government tried and convicted Walters and Bloom of racketeering and mail fraud in a case laced with threats of violence to athletes and with the involvement of organized crime, only to have the case overturned on a technicality.

By way of background, Walters is a flamboyant, silver-haired, fifty-nine-year-old agent who for years booked most of the top black entertainment groups in the country through his New York–based agency, Norby Walters Associates.

Norby is an outgoing person who rides in a Rolls-Royce and is quick to throw a party. He has been known to take over clubs such as Studio 54 and give a bash for hundreds of people. Quick with a buck, he once operated Norby Walters' Night Club, which was located next to the famed Copacabana in Manhattan. Things went well until two wiseguys were blown away in Norby's club. He lost his liquor license—and that was the end of that.

In 1981, he and Lloyd Bloom formed a sports agency and named it World Sports and Entertainment. Between 1984 and 1987, Walters and Bloom started signing highly regarded college athletes, offering to represent them in negotiations with professional clubs.

They used the same technique which they used in their entertainment agency, that is, they concentrated on blacks. Of the forty-four college players signed—forty-two football players and two basketball players—all were black, and while they were from a cross section of major colleges, thirteen were from the scandal-plagued Southwest Conference. Many had also not fared well academically.

It developed that most of the players had been given loans as an inducement to sign contracts while they were still in college; the signings were kept secret until the players left school. And the government further contended that Walters and Bloom had additionally used enticements such as cash, automobiles, clothing, concert and airline tickets, hotel accommodations, the use of limos, insurance policies, plus trips to major entertainment events, and introductions to prominent entertainers.

All of these inducements not only violated NCAA rules, but the government claimed that the agents conspired to conceal the payments. Normally the FBI and the federal government would not have gone after Walters and Bloom for these indiscretions, but there was much more to the story.

Many of the players, for one reason or another, had decided they wanted to split from Walters and Bloom. In 1987, Walters had prematurely signed seven of the top twenty-eight first-round NFL draft picks, the biggest first-round success of any agent in history. But it wasn't as great as it appeared. The word was out that Walters and Bloom were under investigation by the FBI for threatening players and their families with physical harm if they tried to leave the agency.

The investigation also involved the beating in Chicago of Kathy Clements, the wife of former Notre Dame quarterback Tom Clements and an employee of a rival agent, Steve Zucker, who represented then Chicago Bears quarterback Jim McMahon. A man wearing a ski mask entered Zucker's office early in the morning when Ms. Clements was alone, beat her with his fists, and stabbed her in the arm. She was left battered, bruised, and bleeding. Kathy made a full recovery and now has her own sports marketing business in Chicago, but she's no longer a player's agent, and who can blame her?

No one was convicted in the Clements assault, but Steve Zucker, who represented about forty pro football players, says that following the incident, he was the one responsible for getting the investigation into the actions of Walters and Bloom started.

Walters denied making threats, or having any involvement in the Clements beating. But the prosecution—backed up by FBI tape recordings—contended that Walters and Bloom warned some of the players that they had friends who would visit the athletes and do physical harm to them if they tried to back out of deals they had signed.

Despite the threats, players were bailing out like squirrels running ahead of a forest fire. Five of Norby's seven first-rounders had left him, and he had filed breach-of-contract suits against them. Adding to their problems, Walters and Bloom had been decertified by the NFL players union for nonpayment of dues, and the union was cooperating with the FBI in its eighteen-month-long investigation of threats by the agents.

Maurice Douglass, a free safety for the Chicago Bears, testified that Bloom told him in a phone conversation that "somebody might break [my] legs."

Tony Woods, a Seattle Seahawks linebacker, and Everett Gay, a Dallas Cowboys wide receiver, testified that Walters and Bloom had threatened them. Meanwhile, Edwin Simmons, former University of Texas star, told the jury that Bloom said to him, "If Gay leaves us, we've got people who can come down from Las Vegas and make sure that Everett Gay doesn't play football again."

Another player swore that the agents had threatened to have someone break his hands.

And this is sports in America?

As I said in a column in June of 1987, "the charges in this case—fraud and tax evasion, extortion, racketeering, wire fraud and mail fraud—put one in mind of organized crime and godfathers, so severe, so criminal, does it sound. One almost expects to hear next of shoot-outs over linebackers at Umbertos Clam House in Little Italy (in Lower Manhattan)."

One of the key witnesses for the prosecution in the trial against Walters and Bloom was thirty-nine-year-old Michael Franzese, a self-admitted captain in the Colombo crime family, who in 1985 was indicted on fourteen counts—involving racketeering, counterfeiting, extortion, and tax evasion—not related to the case against Walters and Bloom. Franzese, a lifelong friend of Norby Walters, who had for most of his life referred to Walters as "Uncle Norby," is currently serving a ten-year federal sentence after pleading guilty to several counts of racketeering and tax evasion in the 1985 case.

Franzese indicated that his father, John "Sonny" Franzese, also a member of the Colombo crime family and also someone who had served time in prison, was for much of his life an associate of Mr. Walters in the music business. Franzese said he, too, had been involved with Walters in the music business and in 1984 had become a silent partner in his sports agency, giving Walters $50,000 in cash in return for 25 percent of the business. As part owner, his responsibilities would include trying to persuade would-be business associates of Mr. Walters to agree to the agents' business propositions.

According to the FBI, the threats to football players would allude to Franzese, but Franzese himself never made the threats. Franzese agreed to cooperate with the government in its case against Walters and Bloom, hoping his testimony would lead to a shorter prison sentence. It isn't known if his cooperation will help when the parole board reviews his case.

What a business. Sports in America. Will John Gotti be the next sports agent? It's such an outrage.

The federal government felt it couldn't let Walters and Bloom go without trying to bring them to justice, but they had to come up with an unusual hook to be able to get them to trial.

According to Tom DePaso, legal counsel for the NFL Players Association, Walters and Bloom were breaking the rules at will, assuming that NCAA rules are merely rules of a private organization, not laws of any government, and therefore no one can do anything about it.

Wrong. The government decided to go after Walters and Bloom with the RICO (Racketeer Influenced and Corrupt Organizations) Act. To effect this, they threatened to try the forty-four athletes signed to the agency on mail fraud charges, making each of them, if convicted, subject to five-year prison sentences. This threat forced the players, as part of the government deal, to provide testimony against Walters and Bloom, first before the grand jury, and then at the trial. Of the players, forty-three cooperated, and the one who didn't, Cris Carter, former Ohio State star and a former Philadelphia Eagle, was convicted of lying to the grand jury and was given a sentence of three years probation, a $15,000 fine, and six hundred hours of community service over three years.

The following is a list of the players who entered into pretrial agreements with the prosecutors. Included are their schools and graduating classes:

Egypt Allen, Texas Christian, '86; Jeffrey L. Atkins, Southern Methodist, '87; Teryl D. Austin, Pitt, '88; Jerry L. Ball, Jr., SMU, '87; Robert Banks, Notre Dame, '87; Raven Caldwell, Jr., Arkansas, '86; John Clay, Missouri, '87; Terry Coner, Alabama, '87; Kenneth Davis, TCU, '86; Donald Douglas DuBose, Nebraska, '87; Charles Faucette, Jr., Maryland, '87; Robert T. Flagler, Clemson, '87; Kenneth Flowers, Clemson, '87; Brent Fullwood, Auburn, '87; Everett Gay, Texas, '87; Charles R. Gladman III, Pitt, '88; Ronald Harmon, Iowa, '86; Carl Hilton, Houston, '86; Mark Ingram, Michigan State, '87; Mark Logan, Kentucky, '87; James Lott, Texas, '88; Terance Mann, SMU, '87; Timothy McGee, Tennessee, '86; Alvin Miller, Notre Dame, '87; Devon Mitchell, Iowa, '86; Ronald Morris, SMU, '87; Andrew Mott, Southern Miss, '87; Frankie Neal, Fort Hays (Kan.) State, '87; Paul Palmer, Temple, '87; Robert Perryman, Michigan, '87; Tom Powell III, Auburn, '87; Garland Rivers, Michigan, '87; Terrence Roulhac, Clemson, '87; Bradley D. Sellers, Ohio State, '86; Edwin Simmons, Texas,

'87; Timothy Smith, Texas Tech, '87; George W. Swarn III, Miami, '86; Craig Swoope, Illinois, '86; Raymond Tate, Houston, '87; Adrian White, Florida, '87; Lester Williams, Iowa State, '86; Stanley Anthony Woods, Pitt, '87; and Roderick Woodson, Purdue, '87.

In addition to Mike Franzese, the star witness, the prosecution relied heavily on the testimony of the Honorable Theodore Hesburgh, former president of Notre Dame, and Bo Schembechler, then football coach of the University of Michigan.

Ultimately, Walters and Bloom were found guilty on five counts of racketeering and fraud and were acquitted on two counts of mail fraud. Walters received a sentence of five years in prison, followed by five years of probation. Bloom was sentenced to three years in prison and three years probation. Walters would serve three years, four months, before being eligible for parole. Bloom would serve at least two years before facing a parole board.

I do not condone the activities that led up to the trial, but as a lawyer, I am deeply troubled by this case.

In the column from June of 1987, I wrote:

Let's be clear about something here. I do not sanction violation of rules or of law, by any agent or by any player; by any university president, coach, or overzealous alumni. But this investigation fascinates me and intrigues me because of the questions it raises about priorities, about law, about college sports. About the hypocrisy of universities that don't want to lose money. And about how we are willing to spend taxpayers' money to attack, not the heart of the problem, but the surface of it. Not to strike at what is really wrong, everywhere big-time college sports is played, but at a handful of people who may represent the symptoms but not the disease.

... I am a believer in our justice system, a fan of the courts, and a proponent of federal intervention, and to question the usefulness of this prosecution is very unusual. But question it I do. It is time-consuming, expensive, paid for by the public, and it won't cure the ills that afflict us. I doubt it will give one agent or one player pause before they sign a contract tomorrow, next month, or next year. Not until we rid our universities of big-money TV contracts for sporting events; not until we make colleges and universities places of learning, and not farm teams for the NFL and NBA, will we rid ourselves of these scandals; not until university presidents stand up and dump these awful football and basketball programs into the gutter where they belong will we have sport in its proper perspective. There isn't a prosecutor in the world who can accomplish in months of trial what Chancellor John Slaughter could have accomplished in one day, if he had eliminated Maryland's basketball program in the wake of the Len Bias death and scandal.

Perhaps the ugliest thing about this case is not the greed of the agents or the players, but the willingness of schools to join in and indict their own players along with these agents. Nothing in our recent history has so cleanly stripped academia of its pretenses as an educational institution, and exposed it as a money-grabbing business, terrified to lose NCAA and TV monies, should any of the players be convicted in court.

. . . If the government is going to get involved, then I remind you of an appearance I made in 1972 before the Senate to testify in favor of a federal sports commission. It was not a popular idea then. Nor is it now. So-called big government got a bad rap during the Reagan era. But in my view, the time has come for such a federal body. Are we to have federal prosecutors across the nation chasing after a handful of sports agents and college athletes? Are we to have NCAA rules here, state laws here and there, federal law, university policy on the one hand, TV and sports on the other? You think it's just fun and games and federal intervention is unnecessary? Then why are our sports pages filled with rules violations, scandals, court cases, grand juries, convictions, appeals, suspensions, fines, and even death?

Those words, written four years ago, are just as true today as they were then.

One of the things that bothers me most about the Walters and Bloom trial is the fact that the defendants and the players said that based on legal advice, they had no idea they were violating federal criminal laws. So was there actually a crime committed? The prosecutors claimed that Walters and Bloom defrauded the schools of funds the schools paid to the student-athletes in the form of tuition, room, and board. These payments were based on false certification, the prosecutors claimed, because the players had illegally signed contracts with the agents.

My point is, what money did the schools lose? None of the athletes were declared ineligible by the NCAA because of the signing by the agents. None of the schools were forced to forfeit any games, but Temple University did forfeit six games on a voluntary basis because running back Paul Palmer had signed a lucrative contract with Walters and Bloom. Ironically, Palmer claimed that Bloom used $125,000 of the players' money that was meant to be invested in a credit restoration business. Palmer said that Bloom spent the money for his personal use in leasing a Rolls-Royce, clothes, repaying personal debt, and buying karate lessons. The government contended that these actions by Bloom constituted fraud.

But the government was not contending that the players were the victims in the case. As previously stated, the government was threatening charges against the players unless they accepted immunity and turned state's evidence against the defendants. The prosecution's claim was that the NCAA schools were the victim, and I'm not sure that was the case. And as anyone with any legal savvy knows, for there to be a crime there has to be a victim.

I'll admit that Walters and Bloom broke NCAA rules. The government used the broad-based RICO law to prove that and I don't think it was appropriate. Nor do I think that breaking NCAA rules should be a federal crime. If the government wanted to try the case, they should have gone about it in another manner.

After the trial, federal judge George M. Marovich, who heard the case, called Walters and Bloom "bad actors" and predicted they would lose their appeal. He also felt that it was another "bad actor," Michael Franzese, whose testimony was most damaging. During the trial, Walters called Franzese a liar and said that he didn't need his cash to start up the agency. But Judge Marovich said that he felt the jury in convicting Walters and Bloom of racketeering believed Franzese.

All along, I had predicted that based primarily on legal precedent, Walters and Bloom would win their appeals. I told Walters as much when I saw him in the Friars Club in February of 1990. Walters and Bloom were free on bond pending their appeals.

Every time I would see Norby during the months following his conviction on April 13, 1989, I would give him encouragement. Norby would warmly shake my hand and tell me that his attorneys were basing their appeal on views stated in my syndicated column.

In announcing its ruling in favor of Walters and Bloom, the Seventh U.S. Circuit Court of Appeals in Chicago said Judge Marovich improperly refused to call Walters's testimony to the jurors' attention during his instructions to the panel.

The day following the announcement by the appeals court, Walters was flying high. Despite my encouragement, he knew all along that he could be facing five years in prison. Having that lifted is a big load off a person's mind. He breezed into the Friars Club in his flamboyant manner, giving hugs and high fives to friends and members. "We beat 'em. I love everybody. God bless the judges," he said.

Norby slapped me on the back and thanked me profusely for my support. His celebration was spontaneous and you couldn't help but feel happy for the man.

He sat down with Shelby and me for a few minutes before continuing his joyous rounds. Friars Club maître d' Frank Capitelli shook his head and smiled in disbelief and remarked, "Only in America."

In January of 1991, Walters and Bloom were shocked when the government announced that they would be retried in separate trials.

In an effort to control unscrupulous agents, and as a way of protecting the players while at the same time generating some additional revenue, the NFL Players Association in the seventies started a program of agent certification. The pro baseball and pro basketball unions have followed suit. These efforts have met with mixed results.

The union charges an application fee, annual dues, maintains a code of ethics for the agents, and requires them to attend educational seminars.

Mark Levin, the agent-system coordinator for the NFLPA, says that at one point in the eighties, the NFLPA had between 1,500 and 2,000 certified agents. That number has dwindled to 580, and since the football union has decertified and is an association, not a union, the organization no longer offers agent certification, but simply offers agent registration. The application fee is $100 and annual dues are $400. An agent must complete a nine-page application form, which concentrates on the applicant's credit rating and character. If an agent fails to pay his dues, demonstrates unethical behavior, or is convicted of a crime, his name is dropped from the union's list of agents in good standing.

In light of many scandals in recent years involving agents getting athletes to enter into premature agreements, many states, about twenty at the time of this writing, have passed legislation requiring agents to register with the state. These laws are for the most part like other previously mentioned state legislation, self-serving laws designed to protect the big-time state-college athletic programs and specifically, the big money derived from football and basketball. Some states require a registration fee of $1,000 per year, a much larger amount than lawyers pay annually to practice law in a state. Some states even require that agents post bond.

Tom DePaso, legal counsel for the NFLPA, says many states have gone overboard in order to protect the eligibility of the big-time college jock. "It's a nightmare for anyone who wants to abide legitimately by the law," says DePaso. "Administratively and financially, you are out of business before you even get into business. It's crazy. It's nuts."

All legitimate agents are up in arms over these requirements and restrictions. Obviously, because of all this protectionist legislation that's been promulgated by the various states, there is a pressing need for a national law to regulate registration of agents and to eliminate the massive confusion generated by the current state legislation.

One piece of admirable national legislation is the Bill Bradley–Tom McMillen bill, which requires all colleges to publicly announce the percentage of student-athletes who graduate from the school. These two Rhodes scholars understand the importance of education and want to make athletes aware of the deemphasis of education in college sports.

To its credit, the NCAA took the lead from this legislation and now makes it a requirement that the school provide the graduation-percentage information to any youngster before he or she signs a letter of intent to accept a scholarship.

Because of tremendous pressure to win, it's not surprising that college basketball coaches expanded their talent search to areas outside the United States. Maybe Al McGuire started it back in 1977 when he won the national championship for Marquette with Butch Lee of Puerto Rico in the backcourt.

The legendary Bob Knight had strong teams at Indiana with West Germany's 7'1" Uwe Blab at center. And Seton Hall came within a basket of winning the national title in 1989 with Andrew Gaze of Australia in the lineup.

One has to look no further than the Big East Conference to see the influx of foreign stars and the impact they have made on the game. Dikembe Motombo of Zaire is a force for Georgetown. Nadav Henefeld of Israel was instrumental in the Cinderella success of the University of Connecticut, which won the Big East Championship in 1989–90. (Henefeld bowed to pressure from his homeland and didn't return to Connecticut for his second season, remaining home and playing for the Israeli national team.) And Bill Wennington of Canada and Marco Baldi of Italy are past stars of St. John's University.

Personally I have no problem with a foreign athlete's playing for a college in the USA if he qualifies academically and is interested in pursuing an education. I don't agree with CBS analyst Billy Packer, who opposes scholarships to any foreigner based on the grounds that it denies an American youngster a chance to receive a scholarship.

Surely he couldn't mean someone like a Chris Washburn,
who scored a combined 470 on his SATs. Packer, from
North Carolina, Tobacco Road in the heart of Dixie, may be
so provincial that he would have denied landing rights to
Columbus. I was born in North Carolina, and I recognize
that not all people on Tobacco Road, which stretches from
Virginia to Georgia, agree with Packer.

Coaches will go to faraway places to sign a player who
might give their team an edge. The best example is Marist
College in Poughkeepsie, New York. Within the past six
years, Marist has had basketball players from France, Holland, Yugoslavia, Hungary, and Canada. Among them was
towering Rik Smits, a 7'4" center from Holland, a lottery
pick in the NBA draft, and a star player for the Indiana
Pacers. Oh, yes. Marist College also made the NCAA
dishonor roll, probation for rules violations in connection
with their basketball program, specifically in the recruitment of foreign athletes.

Seton Hall University, a Jesuit school in South Orange,
New Jersey, thought for a while in 1989 that it too, might
find its basketball team on probation, thanks to circumstances surrounding a foreign recruit. The Aussie, Andrew
Gaze, had been instrumental in propelling the Pirates to the
championship game of the 1989 Final Four.

No sooner had Seton Hall received its tournament
runner-up check for $1.2 million then Gaze took his three-
point jump shot and hightailed it back to the land of
kangaroos and boomerangs, having decided that he had had
enough of American education. In all, Andrew had completed courses in youth activities, first aid, and creative
movement. No kidding. Outrageous! Seton Hall officials
began to worry that they had a real live boomerang on their
hands. Reports began filtering back to the U.S. that before
Gaze came to America to further his "education" (and to
display his basketball skills), Gaze's basketball club back in
Melbourne had deposited $25,000 in a Gaze family trust
fund. Panic! Would Gaze be declared ineligible? Would the
Hall have to forfeit its wins and return the $1.2-million
tournament swag earned with Andrew in the lineup?

Melbourne Tigers general manager Bruce Ward claimed
that the trust fund did exist, but Seton Hall athletic director

Larry Keating said the trust fund was not for Andrew. He added, "There was a $25,000 general expense fund for *all* the players on the Melbourne team. Most of the money had never been used, and Gaze's father had kept it in case it was needed for club operating expenses."

You'll buy that, won't you, mate?

The NCAA did. According to Shawnee Mission, everything was kosher. Gaze was back home with his trust fund and Seton Hall kept its $1.2 million.

And that, my friends, is college sports in America—with a new international flavor!

Chris Washburn's admission to North Carolina State with a combined SAT score of 470 brings us to Proposition 48, and its offshoot, Proposition 42.

Simply stated, Proposition 48 says that a college athlete must have graduated from high school with a minimum of eleven college preparatory credits and a C average, and must score a combined total of 700 minimum on the SAT (or 15 on the ACT) in order to play sports in college. By enacting this proposition in 1986, the NCAA finally took an appropriate stand in terms of the academic requirements necessary for a student to be eligible to play sports. Certainly, the requirements would seem fair: the standards are minimal; no one is asked to attain anything more than the average. A Prop 48 student—one who fails these requirements— simply misses his first year of eligibility and plays three years instead of four.

So then, what's the problem? The problem is twofold. First, the charges of racism from predominantly black schools came swiftly and sharply. Why? The average white student scores 900 or more on the SAT, while the average black, 709–15. The average white athlete scores about the same 900 plus—but the average black athlete scores 650 or less. Without question, under the proposition the hardest hit would be black student-athletes and predominantly black colleges and universities, particularly members of the Southwestern Athletic Conference—schools such as the famed Grambling State University, Jackson State (alma mater of Walter Payton), and Texas Southern. These schools depend heavily on their athletic programs to provide an image, to help in recruiting students, and to achieve prestige.

Were the black schools right? Do these propositions punish black students unnecessarily? Are they tantamount to racist acts, not in word but in deed? "No," black activist Dick Gregory declares adamantly, "because I'm looking down the road at the future. And we need blacks with education. We need more black doctors, lawyers, scientists, not ball carriers."

"No," says black sociologist and educator Harry Edwards. "It's utterly ridiculous to call it racist. Blacks are pathological about this subject. They refuse to look in the mirror and see themselves as they are. We need education. We need teachers who can teach. Education is the core of the problem, and there is no future for any of us without it."

Digger Phelps also dismisses the charges of racism. Digger has had years of experience as a college coach, working with whites and blacks, and he believes the NCAA ruling, while painful for everyone in the short term, will ultimately be profitable for everyone.

One thing is clear. This is a complicated and sensitive issue. And one thing is certain. No matter what I say about this issue, someone, somewhere, will level charges of racism at me. They will be absolutely without foundation and this distresses me, but I will not remain silent, because the quality of education in this country is a problem that must be faced, by black and white alike. In the end, whatever is done, it is bound to be wrenching.

I believe that Edwards, Gregory, and Phelps are right, and that they make a compelling argument. Basically, they reject a double standard. They feel strongly that the heart of the matter is educational and societal, and not racial, despite the fact that black education historically has been so poorly funded and has handicapped black students in competition with whites. Furthermore, all three of these men long ago dismissed the idea that sports is a way up and out of poverty for young blacks. Certainly only a mere handful of the black population (and virtually all of that male) will make it into professional sports and actually earn a living. When compared with all the hours of practice, all the hours of games, and all the opportunities missed to study and learn to become a doctor or lawyer or accountant or businessman, it hardly seems a fair exchange.

Not that I don't ache for all these youngsters who are suddenly accountable in ways their predecessors were not. Certainly there's an element of unfairness, almost of cruelty in it, in the sense that the rules were changed so quickly. These kids must feel as if they're being punished for some crime they weren't aware of committing. If the American educational system were stronger, there would be no need for these athletic propositions.

But in truth, these black athletes are not the only ones who will pay the price of an educational system that failed them, and a society that prefers to overemphasize its sports at the expense of higher education. White athletes, too, are going to suffer. There are many who do not meet the NCAA standards, but they suffer in other ways as well.

This is the second part of the problem. The state of education has become a national tragedy, with dire ramifications for all students, white or black. It is unrealistic to argue otherwise, or to start from the assumption that whites are receiving a far superior brand of public education nationwide. It is true that they do in some of the wealthiest communities, but that is the exception, not the rule. Just look at some of the educational requirements laid down by the states. Maryland has no eligibility requirements for recruiting athletes—perhaps a contributing factor to the ugly and sad situation in recent years at the University of Maryland. New York has none either. In Florida and Louisiana, one needs only a 1.5 average, a D average, to qualify. Indiana, where Phelps coaches, also has a lower set of state eligibility requirements than those set by the NCAA. Phelps could, if he wished, choose to apply Indiana's standards and then wait to be disciplined by the NCAA—be suspended for a season, thrown out of tournaments, whatever the NCAA deemed appropriate. It's a risk Phelps won't take.

This country is only as good as its educational system and can only survive when education is funded properly, teachers are paid decently, when colleges and universities, white or black, have education as their priority, not football or basketball.

This problem does not discriminate; it cuts across racial lines and class lines to the very heart of what this nation says it's about. If we don't correct this disgraceful situation in our educational system, we will all pay the price—if not today, then tomorrow; and if not tomorrow, then in the years to come.

Nobody, but nobody, feels more deeply for the struggles that face the predominantly black college than I do. However, I had a long talk with Grambling coach Eddie Robinson, and what he said gave me hope: "We're going to be terribly hurt by this, Howard, and sometimes I think it's unfair. But we can do it. We have to do it. It's our task."

Proposition 48 was a step in the right direction—but it didn't go far enough. Some schools were still stockpiling Prop 48 students, nonqualifiers who simply sat out their freshman season and played three years instead of four. In the first year the proposition was enacted, Oklahoma had eight football players who were Prop 48s, De Paul had three basketball players, Michigan had two.

So in 1988, the NCAA, on a highly criticized second ballot at its convention in Dallas, passed the controversial Proposition 42, which eliminated the awarding of financial aid to athletes who did not meet Proposition 48 academic requirements. Now, with Prop 42, the offshoot of Prop 48, the NCAA had finally put some teeth in its efforts to control the schools that went after nonqualifying athletes.

And then the more militant black coaches went wild with screams of racism. Temple's basketball coach, John Chaney, perhaps the strongest critic of Prop 42, told *Inside Sports,* "You can't always say when somebody is a racist that he intends to be a racist. I can take a look at a guy that takes a truck and runs over a guy the first time; you mean the [first] time I'm going to know you're trying to kill me is when you back the wheels up over me? Forty-eight was already directed at a special group of people. Forty-two was the wheels coming over them."

Unbelievable. This man Chaney is a dangerous thinker. He receives absolution from Temple alum Bill Cosby, a man who would better serve blacks by taking a stronger stance on education.

I approved of Props 48 and 42 on very simple grounds. It

is right to have standards for admission to a college or university, and it is wrong not to have standards. Props 48 and 42 were right because not every young person is qualified to go to college, and not every young person should automatically be allowed into college.

The depth of the wrongness is lodged in the philosophy of John Chaney, who has made a name for himself, frequently using racism in the development of that name. He appeared on national television, CBS's "Face the Nation," with a distinguished correspondent, Lesley Stahl, who by giving him a national forum invested him with rights as a spokesman for a point of view that is utterly antithetical to education in this country.

As an illustration of Chaney's philosophy at work, consider the sordid story of Lloyd Daniels, great basketball prospect out of New York City—some say the best prospect out of New York City since Lew Alcindor (Kareem Abdul-Jabbar).

Although Daniels's academic record reflected that he had attended five high schools, had received no high school diploma, had failed at several attempts to attain a junior college degree, and had a history including several drug incidents, he was admitted to the University of Nevada–Las Vegas. After two weeks at UNLV, Daniels was busted for buying crack.

To his credit, Coach Jerry Tarkanian then said, "Lloyd Daniels will never play for UNLV regardless of the outcome of his case."

So who was one of the first to declare he would gladly take Daniels at his school of higher learning? You guessed it: John Chaney of Temple.

Daniels has clearly demonstrated that he is no scholar, that his sole purpose for being on a college campus is to play basketball. The argument presented by people like Chaney, however, is that people such as Daniels are entitled to an education, that because their roots are in poverty and because they are black, they are entitled to use a sport as a basis for "getting an education."

This attitude in my opinion reflects pure racism. You don't help such people in this way; you corrupt them. You lead them to believe that all they need to enable them to advance in this society is the ability to play basketball, which clearly is nonsense. Furthermore, by doing so you corrupt and destroy the educational system.

So much for the philosophy of John Chaney.

This is the same John Chaney, a former national coach of the year, who is famous for holding basketball workouts at six A.M. This is what college is all about?

The same John Chaney who in 1984, in an altercation at midcourt in a Temple game against George Washington University, grabbed George Washington head coach Gerry Gimelstob with both hands around the neck in an apparent effort to choke him.

It is the same John Chaney who in 1990 called Philadelphia sportscaster Howard Eskin of WIP radio a racist and threatened him with physical harm. Chaney said to Eskin's producer, "Tell your motherfucking boss Howard Eskin that he's a racist and that I'm going to punch him in the motherfucking mouth." This was an offshoot of Eskin's criticizing Chaney for the way he handled the situation when 7' Temple center Duane Causwell flunked out of school. Later Causwell would be an NBA first-round draft choice of the Sacramento Kings, who signed him to a two-year contract for $1.4 million.

It's the same John Chaney who in 1990 during a game on the home court of the University of Massachusetts physically pushed U Mass head coach John Calipari during a midcourt argument. Chaney simply has a track record of losing control of himself.

In an ESPN interview that I gave to Dick Schaap, I referred to John Chaney as a "national disgrace." I rest my case.

When it was reported that Atlantic 10 Conference commissioner Ron Bertovich started an investigation amid rumors of a possible Chaney suspension, Temple athletic director Charlie Theokas said, "There's absolutely no truth to the rumor about an impending suspension." Bertovich denied the existence of a formal investigation of Chaney. Theokas is the former commissioner of the Atlantic 10, and many feel he still runs the league.

Another severe critic of Props 48 and 42 was John Thompson, the three-hundred-pound head coach at

Georgetown University, one of the country's truly fine universities. In many ways I have great respect for John Thompson. Unlike Chaney, who fails to develop properly outstanding players such as Mark Macon, and whose teams are poorly coached in that they are very predictable, Thompson is a good coach. The main complaints against John have been that he's overly protective of his kids, and that he has recruited few white players in his almost two decades at Georgetown. I am not concerned with these two charges. His kids may actually benefit from being sheltered from sportswriters, and Thompson is entitled to recruit whomever he wants. Besides, he actively recruited Chris Mullin, who went to St. John's. And he tried to recruit Danny Ferry, who didn't seriously consider Georgetown and went to Duke. And I can't believe that Thompson wouldn't have taken Rex Chapman, who went to Kentucky and then to the Charlotte Hornets. Charles Barkley of the 76ers, speaking at the NBA All-Star Game in Miami, said that Chapman, a white player, had "the legs of a brother." Certainly Thompson would love to have had Rex Chapman at Georgetown. He's one of the few white players who would fit in with John's basketball style. The point should be made that Thompson has had white assistants ever since he's been at Georgetown, so it can't be said with validity that he discriminates in that regard. However, John did admit on my "Sportsbeat" program on ABC television that he might "have a trace of racism."

My main problem with Thompson's program is that Georgetown obviously lowered its academic standards to get some of his players into school. Two of his early stars, Craig Shelton and John Duren, were marginal high school students from the D.C. inner city, and there was much speculation among college coaches who were recruiting the two that neither might qualify for any four-year college. Yet both were quickly accepted at Georgetown. To Thompson's credit, if marginal students are admitted, he does implement an assistance program, offering tutoring help and supervision; as a result, an overwhelming percentage of his players get a degree from Georgetown.

When Thompson came to Georgetown from St. Anthony High School in D.C., he brought along a white biology teacher named Mary Fenlon and made her an assistant coach in charge of academics. That's the woman you've seen sitting near the Georgetown bench for all these years. Over the past couple of decades her duties have been expanded, and Mary Fenlon is the one person more than anyone else who makes John Thompson's basketball program run smoothly.

Mary is largely responsible for the fact that fifty-seven of the first fifty-nine players who played for Thompson for four years have graduated from Georgetown.

One of those who didn't last four years is an embarrassment to Thompson. John Turner, a 6'8" forward, along with center Alonzo Mourning, became friends with Washington, D.C., drug kingpin Rayful Edmond III, who in February of 1990 was sentenced to life in prison for conspiring and running a drug network. Thompson went on ABC's "Nightline" and told about meeting with Edmond in an effort to prevent any of his players from being hurt by their association with him. This is college sports in America, ladies and gentlemen.

Apparently Mourning backed away from the drug lord, but Turner maintained his relationship, and Thompson dropped him from the team and ultimately he dropped out of school. In the summer of 1989, Turner was arrested near his home in Glenarden, Maryland, and was charged with possession of cocaine with intent to distribute. (The charges were later dropped.) Late word, however, is that Turner has been recycled in the basketball program at Phillips University in Enid, Oklahoma, and is doing just great, thank you. The '90-'91 season was his last year of eligibility at Phillips.

Thompson has won the national title at Georgetown, put his school in the NCAA tournament for thirteen straight seasons, but was a bust as the Olympic coach for the USA, finishing third at the Seoul Olympics.

His publicity-seeking boycott of two games at the start of the 1988 season in protest of Proposition 42 was in my opinion not one of the highlights of his career. He walked off the Capital Centre court in Landover, Maryland, before the start of a game against Boston College, then boycotted a second game before believing he had made his point.

Thompson is proud of his boycott, but personally, I feel it

ranks with his performance of 1990 when he was called for three technical fouls, resulting in ejection in the first half of a game against Syracuse. His childish and unforgivable action, a wonderful example for the youth of our country, resulted in an incredible ten-point play for Syracuse and made Georgetown a loser in the game.

Chaney and Thompson are masters of intimidation, both are famous for sneering at game officials, and maybe their ranting and raving about Proposition 42 had some influence on NCAA voters when it came time to review the legislation. Regardless, the convention, again meeting in Dallas in 1990, took the teeth out of Prop 42 by making it possible for a nonqualifier, a Prop 48 student, to obtain financial aid from nonathletic sources within the university. Most Prop 48 nonqualifiers qualify for nonathletic aid scholarships on the basis of need, so in most cases, money that could go toward educating some deserving, qualified student will go to supporting some jock who is just waiting to play ball his sophomore year—another victory for athletic corruption, and in this case, racism, too.

The argument that Georgetown can use in lowering its admission standards for basketball players is simple: everyone else is doing it. Sad but true; most are. If an up-and-coming Moses Malone or Patrick Ewing can just get a high school diploma, any of 150 to 200 schools throughout the country will quickly get him past the dean of admissions. Don't be surprised if John Thompson brags, "We've never recruited a Prop 48 student." They'll never show you the students' records, so we can just give John the benefit of the doubt on that one. But don't let him tell us that over the last two decades Georgetown has never bent its admission standards for any of his players.

I was delighted to see Arthur Ashe, the tennis star and author, endorse Prop 48 and Prop 42 in an op-ed piece in *The New York Times.* Ashe knows what education is all about.

No one knew Jackie Robinson better than I. Had Jackie been alive, he would have been one of the first to say that Props 48 and 42 were correct. He was a man of vision, unlike some basketball coaches concerned with twenty wins and a tournament bid. Unlike some John Chaney dreaming of Lloyd Daniels taking him to the Final Four. (Incidentally, Chaney can forget Daniels. After being shot three times in a drug deal gone sour, Daniels recovered and turned professional. He's playing in various leagues, with hopes of making it to the NBA.)

Those who claim we don't need to maintain minimum standards for admission of student-athletes are just as wrong as those who claim we should pay college athletes. Every time some player is caught taking some large amount of illegal money—or every time college basketball has one of its patented little point-shaving scandals—sportswriters will start crying, "Let's pay the student-athlete. The universities are exploiting the athletes, making large sums of money off them, and they deserve to be paid."

Dr. Bart Giamatti answered this preposterous proposition best: "That is not what a college or a university is for. Don't pour more fuel on the fire. Big-time college athletics must be seriously reformed, or abolished."

John Nash, the fine general manager of the Washington Bullets, agrees. When he saw me at the 1990 NBA All-Star Game in Miami (he was general manager of the Philadelphia 76ers at the time), Nash hugged me and said, "Howard, you seem to be one of the few who understands. Don't pay the college kids a stipend. No. No. No. Reform the messy situation which now exists. The Ivy League does it the right way. If a kid wants to be a pro basketball player and is not ready for the NBA, let him play in the minors, the CBA, or in the European leagues."

John Nash is a pro executive who recognizes the college problem. He is a breath of fresh air.

<u>CHAPTER</u> SEVEN

From Campanis to the Greek to Kiam to Wyche

There is really no bigotry in sports . . . if there were more qualified blacks to go into sports management, you would certainly see more of them in sports management jobs," said publisher Roger Stanton in a letter to NBC's Tom Brokaw.

Garbage! Ludicrous!

In his letter, Stanton indicted himself as either one of the world's dumbest men, one of the world's biggest bigots, or both.

First, let's review a few incidents that happened within one month in early 1989. They will certainly demonstrate that racism, in many forms, is alive and well in the American sports structure. It raises its ugly head in many ways, some subtle, some not so subtle. At the same time, I will demonstrate that a supersensitivity exists, one that clearly reflects a double standard.

In January, Georgetown University played the University of Connecticut in basketball. During the game, Georgetown center Alonzo Mourning, a black player who was struggling through a personally disappointing season, allegedly had some nasty things to say to Nadav Henefeld, the rugged Israeli star who led the U Conn team to thirty-one wins.

At one point in the game, Mourning, who is known for

talking trash to opposing players during play, reportedly called Henefeld "you dirty Jew." It didn't seem to bother Henefeld, who had three years training in the tough Israeli army, an outfit that specializes in "six-day wars." Henefeld went on to lead Connecticut to a win over Georgetown, the first of two wins for the Huskies over the Hoyas that season.

The next week, the New York Rangers played the Boston Bruins in the Boston Garden. In that game, during the heat of battle, Rangers left wing Chris King reportedly called Bruins right wing Graeme Townshend, one of only six black players in the National Hockey League, "a fucking nigger." King denied it, but some players insisted that he had said it. It was a tough week for Townshend. A few days after suffering the racial slur, he was sent back down to the minor leagues.

If you thought racial epithets ceased after the Jackie Robinson era, you were wrong.

College basketball got back into the racial spotlight a couple of weeks later; once again, the infamous Tates Locke was cast in the role of a villain. His Indiana State club hosted Wichita State at Terre Haute, Indiana, ultimately losing (one of the twenty games it was to lose in the '89–'90 season).

During the contest, which Indiana State lost by a score of 67–60, Tates protested a traveling call by throwing his money clip and wallet onto the playing court, an action that resulted in two technical fouls for the Sycamores coach. Locke will soon learn that it's more prudent to be winning twenty games instead of losing twenty games before one starts throwing things; authorities somehow seem to take a more lenient posture with a winner.

Locke's troubles didn't stop with the throwing of his money clip and wallet. He told a postgame news conference, "The officiating in our league [the Missouri Valley Conference] is awful, but that was the worst out there. The officiating in our league is a terrible problem that has to be addressed."

But what a way Locke decided to address it. Referring to referee Willie Sanchez, who made the disputed traveling call, Tates said, "I did find one thing out today: why it took so many Mexicans to win, to beat our guys at the Alamo. I just found that out today, because one of them was working the game."

Unlike the first two racial slurs I had detailed, mumbled during the heat of play, this one was made publicly, to the press. Obviously it required some action. Missouri Valley Conference commissioner Doug Elgin said Locke was officially reprimanded by the league for his remark.

The following day, Indiana State University president Richard G. Landini, known as a law-and-order hard-liner who shocked observers when he hired renegade Locke, covered for Tates a bit by issuing the following statement: "Locke's ethnic allusion lacked taste and sensitivity. Indiana State does not condone such behavior. It is inappropriate among people of good will and completely out of place within a university."

In more of the prepared statement, Landini said Locke "has expressed his regret." The statement continued, "He has expressed his apologies to the public at large, and to all who were offended, justifiably, by his allusions. I take him at his word when he tells me that his remarks were an ill-considered attempt at wry humor under stressful circumstances. I do not believe that his allusion is a true reflection of his thought and character."

Some humor, Tates!

A few days after the Locke affair, former New York Knicks star and pro basketball Hall of Famer Walt Frazier, now an analyst for Madison Square Garden cable and the New York Knicks radio network, committed a faux pas. Frazier, during a broadcast in which he was describing the progress made by former Georgia Tech all-American and Cleveland Cavaliers star guard Mark Price, said some felt that Price was "too short, too slow, and too white to make it big in the NBA." Listeners protested with calls and mail.

Of course, I know Walt didn't mean anything derogatory. He knows about Larry Bird, Jerry West, Bob Cousy, John Havlicek, Bob Pettit, Pete Maravich, Tom Heinsohn, George Mikan, Bill Walton, Dave DeBusschere, and Bill Bradley. Those white boys could play!

Then there was the case of little Billy Packer saying on CBS, "I didn't know Jews could play basketball." Maybe Packer was kidding. Maybe not. Regardless, some viewers were offended. How about Dolph Schayes, Nat Holman, Art Heyman, Tal Brody, Larry Brown, Lenny Rosenbluth, Ernie Grunfeld, Neal Walk, Sid Tannenbaum, Donnie Foreman, Harry Boykoff, Hy and Java Gotkin, Marty Friedman, and Red Holtzman. You see, Billy, not all Jews are doctors, lawyers, accountants, and bankers. And all of these athletes accomplished their on-court greatness without the aid of the Pump!

It's true that most Jewish students are encouraged to concentrate on academics, and Jewish athletes are considered rebels from Jewish tradition. Normally sports is not the sphere in which Jews strive to excel. But for some, sports does prove to be a passport to a better life.

Accordingly, there have been some great Jewish athletes besides the basketball players listed above. Sandy Koufax, Barney Ross, Mark Spitz, Hank Greenberg, Sid Luckman, Al Rosen, and Sid Gordon were tremendous athletes. And there were no better front-office people than Gabe Paul, Red Auerbach, Al Davis, Abe Saperstein, and Sid Gilman.

Of course, Jews have been subjected to anti-Semitism in sports as in other fields. Unfortunately, some things never change.

Some white people are fond of saying about blacks, "I've never walked a mile in a black man's shoes." But I was associated closely enough with Jackie Robinson and Muhammad Ali, and was so supportive of their unpopular crusades—Jackie's integrating baseball and Ali's fighting the military draft—that I probably came as close as any white man will ever come. I doubt that any man, through the mail, has ever been called a "nigger-loving Jew bastard" as much as I. Throughout my entire life, I have endured ethnic and racial slurs—and growing up in Brooklyn, I took some physical beating simply for being a Jew. So I have empathy for those who encounter racial intolerance, and I'm happy to say that much of my entire life has been dedicated to correcting injustices and inequities in society.

The flip side of all this, however, and one of the many things that disturbs me in connection with racism, is oversensitivity. Minority groups are so sensitive to racial intolerance in America today that anyone in public life must constantly be on guard, sometimes to the point of absurdity, so as not to offend certain groups or races with what one says or writes.

I have purposely written some examples into the past few pages to illustrate my point, which includes racial inconsistencies and double standards.

When I alluded to the Six-Day War, it is likely that I antagonized those of Arab descent or those of Arab sympathies. And can you imagine the furor if I had referred to a group of black athletes as "black boys"?

In many cases, it depends on who is doing the talking or writing. When Temple basketball coach John Chaney, at a news conference, referred to his predominantly black team as "spineless and brainless," it didn't create much of a ripple. But had a white coach referred to a predominantly black team as "spineless and brainless," there would have been humongous cries of racism and discrimination.

In 1983, *The Washington Post* tried to paint me with its racism brush when I innocently made the "little monkey" remark about the Redskins' Alvin Garrett, a person for whom I had great admiration. It was a term that I affectionately used when talking to my grandchildren. I detailed all this in my last book, *I Never Played the Game*. And even some of my harshest critics admitted that *The Washington Post,* one of the two greatest newspapers in the country, took a cheap shot.

A decade earlier, Shelby Whitfield wrote in *Kiss It Goodbye* that "from a racial standpoint, all was not well with the Senators when Jim Lemon was manager. Black outfielder Ed Stroud once told me, 'That man Lemon called us monkeys.' When Hank Allen would run after a fly ball, according to Stroud, Lemon would say, 'Look at that monkey go.'"

I know that plenty of people from *The Washington Post* read that book, but none of them followed with articles about Lemon. When Howard Cosell was involved, however, the *Post* made it a federal case. As I indicated, it all boils down to how someone in editorial control wants to play the game.

Up to this point, I have referred to mostly superficial issues. By saying this I don't mean to minimize racial slurs or racial innuendo, because any recipient of a racial epithet knows that it is not a minor or inconsequential thing. There are, however, far more important issues. Issues such as where a person can live; what organizations or clubs a person can join; where a person can work; and whether a person has opportunities to advance professionally and socially and to develop abilities and potential. These are the important issues. And in the fantasylike atmosphere of the sports world, pitiful conditions exist.

It's shameful that woman reporters were still being abused in the National Football League during the 1990 season. New England Patriots owner Victor Kiam, who also owns the Remington razor company, made a total fool of himself with his flip reaction to some of his players' harassing and abusing reporter Lisa Olson in the locker room. Cincinnati Bengals coach Sam Wyche came off as a total idiot when he banned female reporters. Both Kiam and Commissioner Paul "I'm Too Tall" Tagliabue were forced into damage control. For financial reasons, Kiam and the National Football League need the support of women in this country.

And wasn't it a disgrace that it took a PGA golf tournament at the Shoal Creek Country Club in Alabama to call to the attention of the world that blacks are still not allowed to be members of certain clubs. So, the PGA pressured Shoal Creek into rushing out and signing a token black. At about the same time, the organizers at the Augusta National Club in Georgia rushed out and signed a token black so as not to encounter the same problems with the famed Masters tournament that the PGA encountered with its championship. How sad it is.

An old friend of mine, pro basketball Hall of Famer K. C. Jones, then an assistant coach with the Seattle Supersonics, told me in 1990, "Howard, there will always be racism. I've experienced it all of my life, it's there now, and it will be there in the future. I'm not saying that ten percent or that fifty percent of the people are racist. But it exists in America by degrees, and I have personal knowledge and I've had personal experiences of racism across the country." K.C., a former San Francisco University and Boston Celtics star, continued, "When I was looking to purchase a house in Framingham, a suburb of Boston, the realtor drove me by a nice home with a for-sale sign out front. 'That looks nice,' I said, but the realtor replied, 'I can't show you that one because they don't want any niggers; the neighbors will be mad.'"

Jones said, "That's the type of racism I'm talking about. I bought another house in that community and lived there for ten years. But it's not just a real estate problem. There are still some clubs I can't go into, and I was turned away from a restaurant in Andover, Massachusetts. Also, I had black friends in Chicago who had a cross burned on their lawn, and black friends in San Francisco who had a brick thrown through their window."

Continuing to open his heart to me, Jones continued, "The important point is how you deal with racism. If you allow it to consume you, then you are not going to live your own life or do the best you can in life."

K.C. admitted to being angry and undergoing a serious depression for a number of years after his dismissal as head coach of the Washington Bullets. He was head coach of the Bullets for three years, finishing first in his division twice and second in the division the other year. Jones was bitter that he had to wait seven years for another head-coaching job to come his way when Red Auerbach, who had brought him back to Boston in 1977 as an assistant, promoted him to the head job. Auerbach has an admirable record in this area. In 1950, he brought the first black player, guard Chuck Cooper of Duquesne, into the NBA, and in 1966, he hired the first black head coach, Bill Russell.

After five years of coaching the Celtics, K.C. moved into the front office. But he said, "My job was only titular, because General Manager Jan Volk was running a one-man show."

When K.C.'s old friend and former assistant coach with the Bullets, Bernie Bickerstaff, realized he was unhappy, he offered Jones an assistant coaching job in Seattle. In a move that surprised many, K.C. jumped at it. (Jones was elevated to the Sonics' head-coaching job after the '89–'90 season when Bickerstaff, citing bad health, moved up to the general manager's job. Later in 1990, Bickerstaff would leave the Sonics to become general manager of the Denver Nuggets.)

The coaching situation for blacks is far better in the NBA

than in other sports, but K.C. points out that only six of the twenty-seven franchises have black head coaches. And he made the point that Bickerstaff had to wait twelve years as an assistant coach before getting a head-coaching interview with any club. He added, "Some white assistants come in and spend a year or two on the bench and get a head job. Boom! Nobody called Bernie. He had to go out and use the network system. He was persistent and finally got a friendly ear in Seattle. No, it's not as easy as it looks for a black to get a head-coaching job in the NBA." (And remember, basketball is light-years ahead of football and baseball, which I have not yet addressed.)

You'll find racism in the front office and on the field, but unfortunately, it doesn't stop there. It spills over into the press box.

One person who left little doubt about his racist feelings was the late Roger Stanton, a Detroit-based publisher of two national sports publications, *Football News* and *Basketball Weekly,* both of which rely heavily on gambling-related advertising, and both of which cover college and pro football and basketball. In June of 1990, Stanton died of cancer.

Stanton and his wife, Pam, were comfortable mixing with club owners, front-office types, plus NFL and college administrators. For nineteen years, Pam wrote a frivolous column in the publications, naming the best-dressed people in football and basketball. When Roger died, she gave up the weekly column, but continues the inane best-dressed ratings.

Had she done an all-racist list, it would have been hard to keep her husband from the top.

In his infamous letter of April 26, 1989, to NBC's Tom Brokaw, Roger wrote that "black players traditionally lack discipline and they are the ones most likely to get into trouble. . . . Generally speaking, black players have not had the same discipline at home that white players have had and consequently are much harder to control when they are participating in college athletics. The vast majority of problems that face college athletics today involve a black player. These include drugs, petty crimes, and breaking the rules. The black player in general pays less attention to such things as showing up on time or following a rigid routine."

Astoundingly, Stanton continued, "The black athlete has greater emotional swings than the white athlete. While the white player also has highs and lows, it is not to the degree of the black player."

After calling Prof. Harry Edwards of the University of California "one of the biggest black bigots in the country, who is hiding under the guise of respectability as a college professor," he charged Dr. Edwards with seeing racial bias everywhere, even in places where it doesn't exist.

Of blacks, Stanton wrote, "They can be doctors, lawyers, or businessmen if they so desire. But it takes a lot of hard work and discipline, and in many cases they are not willing to pay the price."

Citing a tired and indefensible argument, Stanton continued, "We now have black quarterbacks but we have few of them, and only one has made it to the Super Bowl. That was Doug Williams of the Washington Redskins and that may have been a fluke. Frankly speaking, the quarterback is a very intricate position and there are not very many blacks who are qualified to be quarterbacks. You can call it racial prejudice or anything you like, but it is a fact. There has been no great quarterback yet in the NFL to compare to Roger Staubach, Bob Griese, Fran Tarkington [sic], Joe Namath, Terry Bradshaw, or any of the other super quarterbacks, and I don't think there will be one soon . . . the best players get to play because that is the American way and the prejudices of long-gone years have been forgotten."

Incredibly, Stanton proceeded, "I will guarantee you that if you gave twenty white college football players an IQ test and twenty black college players an IQ test that the whites would outshine the blacks every time."

It was the most remarkably stupid letter that I have read in my thirty-eight years of sports journalism.

I spoke with Brokaw about the Stanton letter and he said, "Howard, it was so ridiculous, so off base, that I didn't dignify it with any on-air rebuttal."

Under the First Amendment, Roger Stanton was free to express his beliefs. He was also free to expose his character and moral fiber. He was also free to show the world that, as a not-so-distinguished sports publisher, he couldn't spell the name of Fran Tarkenton, whom he admitted to being a super player, and I might add, a very well-known quarterback, a Hall of Famer.

The college basketball coaches' association responded with an open letter to Mr. Stanton in which it called his letter to Mr. Brokaw "totally irresponsible, highly inflammatory, unfounded, in poor taste, and completely out of line."

Stanton, recognizing his public relations blunder and the financial ramifications it might cause, undertook some efforts at damage control. He went on a Detroit radio show hosted by former baseball all-star Denny McLain and issued an apology. How appropriate and how ironic that Stanton would go on with McLain. The former Cy Young Award winner and last major leaguer to win thirty games in one season (he won thirty-one for the Tigers in 1968) was twice suspended from baseball (for carrying a gun and for gambling-related activities). After baseball, he was sentenced to twenty-three years in federal prison for loan-sharking, racketeering including bookmaking, and cocaine possession (Denny served twenty-nine months). Certainly he was not one of those white athletes who never got into trouble. How ironic that McLain could leave prison and become a radio star, a fact that tells you something about the listening audience.

If Denny could have had Bob Probert of the Detroit Red Wings and ex–Michigan State basketball star Scott Skiles on at the same time, Stanton could have led a seminar on clean Caucasian culture, for like McLain, Probert and Skiles have records of run-ins with law officials. Probert went from the penalty box to the big house for cocaine smuggling. Skiles had trouble staying out of jail at Michigan State before joining the NBA, where he now plays for the Orlando Magic.

Stanton belittled Doug Williams for a Super Bowl MVP performance and failed to recognize his impressive professional career over a decade, half of which was with a mediocre Tampa Bay team. And I'll bet two of the NFL's better quarterbacks, Randall Cunningham of the Eagles and Warren Moon of the Oilers, both black quarterbacks with riflelike arms, would love to have had Roger Stanton as a pass-receiving target.

Ironically, in 1989, the year of Stanton's incredible letter, Roger's three home-state football teams—the Detroit Lions, the Michigan State Spartans, and the Michigan Wolverines—had black starting quarterbacks. And I'm sure Roger was happy to see Andre Ware, the black quarterback from the University of Houston, win the Heisman Trophy in 1989. And wouldn't you know it, Ware was drafted by the Detroit Lions.

It was interesting to see Roger Stanton, after his letter, give an award to black sportscaster Lynn Swann of ABC as the year's most improved sportscaster. I wonder if Swann was aware of the racist views Stanton expressed in his letter to Brokaw.

On one occasion, Emmy and I attended a Super Bowl party hosted by Stanton and his wife. That was before I learned of the man's racist views. Roger Stanton should have limited his invitations to Lester Maddox and Bull Connor types.

I recognize that it's popular to say and write kind things about people after their death, but in view of the racist letter by Roger Stanton, some of the eulogies printed in the *Football News* following Roger's death were incredible. Hugh Culverhouse, owner of the Tampa Bay Bucs, wrote, "He was a great friend to the Buccaneers and the National Football League. He will always be remembered as someone who was interested in all the facets of our sport, not just the negative aspects that some journalists dwell on."

Billy Sullivan, Jr., president of the New England Patriots, wrote, "Since Roger was such a complete success as a human being, the rewards that will come to him in eternity will serve to compensate for the manner in which he devoted his mind and body to those who were not as fortunate as he."

Lee Iacocca, chairman of the board of the Chrysler Corporation, wrote, "Roger was a great friend and an asset to the Detroit community. He will be missed." I wonder how black workers at Chrysler feel about that.

Mike Lynn, the general manager of the Minnesota Vikings, wrote about Stanton, "He really loved the NFL and it showed. He was always making suggestions about things we [the league] should do, and he wasn't afraid to put them into print. He will really be missed, not only by this team but by all teams. He was a true friend and supporter of the NFL."

Former commissioner Pete Rozelle wrote of Stanton, "Our friendship went all the way back to my days with the Rams. I hope and pray it'll be possible for you [Pam Stanton] to keep the paper going and continue what Roger started so many years ago. His buoyant optimism and generous friendship with me will be sorely missed."

As I read each letter, I cringed at the thought of Stanton's racist position in his communiqué to Tom Brokaw.

One could continue recounting revolting race-related incidents ad nauseam. So I'll regale you with just a couple more before addressing the more important issues of this chapter.

In November of 1989, there was an investigation of an illegal slush fund at the University of Minnesota. In the course of the investigation, former Golden Gopher football player Andre Gilbert of Chicago testified that he was called a "supernigger" by members of Joe Salem's coaching staff before Salem was replaced by Lou Holtz in 1983. Gilbert said the white coaches would tell him, "We need a couple more superniggers like you." When reached for comment, Salem said, "There was a lot of tension that last year, but I don't know if it was racial."

Don't think the players have a monopoly on racial controversy. The racial mix of cheerleaders, whether high school, college, or pro, is always a hot potato. For example, in March of 1990, *The Washington Post* reported that more than half of the forty-member Redskinettes had charged management of the cheerleading group with favoritism, nepotism, verbal abuse, and racism. One of the charges was that management did not include black members of the squad in personal appearances in such places as Atlantic City.

For a while there in the eighties, it appeared that the public had become complacent about racism in sports. Then Al Campanis came along to shock the nation. The Los Angeles Dodgers vice president for player personnel accepted an invitation to go on ABC's "Nightline" with Ted

Koppel, a show meant to be a tribute to Jackie Robinson, who broke baseball's color barrier forty years earlier. Little did the seventy-year-old Campanis, who had been a Dodger front-office employee for thirty-seven years, know that the TV appearance would end his career.

On the program, Campanis said, among other things, that blacks lacked the "necessities" to become field managers and top-level club executives. Koppel gave Campanis every chance to reverse his comments, but incredibly, Campanis dug himself a deeper grave by implying that blacks didn't have what it takes to be pitchers or quarterbacks, and that they lacked the buoyancy to be good swimmers.

Campanis offered an apology the next day, and Dodger owner Peter O'Malley initially indicated that he would support his beleaguered VP. However, intense pressure from Commissioner Peter Ueberroth and others prompted O'Malley to fire Campanis the following day. At the time, baseball had no black managers, no black general managers, and no black owners, a situation that suddenly became an additional part of the controversy and one that could not withstand the fallout of the Campanis explosion. As it developed, Al Campanis, unwittingly, would do more for blacks in baseball than anyone could imagine.

On a personal level, the almost unbelievable Campanis statements were a sad thing for me. He's an old friend. We were classmates at NYU. His words were reprehensible and indefensible, but there is goodness in the man. He was a friend of Jackie Robinson's and they played together on the Montreal team in the minor leagues. As a matter of fact, he was one of few players who befriended Robinson in stressful times. Al worshiped Branch Rickey, the man who brought Robinson to the majors, and he has collected all the old Branch Rickey tapes.

I feel that Campanis's statements were more of an expression of sportsworld management than a statement of his personal feelings. But how could he say such things? Before his "Nightline" appearance, I had always thought that Al's biggest screwup came in college, when he cost our team a football bowl invitation. Georgetown was kicking off to NYU. The ball went into the end zone, and Campanis screamed to his teammates, "Don't touch it! Don't touch it!" Georgetown fell on the ball for a touchdown, the only score of the game. Al denies the incident, but it happened. Generally, however, he was a hell of an athlete, a great college second baseman.

Al Campanis and his racist statements on TV brought racism in sports back into the white public consciousness. It had never disappeared, of course, but for a while it had no longer been fashionable to talk about racism. White America had tired of the subject, and those of us—black and white—who still hammered away at racism were accused of being tiresome or embittered. Besides, isn't sports where young blacks get their chance to "make it"? Sports were viewed as the big equalizer, the road to success for blacks, and that attitude sneaked back into fashion somehow, even though statistics have long proven what a dangerous falsehood that notion is.

The Campanis incident led me to rethink my past, the roads I have traveled in sports for thirty-eight years, and to reflect on what, if anything, has changed, on what progress, if any, we have made. Yes, outwardly sports have changed in my lifetime. If you travel south in the spring to watch your favorite team work out, you will not see water fountains labeled "whites only" and "colored." Darryl Strawberry and Howard Johnson drink from the same public water fountain. They use the same public rest room at the airport. Yes, that is progress.

Nor will you find Rachel Robinson climbing through a broken slat of fence to get into the ball park to watch her husband play. No one will throw a black cat at him on the field. No teammates will refuse to play on the same diamond with him. The crowd won't insult him on racial grounds, not anymore. No one will throw garbage at Hank Aaron. Larry Doby and Monte Irvin won't have to be bused to a special part of town to eat and sleep and call it home. Now Tony Gwynn travels with his teammates, stays in the same fine hotels, eats in the nicest restaurants with them, and no one has refused to play on the Padres with him because of his skin color. Yes, one has to call all these examples of progress.

They do not, however, represent enough progress. Not enough has changed. We cannot, those of us who constitute white America, comfort ourselves with visions of integrated playing fields and black players checking into the Hyatt for an overnight stay.

Spend thirty-eight years in sports and you will see, like me, the face of racism in all its ugliness. And if you are a decent and caring human being, you feel it in your bowels and it makes you sick. I watched racism surface in one form with Jackie Robinson. I felt the full, horrible weight of it—as much as a white man can feel—with Muhammad Ali.

The storm of hatred and racism unleashed across this land by one young black man who exercised his right to refuse induction into the armed forces can, to this day, wake me with nightmares. My defense of Ali brought me dreadful telephone calls, even ads in newspapers demanding that I be deported—it was an America I only suspected existed. To have my suspicions confirmed and turned into the reality of my life—American life—was an education whose lessons stay with me every day.

Yes, progress has been made, but we are not yet far enough away from the mentality that struck at Ali and all who fought for him, not by a long shot.

The Al Campanis remarks and the subsequent publicity put the heat on baseball. Commissioner Peter Ueberroth knew he had to move and move quickly. Politician extraordinaire and outspoken black activist Rev. Jesse Jackson, among others, was breathing down his neck, demanding changes.

One of Peter's first moves was to name Dr. Harry Edwards, University of California–Berkeley professor and a man I have known closely since he plotted the black activists' protest at the Mexico City Summer Olympics, as a special adviser to Ueberroth for racial affairs. I applauded the appointment as one of the best things to happen in sports in my lifetime.

Why? Because Edwards was big and hulking and smart as hell. He never stopped talking. He hammered away at the lies, the injustices. He told the truth. He was the kind of black man, at 280 pounds, who scared the hell out of a certain kind of white. So confident. A former track star who made such a powerful presence. A man who didn't know how to bow down or back down. It was time for such a man to become involved in baseball.

Efforts had been made in the past to bring in such a presence, but they had met with little success. Former commissioner Bowie Kuhn had tried hard to move highly qualified black Donn Clendenon into the Chicago White Sox front office with the idea of getting him promoted into the general manager's job. His efforts failed.

Clendenon had been the hero of the 1969 Mets, one of the powers on the miracle team that won the World Series. By 1987, he was even more powerful. Among other things, he was a lawyer, and a member of the editorial board of the Duquesne Law Review. He was also president of his own building and construction company, and president as well of the Chicago Economic Development Corporation, an organization dedicated to training and employing minorities.

I saw Clendenon at a dinner honoring key industrialists, a dinner given by Clendenon's organization. Clendenon is a distinguished man, enormously articulate, and with his gradually whitening hair, he looked to be the soul of dignity—a dignity he retained even amid his rage.

Why was he so angry? Because he was sick and tired of picking up newspapers and reading lists of minority players who just might be qualified to manage a baseball team. He had read, or heard, this garbage for years. The list appears periodically. Fuss and noise is made. Little changes.

I was outraged, too, by these listings. They were a consummate affront to anyone even remotely conversant with the history of major league managers, or with the game of baseball itself. Let's tell it like it is, once and for all. I don't ever want to read again, or hear, that managing in the minors is necessary training before managing in the majors. Larry Bowa, Lou Piniella, and Pete Rose—to name just three—had no such minor league training. And I don't want to hear about the great intellect it takes to manage a ball club. The great Dodger catcher Roy Campanella said it all when he said, "To play this game you've got to have a lot of little boy in you."

Baseball is a child's game in the sense that it is simplistic, orderly, traditional, easy to learn, and easy to play. Children of ten fare very well on the diamond. The essentials are easy to grasp. But if one were to judge by the baseball establishment's managerial hype, one would assume a doctorate to be a minimal requirement, along with fifteen years' prior experience in the minors. What hypocrisy!

Through the years far too many managers have been tobacco-chewing and spitting slobs. Men without literacy, culture, proper education, or managerial ability. Historically, managers have been steadily rotated, the same handful, the same clubs, over and over, in a game of musical chairs that the owners like to play. So it is understandable that Donn Clendenon was outraged and affronted by the periodic appearance of a list of qualified blacks. Especially since he was plenty familiar with the questionable quality of many of the whites who had worn a manager's cap. These lists are an affront to every minority player in every sport.

Sadly, in 1987, Donn Clendenon's life came tumbling down. That was the year he was diagnosed to have leukemia, and additionally—although it was not publicly known at the time—he had become addicted to freebase cocaine. In a complete and heartrending explanation to me in a phone conversation on March 28, 1990, Donn revealed that he had checked himself into St. Benedict's in Ogden, Utah, for drug treatment. At the same time, a bone-marrow examination in Utah confirmed that his leukemia was in remission, but remained a constant threat.

Plagued by the double tragedy of cocaine addiction and leukemia at the age of fifty-one, Clendenon's dreams of a baseball management position were shattered.

The Reverend Jesse Jackson met with Commissioner Peter Ueberroth in the aftermath of the Campanis affair. Pressure of this nature could only help as baseball attempted to improve its minority-hiring record.

The late Edward Bennett Williams, the president and owner of the Baltimore Orioles, a good friend of mine and one of the country's great lawyers, was one of the owners who responded in a positive manner to the controversy over minority hiring. He named Frank Robinson, the Hall of Fame great who was the first black manager in baseball, to be his special assistant, with key responsibilities in the areas of scouting and developing all future Orioles talent from Latin America and the Caribbean.

Williams also kept his word—and the word of baseball in general—on the development of black talent for the front office. He named Calvin Hill, former NFL star, to the Orioles board of directors and gave him the title of vice president for administrative personnel. Hill was charged with monitoring the employment program, to ensure that every consideration was given to minority talent in filling jobs.

It was my feeling that Williams eventually wanted to split the general manager's job between incumbent GM Roland Hemond and Robinson, but in 1988, after the Orioles got off to their worst start in thirty-three years by losing their first twenty-one games, Williams fired Cal Ripken, Sr., and gave Robinson the job as field manager.

Robinson had experienced mixed results in previous managerial stints with the Cleveland Indians and the San Francisco Giants. He originally came back to Baltimore as a coach in the Orioles organization. His career reflected a legacy of pride and victory, but also a legacy filled with charges of being difficult to work with, of being arrogant and too hard on people. It was a reputation that had dogged him for his entire professional life, even before the majors. Once in the South, when he played in the minors, he went after a group of fans who were hurling racial slurs at him. As a major leaguer, he had a reputation of being tough in more ways than one. He didn't take anything from anyone. When he began in baseball in the fifties and in the early sixties, black men weren't supposed to have pride or, if they did, to exhibit it. Robinson always showed pride, never took guff from anyone—the fans, press, or management, not even his own teammates. He seemed to frighten people. In the days when "uppity" was a term people dared to use, they used it to describe Frank Robinson.

I recognize that Frank is not always easy to get along with, but he is intelligent, articulate, and opinionated about baseball and about many other more important things. Such personalities are frequently difficult to deal with, but it is the price one pays for his talent. It is a price often paid with talented people. Frank Robinson belongs to baseball. He is the only person to win MVP in both leagues. He won the Triple Crown. Edward Bennett Williams was wise in bringing him back to the game, and it's a shame that Williams wasn't around to witness Frank Robinson's unbelievable turnaround of the Orioles in the 1989 season. Under Robinson's superb management, the club went to the final game of the season before losing the divisional crown to the Toronto Blue Jays, who were managed by another black man, Cito Gaston.

The Gaston story is fascinating. In 1989, six weeks into the season, the Toronto Blue Jays, after an awful start, relieved Jimy Williams as field manager, making him the first manager the Jays had dismissed within a season. Toronto management named hitting coach Clarence "Cito" Gaston as interim manager, but Cito said he wasn't interested in becoming the full-time skipper. It was also known that Toronto GM Pat Gillick only wanted him for a few days, until he could sign ex–Yankee manager Lou Piniella, who was still under contract to the Yankees.

Gaston declined even the interim job at first, but under some pressure from several quarters, including the commissioner's office, changed his mind. And when George Steinbrenner refused to release Piniella, Cito became manager for the season and maybe many seasons after that. His success delighted the commissioner's office, which wanted to see two black managers in the majors at the same time, something that had happened only once before in the history of baseball.

After a few months on the job in Toronto, with his club on the move to the top, Gaston proved my point about managers when he said, "The worst part is the questions from the press. When the game starts, I relax."

Gaston was only the fourth black man to manage in the majors, and he won the American League Eastern Division Championship in his first year. It makes one wonder what men such as Joe Morgan, Bill Robinson, Don Baylor, Tony Taylor, Hal McRae, Bob Watson, Sandy Alomar, and Donn Clendenon could have done as managers if only they had been given a chance.

The 1989 season was a history-making season for black managers in another way. Never before had two black managers gone into the final series of the season with one of them about to become the first black manager to win a division championship series.

In 1990, in another sport, college basketball, the University of Minnesota fell three points short of going to the Final Four under the leadership of its black head coach Clem Haskins. He came close to joining Nolan Richardson of the University of Arkansas as the first two black head coaches to make it to the same Final Four. The only two black head coaches to reach the Final Four are Richardson and John Thompson. There are thirty-two black head coaches in Division I basketball, which is played at 292 schools.

Richardson said about taking over the Arkansas team in 1985 that "the pure racists hated me and let me know it. I forgave but I will not forget. I think that every dog has its day, and that a good dog has two. Now the ones that were barbecuing me have run out of sauce."

After the Hogs phenomenal success, Nolan said, "I have to think of myself as more than a basketball coach, but as an instrument to bring people together. The role that the basketball team has played in Fayetteville, Arkansas, is awesome. We are changing longtime attitudes and perceptions. It is an overwhelming occurrence."

Baseball did itself proud in 1989 by naming Bill White to be president of the National League. It was history-making in that White became the first black man to hold such a high position in professional sports. He succeeded Bart Giamatti, who replaced Peter Ueberroth, who had resigned as commissioner.

White had been an outstanding major league player, and following his playing career, he became a solid major league broadcaster. He had done off-season radio work for ABC, his last assignment for Shelby Whitfield being the Winter Olympic Games in Sarajevo, Yugoslavia. I had been instrumental in getting White into the Yankee broadcast booth, and it did my heart proud to see Bill promoted to the National League presidency. He is a fine man, a likable, fair, intelligent person who will distinguish himself as head of the National League.

The 1989 World Series will be remembered for the devastating earthquake, but forty-eight hours before the start of the Series, the Giants were shaken by claims of a former teammate, Jeffrey Leonard of the Seattle Mariners, that the Giants' all-star first baseman, Will Clark, was a racist.

What an unfortunate bunch of rubbish from a disgruntled ex-Giant who obviously was jealous of his old team's success. Some sportswriters, of course, ate it up.

During the delayed spring training of 1990, from the Giants training camp in Arizona, Giants general manager Al Rosen, a close personal friend for all of my sports life, told me in a phone conversation, "There is not a racist bone in Will Clark's body, and you can quote me. Nobody has better interaction with the blacks and Latins on this ball club than Will Clark. Was there friction between him and Jeff Leonard? When Jeff Leonard was here, he was the acknowledged leader of the ball club, and when Will Clark came here, after only sixty games, it was clear that he was a budding superstar, and Leonard didn't like that. So the two used to razz each other. That's all there was to it."

So that sets the story straight about Will Clark.

Equally ridiculous are the charges from the uneducated and misguided that the New York Mets is a racist organization. What an outrage! I know Mets president Fred Wilpon and Mets general manager Frank Cashen on a personal basis. One of my proudest moments came when Wilpon established a journalism scholarship in my name at Brown University. Neither of these men would tolerate racism of any type in his organization. Yet when a disgruntled George Foster, the last National Leaguer to hit fifty home runs (he had fifty-two with the Reds in 1977), left the Mets organization, he let it be known he felt the Mets were racist.

Nonsense!

Some have pointed to the run-in between Mets star Darryl Strawberry and scrappy Wally Backman as evidence of racism on the team. Strawberry called Backman a "redneck" and threatened to punch him in the face. Backman was subsequently traded to the Minnesota Twins and later went to the Pittsburgh Pirates. Others chastised the Mets because they have so few blacks on the roster. It's true that at the start of the 1990 season, Darryl Strawberry and all-star pitcher Dwight Gooden were the only blacks of note on the club, but the insinuations that the Mets are racist are crazy. (Later the Mets would sign black center fielder Daryl Boston.) It's the same as those who have charged the Boston Celtics with racism because they have a lot of white players on the roster. The Celtics have had great white players. So have the Mets. I'm incensed when I hear someone impugn the reputations and integrity of people such as Fred Wilpon, Frank Cashen, and Red Auerbach with these inane charges.

Yes, baseball is rife with racism—Hank Aaron, the greatest home run hitter of all time, will attest to that. But one must be aware of wild charges against innocent people. Reputations are easily ruined.

Aaron has done much to combat racism in baseball. I have been close to Henry Aaron over the years. He is not a bitter man, but if he were, it would not be without reason, and it is a measure of the man's character that he is not. He does feel hurt, however, deep within. Henry told me that a day doesn't pass without his thinking about Jackie Robinson. The two men were very close and Henry still misses him.

It reminded me of a conversation Jackie and I once had when he was driving me home after a game at Ebbetts Field. "They'll talk about me, they'll talk about Willie Mays, but when it's all over," Jackie said, "the one they're going to really talk about is that guy in right field. He's greater than us all. Howard, there isn't anything the man can't do, including run the bases." That's the way Robinson felt about Henry Aaron.

Henry is a kind and quiet man of enormous dignity. Over the years, his demeanor has grown more assured, more graceful. Once he was shy and withdrawn in company and as a result, was always misread and inaccurately described as sullen or hostile by sportswriters. He is now more relaxed. He is not, nor was he ever, sullen, hostile, or bitter.

He is, however, a man convinced that he's never quite gotten his due. I could not agree with him more. He never received the acclaim he so justly deserved, both as an athlete and as a human being. Had he played in New York or perhaps Los Angeles, instead of Milwaukee and Atlanta, things might have been different for Hank. The attention of the dominant New York media might have resulted in the acclaim he so richly deserved.

But then again, perhaps not. Don't forget, Henry Aaron was so gifted at his profession that he became the man—the black man—to have the audacity to challenge the home run record of that long-gone Yankee with a drinking problem, Babe Ruth. Oh, how I remember that time with distaste. What the media did to poor Roger Maris, a white man who broke Ruth's single-season home run record; they nearly destroyed Roger.

But Hank Aaron took double the abuse Roger suffered. What should have been the crowning glory of his career, and the happiest time of his life, he still describes as one of "the ugliest, most painful" of all his years in baseball. When Aaron approached Ruth's record of 714 homers, his life was threatened; his children were the targets of kidnapping threats. It was America at its most vile, and it tore to shreds all the myths about sports being a place where everyone is equal, where we see no color, where men and women are judged on their performance alone. It was a truly disgraceful chapter in sports history. Incidentally, Aaron finished with 755 career home runs, a record for the ages.

Hank Aaron and others have worked hard in efforts to reduce racism in baseball, and some progress has been made. But don't think a major problem doesn't remain in most sports.

In the post-Campanis era, there are more minority employees in front offices. All baseball clubs are more race conscious now, oddly enough, because of Al Campanis.

Sadly, it's a different story in football, and in particular, in the National Football League. The NFL has a shameful record of minority hiring! A disgraceful record!

To think that it took until 1989 for the NFL to hire its first black head coach in modern history boggles the mind.

In a remarkable double standard, while baseball was taking a horrible beating—and rightly so—for its record of minority hiring, football was left unscathed. In fact, it was the NFL, when compared to baseball, that made few efforts, and almost no progress, toward eliminating its prejudices and integrating its front office and coaching positions.

At a meeting in his Park Avenue office in 1987, NFL commissioner Pete Rozelle talked privately with a handful of black employees of the league, employees dissatisfied with the league's treatment of black personnel. Several attendees said that Rozelle began that meeting by stating flatly to the assembled men, "I want to tell you right off that we are not even going to discuss coaches." What a way to start the meeting.

That statement set the tone of the meeting, and that statement was made to, among others, Paul "Tank" Younger, then the assistant general manager of the San Diego Chargers; to Theo Bell, then director of community relations for the Tampa Bay Bucs; to Paul Warfield, then the director of player relations of the Cleveland Browns; and to Bobby Mitchell, assistant general manager of the Washington Redskins. After that meeting took place, Tank Younger was asked to leave his job with San Diego. And Theo Bell was asked to leave Tampa Bay. Were these dismissals mere coincidence?

When no. 42, the great wide receiver Paul Warfield, joined the front office of the Cleveland Browns, the team he began his career with, Warfield was led to believe that when the job of director of player personnel finally opened, it would be his. Instead, Warfield was passed over. It was a terrible injustice. His reaction, understandably, was to resign. He had been dignified, quiet, circumspect; he raised no fuss, which was Warfield's way. But why didn't someone else raise a cry? Where were all the good liberals, the ones who yelled loudly about baseball? Where was Browns owner Art Modell? And where, oh, where, was Pete Rozelle?

Where are the black head coaches in the NFL? It's 1990 and the NFL has one. Why hasn't Eddie Robinson, the greatest college football coach of my lifetime, the coach at Grambling State University, the winningest football coach of all time, been offered a head coaching job in the NFL? Robinson has coached over 360 victories and has sent over 250 players to the NFL. Among Eddie Robinson–coached players who became NFL stars are: Paul "Tank" Younger, Willie Davis, Willie Brown, Buck Buchanan (Davis, Brown, and Buchanan are all Hall of Famers), Roosevelt Taylor, Ernie Ladd, Charlie Joyner, Trumaine Johnson, Goldie

Sellers, Doug Williams, James Harris, Frank Lewis, and Henry Davis.

What happened to Calvin Hill, a Yale graduate, when he applied for the general manager's jobs at New Orleans and Atlanta? He received no reply, no acknowledgment of his application, from New Orleans, and he received an after-the-fact letter from Rankin Smith, owner of the Atlanta Falcons. That's what happened to Calvin Hill, who left the Cleveland Browns front office because there was no place left to go there. As mentioned earlier, the Baltimore Orioles rescued Hill and gave him a job in their front office.

And how about other blacks who could have been named head coaches? Where is no. 87, Willie Davis, who would've made a spectacular head coach? He's a wealthy businessman, but not in football. How about Willie Wood, the great Packer free safety, another man who would have made a fine head coach. How about perennial assistants Elijah Pitts and Tony Dungy? For years, Dungy has been rumored to be in line for a head-coaching job, but openings come and go and Dungy remains an assistant.

This is a sport that practiced "stacking," where blacks could only be played in certain positions—primarily wide receiver and defensive back—because the racists thought blacks didn't have the brains to play quarterback or middle linebacker. Well, stacking may be gone, but the prejudice behind it isn't.

Perhaps the saddest fact of all is that there's nothing new here—it's all business as usual. Jim Brown, in my estimation the greatest running back of all time, willingly tells anyone who asks, and has for years, that the NFL is still rife with racism. Usually he is accused of sour grapes, or of having become a terrible bore on the subject.

It was in February of 1990 that Jim Brown charged the Pro Football Hall of Fame in Canton, Ohio, with racism—and threatened to have his name removed from the Hall. Upset over certain blacks being passed over in the voting, Brown told the (Dayton, Ohio) *Daily News,* "How can John Mackey not be in it? How can Lynn Swann not be in it? It's racist." Brown later added cronyism to his racism charge.

Less than a year after Al Campanis committed professional suicide on "Nightline," football countered with its own version. Little did Jimmy "the Greek" Snyder know when he went to the famous Washington eatery Duke Ziebert's with his family for lunch that he would ruin his TV career with a few ill-chosen and repulsive remarks.

Ed Hoatling, a local writer/producer from WRC, the NBC affiliate in Washington, approached Jimmy at his luncheon table for some comments about civil rights in sports. Hoatling was gathering taped comments on the significance of Martin Luther King's birthday.

Jimmy, seventy, the same age as Campanis when he took his racial TV plunge, said, "Blacks are better athletes than whites because they have been bred that way, because of his high thighs and big thighs that go up into his back. And they can jump higher and run faster because of their bigger thighs, you see."

Jimmy continued, "I'm telling you that the black is the better athlete and he practices to be the better athlete and he is bred to be the better athlete, because this goes all the way back to the Civil War, when, during the slave trading, the owner, the slave owner, would breed his big black woman so that he would have a big black kid, see. That's where it all started."

Like Campanis, the Greek got himself deeper and deeper the longer he talked. When asked about coaching jobs for blacks, he replied, "Well, they've got everything; if they [blacks] take over coaching like everybody wants them to, there's not going to be anything left for the white people." His comments made all the network news programs that night, and Jimmy was a goner.

He was in Washington for the NFC championship to be played on Sunday. His remarks were made on Friday, and CBS fired him the next day. Brent Musburger never really liked Jimmy—they once had a tiff in a New York bar—and gave him no support. Neal Pilson, the head of CBS Sports, dropped the Greek like a hot potato.

I was very disappointed in Jimmy's remarks. They were obnoxious, distasteful, insulting, and indefensible. Besides the myriad of questions those remarks raise about institutionalized racism in this country, they also raise another very basic question that must be asked: What in the world was this oddsmaker—or *any* oddsmaker for the matter—

doing in a broadcast booth in the first place? What is an oddsmaker doing on national television representing the unholy alliance of network television sports and the National Football League? It is not a healthy marriage. What is it about football that produces network oddsmakers when the NBA and baseball do very nicely without them? Many of the ills of the sports world seem to be closely interwoven with the vices of different natures.

Jimmy the Greek has been a friend of mine for many years. He has some likable qualities, and there have been many hardships in his life. Still, an oddsmaker or bookmaker doesn't belong on the air.

The question of his dismissal is an altogether different story. Jimmy was not a front-office member of football, in a position to make personnel decisions, as was Al Campanis in baseball.

Jimmy the Greek worked for a medium that practices the First Amendment. Maybe Ed Koch, the ex-mayor of New York, now a newspaper columnist and radio commentator, said it best on one of my radio programs: "Under rights granted us under the First Amendment, is it right that one lose a job for expressing views considered heretical, bigoted, or ignorant?"

Perhaps Ed Koch is right.

Should Roger Stanton be deprived of the right to publish a paper just because he expresses bigotry and ignorance? No, of course not.

CBS got burned when it suspended Andy Rooney for allegedly making racist remarks, remarks that he denied making. After a public outcry, the suspension was lifted.

The Greek issued an apology the same afternoon that he made his remarks. "If what I said offended people, I apologize. I didn't mean for my remarks to come out the way they did. I was trying to emphasize how much harder so many blacks work at becoming better athletes than white athletes. And they work harder because they're hungrier, too. That many black athletes run faster and jump higher than whites is a fact. Using the term 'bred' was wrong on my part and I apologize for that, as I do for suggesting coaching was the only domain left for whites. Blacks could do well in that area, too, if given the opportunity."

The apology was not enough to save Jimmy the Greek. CBS took the easy way out.

It is likely that the Greek's views are shared by many in television sports—views, in fact, that are often spoken, but not in front of a live TV camera.

Jimmy has made a bit of a recovery from the loss of his $400,000-a-year job. He got some writing with King Features, has done some cable work, and to his discredit, has been visible in the touting business. In 1990, Jimmy said he was "out of work, blackballed, and need[ed] a job." But he will never live down his remarks made at Duke Ziebert's. In February of 1990, Phil Donahue called me to invite me on a program that would rehash the Jimmy the Greek issue. I declined.

In 1989, Minnesota Vikings general manager Mike Lynn called me for advice. He said, "Howard, Joey Browner has accused me of being a racist. What should I do?"

"Is it true, Mike?" I said.

"No, Howard, you know it's not true. It's just a negotiating ploy."

My advice was to deny the charge and not worry about it. Later, Browner would sign a series of one-year contracts making him the highest-paid player at his defensive position in the NFL. In the middle of the 1990 season, when Lynn announced that he would be leaving the Vikings to replace the fired Tex Schramm as head of the new World League, Browner repeated his charges that Lynn was a racist.

Hugh Green, the former Tampa Bay Bucs linebacker, tells a story of how he complained to Bucs owner Hugh Culverhouse about how the white players got most of the publicity, endorsements, and speaking engagements. According to Green, Culverhouse replied, "This is America, Hugh. What do you expect?"

When the NFL did hire the first black head coach in the modern history of the league, the move was made by Al Davis—a renegade owner, an adversary of Pete Rozelle, and a longtime friend of mine. I had hoped that Al would do it when Tom Flores retired, but in a move totally out of character for him, he went outside the Raiders organization to hire Mike Shanahan from the Denver Broncos. When the

Raiders floundered, Al admitted to me, "Howard, I made a terrible mistake."

On October 2, 1989, Al Davis made me a happy man when he called me to say that later in the day he would name Art Shell to be the first black NFL coach of our time. The former Maryland–Eastern Shore and Oakland Raider great was just what the NFL needed.

The old guard, the old boy network, the football establishment, would always have you believe that coaching football is so complicated, so technical, that only men of Mensa can handle the job. Implicit in that idea is, of course, the notion that intellect belongs to whites only. That old system of sports thinking is so revolting, smacks so much of institutionalized racism, that it turns my stomach.

Shell, a hulking black man as big as a house, with no prior head-coaching experience, took over a struggling team that had lost three of its first four games, then promptly won four of the next five. The old guard must have been squirming—even more so when he led the Raiders to the playoffs the following season.

I was proud of Al Davis and Art Shell. And even though Al makes me angry with the way he plays or threatens franchise chess, the NFL would be better off with more Al Davis types.

Only time will tell when other qualified black coaches will get their chances. One solution, easier said than done, is for blacks to purchase franchises. Former Chicago Bears great Walter Payton is attempting to obtain an NFL franchise for St. Louis, which lost the Cardinal football franchise when the greedy Bidwells took the money and ran to Phoenix. Payton says he has an open-ended deal with Johnny Roland, a black assistant coach with the Bears and a former St. Louis running back, for Roland to be the head coach of the new franchise.

Currently, sports is devoid of black ownership, excluding the NBA's Denver Nuggets, but that may change. Besides Payton, Magic Johnson has indicated that he wants to own a basketball franchise once his playing days are over.

The NFL is making some superficial, cosmetic efforts to improve its racial image. One example, which was really a joke, was for the search committee to list Willie Davis as a finalist in the long and troubled effort to name a successor to outgoing commissioner Alvin Pete Rozelle. Davis is a fine man with excellent qualifications, but it's my learned opinion that Davis had about as much chance of being named commissioner of the National Football League as I. And you know how much I've endeared myself to the oligarchs of the National Football League.

And when the NFL awarded the 1993 Super Bowl game to Phoenix, it did it on the condition that the State of Arizona must honor the birthday of Martin Luther King, Jr., as a holiday. Faced with demonstrations and boycotts, the NFL would be crazy to attempt a Super Bowl in Arizona without recognition of the King holiday. This position was not a racial consideration by the league; it was just a cold, hard necessity.

Blacks have been able to integrate basketball, football, boxing, and baseball with great success. The same can be said for track, but for one reason or another, there has been little integration of hockey, all winter sports, swimming, golf, and tennis.

Althea Gibson, who in the fifties won both the U.S. Open and Wimbledon singles championships, was the first black female to win either of these events. She grew up in Harlem playing stickball, not in some country-club atmosphere playing tennis. In 1975, my good friend Arthur Ashe became the first black man to win the U.S. Open and Wimbledon. But those have been the only two black tennis stars, even though Zina Garrison and others are making an impact.

Golf, like tennis, until only recently was known as a white man's game. Charlie Sifford, in 1960, became the first black man who received approved status in the PGA. In the seventies, Lee Elder became the first black to qualify for the Masters, which under the direction of the late Cliff Roberts was a bastion of racism. And Calvin Peete, winner of many golf tournaments, is likely to be remembered as the first black star on the links.

(Incidentally, even now, it wounds the diehards of Augusta National when foreigners such as Seve Ballesteros,

Bernhard Langer, Sandy Lyle, and Nick Faldo—twice—win the Masters. If a black were ever to win it, surely the trees on Magnolia Lane would fall dead.)

Lee Elder and his wife, Rose, are dear friends of mine. He always plays in my charity golf tournament in Palm Springs. One of the heartwarming stories is Lee Elder's sponsorship of a school for black children in Durban, South Africa. When he started the school, critics said he was crazy, but it has been a huge success.

Lee Elder means a lot to me. I was overjoyed when he won Pensacola for his first victory, and I was equally pleased when he won Westchester for his biggest payday.

I hope this doesn't seem self-serving, but no one has befriended the black golfers the way I have.

One of the fascinating stories in sports is the absence of black jockeys in Thoroughbred racing. Black jockeys dominated racing in the early days of the sport. In the first Kentucky Derby, run in 1875, fourteen of the fifteen jockeys were black. Isaac Murphy was the first black superstar in any sport and was considered the best jockey before the turn of the century. The record shows that among those who critiqued his riding, it was thought that when it came to riding a horse, Murphy had no peer.

I have long been on record as feeling that jockeys are the best athletes pound for pound in the world. It takes uncommon strength to handle a 1,200-pound animal, and it's extremely dangerous. The risk of death is not the greatest fear, however; what the jockey fears most is paralysis. They risk death and paralysis every time they race. Every muscle, every sinew, is subjected to severe strain, yet jockeys somehow put it all together, make it all work, know when to take the risk, when to move the mouth, when to employ the whip, and how to use it. I know of no other athlete who has to synchronize so closely the functioning of the human mind and body.

How did black jockeys go from dominating the sport to almost complete disappearance? When a group called the Jockey Club was founded in the 1890s and started to license and relicense jockeys, the blacks were simply squeezed out, so black jockeys went from 90-percent dominance to virtually no participation in the sport within a twenty-year period.

But why black American jockeys remain practically non-existent now is a baffling question. Hispanics dominate a large part of Thoroughbred riding, and I don't understand why blacks can't ride if they so desire.

In boxing, one has to look no further than Don King to find racism. He plays blacks against whites, whites against blacks, whites against whites, and blacks against blacks. No one is more skilled at turning boxers against trainers, boxers against managers, and boxers against family members than Don King, something he accomplished with Tyson and his trainer Kevin Rooney, and Tyson and his manager Bill Cayton.

After trying to deprive Buster Douglas of his duly-won heavyweight championship, King took him to court and tried to split his professional family and paternal family.

Don came out of the rackets in Cleveland. He killed two men—one was ruled self-defense, but for the other, which was ruled manslaughter, he served time in the Marion Correctional Institution. Don King. Boxing's finest. Nowadays, he makes millions in a highly visible position. As King himself is fond of saying, only in America!

As earlier indicated, this book is meant primarily to be an overview of sports in the last six years. Any chapter on racism would be incomplete, however, without a brief review of the black athlete and his impact on America.

Arthur Ashe, who has written a series of books encompassing an extensive study of the black athlete, feels that Jack Johnson, the former heavyweight boxing champion of the world, was the most significant black athlete of all time. I vehemently disagree.

Admittedly, Johnson's history is colorful. He won the heavyweight championship from Tommy Burns in 1909, and in 1910 he KO'd Jim Jeffries; it was this later bout and Johnson's subsequent years that served as the basis for the Broadway play *The Great White Hope*. Ashe feels that when Johnson won that match, he wiped out the pillars of white supremacy. What Ashe ignores is that Jack Johnson was a controversial figure. He held the boxing title for six and a half years after being convicted under the Mann Act, charged with transporting a white woman over a state line for the purpose of prostitution. Actually, it was a trumped-up charge, as he was planning on marrying the woman and later did. (During his life, Jack had one black wife and three white wives.)

Johnson was despised by whites for his personal life and his success, but blacks loved him because he was the most famous black person of his time. And for having come to the forefront as the world's best fighter and strongest man, Ashe rates Johnson as the person who did the most for his people.

Again, I respectfully disagree. I think this distinction goes to Jackie Robinson, followed closely by Muhammad Ali.

When I was teaching at The New School for Social Research in New York, I had Ashe speak to my class. The class also did not agree with his theory about Jack Johnson and felt Ashe belittled the significance of Jackie Robinson.

Two other great sports figures who were black were Jesse Owens and Joe Louis. Jesse's remarkable performance in the 1936 Olympic Games in Berlin stood as an outstanding rebuff to Hitler and his Aryan theory of white supremacy. Jesse won four gold medals at those games. I was master of ceremonies for six consecutive Jesse Owens dinners in New York. He was accused of being an "Uncle Tom"—a white man's black man—by a new generation of black Americans, but I always had the utmost respect for Jesse Owens.

Joe Louis likewise did his country proud in the thirties by KO'ing Max Schmeling of Germany in round one before seventy thousand in Yankee Stadium. Schmeling was a good man, but Hitler was using him for his own sick, twisted ideology. It was a joyous moment for Americans, tempered by victory celebrations that turned into riots resulting in the deaths of eight people.

Louis, the Brown Bomber, had serious trouble in his old age—debt, drugs, and bouts of delirium. I emceed the last big benefit dinner for Joe in Las Vegas. My final memories of him were not pleasant, especially those involving promoter Don King's exploitation of him by rolling his wheelchair out to the ring apron for celebrity introductions before championship matches.

Maybe Muhammad Ali had a good perspective. He said, "I looked up to Sugar Ray Robinson and Joe Louis as boxers, but Jesse Owens and Jackie Robinson were my heroes."

There's no doubt in my mind that Ali and Robinson were the two most important athletes of my lifetime—and I think of all time.

The basic reason is clear. Both are in American history books, not mere figures to be lionized in a sports tome.

Jackie overcame the problems of integrating baseball while still coping with a great deal of personal tragedy in his life. His son, Jackie junior, a veteran of Vietnam, developed a hard-drug problem during his military service, a problem he would later defeat, only to be killed in an automobile accident.

I remember Jackie junior's parents telling me they should never have saddled him with Jackie's name. It was too much for him to live up to. I remember seeing him, after returning from Vietnam, walking close to the walls of buildings, as so many Vietnam veterans did, feeling the walls provided security. It was as though they feared an ambush attack. And I remember at his funeral, when they played "Bridge over Troubled Water," a fitting tribute to his whole life and his whole being, I cried like a baby. Somehow Jackie and Rachel Robinson rose above this tragedy.

Ali didn't have the same background as Robinson. He was uneducated, but he was young, exuberant, and was gifted with a wisdom and understanding that was unbelievable. How else can you explain a man with his background rising to move in the highest circles of government, in the White House, in Buckingham Palace, and in the Kremlin? How else can you account for a man who defied the whole society, rejected military induction, took the slings and barbs of an outraged public, and never knuckled under? He seemed to draw strength from the abuse heaped upon him, and on the day he rejected military induction, I found him to be stronger than ever—unbowing, unworrying, with a secure knowledge inside that he had done the right thing and that he would win.

Despite the hostility shown him, Ali never experienced the racial epithets known to Jackie Robinson, but when he came back from winning the gold medal at the 1960 Rome Olympics, he told me several times, "That medal meant nothing. Nothing. I came back and I was just another black." People have disputed the story that he threw the medal into the Ohio River, which borders his hometown of Louisville, but Ali confirmed to me that he did so.

Racism is not an easy thing to overcome. Some barriers have been lowered, but the fact is the face of racism has changed. Today it is not usually so open, but is implied and covert and subtle—witness the blacks on the playing field and not in the front office.

For the most part, backlash was the racism of the eighties: attacks on affirmative action. Assaults on equal rights. Euphemisms, instead of slurs. Pleasant smiles and firm handshakes and blind eyes and deaf ears instead of mouths screaming insults and eyes blazing hate.

Well, let the backlash come, if it must. There is no gain anytime, anywhere, without discomfort and without pain. The voices of reason and compassion may be fewer than the voices of illogic and hate, but we are stronger. The sports world must, and will, be purged of its racism one day.

<u>CHAPTER</u> EIGHT

Gaming Cancer Runs Amok

When the Cincinnati Reds met the Oakland A's in the 1990 World Series, Pete Rose was in prison. He was earning eleven cents per hour working in the prison machine shop, and he watched the World Series games on TV with the other inmates in the prison recreation room at a minimum-security federal prison camp located in Marion, Illinois. Gambling was the ruination of Pete Rose, as it has been for many people. Before his conviction on two counts of filing false income tax returns for failing to report more than $350,000 in income from gambling, autograph-signing, and baseball-memorabilia sales, Pete was given a lifetime ban from baseball by Commissioner Bart Giamatti for betting on baseball games, including Reds games while he was the team's manager.

Pete Rose is a compulsive gambler, who I believe does not belong in the Baseball Hall of Fame.

There is no evidence that Pete fixed or attempted to fix the outcome of baseball games, but there is undeniable evidence that he ignored and/or violated clear and simple baseball rules that pertain to betting. And if one will read the Dowd Report, the summary of the official baseball investigation into the Rose matter, and if one will accept the testimony of the people closest to Rose, then it is clear to anyone with an open mind that Rose not only bet on baseball, but bet on his own team, the Cincinnati Reds.

Pete, however, had denied the charge. He knows that to acknowledge personally that he bet on baseball and the Reds would in all likelihood prevent him from ever being reinstated to baseball and from being voted into the shrine at Cooperstown, New York.

Simply stated, I believe the man is a liar. And there is much evidence to support that opinion.

It is my opinion that never in the history of baseball has a person used such poor judgment and committed so many indiscretions in selecting his inner circle of friends and engaging in illegal gambling activities.

Rose's arrogance and disdain for the law—including federal, state, and baseball—is appalling. Just because he could successfully connect with 4,256 baseballs for hits, and therefore felt he was an untouchable American hero, he was led to think falsely that he was bigger than it all.

Don't get me wrong. The man was a great baseball player. He showed guts with his headfirst slide. But his racing to first base on walks was a showboat move, false hustle that helped earn him the nickname Charlie Hustle, a bona fide hot dog.

Pete Rose and I always had a great relationship. I've known him for so many years, they're almost uncountable. And I have always cared about Pete Rose. I was the only person he talked to at the 1983 World Series when the Phillies benched him. He came on the air with me to talk about it. So I know Pete Rose.

Ted Williams, at the height of Rose's career, said, "He's nothing but a singles hitter. If he's content with being that type hitter, fine." Now come, Ted, I know you were the greatest hitter, but let's give Rose his due. The man was a great player. Most hits. Most games. Most at-bats.

Everything considered, Rose was a fantastic ballplayer. That, however, is where his greatness stops. He was not a good manager, and he set a terrible example for the youth of America.

One incident that best describes Rose as a sportsman occurred when he had his consecutive hitting streak stopped at forty-four games in Atlanta's Fulton County Stadium.

After the game, Rose was bitter and critical of Atlanta relief pitcher Gene Garber for showing emotion and bearing down in an effort to stop Rose's streak. Pete the Competitor couldn't recognize the right of Gene Garber to be a competitor. He held the National League record of forty-four consecutive games—an amazing feat in itself—so at least Pete could have been gracious and complimented the pitching of the Atlanta Braves. Instead, he was critical and bitter. It was a demonstration of Pete Rose the spoiled brat.

In the book *Hustle: The Myth, Life, and Lies of Pete Rose* by Michael Sokolove, it was revealed that the security section of the baseball commissioner's office had investigated for almost decades Rose's gambling with bookmakers. Security Director Henry Fitzgibbon would give Commissioner Bowie Kuhn periodic reports on Rose's gambling activity, but Bowie, the world's biggest opponent of gambling, did nothing. Neither did Bill Giles of the Phillies and Bill Bergesch of the Reds, key executives who knew of Rose's gambling, but elected to do nothing. Rose was such a big star, a meal ticket, that Kuhn, Giles, and Bergesch simply stuck their heads in the sand.

The Pete Rose gambling investigation started during the reign of Commissioner Peter Ueberroth. Rose was called to the commissioner's New York office in February of 1989 to explain his gambling activities. At that time, Rose started his pattern of denial and lies by saying, "Gambling was not the reason I was asked to come there. Ueberroth and Commissioner-elect Bart Giamatti wanted my input and advice on a couple of things, and I gave it to them. It took an hour. I left, and that was it."

During his six seasons as manager of the Reds, Rose made no secret about his love for gambling. He was known to be a frequent and heavy bettor on horses, dogs, college basketball and football games. From time to time, he would remark, "I'm not supposed to gamble. They have talked to me about it."

The Dowd Report reemphasized how much Pete Rose liked to gamble. The Reds manager bet more than one million dollars with an Ohio bookmaker named Ron Peters. Peters, who was facing drug and tax charges, cooperated with the baseball investigation, and for that support was the beneficiary of the famous letter from Bart Giamatti to Judge Carl Rubin, who was scheduled to pass sentence on Peters.

Bart was to come in for much criticism about that letter. Absurd criticism, in my opinion.

John Dowd, a Washington lawyer and the author of the Dowd Report, composed the letter for Giamatti's signature. Letters of this nature to judges are common and are considered ethical in legal circles. Rose supporters, however, proclaimed the Giamatti letter to be highly unethical, and to be evidence of a Giamatti vendetta against Pete Rose.

I've already mentioned that I approved of the fair and evenhanded manner in which A. Bartlett Giamatti handled the Rose affair. I have also mentioned that I was very close to Bart Giamatti. We talked to one another at least once a week, sometimes several times a week, and I was happy to be his friend, confidant, and trusted adviser.

As a lawyer, I knew that Bart was meticulous in following the course of due process Peter Rose was entitled to under the Fifth and Fourteenth Amendments. Bart Giamatti was right on the money every step of the way. Criticism by Judge Rubin, and later, Judge Norbert A. Nadel, simply smacked of Rose favoritism.

Nadel, a joke of a judge from the Hamilton County (Ohio) Common Pleas Court, cited the Giamatti letter to Rubin in blocking a Giamatti hearing on Rose's betting charges. What a laugh. Ridiculous. Anyone critical of that letter simply knows nothing about the legal system. The Nadel ruling was a travesty of justice and was destined to be overthrown by a higher court.

Judge Robert Bork, on a radio program of mine in April of 1990, said, "The judge, up for reelection later in the year, didn't even cite any law when he stopped the Giamatti hearing."

Had Nadel ruled against Rose, it might have been political suicide for the judge, who sits in the middle of Rose country. Oh, yes, Judge Nadel was reelected.

It was apparent to anyone with legal savvy that Giamatti was right and would succeed with the case against Rose. Attorney Reuven Katz and the rest of the Rose lawyers tried from the very beginning to make the Rose affair a Muhammad Ali–type constitutional case. Nonsense: the two cases were in no way similar, and Rose was afforded the right of due process every step of the way. The Rose matter was not a case of constitutional law, and I warned Giamatti about falling into that trap.

In the middle of the investigation, ex-commissioner Peter Ueberroth told me, "Howard, Rose is guilty. There is too much denial on his part. He's not telling the truth." Time would prove that Ueberroth was correct.

When Katz and his legal associates realized that they were fighting a losing battle, they moved to plea-bargain with Giamatti.

Rose was not in a position to gain much leniency; it was to be a lifetime ban. Good riddance to bad rubbish.

Bart Giamatti called me at my Manhattan apartment the night of his agreement with Rose. I was speaking with Shelby Whitfield on the phone when Bart's call came in, so I kept Shelby on one line and talked with Bart on the other, listening as he filled me in on the signed agreement with Rose.

Bart was a relieved and happy man. "We are ridding baseball of a cancer," he said. "I am proud that we are able to uphold the integrity of the game." Bart wasn't too happy that Rose could apply for reinstatement after a one-year period, but that was part of Rule 21 (d), under which they based the agreement.

I was just as relieved and gratified as Bart. I had felt for him, encouraged him, and consoled him all along the way. I told Bart that history would reflect he had been wise, patient, and fair, and that I would see him at the news conference the next morning when he announced Rose's banishment from baseball.

Shortly after Bart's call, reports of the ruling began running on television and radio, many of which contained erroneous information about the deal struck between Giamatti and Rose. CNN was saying it was a five-year suspension. So was UPI. Shelby Whitfield, by phone, cautioned ABC and certain friends in the media that the five-year reports were inaccurate. At the news conference the next morning at the New York Hilton, Bart was to chide the reporters who went with inaccurate information.

I visited with Bart in an adjoining room before the news conference started, and it was even more apparent that he was a relieved man, happy that the six-month-long ordeal was over. As I sat with Shelby during the news conference, it all seemed so anticlimactic. I had lived so close to the case for six months; now it was over and justice had been served.

The Pete Rose case had been a nasty and sordid affair. It was a case that included betting slips on which the FBI found Rose's fingerprints, and alleged losses of $400,000 to a New York bookmaker over a three-month period in 1987.

It was the story of Pete's closest friends, a collection of hustlers with questionable character who were themselves facing various charges of gambling, tax evasion, and drugs. In the end they turned on Pete Rose when the going got tough. Ron Peters and Paul Janszen were not "stand-up" guys, and their testimony against Rose was damaging. His close friend and former houseguest Tommy Gioiosa didn't cooperate with the investigation, but ultimately, he confirmed Rose's gambling, including bets on baseball and in particular on the Cincinnati Reds.

Rose and people who blindly support him—such as Cubs broadcaster Harry Caray—claim the commissioner had no evidence against Pete except the testimony of some felons. Such is not the case, and anyone who reads the 225-page Dowd Report knows it. There is insurmountable evidence, and as time passes, the testimony of the felons looks better and better.

Perhaps Paul Janszen, one of Rose's chief accusers, said it best. In a copyrighted interview in the *Dayton Daily News,* Janszen said, "When all this started, Rose denied at least five things I told John Dowd. Now he has admitted to four of them. One, he said he never won any Pik-Six tickets. Two, he said he never bet with bookies. Three, he said he always paid his taxes, never evaded them. Four, I said Pete had a gambling problem. He denied it. Now he says he's getting help for a gambling disorder. Five, he said he never bet on baseball. Right now, I'm four for five—and they say I have no credibility."

Pete Rose's average in the untruth department is better than his batting average. I say he's a perfect five for five.

Rose's credibility was further eroded when he, with Roger

Kahn, wrote a book entitled *Pete Rose: My Story*. It turned out to be far from his whole story. The book contained one chapter on Rose's gambling, but contained no major revelations. His publisher, Macmillan, promised that Rose would provide answers to heretofore unanswered questions, but there were no answers. Later, Kahn was to say that he felt Rose had deceived him.

As time passed, Kahn became even more outspoken. On April 23, 1990, he told me:

I was blatantly misled by Rose and others who were associated with Rose, in regards to Pete's tax situation and his gambling. Pete didn't want an honest book. There was a dark side. He was simply looking for quick cash to pay debts. What they really wanted was a self-serving book which would help Rose gain admission to the Hall of Fame.

When I was writing the book, stories were flying about Pete's gambling debts, tax problems, and memorabilia sales. When I asked Rose about the Internal Revenue, I was given a completely erroneous story. Pete said, "I have done nothing wrong with Internal Revenue." Reuven Katz told me, "The IRS simply wants Pete to finger some Cincinnati-area bookmakers. He knows them all, and the IRS wants the names."

When Rose refused to give me answers to gambling questions, Macmillan [the publisher] threatened to cancel the book and said it would consider a fraud suit against Rose. After that, Pete did give me some time, but he never really leveled with me about taxes or gambling.

When I asked Pete about selling memorabilia, he said, "Nothing much, nothing much. Maybe a couple of shirts." Later, I found out he sold a bat for $129,000. When I asked Pete for a statement of financial worth, he said, "It's nobody's fucking business what I'm worth." I countered, "Pete, you are running for the Hall of Fame. You need to be candid." It wasn't to be. Every time I mentioned the gambling, Pete would say, "Everybody does it." I think that may have been Pete's self-delusion, but I know that management people around Rose knew that he had a very serious gambling problem. It was apparent to me that Pete Rose had a bodyguard of lies.

After the book came out and I started learning the truth, too late, I told Reuven Katz and Pete Rose that down the road, when everyone was prepared to tell the truth, they should do a very gripping book about Rose's gambling. They should call it *My Life as a Gambler,* along the lines of Lillian Roth's *I'll Cry Tomorrow,* which was a book about obsessive-compulsive behavior. I would not be interested in doing the book, or being involved in any way with Rose or any of his people again, because once misled is enough.

Kahn concluded our conversation by saying, "I'm concerned about what the Rose book did to my credibility. It surely didn't help it. I hope people will forget my involvement with the Pete Rose book and remember me for *The Boys of Summer.*"

Strangely enough, the week before the Rose book hit the stands, Pete Rose told the Associated Press, "I'm no longer interested in telling my side of the gambling scandal that led to my ban from baseball."

At the height of the scandal in the summer, Rose had promised to someday give his side of the story. He repeated his desire to do so at a news conference on the day Bart Giamatti banned him from baseball. But on November 9, 1989, Pete said, "I've changed my mind. I'm not really interested in telling my story." The publishers of *Pete Rose: My Story* must have died a thousand deaths; the book was due in six days.

It was also about that time that Rose admitted that he was receiving psychiatric help for a gambling problem. He said, "I bottomed out by losing my occupation." Until then, Rose had insisted that he was not a compulsive gambler and did not require help. There are those who question the reasons for Rose's treatment. Some feel it's a ploy, an effort to speed his chances of reinstatement to baseball.

Additionally, there are those who question the effectiveness of Rose's treatment, which has consisted solely of a series of talks with Dr. James Hilliard, a University of

Cincinnati psychiatrist. In the first six months of treatment, Rose told *USA Weekend* magazine, a newspaper supplement, he talked with Hilliard twelve to fifteen times, mostly in person, but sometimes by long-distance telephone. Rose told the magazine, "We got it under control. I can't remember the last time we bet—but you're always on the edge."

"That's not enough," says Arnie Wexler, executive director of the Council on Compulsive Gambling of New Jersey. "You can't do it with a therapist alone. Lifelong group therapy, like Gamblers Anonymous, is the only way to overcome this addiction. I've never seen it happen any other way."

Pete spent the winter of 1989 playing golf in Florida with people such as Cincinnati Reds broadcaster Joe Nuxhall. Rose, like Lawrence Taylor, feels that golf is good therapy.

In an attempt to improve his public image, Rose hired a PR person, Barbara Pinzka. His first speaking appearance was at the University of Florida for a $10,000 fee, and he agreed to do a series of broadcasts during the 1990 baseball season for Cincinnati radio station WCKY.

However, Rose is still persona non grata with baseball. He can't be a broadcaster on any club's games, either locally or nationally. And Commissioner Fay Vincent, in his first dealings with Rose as commissioner, ruled that it would be inappropriate for the Philadelphia Phillies to invite Rose to take part in a Phillies 1980 World Championship team reunion during the 1990 season.

Actually, the one thing Pete Rose was trying hardest to do in 1990 was to stay out of jail for income tax evasion. The *Cleveland Plain Dealer* reported that Rose apparently owed more than $100,000 in taxes from unreported income. Rose's PR person, Ms. Pinzka, confirmed that a federal grand jury was investigating whether Rose owed taxes from cash earned at baseball card and memorabilia shows.

It's a matter of fact that Rose frequently took his payoffs at baseball card and memorabilia shows in cash, sometimes bills in a paper bag. Pete is high-profile, and it shouldn't have taken the IRS long to build a case if it wanted to do so.

For his part, Rose denied selling off personal property and baseball awards to pay gambling debts, despite rumors that he had sold a car and a World Series ring for that purpose.

Court records, however, indicate Rose was lying. From a federal court document called a Statement of Fact, which was signed by Rose and his attorneys, "in the early 1980's, unknown to his advisers, Rose began to sell memorabilia and to take fees for card show appearances to cover his gambling losses."

One major item involved the bat Rose used to break Ty Cobb's record for career hits in 1985. The document continued, "Rose received $129,000 from an individual who purchased his '4,192' bat by requesting and receiving (as partial payment) 11 checks for $9,000 and one check for $5,000," said Assistant U.S. Attorney William E. Hunt. "These checks were cashed at the bank on separate days in order to avoid the filing of currency transaction reports."

The remaining payment—from a man Rose identified as Steve Wolter, his insurance man—was made in the form of a $25,000 check. This check was used to pay a personal bank note and therefore did not require a currency transaction report.

One of the funny Pete Rose stories is told by memorabilia collectors and promoters. It is said that Rose will sell anything with any type of representation. Memorabilia promoters joke about the patron who wanted to know if he could buy the authentic Pete Rose uniform blouse worn when Pete set a certain record.

"Sure we have it," the promoter says. "What size do you wear?"

For many months in 1989 and 1990, Rose was the subject of a federal grand jury investigation and an IRS investigation. And again, it was time for Rose and his attorneys to plea-bargain. He could have been hit with income tax evasion charges, meaning a certain jail sentence, but the government decided it was appropriate to cut a deal with Pete, allowing him to plead guilty to the lesser charges of filing false tax returns. Under the reduced charges, still felonies, America's hero was permitted to pay his back taxes, plus interest and penalties, and then take his chances with U.S. District Judge S. Arthur Spiegel in regards to a fine and prison sentence.

On April 19, 1990, Rose pleaded guilty to two felonies, reporting false income tax returns for the years 1985 and

1987. He understated his income by $354,698 and owed tax of $162,703 before interest and penalties. When he entered his guilty plea, Rose paid the back tax, plus $66,984.64 in interest and $129,715.25 in penalties. He faced a possible $500,000 fine, plus a jail sentence of up to six years, but after plea bargaining by Rose, the judge gave Pete five months in jail, followed by three months in a halfway house and a fine of $50,000.

Before the ruling, the government, expecting criticism for cutting a deal with Rose for a light sentence, took the offensive. U.S. Attorney D. Michael Crites, the architect of the plea-bargain arrangement, said it was no "sweetheart" deal.

Crites also called it "a sad day for major league baseball, a very sad day for the city of Cincinnati, Ohio, certainly a very sad day for Mr. Rose and his family, but particularly a sad day for those young Americans to whom Pete Rose was an idol."

Despite all the rhetoric, however, it's obvious that jocks do enjoy the benefit of a double standard in this country. It's the American way. Leona Helmsley, the New York hotel queen, a senior citizen, who has paid literally hundreds of millions of dollars in taxes (she wrote one federal tax check for over $40 million in 1990), can go to jail for tax evasion without sympathy, but when an athlete is sentenced, there's an abundance of concern. Perhaps even more damaging than the failure to report income from the sale of memorabilia, there is the clear evidence that Pete Rose won large amounts at the racetrack and took steps to evade taxes.

Paul Janszen and Tommy Gioiosa testified in a Cincinnati courtroom that Pete Rose was the primary owner, 75 percent, of a winning Pik-Six ticket that paid $47,646 on January 14, 1987, at Turfway Park in Florence, Kentucky.

Rose was a bigger winner on other Pik-Six tickets. On his deposition taken by John Dowd, Pete alluded to two winning Pik-Six tickets at Turfway Park that totaled $265,069. Initially, he denied owning part of the tickets, but later admitted to having a share of them. Rose would have friends and hangers-on, most of whom had little reportable income, cash the tickets for him in an effort to avoid tax liability. The Reds manager was a regular at Turfway Park. A room there where Pete did his wheeling and dealing was referred to as "the Rose room." Strangely enough, one of the owners of the track was partners with Rose on a huge Pik-Six winning ticket. The Kentucky State Racing Commission indicated that it was not illegal for a track owner to be betting with Rose.

Pete didn't confine his horse action to little Turfway Park, a track lacking in prestige. Janszen testified that Pete hit a winning ticket of over $94,000 at the famous Churchill Downs and true to his form, had someone else sign for the winnings.

While Rose clearly tried to hide his track winnings, he told the IRS that he didn't think he had to report his winnings because over the long haul, he always lost more than he won. That may have been the case, but by law, one must report all substantial racetrack winnings, then deduct track losses against those winnings reported to the IRS. Rose's tax case records revealed that he won at least $136,945 by entering into partnerships on Pik-Six horse track bets.

Like most bettors, of course, Pete Rose lost money on his gambling, and indications are he was a heavy hitter. Records show that for the most part, Pete would bet $1,000, $2,000, or $3,000 per game, and it was not unusual for him to wager from $8,000 to $10,000 per day.

Besides his betting, Rose chose to consort with known gamblers. One of his closest friends was Joseph Cambra, a convicted bookmaker from Somerset, Massachusetts. Rose, through the Reds, arranged for hotel reservations for Cambra at the team's spring training headquarters in Florida, and he even permitted Joe to enter and visit in the Reds dugout. For these actions alone, Kenesaw Mountain Landis, and maybe even Ford Frick, would have given Rose a substantial suspension, perhaps a lifetime ban.

A man who so blatantly defied baseball and society as a whole with his disgraceful behavior would continue to defy Bart Giamatti, even after signing his lifetime ban agreement. At his news conference in Cincinnati, which started before Giamatti was even finished with his news conference in New York announcing Pete's ban, Rose continued to stonewall. He refused to admit to guilt in betting on baseball, then a few hours later, said that he was dumb-founded that the commissioner would express an opinion that he had bet on baseball games.

The day after the Rose announcement, Giamatti went to his summer home in Edgartown, Massachusetts. On the phone, Bart said, "Why is Rose saying these things? He's a sad case. I was very clear about the fact that I was not going to be constrained from saying what I thought was the truth. I'm not about to change anything that I have said."

It was crazy. Here was Pete Rose agreeing to a lifetime ban—and refusing to admit that there was any reason for him to enter into such an agreement.

To this day, Rose has derogatory things to say about Bart Giamatti. When he talks about 1989, Rose seethes with anger and claims that he was the victim of a one-sided investigation. He told *USA Weekend*, "Giamatti had no evidence. He had hearsay. I spent twenty-five years in the game, twenty-four more than Giamatti. A lot of people forget that."

And this statement comes from a man some people felt contributed to the condition that led to a great man's having a heart attack. It makes my blood boil!

Many fans turned against Pete Rose when it became clear that he had lied about his gambling activities. Others defected from Rose's fan club when he was convicted of filing false tax returns and went to jail. Cincinnati fans certainly didn't miss him as a manager. The Reds finished fifth under the direction of Pete Rose in 1989, but under Lou Piniella, the club opened the season with nine consecutive wins, remained in first place all season, polished off the Pirates to move into the World Series where they swept the highly favored Oakland A's. Of course, Rose claimed that the kids he developed were simply maturing in 1990, and that Piniella benefited from the fruits of his work. Few fans believed Rose.

As insignificant as it may be, maybe a development in New York City best illustrated Pete Rose's demise. In 1990 a popular eatery, Manhattan's Stage Deli, which names sandwiches for celebrities, polled over seven hundred customers about which celebrities should be dropped from the menu. There is no more Pete Rose sandwich. He was one of the first to go. They didn't even keep a Pete Rose hot dog with lots of mustard.

Even if he doesn't get back into baseball, Pete Rose has a burning desire to be elected into the Baseball Hall of Fame when—and if—he becomes eligible in 1992.

After Pete pleaded guilty to income tax felonies, he released a statement through his press agent. Impressive and well-written, it was far more repentant in tone than Rose had been in his own speech. "I am truly sorry. My family and friends have suffered as well, and I regret the pain it has caused them. I am not a bad person, but I did some bad things."

This statement, under the name of Rose, came at about the same time he was showing defiance and anger by snapping at reporters and threatening cameramen and photographers.

More of the written statement seemed aimed at Baseball Hall of Fame voters. "There's no question that my baseball records earned me a place, but I understand that the Hall of Fame means more than 4,256 hits," Rose said. "In a year and a half, the baseball writers will have to make the decision of whether or not I'm worthy of the Hall, and I hope they understand that the mistakes I made off the field were caused by my gambling disorder."

In more of his statement, Rose asked for tolerance and forgiveness of his sins:

> I just hope that you will understand that I have a sickness. I first realized last October that I had a gambling problem, and I made that public last month. I have been able to stop gambling since then—but I will need help for the rest of my life.
>
> Gambling relaxed me and I enjoyed it. About six years ago, though, when my playing career started to wind down, gambling became more and more important to me. Every gambler thinks he's going to be the one to beat the house, and I was no different. But the house does win in the long run, and so I needed more and more money to bet more and more.
>
> I'm very lucky that I'm still financially well-off, because my advisers made it embarrassing for me to get

at all of my savings to use for gambling. I didn't want anybody I cared about to know how much I was gambling. The so-called friends I had back then didn't care about my gambling or me, so I was ready to hang out with them. They even made money off of me. When the chance came along to get gambling money by signing autographs and selling memorabilia, I grabbed it.

When one is facing six years in prison, the statements had better sound good. It's the proper time to show remorse and generate sympathy.

Does Pete Rose belong in the Hall of Fame? If the sportswriters who vote on entry follow their own rules, the answer is a resounding "No!" It clearly states in the Hall's criteria for election that in addition to a player's ability and playing record, voting shall be based upon a player's "integrity, sportsmanship, character."

Enough said. No convicted felon has ever been admitted to the Baseball Hall of Fame.

Yet, it is very possible that the writers will forget the rules, forget the facts, and vote Rose into the shrine. Some will say you can't have a man in the Hall of Fame who was kicked out of baseball for gambling and who was convicted of tax fraud felonies. Others, as misguided as they may be, will say that you can't have a Hall of Fame without a great player like Pete Rose.

More than 450 writers are expected to vote in 1992, when Tom Seaver and Rose both become eligible. There seems to be no doubt about Seaver's election, but the Rose question will be one of sport's hottest debates right up until election time.

In 1991, the Hall of Fame changed its rules, making any player on baseball's banned list ineligible for election to the Hall.

The Baseball Writers Association of America is an organization with over 800 members. But only those with at least ten years' tenure are allowed to vote in the Hall of Fame election. An eligible player must receive at least 75 percent of the votes to be elected.

Then there's the question of why only baseball writers

elect members into the Hall of Fame. Why does baseball give the baseball writers this right? Are all of them qualified to vote? Why aren't other segments of the media allowed to participate in the voting? Should retired players and managers be allowed to vote on the Hall of Fame? These are legitimate questions for baseball.

Many baseball writers would vote for Pete Rose because he was always friendly with the writers. He always had time for them, and he gave them what they wanted to hear. He was good copy. As a whole, Cincinnati beat writers loved Pete Rose, so for many, it will be a vote of favoritism with no regard to the integrity or character requirements.

I was surprised to see George Vecsey, a *New York Times* columnist and one of the country's great sportswriters, in a column on August 26, 1989, state that Pete Rose belongs in the Hall of Fame. (Since then he has changed his mind.) Based on playing ability, yes. Based on the other areas, no.

I was amused to see *New York Times* columnist Dave Anderson, a Pulitzer Prize winner, write that a one-year suspension was long enough for Rose, even if he bet on baseball, and even if he bet on his own team. Amazing. Has Anderson no regard for the rules of the game?

Want a bigger shock? Remember how Commissioner Bowie Kuhn despised gambling so much that he had to wash out his mouth with soap if he even said the word? Many felt the commissioner was conservative, pompous, and out-of-bounds when he suspended Mickey Mantle and Willie Mays from the game because of their employment by casinos, which paid the ex-players to socialize and play golf with high rollers. Hang on to your hat. Bowie, the paragon of morality, favors Pete Rose's election to the Hall of Fame. He says he always liked Pete. Bowie is an old friend of mine and is very dear to Emmy and my daughters, Jill and Hilary, but I must say it—his position on Pete Rose disappoints me.

Pete Rose shouldn't be kept out of the Hall of Fame because he's an uneducated, colossal bore. He shouldn't be kept out of the Hall of Fame because he was a bad father or a cheating husband during his first marriage. (His bitter divorce action from his first wife, Karolyn, revealed Rose as one who flaunted other women in front of his wife, and one who was not a good father to his son, Petey, and his daughter, Fawn. And who can forget Pete's highly publicized paternity suit?) But he should be kept out of the Hall of Fame because he does not meet the entry standards of integrity and character that were set by the writers themselves. A man barred from baseball for life because of illegal, wholesale gambling simply doesn't qualify for reasons of character and integrity.

If Rose is reinstated to baseball or makes it into Cooperstown, two great commissioners, Judge Kenesaw Mountain Landis and Dr. A. Bartlett Giamatti, will roll over in their graves.

Remember, however, it's a permissive society we live in today, one in which the outlaw is a hero. Who receives the most fan adulation and attention when he attends the fights at Madison Square Garden? John Gotti, that's who, the king of the mobsters. It's sad but true.

Just as sad as the Rose case is the case of Chet Forte. Chester was an all-American basketball player at Columbia and became the best director in the history of TV sports. Flamboyant little Chester, 5'9", with a bubbling personality, gained fame as the director of "Monday Night Football." As the top director at ABC Sports, his salary escalated to $900,000 per year. Unfortunately, throughout his thirty years in the broadcasting business, he was a compulsive gambler.

Forte was primarily a sports bettor, but he did lose hundreds of thousands of dollars at the casino tables. While he claims he wasn't very big as a casino player, he lost enough that any casino would be happy to send a plane if Forte wanted one.

He lost millions of dollars betting on sports. On a given day, Chet would bet the entire card, the worst thing a gambler can do. He was the bookmaker's best friend. He would lose $10,000 or $20,000 a game. It was not unusual for him to lose $100,000 on NFL games on a Sunday. He would wager as much as $50,000 on the Super Bowl, and it was common for him to have $20,000 riding on a Monday-night game that he was directing.

That was a violation of ABC policy, but for years Forte openly defied the policy. The company does not condone illegal gambling, or wagering on games on which one is working. But for decades, the policy was not rigidly enforced.

Everyone knew Forte was gambling—he was open about it. He freely tells the story about how his coworkers wanted to know his selections so they could bet the other way. It was common knowledge that Chester often got in deep debt and therefore deep trouble with bookmakers. On at least one occasion, Roone Arledge bailed him out of a desperate situation.

I maintained a good working relationship with Chet Forte. As a director, he was the best, and I never knew his bets to affect his performance. Indeed he did seem to have the ability to block out his wagers from his mind when he worked.

When I wrote about Forte's gambling in my earlier books, it irked him, but it didn't seem to stop him or even faze him.

Chet could be a shrewd office politician, and nobody knows that better than Ed Silverman, an award-winning producer on my "Sportsbeat" program, and a man who goes back with me to my early days in radio. He used to work the Bill Stern radio show and is the man who first started using taped comments on radio sports shows.

Ed used to tell me, "That little Forte is a dangerous snake, Howard. He stirs up things on the twenty-eighth floor [the executive sports floor of the old ABC building]. Look out for him."

Forte won nine Emmys for his brilliant work, but his star had fallen at ABC when he left the company in 1986. His salary had been cut back to $300,000, and he left with a year remaining on his contract. He took a buyout on his final year in order to obtain quick cash to apply to his massive gambling debts.

Forte's world came crashing down in 1990. He lost his Saddle River, New Jersey, home for nonpayment of the mortgage, and the hosue was sold at a sheriff's auction for $908,000. Worse, he was charged with bank fraud for falsifying bank loan applications when he borrowed money for gambling purposes. Authorities claim he fraudulently obtained $1.5 million in loans.

The fifty-four-year-old Forte pleaded guilty to mail fraud,

wire fraud, and income tax evasion for not filing a 1987 return. He faces a maximum penalty of eleven years in prison and a $27,000 fine. Forte is broke. His family has stuck with him, and he lives near Richmond, Virginia, with the financial help of relatives. He is being defended by a public defender, a thirty-four-year-old Harvard graduate, Lawrence Lustberg.

Forte is scared to death of going to prison. He openly admits his gambling problem, joined Gamblers Anonymous, and has started a media campaign aimed at generating sympathy and obtaining job possibilities. He is praying for probation and a chance to rebuild his life.

On October 4, 1990, Chet called me at my ABC office. First, he called our apartment and talked with Emmy for half an hour. She was sympathetic in response to his sad story and told Chester that he could reach me at the office. It was the first time I had heard from Forte in years. He told me his sad story, and I encouraged him and attempted to give him some job leads. At the same time, I cautioned Chet that his planned media campaign might backfire on him. I was especially concerned about Chet's asking for help from Stan Isaacs of *Newsday*, a writer who has vilified me for decades. (Isaacs had the gall to show up at my Olympic venue in Los Angeles to tell me that I was finished and would have no impact on those Olympic games. As usual, Isaacs was wrong, and I actually got ovations from the crowd when I would enter the boxing arena.)

On October 16, Shelby called Arnie Wexler, the New Jersey chairman on the Council for Compulsive Gambling. He wanted to check out the stories about Forte's involvement with Gamblers Anonymous. Ironically, Chet was with Wexler in his Trenton, New Jersey, office, and Chet got on the phone with Whitfield for half an hour. Then Wexler got back on the phone and assured Shelby that Forte is serious about GA. "I can spot the phonies, and believe me, Chet is sincere about his sickness."

Both urged Whitfield to listen to WFAN Radio in New York later in the day, when Forte would be on the air discussing his situation. Chet stated his case on the program and broke down and cried when discussing the problems he had caused his family. Oddly enough, one of the program hosts, Mike Francesa, who also works for CBS-TV, had been a handicapper for the *College & Pro Football Weekly* and now handicaps for WFAN.

There's no doubt that Forte's trying to save his hide, escape prison, and rebuild his career. Some people join GA because they want help. Others join the organization for protection from unfriendly and dangerous debt collectors. The first thing a new member does is to make available to the organization a list of creditors, and this serves as an insurance policy. It tends to deter musclemen from collecting. If anyone came up hurt or missing, GA would know where to send the cops. Unfortunately, some members simply use the group for protection and have been known to continue gambling even though they are attending meetings. Incidentally, Forte, despite losing millions, claims that no one ever threatened him with muscle.

Wexler seems sure that Forte is serious about his GA meetings, and Chet claims not to have gambled for two years. Forte admits he's cooperating with authorities on a big case that he won't discuss. He's hoping for leniency in exchange for his cooperation. The mere fact that he admits this to the media does not seem wise. Give up the wrong people to the authorities and one might need the federal witness protection program.

The Pete Rose and Chet Forte cases brought back memories of one of the National Football League's biggest gambling scandals.

In 1987, former Indianapolis Colts quarterback Art Schlichter, now a sporting goods salesman in Columbus, Ohio, was arrested and charged with wagering $230,000 with bookmakers in Indianapolis.

Schlichter had been suspended from the National Football League in 1983 after running up gambling debts of more than $750,000 while playing for the Baltimore Colts. The former Ohio State quarterback, who had experienced problems with compulsive gambling dating all the way back to college and high school, was reinstated by Pete Rozelle in 1984.

He was undergoing treatment with Gamblers Anonymous

when he was cut by the Colts in 1985 and again in 1986 by the Buffalo Bills, who had briefly added him to their roster.

His 1987 arrest raised a very interesting question: How could bookmakers in their right minds let Art Schlichter bet over $230,000 when they knew the guy lost over $750,000 to Baltimore bookies, failed to pay them, and snitched to the cops about their activities? It didn't say much for the intelligence of the bookmakers of Indianapolis.

The case raises another good point: Does anyone think Pete Rose and Art Schlichter are the only people in organized sports who are betting on games? Of course not. It's a betting society we live in, and you can be sure that there are plenty of players, coaches, and front-office people who bet on a regular basis.

Baseball commissioner Fay Vincent has been quoted as saying that he isn't interested in pinpointing all members of baseball who have bet with bookmakers. That's a strange stance for a commissioner to take.

It was no secret that football owners Leonard Tose of the Philadelphia Eagles and the late Carroll Rosenbloom of the Los Angeles Rams were legends when it came to wagering. And it's also a known fact that bookmaking produced seed money for the ownership of the New Jersey Giants by the Mara family.

So why should people be surprised when gambling cases come to light in the National Football League?

It has long been my position that the NFL's posture on gambling has been suspect. Publicly they denounce gambling; privately, their own actions seem to contradict their public stance.

Earlier in this book I raised the point about Jimmy the Greek's being permitted to act as commentator on NFL shows. Had Jimmy the Greek not made the racial remarks, he might still be touting teams on CBS. And NBC couldn't find an oddsmaker they liked. The late Pete Axthelm, the ex-*Newsweek* sportswriter, was dropped by NBC, only to be picked up by ESPN, where he enjoyed top-tout status. NBC tried former player Paul McGuire picking against the spread, but he proved to be no more than a barroom buffoon.

Pete Rozelle always said he didn't like the idea of oddsmakers being identified with the NFL, but he said he wouldn't interfere with the networks because of their rights of "freedom of the press."

On the surface, the commissioner's argument has merit, but it does not withstand close scrutiny.

NFL Films is a subsidiary of the NFL. For years it has produced a weekly NFL cable show with Nick Buoniconti and Len Dawson as cohosts. In years past, in the course of each show, Larry Merchant, a sportswriter, would appear in front of the Caesars Palace oddsboard in Las Vegas and discuss the point spreads for weekly NFL games and the over-and-under point totals for such games. He would tell viewers whom he liked and why. Merchant is a recognized expert on gambling, has even written a book on the subject, and is a perfect choice if you wish to lend credibility to gambling information. There can be no league disclaimer about that show, since it was an NFL product.

I discussed the matter at length with Buoniconti, who told me, "It killed Lenny and me to have that junk on the show." He called it "a disgrace to the league." Remember, too, what Dawson went through the week before the 1970 Super Bowl. Dawson was linked to gamblers—all of it rumors—and he went through hell. He was vindicated by a superb performance as he led the Kansas City Chiefs to a 23–7 victory.

At a benefit for his now-paralyzed son, Buoniconti added, "I hope it doesn't happen to us again." Merchant was removed from the show.

Back in 1986, *Sports Illustrated* did a whole issue on gambling and quoted a CBS Sports executive as saying exactly what I have already stated—that the NFL's public position on gambling is one thing, but privately, "they encourage it."

NBA commissioner David Stern has told me flatly that CBS wanted to put Jimmy the Greek on the NBA pregame shows, but Stern would have none of it. Even though Neal Pilson of CBS Sports denied this to me, I believe David Stern.

On ABC, I interviewed Pilson and Arthur Watson, then head of NBC Sports, about the policy of using oddsmakers on their networks. Each said they didn't think using oddsmakers on the air encouraged gambling. I think it's clear that it does.

All of which takes us back to Rozelle's reliance on freedom of the press and noninterference with what the networks put on the air. In general, his position is correct. There should be no right of approval over selection of announcers, and there should be no censorship over what announcers may say. But when it comes to the encouragement of gambling, which strikes at the integrity of the sport, or even the cleanliness of the climate that is essential to public trust, the league has no right to take a laissez-faire attitude.

I know the network sports business inside out. If Pete Rozelle or Paul Tagliabue didn't want oddsmakers on the air, they wouldn't be there. (At the urging of the NFL, CBS and NBC did not use touts in 1990.) The cold, hard truth is that widespread gambling has created much interest in the NFL. Violence and gambling are two of the main reasons for the popularity of the sport.

Gamblers want the latest in information on player injuries—and the National Football League obliges, even fining coaches who withhold information. The NFL releases the latest injury rundown, and newspapers regularly print that information. The injured will be listed as "questionable," "doubtful," or "out." When an injured player's status changes during the week, the league immediately announces that change. Gamblers love it.

By now, you have no doubt detected my disgust for gambling. However, I have no personal dislike for the Pete Roses and Art Schlichters of the world. I have sympathy for them.

Gambling is a national disease. I'll go even further, however. Gambling is a national disgrace. It can't be eliminated entirely. It probably can't even be seriously curtailed. But one thing must be remembered: most forms of sports gambling are illegal everywhere, except in Nevada and Oregon.

The touts and oddsmakers tout themselves and their expertise, and by doing so encourage the spending of money on a distasteful and dangerous dream. This gambling obsession is no joke. This isn't a case of betting two dollars to win, for fun, at the track one Saturday. The kind of gambling we are talking about governs people's lives; it destroys marriages and families.

There's no better example than the tragic and infamous case of Robert O. Marshall, the Toms River, New Jersey, man who was convicted of hiring a killer to murder his wife, so that he could collect insurance money. He planned to use the money to liquidate more than a quarter million dollars in gambling debts.

And there's the sad story of boxing trainer Kevin Rooney, the former trainer of Mike Tyson. Rooney got a bad break when Tyson unceremoniously dumped him, but his financial problems were of his own creation. The IRS seized one of his homes for failure to pay taxes, and Rooney filed for bankruptcy, claiming $1.4 million in debts and no assets. It emerged that Rooney owed huge gambling debts to a number of casinos, making his another sad and all-too-common story.

As we've stated, gambling is an illness, something to be treated by doctors and psychiatric counselors. Yet the networks have chosen to promote it on their shows.

How about "Monday Night Football" in the 1989 season? The announcers frequently mentioned the point spreads, and even the over-and-under, the point total used for betting. In fairness to ABC, it's the only network that never permitted an oddsmaker on the air.

The networks, however, are not alone in this malfeasance. Newspapers are equally culpable, many of them acting like toutsheets, pure and simple, with the odds, the line, the point spread, whatever you want to call it, featured on a daily basis. Indiana basketball coach Bob Knight, a vocal opponent of gambling, says that if a newspaper is going to publish the betting odds and thereby encourage illegal gambling, the newspaper might as well publish the telephone numbers of prostitutes.

Additionally, some newspapers offer their own special experts with their special picks. If you're not expert enough to bet the rent money on the game, just take the advice of the newspaper experts. It's nice and easy, all right there in black and white, very easy for you to consult from the warmth of your family room. Bet with enough of these experts, and you'll wind up sleeping in the street.

I once met a man who made his living as a tout, a man enormously proud of himself and his career, one who brownnosed endlessly along network corridors, looking for a featured role on a pregame show. He was arrogant and obnoxious beyond belief. He had an answer for every statistic about the dangers of gambling, a smart remark for every criticism of his work, a flippant dismissal of medical evidence that gambling is a disease. He maintains that the only reason people watch sporting events is because they gamble. They don't watch for the fun or excitement, or even to alleviate boredom. No, they watch because they gamble.

Well, a certain section of the population watches for that reason, I'm sure. But this tout's belief that gambling is the only reason people watch seems to me to be a measure of how deeply disturbed and dangerous the proponents of gambling in this country have become. They are determined to gain recognition as a legitimate, respected part of sports coverage in this country.

During the football season, it's sickening to see the number of cable TV shows from Las Vegas and other cities featuring so-called gambling experts. They include panelists who tell viewers how to bet on games. Most are come-ons for the dozens of gambling services across the nation, many of which run blatantly false advertising on cable TV, radio, and in newspapers. The ads are ludicrous, misleading, and frequently filled with lies.

In February of 1990, the New York City Consumer Commission finally said enough is enough. It announced the assessment of over $40,000 in fines for bogus newspaper advertising and for deceptive claims made via telephone by what it calls "scamdicappers."

Among the companies fined were Point Spread Consultants, Inc., aka Kevin Duffy ($13,000 fine); Tony Montana Sports; Stu Mitchell's Locker Room Report; Final Spread, Inc.; Super Scout, Inc.; Duke Action Line; the Hammer and Sports Pick, Inc.; Systems Sports, Inc.; and Linemasters, Inc.

Later, the department took similar action against tout

services represented by Jimmy "the Greek" Snyder, former New York Jets coach Walt Michaels, and Mike Warren, a Baltimore-based tout who spends millions in print advertising. Warren has appeared on USA Network, FNN/Score, and Larry King's CNN show as an expert on gambling and handi–capping.

Ex–New York City consumer commissioner Angelo Aponte said, "Thirteen years ago, Jimmy the Greek was quoted in *The Washington Post* saying what a rip-off these operations are. He spoke of how claims of 81 percent winners and money-back guarantees are preposterous. Now, Jimmy the Greek's part of this very same industry making similar claims, like 90 percent winners on his Lock-of-the-Year games over the last five years."

Aponte was critical of the *New York Post* and the New York *Daily News,* which accept the gambling ads. He told the *Post,* "On page one, the papers will expose a scam, but on page eighty-three, they'll accept money to promote one."

It's believed that some papers take in revenue of as much as one million dollars per year from these gaming advertisers. Two national dailies, *USA Today* and *The National,* print these hideous gaming-related ads for tout services. Aponte was quoted as saying, "On one hand, the papers have an internal conflict because they draw revenue from advertisers; advertising keeps them in business. But on the other hand, the papers are lending themselves to those who want to separate readers from their money in a most unscrupulous fashion."

This is not to say that some tout services are not legitimate; some do sell authentic gambling information. The exploding business does, however, include some outright cheats who follow dubious practices. For example, some services will give one team to win a game to half of their customers, then will give the other team to win the same game to the other half of their telephone customers. This assures the tout of a winning selection with many customers, and even most of those customers who have the losing side will come back and pay more hard-earned dollars for more selections.

Some services sign up former players to attract customers

or suckers. Former Baltimore Colts star Johnny Unitas and ex-quarterback Billy Kilmer are among players who have lent their names to touting services.

And the phone companies are also actively encouraging the gaming business: 800 numbers, 900 numbers, and 976 numbers are saturated with gambling information such as point spreads, injury and weather info, tout selections, and up-to-the-minute scores for the gaming addict.

I find this gaming craze disturbing. I think the public—the non-gambling public—should be disturbed by it, too. The taint of gambling reflects on the sport, on the game itself.

That gambling scandals will continue to touch sports periodically is a certainty. In today's society, many people would say you can make book on it. How is the public ever going to be sure that the game on the field is an honest one when gambling is implicitly encouraged by the football establishment, the television industry, and the newspaper industry? Why should the players themselves, whatever the rules say, be above gambling? Why should they be above making a huge sum of money one weekend in exchange for fumbled balls, dropped passes, or endless overthrows of pass receivers? How can you keep a sport clean if the atmosphere around it is so sullied?

You can't. Sooner or later, it catches up with you. Sooner or later, the sport becomes infected by it. Sooner or later, there's a scandal. Again.

Point-spread—more precisely, point-shaving—scandals date back as far as one can remember. In the past decade, there was Boston College in the early eighties, where basketball players were alleged to have ties to the Mafia, for whom they were dumping games.

Tulane University was hit in 1984, when point-shaving was alleged. John "Hot Rod" Williams, now with the Cleveland Cavaliers, was found innocent of taking part in the point-shaving scandal at Tulane, but his defense in two trials was as embarrassing as the charges.

He was described as a youngster from a deprived environment, horribly unprepared for college, hidden out in puff courses to keep him eligible, cut off from the mainstream of campus life, and victimized by sharp, rich fraternity boys from the East.

The scandal nearly destroyed Dr. Eamon Kelly, the Tulane University president, who is a former assistant secretary of state, a former head of the Ford Foundation, a great American.

Tulane itself is an outstanding institution. In recent times, it ranks near Harvard and Yale in turning out Rhodes scholars. Dr. Kelly didn't want a rotten basketball program to detract from the greatness of the school, so he did the smart thing and after the 1985 season dropped the basketball program. He knew that no matter how hard he tried to control it, the blandishments and temptations and corruptions were just too widespread by now, too inherent in the big-time college sports establishment, for any conscientious university president to handle.

Over the next few years, however, Dr. Kelly was subjected to much pressure and strong-arming from Tulane alumni and supporters who wanted the program reinstated. Yielding to that relentless pressure, Dr. Kelly reluctantly agreed, and with new coach Perry Clark and a roster of eight freshmen, Tulane returned to big-time competition (Metro Conference) in 1989, promptly losing twenty games.

The next alleged point-shaving scheme was targeted at North Carolina State's basketball program. ABC News, using a young reporter who specializes in exposé-type journalism, Armen Keteyian, charged that a $65,000 loan made to Charles Shackleford, the ex–N.C. State star, was part of a plot to fix games. Shackleford denies it. As of this writing, no one has been able to prove anything, and if I were Roone Arledge, who in 1990 signed a new five-year contract as president of ABC News, I might be a little worried that Charles Shackleford, a former member of the New Jersey Nets, might obtain a good lawyer and wind up owning ABC News. Don't get me wrong. I won't be shocked if the point-shaving charges pan out. The environment is always ripe for a scandal.

Many coaches try to pound the danger of fixers into their players' heads. Bob Knight hammers with a warning to his Indiana kids. Even Lou Carnesecca of St. John's finds time between recruiting junior-college players to show his team the album of old newspaper clippings depicting point-shaving tragedies.

Tates Locke, the Indiana State coach, stated in his book, *Caught in the Net,* "There are two things in coaching I will never swear to: that no one on my ball club doesn't deal with drugs. Two, that a player of mine never dumped a game. I'm talking about point-shaving. Personally, I've always feared the dumpers. I mean, look at it this way, if a school can buy the services of a player for a certain amount of money and promises, what makes you think a gambler out on the street can't also buy him?"

The pros seem to keep a little better handle on fixed or "funny" games. Football, baseball, and basketball have security forces that follow the point spreads and money line in an effort to detect any big money moves that might signal tampering by would-be fixers. League officials, and some wiseguys in the gaming industry, invariably say that it's impossible to fix games without detection at the time, but every few years, like clockwork, a scandal breaks indicating that despite precautions some games were rigged.

In truth we'll probably never be free of gambling scandals so long as wagering is such an accepted practice in our society.

Did you know that one of the country's top cardsharps, a bona fide card counter at blackjack, is also one of the top college basketball coaches in the country? Bill Frieder of Arizona State University, the former University of Michigan coach, has been banned from many casinos because he is too sharp. It is a standard practice for casinos to bar card counters who play twenty-one. Card counters simply beat the house dealer, and casinos don't like to lose. Some feel that one of Frieder's priorities in moving to Tempee is its proximity to Las Vegas.

And in 1990, John Thompson, the Georgetown University coach, created a stir when he purchased a home in Las Vegas. Some read the acquisition as an indication that Thompson was angling to replace Jerry Tarkanian as coach at UNLV. It turned out that Thompson wanted the house because he frequently visits friends in Las Vegas and loves to gamble in the casinos. He admits to a strong attraction to the slot machines. It must be a sight watching Big John trying to intimidate a one-armed bandit.

When officials at the University of Oklahoma decided to dismiss head football coach Barry Switzer, they had to wait for him to return from a gambling trip to Las Vegas before they could inform him.

Seemingly, the whole world likes to gamble. Some of my best friends gamble, but I still oppose it.

My collaborator on this book is an outstanding sports handicapper, with key contacts in Las Vegas. People seek Shelby's opinion, and with justification—he knows his sports. He's also been known to make a wager on occasion. On Derby Day at Churchill Downs in 1987, Shelby correctly selected nine straight winners, including Alysheba, the Derby winner, who paid $18.80. ABC Radio advertisers, who were being entertained at Churchill Downs, were betting his picks. They thought they'd died and gone to heaven.

At one time or another, most of us have wagered on some type of sport, but playing the races once or twice a year and entering the World Series or Super Bowl office pool is not what serious sports betting is all about.

The annual sports take in Las Vegas grows every year. In 1989, Las Vegas took in $1.35 billion. Sonny Reizner of the new Rio Suite Hotel and Casino, formerly the sports gaming head of the Castaways Hotel and Casino and later the Frontier Hotel and Casino, says sports gambling in America has proliferated to the point where it generates greater revenue than U.S. Steel.

And the $1.35 billion bet in Las Vegas is only a drop in the bucket compared to what is bet illegally across America. The FBI estimates the annual illegal sports betting to be close to $50 billion per year; Reizner's estimate is a slightly more conservative $40–50 billion a year. As stated earlier in this book, legitimate income from organized sports makes it a $50-billion-per-year business in this country, and it appears that more than that amount is wagered on sports each year. No wonder some, such as the National Football League, treat gambling with reverence. That type of money has an impact.

No one loves to bet more than New Jersey Giants coach

Bill Parcells. He can't go through a day without betting. Some of his players claim Portly Bill (my favorite nickname for Parcells before he went on a diet) will bet on anything, whether a thin man or a fat man next walks through the door—or whether a frog will jump two or three times.

One man who doesn't want his players betting at all is David Stern. When Charles Barkley of the Philadelphia 76ers and Mark Jackson of the New York Knicks engaged in some friendly $500 bets, Stern fined them $5,000 each and told them to stop it. Jackson had won $500 from Barkley during the 1989 playoffs, and Barkley won it back in a game between the two teams the following season. Barkley popped off to the press about the wager, and it got back to Stern. For Barkley, the $5,000 fine was like a spit in the ocean. After he was fined $20,000 for fighting later in the season, he said he didn't care because he earned $3 million in a season. I'll bet the Commish loved that.

To further demonstrate just how far out of hand this sports betting business has gotten, here are a few examples from 1989.

The University of Florida, with a 5–1 record in midseason, suspended its starting quarterback, Kyle Morris, and reserve quarterback Shane Matthews, for betting on games. The school said that during the 1989 season, the two players bet up to $100 per game on college games, a violation of NCAA rules.

Meanwhile, two University of South Carolina football players were arrested for betting on college and pro basketball and pro football games. Officials said Gamecock nose guard Tim High bet up to $500 per game, and offensive lineman Wes Pringle was betting up to $375 per game. One legitimate question is where are the college kids getting that kind of money to bet on sporting events? South Carolina athletic director King Dixon said, "We were truly shocked and upset."

At Austin, Texas, it would have been easier to name the University of Texas Longhorn football players who were *not* betting on football games than to name the ones who were. Twenty University of Texas football players were found to place bets regularly on games with a bookmaker through a teammate. Longhorn officials held their breaths, but the

NCAA did not declare the players ineligible for the 1990 season. Perhaps it would not be too cynical to assume that pro gamblers might think twice before betting on a team that had twenty players who were themselves betting with both fists.

One of the saddest gambling investigations came to light in July of 1989, when the FBI and Alabama law enforcement officials were investigating the possible fixing of high school football games.

The investigation became public after law officers shadowed for two years a sports gambling ring that may have had a role in fixing high school games in the so-called Quad Cities area of Florence, Muscle Shoals, Sheffield, and Tuscumbia, Alabama.

In April of 1990, Richard B. Thompson, the Florence chief of police, told me, "The only indictment so far was a perjury indictment against Ronald G. Bowling, chief of police of Muscle Shoals. Another member of the Muscle Shoals Police Department remains under investigation."

At first, it was believed that the allegations involving tampering were restricted to game officials—people running the clock, spotting the ball, running the yardage marker—but Chief Thompson said that players and coaches were involved in the investigation as well, and one high school coach admitted placing bets on games involving his team. The chief added, "This is no small-potatoes investigation. Using a total of one hundred FBI and police officers, we seized nearly one million dollars in cash and stacks of gambling records in our searches of homes and businesses. The FBI in Washington is studying the gambling data. I expect an indictment of ten to twenty people. This case will have national ramifications."

I ask you, how low can you go? You have to be the dregs of society to fix a high school football game.

Strangely enough, many law enforcement agencies now treat gambling offenses like "nuisance" crime. The FBI seldom involves itself with bookmakers anymore, unless there are aggravating circumstances. In 1990, one agent told me, "We are so busy with drugs, we just don't have time to concern ourselves with gambling." New York City police seem to have the same philosophy.

Fortunately there are occasional exceptions. In May of 1989, police in Manhattan, Queens, Staten Island, and Nassau County, New York, arrested sixty-eight people in a single betting ring that police say brought in $300 million in illegal sports bets a year. That arrest resulted from the work of an undercover detective, but for the New York police or the FBI to get involved in a gambling case, there usually has to be some evidence of organized crime.

In thirty-eight years of broadcasting for ABC, I have been aware of many bizarre happenings. Few top the time an old radio producer got into trouble with a bookmaker of the mob, the son of a well-known figure in the Lucchesi family. The producer's name is not important, he has long since left ABC, was rehabilitated by Gamblers Anonymous, and is now in another line of work. He incurred the wrath of the mob for failing to pay $22,000 in gambling debts and for calling in bets to the bookmaker's office after he had been told to stop. The result was a severe beating, followed by hospitalization and surgery to repair broken bones of the cheek and eye socket. A verbal threat of even more violence, specifically one to kill him and members of his family, was enough to send the producer to Gamblers Anonymous for help.

Another tragic gambling case is the one involving self-admitted New York gambler Howard Spira. (I don't know how Pete Rose missed Howie Spira as a member of his inner circle of trusted friends. Howie would seem a natural.) Spira claims he stiffed New York bookmakers for $2 million, betting both sides of games with different bookies, collecting winnings from one and refusing to pay the losses to the other. It seems highly unlikely that New York bookmakers, many of whom are mob-connected, would allow him to lose that much money before cutting off his wagering or resorting to the same tactics used in the producer's case. Remember, truth is not a strong suit of most sick and compulsive gamblers, and Howard Spira certainly seems to fit that description.

I find it difficult to understand why so many people support gambling. In so many documented cases it has destroyed lives and families, has resulted in lost cars, homes, and jobs. Yet, wherever you turn in the United States, there is some symbol of gambling. A state lottery (thirty-four U.S. states now have lotteries), off-track betting parlors, numbers games in the neighborhood, weekly poker games at home, community bingo, local dice games, casinos in Las Vegas, Reno, and Atlantic City, office pools, legal bookmaking in Nevada and Oregon, and illegal bookmaking everywhere in the U.S. Surprisingly enough, there is some form of legal gambling in forty-eight of the fifty states.

Back in the seventies, the federal government named a commission on gaming, which conducted three years of research and hearings. The National Commission concluded that gambling is "inevitable" in this country, and that 80 percent of adult Americans favored one form or another of legalized gambling. The executive director of that committee, James Ritchie, said, "We determined that two-thirds of all Americans gamble."

That it's a widespread practice still doesn't make gambling right. Many people use illegal drugs. That doesn't validate drug usage.

In 1989, Christiansen/Cummings Associates announced research that showed that in 1988, Americans bet $253 billion, more than half of that on casinos, lotteries, bingo, and numbers, and about $56 billion of that total on sports. It's pathetic. Can you imagine what good could be done with that money? The things that could be accomplished for the sick, for the needy, and to educate the young people of our country. Supporters of legalized gambling will argue that much of the money (from lotteries) is directed to those areas. I say most gambling monies go either to the casinos or to the underworld. This debate can go on and on.

Gambling, of course, is not unique to this country. It is practiced, with variations, all over the world. European countries have had lotteries and soccer pools for decades. History tells us they even played something that resembles our present-day dice game during the days of Julius Caesar, and it is very likely there was some type of wagering in the Colosseum when they held the chariot races and staged the terrible battles, to the death, between slaves, who were sacrificed for amusement.

The British may be the bettingest people of all. Their bet shops—their bookmakers are usually called turf accountants—are scattered all over the country. The betting chains include Hills, Ladbrokes, Mecca, and Coral, and their hundreds and hundreds of betting shops offer wagers on just about any sport in the world. The soccer and cricket games command the most play, but horse betting and dog betting are popular in England as well. The Wimbledon championships and the British Open offer diversion. You can bet on any player to win Wimbledon, bet on any individual match, and bet on the number of sets in any match. British Open odds are posted before the tournament and change after each of the first three rounds.

One can sometimes get odds of up to 500 to 1 on a very lightly regarded horse. Of course, not many of those tickets get cashed.

The British have one very unfair betting practice. If your horse is scratched, you don't get your money back. Tough luck, your lordship. Equally unfair is the British policy of not refunding money on sporting events that are rained out.

The Brits can get a little innovative with their nonsports wagering. You can bet on political races, in the U.K. or in other countries, including the U.S.A. One can bet on the weather, bet on whether it will rain, bet on how much it will rain.

Some British bookies will even offer bets on prison breaks. The tougher the escape from a certain prison, the higher the odds. Additionally, there are odds for single or multiple prison breaks. It's crazy. Sometimes the whole world seems insane.

Bingo parlors seem to be located in every block of London, and many of them are crammed with little old ladies losing the grocery money. It's as bad as people on a fixed income, social security, riding the buses to Atlantic City and blowing their money.

Americans haven't come close to the British in their zest for wagering, but legalized gambling of all kinds seems to be spreading in the U.S. as well.

Atlantic City doesn't have sports betting yet, but bills to legalize sports wagering have been introduced in the New Jersey and New York legislatures.

Oregon, in 1989–90, offered wagering on the NFL and the NBA; it was met with mixed results. The state took in $7.1

million, after setting a goal of $10 million. Wagering on the NBA was light, and Oregon dropped NBA betting in 1991. The league, which had sued the state, claiming that betting infringed on its rights, dropped its suit after Oregon agreed not to offer NBA wagering for a five-year period.

Sonny Reizner is the innovative Las Vegas gaming director who pioneered legal betting on such events as the Boston Marathon and the Academy Awards.

Those events are lightly wagered, but there is no doubt about the world's single biggest betting event. It's the Super Bowl. It's estimated that up to $2 billion is wagered on the Super Bowl each year.

Some Nevada sports books listed as many as forty-nine betting propositions on Super Bowl XXIV. One can wager on the coin toss; on which team will score first; on whether the first score will come by field goal, touchdown, or safety; on the number of points scored in each quarter and each half; on which team will have the most fumbles and pass interceptions; on which team will miss the most field goal attempts; and it goes on and on and on.

It's ridiculous.

The whole picture is a sad one. Too many people can't bet with restraint. Too many bettors are out of control. The slogans, such as "Bet with your head, not over it," simply don't work. There are too many Pete Roses and Art Schlichters of whom nobody is aware.

The gambling-related divorces, bankruptcies, lost homes, lost businesses, fixing scandals, and murders—yes, even murders—are on the upswing. The calls to Gambler's Anonymous increase. More and more high school students are becoming involved with problem betting.

The public must become aware of this increasingly troublesome situation.

You can't eradicate gambling, no. But you can at least relegate it to the cellar where it belongs. Take it off the air and out of the pages of newspapers. Make it harder for gamblers to gamble, then we'll see what happens.

CHAPTER NINE

Alvin Pete Purged; "Too Tall" Anointed

If Alvin Pete Rozelle wasn't fired as commissioner of the National Football League, he was certainly pushed. It is unequivocally fair to say that Pete was forced into early retirement.

These are the facts. Rozelle's ten-year contract was due to expire in 1991. For most of his almost thirty-year career, Pete had generally been acclaimed as the most successful commissioner of any professional sport, and at age sixty-three, many observers felt that he might like to continue in the job past 1991. However, his effectiveness and his support among the owners had diminished. It would be difficult for a layman to detect this situation because Rozelle's massive, Madison Avenue–slick public relations machine was more effective than ever. The National Football League's public relations department and its enormous lobby make it the strongest and most persuasive of all organizations in this country—yes, stronger than the NRA (National Rifle Association) and the AMA (American Medical Association).

Rozelle was approaching the end of a chaotic decade, and despite receiving most of the credit for bringing the NFL from a "mom-and-pop" operation to twenty-eight franchises worth a combined total of at least $2.5 billion, many of the owners felt Rozelle was no longer a strong asset. The most alarming aspect of the situation, however, was that many of those same owners were among his strongest friends and supporters.

In the early part of 1988, five of the old-guard owners—Art Modell of the Cleveland Browns, Wellington Mara of the New Jersey Giants, Leon Hess of the New Jersey Jets, Tex Schramm of the Dallas Cowboys, and Dan Rooney of the Pittsburgh Steelers—held a top-secret meeting in Phoenix, Arizona, to discuss Rozelle's responsibilities and the possibility of naming an assistant to help him, and/or the possibility of lining up the person who might be his successor. Another of the topics discussed at the meeting covered the possibility of naming two men to succeed Rozelle—one to deal with ceremonial and PR-oriented matters, as well as discipline and rules; the other a lawyer, a business-oriented type, to deal with labor negotiations, TV and radio negotiations, and congressional and political affairs.

Rozelle didn't learn of the meeting until well after the fact, but surely the mere existence of such a meeting was devastating to Rozelle's ego. What made it even more shocking to him was the questioning of his effectiveness by this particular group of men. If Mara, Hess, Modell, Rooney, and Schramm were concerned about the leadership of the National Football League, how did the Young Turk owners—already lukewarm supporters at best—and his outright critics feel about Alvin Pete Rozelle at this point? Eight new owners entered the league during the eighties, and some of those were not enamored of Pete; certainly they had no long-term allegiance to him.

It's an absolute fact that Pete was weary from the stressful court fights, two brought by Al Davis and the other by the United States Football League. Davis left Rozelle and the NFL battered, bleeding, and losers in court, and you wouldn't know it from the nation's media, but the NFL's losses in the USFL case were far greater than the $3 monetary award. The league was formally branded a duly adjudicated illegal monopoly and had to pay the USFL legal fees exceeding $5 million. The National Football League appealed the ruling on legal fees, and when it lost the appeal, there was hardly any mention of this fact in either the electronic or the written press.

Rozelle's record out of court wasn't too hot either. There was labor strife: player strikes in 1982 and 1987, and no collective bargaining agreement since 1987. The league's drug policies were a joke. Cocaine and steroid use flourished in the National Football League in the eighties. Therefore, things were not exactly a bed of roses for Rozelle as he approached Super Bowl XXIII in Miami, and they would only get worse. Super Bowl week is a spectacle and a national celebration, but it is also vulgar and obscene with its gaudy extremes, including ticket-scalping (up to $2,000 per ticket), and the commissioner's party, costing up to $1,000,000, money aimed at getting the propaganda hooks into a hungry national media corps.

Since the National Football League is quickly identified with racism and violence, it seemed ironically appropriate that Miami would supply a liberal dose of racial violence for the Super Bowl festivities. A Miami policeman shot a black man to death on Monday of Super Bowl week, touching off riots that featured Molotov cocktails and fires in the Overtown, Liberty City, and Coconut Grove sections of the city. The Cincinnati Bengals could watch the fires from their downtown hotel rooms. One Bengal remarked, "We went to see the movie *Mississippi Burning* and came back to the hotel to watch Miami burning."

Rozelle and his underlings were worried about what the rioting might do to the Super Bowl itself, and how it might affect the festivities. Later in the week, at what was to be his final "State of the League" address to the media, Rozelle said the violence would have no effect on the Super Bowl, one that was to be the last under his commissionership. And in a shocking development, Pete defended the NFL's record on racial relations. He said, ". . . in some ways we have a great track record. We were the first to integrate in sports, the first to have a black game official, and the first to have a minority official in a key role." Quick, who were they?

Don't feel bad. No one else knows their identities either. (Rozelle was referring to Leo Miles, the official, and David Cornwell, who held a minority coordinating position in the league office).

Thankfully, the racial violence subsided, but the Super Bowl nightmare in Miami wasn't yet over for Alvin Pete Rozelle. Cincinnati Bengals starting running back Stanley Wilson, the former Oklahoma Sooner star, went on a cocaine binge and was suspended from the game. He would later be banned from pro football as a three-time cocaine loser.

Tragically, it was during Rozelle's half-million-dollar party, his annual bash for media and sponsors, that Pete's wife, Carrie, was informed of the death of her son from a drug overdose. The boy, a hard-drug user for years, was from Carrie's prior marriage to the son of Washington Redskins owner Jack Kent Cooke. The telephone call was a shock to Rozelle and his wife. Carrie Rozelle had been close to Emmy and me down through the years. She's a great lady who has done wonderful work on dyslexia, the reading disability, receiving national acclaim for her work in this area.

Two days later, on the morning of the Super Bowl, Rozelle had a labor meeting aimed at settling the long dispute between the players' union and management. This problem was of great concern to the commissioner, and he hoped that both sides would agree on a collective bargaining agreement. Rozelle knew that having gone so long without an agreement reflected unfavorably on his record as commissioner. He was tired of the court fights and the litigation and was willing to make certain free-agency concessions in order to reach an agreement with the players.

Gene Upshaw, the former Oakland Raider great and the executive director of the NFL Players Association, a long-time friend who has considered me a confidant and trusted adviser for many years, told me, "Pete was ready to make us a deal which would have been acceptable to the union, but Hugh Culverhouse killed it on the spot, rebuffed Rozelle and said he was finished as commissioner."

Hugh F. Culverhouse is one of the most powerful men in the National Football League, a wealthy tax attorney and owner of the Tampa Bay Buccaneers. At one time, he was a powerful official in the Internal Revenue Service, the head of the IRS Southeastern Region of the country.

Culverhouse made an attempt to purchase the Los Angeles Rams in 1974, but was unable to complete the deal. A few months later, he landed an expansion franchise in Tampa Bay for $16 million. His club has struggled on the field, having made the playoffs only three times, but his franchise is considered a gold mine. In addition to the Bucs, Culverhouse owns extensive Florida real estate and is worth in excess of $325 million. He is a brilliant man who became a power in the National Football League by doing favors for other owners. To this day, he is the chief executor of the will of Carroll Rosenbloom, the late owner of the Los Angeles Rams. He authored the tax base for the Rams when they moved from Los Angeles to Anaheim to become the Anaheim Rams, and he lobbied for Rams owner Georgia Frontiere when the Rams were in trouble for Super Bowl ticket-scalping. Georgia remained free, but her husband went to prison in that case. And it was Hugh Culverhouse who saved Leonard Tose's neck, loaning him a huge sum of money to pay off gambling debts. Tose ultimately was to wiggle out of the noose, sell his Eagles club to Norman Braman, and walk away with a profit of $33 million.

It's plain to see from this brief career history that Culverhouse is a man who has some due bills around the league. His positions as chairman of the Executive Committee of the NFL Management Council and as chairman of the league's Finance Committee carry much clout. Culverhouse dealt from a powerful hand when he killed the proposed bargaining agreement and rebuked Rozelle.

According to Upshaw, Culverhouse told Rozelle, "Hell, no, we are not making that deal. We are going to crush this damn union."

Alvin Pete Rozelle knew that from that day, Super Bowl Sunday, January 22, 1989, that his days were numbered; his power had diminished, and he knew in his heart that he could no longer be an effective commissioner.

The same day, *The New York Times* hit the street with a lengthy story, by-lined by Michael Janofsky and headlined "Owners Contend Rozelle Is Slowing." The piece in effect said that many owners felt Rozelle was slipping, and that the league was being run by committee member/owners and lawyers. Coming on the same day as the humiliation by Culverhouse, the story had a devastating effect on Rozelle.

Combined with the Miami racial disturbances, the Stanley Wilson cocaine case, and the death of his stepson to a drug overdose, it was not a week to treasure. At that time, Rozelle surely knew that it was time to bail out.

His idea to compromise with the players and grant some reasonable form of free agency was a good one. He wanted to get the NFL labor problems out of the courts. Pete had seen enough litigation and acrimony. But it was not to be, however.

The NFL establishment and the media treated it as a great shock when Rozelle, at a league meeting in Palm Desert, California, on March 22, 1989, announced his early retirement. Pete had been through enough. He said his health was good, except for the twenty pounds he had gained after stopping smoking, and he announced he would stay on in the job until a new commissioner was named. Little did he know that it would take six months, and that he would gain another ten pounds during the smokeless ordeal.

His announcement came two months to the day after the fateful Super Bowl–morning meeting with Upshaw and Culverhouse. All owners, including Pete's critics, professed shock at his "surprise resignation" and dusted off their most glowing accolades and laudatory phrases. What a charade. Culverhouse, with hypocrisy spewing from every pore, said, "It's too much of a shock. You are not going to replace Pete Rozelle because he is too much to replace. But we will be diligent in our search."

Were they ever. It was to be a six-month comedy of politics, backstabbing, and acrimony.

Denver Broncos owner Pat Bowlen on Pete's resignation said, "I was very much shocked, like someone had dropped a bomb." Any owner surprised at Rozelle's announcement simply was unaware of what was happening or was totally out of touch with reality.

Rozelle said, "When you talk about three trials in five years, it seemed for a while they were never going to end. And we had to do our jobs on top of that. These have not been pleasant times for the owners, myself, or a lot of people close to football."

If the NFL players wind up winning free agency in court, they can thank Hugh Culverhouse. It will likely be a greater degree of free agency than what they would have accepted under the Rozelle concessions of January of 1989.

Outside of failing to conclude a labor agreement, the one thing that Rozelle regretted most was his inability to expand the league from twenty-eight to thirty teams by 1989, something that had been a long-standing goal of his. The owners wouldn't agree, so cities such as Baltimore and St. Louis, cities that were robbed of franchises by the Irsays and the Bidwills, greedy owners who skipped town for more lucrative deals, must wait to replace their franchises.

The cold, hard truth is that Rozelle could have stopped these franchise relocations, but had he done so, the owners might have forced an even earlier resignation. National Football League owners insist on what is best for their pocketbook. It's a sad but real truth in the National Fantasy League.

My friendship and personal relationship with Pete Rozelle goes back almost thirty-five years. My first dealings with him came when he was a young PR man at the University of San Francisco. I had continuous dealings with him since in his tenure with the Rams, and then as league commissioner. Most people who know anything about sports know that for much of the last decade, Pete Rozelle and I were estranged. As detailed in my last book, Pete resented my position on both Al Davis court cases brought against Rozelle and the National Football League, and he bitterly resented my testifying for the USFL in its 1986 trial against the NFL.

But I can't forget thirty years of friendship. Emmy and I were in the Rozelle home so many times, and in the old days, Pete and Carrie frequently came to our home. People can't forget those things, and I recognize and appreciate the fact that it was Pete Rozelle who first recommended to Roone Arledge that I do "Monday Night Football."

So it's with candor that I write that our estrangement for much of the eighties pained me. And that's why I was happy when Pete invited me to join him for cocktails in the last few days of his commissionership.

Before Rozelle was able to leave his Park Avenue office, he had to go through the ordeal of waiting for the owners to amuse America with their efforts to choose a new commissioner.

At first, it appeared that former congressman Jack Kemp, the ex–NFL quarterback, would get the job. Kemp, however, didn't want to go through a lengthy election process, and since the NFL owners were not about to quickly hand the job over to anyone, Kemp announced that he was not interested. It is my personal feeling that Kemp, as the secretary of housing and urban development in the Bush administration, has a far more important job, and he probably still harbors presidential hopes.

After Jack Kemp dropped out of the running, many men were mentioned for the position, among them U.S. Senator Bill Bradley, broadcast executives Roone Arledge and Neal Pilson, and Cap Cities/ABC executive Michael P. Mallardi. The most ludicrous candidate was Robert Mulcahy, the president and CEO of the New Jersey Sports and Exposition Authority, which controls Giants Stadium. His selection could have created a blatant conflict of interest. And if Mulcahy wasn't acceptable, Mara wanted Jon Hanson, chairman of the New Jersey Sports and Expo Authority. At a Yankees cocktail party at the 21 Club, both Mulcahy and Hanson publicly stated that they appreciated my position about Mara's pushing them for the NFL job, and they explained that it made them feel uncomfortable.

What an outrage! A blatant conflict of interest. Mara and Leon Hess would like nothing more than to have their former landlord and stadium partner in the commissioner's chair. Talk about a good ol' boy network. Ethics be damned! But did anyone in the New York or the national media raise an eyebrow? No!

Sports are all crazy. It's such a complicated and interwoven mess. It boggles the imagination.

Finally it began to look as though Jim Finks, the New Orleans Saints president and general manager, and the man I felt to be best qualified, would get the job. He was to come close, but couldn't garner the necessary nineteen (out of twenty-eight) votes.

Many of the old-guard owners were backing Finks, but they fell three votes short. Actually, close scrutiny reveals that the old owners and the new owners were split on Finks.

There was a feeling among some, including a substantial number of the newer owners, that the committee was attempting to ramrod Finks through. As a result, they became polarized.

Here's the breakdown of a Chicago vote, with the year representing when the current owner or owner's family took over the club:

Voted for Finks

Falcons	Rankin Smith, Sr.	1965
Bills	Ralph Wilson	1960
Bears	Mike McCaskey	1920
Bengals	Paul Brown	1968
Browns	Art Modell	1961
Lions	William Clay Ford	1963
Packers	Robert Parins	1982
Chiefs	Lamar Hunt	1960
Raiders	Al Davis	1963
Saints	Tom Benson	1985
Giants	Wellington Mara	1925
Jets	Leon Hess	1963
Cardinals	William Bidwill	1932
Steelers	Dan Rooney	1933
Chargers	Alex Spanos	1984
Redskins	Jack Kent Cooke	1974

Abstained

Cowboys	Jerry Jones	1989
Broncos	Pat Bowlen	1984
Colts	Robert Irsay	1972
Rams	Georgia Frontiere	1979
Dolphins	Joe Robbie	1967
Vikings	John Skoglund	1961
Patriots	Victor Kiam	1988
Eagles	Norman Braman	1985
49ers	Ed DeBartolo, Jr.	1977
Seahawks	Ken Behring	1988
Bucs	Hugh Culverhouse	1974

Not Present

Oilers	Bud Adams	1959

Indications were that had Bud Adams been in attendance, he would not have voted for Finks.

Even though I have great respect for Finks as a football man, I told some that it didn't really matter who the commissioner was, it's tweedledee or tweedledum. The owners are going to run the show anyway. The commissioner doesn't represent the players or the fans. He is selected and paid by the owners, and when they say "Jump!" the commissioner will say "How high?"

Someone, of course, has to fill the job, and while much of the country laughed at the inability of twenty-eight owners to select a commissioner, the traveling road show went from Chicago, where the first vote had been taken, to Grapevine, Texas, where the next vote had Finks and league lawyer Paul Tagliabue tied at thirteen votes each with two owners abstaining. Finally, in midseason, on October 24, 1989, the owners convened in Cleveland on the shores of Lake Erie and gave the job to Paul "I'm Too Tall" Tagliabue. The 6'6" Tagliabue had been the captain of the Georgetown University basketball team before that school played big-time basketball. He held the school rebounding record before a center named Patrick Ewing came along. Like myself, Tagliabue is a graduate of the New York University School of Law. He seemed like a logical choice for the National Fantasy League owners. Named commissioner at age forty-eight, he had been a lawyer for the league since 1969 and was already well versed with the operation of the incredibly powerful NFL congressional lobby: people such as Bob Strauss, former national chairman of the Democratic Party; Marlow Cook, former U.S. senator from Kentucky; and Anne Wexler, who was a member of President Carter's administration.

Even though he and I are fellow alumni, I haven't seen too much to get me excited about the talents of Paul "I'm Too Tall" Tagliabue. When he was the NFL attorney, we appeared the same day before the American Bar Association convention in August of 1986 at the New York Hilton hotel. He was supporting antitrust exemptions for the National Football League, and there were a lot of judges in the room. At the same time, then baseball commissioner Bowie Kuhn was in the room, and since baseball enjoyed exemptions from antitrust laws, Bowie was aligned with the NFL.

In the middle of the proceedings, as I was talking, a man in the back of the room got up and started to leave. It was Joe Browne of the National Football League. "You, the members of the judiciary— Don't go, Joe," I hollered. "I want them all to see you," and Browne turned around.

I said, "You see, gentlemen of the judiciary. That man is Joe Browne, director of communications for the National Football League. Every word I utter, every show I do, he has a copy of. Implicit censorship, gentlemen of the bench. Implicit censorship!" (Some reporters might be intimidated when a commissioner monitors sportscasts and obtains copies of speeches, but it only makes me more determined to speak my mind and tell the truth.)

"Now, Mr. Bowie Kuhn knows about this. Because at Mr. Kuhn's behest, I went down to Charlottesville, Virginia, to speak before his law school at the University of Virginia, a very distinguished university in our country. And I was sharply critical of Commissioner Rozelle, in many areas, especially in regard to franchise removal. And the very next morning, and correct me, Bowie, if this is not true, you got a call from Commissioner Rozelle, asking for a copy of my remarks. Is that true, Bowie?"

"Yes, that's the truth," answered Kuhn.

"Gentlemen of the bench, did you ever see anything like this?" Then I turned to Paul Tagliabue. "Mr. Tagliabue," I said, "you are a graduate of my law school, NYU. Like me, you were an editor of the Law Review. How can you countenance this? Okay, Joe," I said to Browne. "You can go now and report what I have said."

And the judiciary went wild.

Joe Browne is funny. A couple of Christmases back, I received a greeting card from him with a note. He wrote, "We miss you. It was more of a challenge when you were around." Apparently some people feel that when you give up TV, you die. Not so, Joe.

So far, I give "I'm Too Tall" Tagliabue mixed grades on his commissionership, which is still in the honeymoon stage.

His first big decision was to fine Cincinnati Bengals coach Sam Wyche for not letting reporters into the locker room. That's some big decision, isn't it? Why shouldn't he have a right to keep them out? The late Yankee catcher Thurman Munson was pilloried for not talking to the press. Didn't he have a perfect human right—as did Phillies pitcher Steve Carlton—a constitutional right, to talk to whom he wanted? Why do some reporters feel that all athletes have a responsibility to give them quotes? Isn't performance on the field enough? If an athlete wants to talk with someone, fine. If not, fine.

I agreed with Tagliabue when he proposed random drug testing of athletes for steroids. I'll elaborate more on this in the chapter on drugs.

The NFL held up the networks and cable companies for a record $3.2-billion contract, but I don't think Tagliabue had much to do with that. Art Modell usually orchestrates those deals. During games, haven't you seen the networks showing him hundreds of times on camera? Keep Art happy and on camera, and maybe those negotiations will go smoother. Modell, whom I've known for over thirty years, is a good man, who underwent serious heart surgery in 1990.

Commissioner Tagliabue showed some character flaws when he refused to attend the 1990 Maxwell Club dinner in Philadelphia to accept an award, the Rozelle award, because I would be on the program. How juvenile. No, he didn't have another commitment. No, he wasn't sick. He told the organizers that my presence kept him away. Tagliabue sent another of his smooth PR-types, Jim Heffernan, to accept the honor on his behalf.

Some things about the National Football League never change. It's still a monopoly, and I don't know of anything that's more indicative of their antique attitude than Tagliabue's boycotting the Maxwell Club dinner. Again, this is another example of how sports interrelate. It's unbelievable that he wouldn't attend because of me. How could he take that position? You can't tell me that's not a form of attempted censorship. Of course it is. It's outrageous, but he did it.

I was the honored guest speaker at the Maxwell Club

dinner, and it was great seeing the old baseball announcer By Saam, one of the true giants in our industry. And Emmy and I had a wonderful time renewing acquaintances with Bo and Millie Schembechler. The former Michigan football coach had accepted a new position as president with the Detroit Tigers. We didn't miss Paul "I'm Too Tall," who told the organizers he knew Pete Rozelle would never attend an affair that featured Howard Cosell.

Nonsense. Pete and I had our differences, but he was a bigger man than that.

I was pleased when Don Weiss of the NFL called, back in the final week of Rozelle's commissionership, and said Pete wanted to meet me for cocktails. My rapprochement with Alvin Pete Rozelle was to take place at the Laurent Bar in the Lombardy Hotel, Pete's favorite hangout. He seemed genuinely happy to see me, and the feeling was mutual. He seemed more relaxed than in recent years. Carrie was already at Rancho Santa Fe in the California desert, where they had built a new home. Pete had been living in a New York hotel for six months while the incredible fight to name a successor dragged on.

Pete had nice things to say about Paul Tagliabue; several times he mentioned to me that he thought Paul would be a great commissioner. He seemed to agree with me that Jim Finks is a better football brain, and I think Pete would have liked to see Finks accept the face-saving offer of a number two job to head up operations. Finks refused it, however.

We talked about our families and we talked about football. You just can't wipe away all the years. We were never buddy-buddy the way Rozelle is with Frank Gifford and Herb Siegel, the president of Chris-Craft, but I would never have wanted that type of relationship with the commissioner of the National Football League. Gifford and Pat Summerall were always too close to Rozelle to be objective about the commissioner or the league.

In our football discussion, Pete cleared up one misconception. After his "surprise" resignation, there was much talk that Rozelle and Al Davis had buried the hatchet. No way. Rozelle made it clear that he still harbors deep resentment for Davis's lawsuits and his testimony in the USFL suit, which was unfavorable to the NFL. I'm sure Pete still resents my testimony in that suit as well, but I had to tell the truth.

Rozelle had no positive things to say about Hugh Culverhouse. I didn't press the issue, but he gave me no reason to believe that Culverhouse hadn't caused him to accelerate his resignation.

Pete and I had an interesting conversation about Leon Hess. As outlined in my last book, Hess and I had become adversaries, so I was surprised when Leon came up to me at a closed-circuit showing of the Mike Tyson–Michael Spinks "fight" on June 27, 1988, at the New York Athletic Club. He started acting like my long-lost buddy. In the presence of then ABC Radio Network president Aaron Daniels, ex-ABC Radio Network president Ed McLaughlin, and ABC Radio Sales senior vice president Lou Severine, Leon said, "Howard, I was just telling Peter Jennings and Leonard Goldenson that you have always been very fair to me. That you told the truth in the courtroom. I said I would never sell Monmouth Park [a racetrack] to the State of New Jersey, and then I did."

I stopped him. "Leon, why are you saying all of this now?"

"Because I need your help," he responded. "I want Bobby Beathard to run the Jets."

Bobby Beathard and I are close friends. I was heavily instrumental in getting him the general manager's job with the Washington Redskins when he was in charge of scouting for the Miami Dolphins. Redskins owner Edward Bennett Williams was ready to hire Al LoCasale of the Raiders as his GM when I telephoned to say it would be a mistake not to hire Bobby Beathard. The rest is history.

I called Bobby and told him to expect a call from Leon Hess, who wanted to talk to him about running the Jets.

The next day, two days after my discussion with Hess, I called Leon back to tell him that Beathard was expecting his call. I was amazed when Hess said, "Oh, that's on the back burner now, Howard. I decided to stick with Joe Walton and the people we now have."

Leon Hess made his millions in oil, petroleum. He is eminently qualified to have been in snake oil.

Pity the poor New Jersey Jets fans. They had to wait and suffer through another two seasons of Joe Walton–induced agony. Finally, the public outcry forced Hess to run Walton out of town and bring in Dick Steinberg of the New England Patriots to run the club.

Rozelle was interested in the story, but was not too surprised at anything Leon would do.

Pete and I left each other with a good feeling. Emmy and I have a standing invitation to visit Pete and Carrie in their new California home. And I must say this for Carrie Rozelle—she's absolutely an amazing woman, indefatigable, so determined with the work that she's done with learning disability in this country. I give her all the credit in the world for that. Plus she's never held the things that I've said about Pete against Emmy and me. For that, I also give her full marks. Full marks!

CHAPTER TEN

Duly Adjudicated Illegal Monopoly

The National Football League engaged in monopolistic practices for decades before it became a duly adjudicated illegal monopoly. This ruling was delivered in July of 1986 in Room 318 of the U.S. District Court Building located at Foley Square in lower Manhattan.

It took an antitrust lawsuit brought by the United States Football League to make it official.

After forty-nine days of testimony and thirty-one hours of deliberation, a six-person jury found twenty-seven of the twenty-eight National Football League teams guilty of conspiring to monopolize professional football. The L.A. Raiders were not named in the suit. Raiders managing partner Al Davis had already beaten the NFL in a couple of lawsuits and was subpoenaed by the USFL to testify on its behalf.

The USFL was seeking $1.32 billion in its suit—actually $440 million, which under the law regarding antitrust legislation would be trebled to $1.32 billion. What the fledgling league got was $1, trebled to $3. That's right. Three lousy bucks! In my opinion, the award represented a miscarriage of justice by the American judicial system and turned a solid and valid case into a travesty.

The jury of five women and one man stated what most everyone had known for years—the National Football

League was a bunch of oligarchs who for years have monopolized pro football in this country.

When the USFL owners filed a federal suit against the NFL, they hoped to receive enough money in damages to keep their league alive, and to force the NFL owners into gentlemanlike behavior. In other words, they wanted to convince the NFL to stop trying to monopolize the TV market, stop hogging players and tampering with USFL players already under contract, stop denying the USFL the use of stadiums, stop monopolizing the coaches and referees, refrain from insulting the junior league in public, and in general, cease attempts to snuff out the new league.

It didn't happen. When the jury didn't establish a realistic monetary penalty, and when the trial judge failed to correct the situation, it meant two things became certainties: the USFL would die, and the NFL bullies would continue their monopolistic agenda, remaining the only professional football game in town.

I'm not so sure the jury wanted it to turn out that way.

According to juror Miriam Sanchez, there was a hung jury, split evenly at three and three. It was a jury that fought and haggled over the case and the verdict, a jury that was ultimately determined to compromise in order to avoid a hung jury and a retrial.

On the surface, it seems that nearly everyone believed that the verdict was a total victory for the NFL. It was reported that way on television, on the wire services, and in the newspapers. However, the outcome may not have been as clear and simple as that.

Ms. Sanchez said openly—and this is key—that the jury chose to set damages at $1 because they were unsure about how high the damages should be, and they wanted Judge Peter K. Leisure to set the damages for them. Judge Leisure had the right to do this, but to the delight of the NFL, he refused.

One juror said afterward that she wanted at least $1 million in damages for the USFL and would have gone as high as $300 million. Another said she felt the damages should be at least $300 million, trebled to $900 million. Had Judge Leisure assessed the latter, it's safe to assume that the USFL would be in business today. The league would have been in a strong position to negotiate a TV contract, and the NFL would have suffered a substantial monetary loss. It would have been a serious wound to the NFL.

When Judge Leisure failed to revise the award for damages, the only hope left for the USFL rested with the Appeals Court.

More than a year later, in January of 1988, a panel of three federal judges in the Second Circuit of the U.S. Appeals Court refused to change the verdict. They agreed that the NFL was a monopoly, but would not give the USFL monetary relief.

The jury in the trial had not accepted the USFL's charges of restraint of trade and monopoly of television, clearing the various television licensors of all charges of monopoly. The jury found that all contracts had been negotiated individually, and prior to the birth of the USFL. Commissioner Pete Rozelle, who had been named as an individual defendant, was found innocent of conspiracy charges.

The unanimous Appeals Court decision touched off wild celebrations throughout the NFL. This, despite the fact that the league remained an illegal monopoly, a finding the trial judge would not vacate. To this day, the NFL remains a monopoly.

It is no secret that I was closely involved in this case; many called me the key witness for the USFL. I cannot quarrel with that assessment, and I will discuss my trial experiences in depth. First, however, let me further address the appeal opinion written by Judge Ralph Winter.

I carefully studied the opinion by Judge Winter, an opinion that is now the law of the land. The decision is what is known as a narrow decision in terms of the antitrust laws. Briefly stated, the Appeals Court said the USFL's failure was not caused by the NFL's contracts with the three television networks, or by the monopoly practices of the NFL. The court decided that the USFL failed because of its own mismanagement and mistakes, and those had nothing whatsoever to do with the NFL monopoly. Therefore, the monopoly practices of the NFL technically were not relevant.

So that is how an illegal monopoly escapes punishment. The decision is narrowed to a small area and dealt with

accordingly. It's less complicated. Less messy, if you will.
And it is, of course, a common and perfectly acceptable
form of judicial practice. Judges vary in their interpretation
of the law, and vary in how narrowly, or widely, they wish to
deal with a case on appeal before them. In this case, Judge
Winter chose the narrow view, and he chose to consider the
evidence in that matter.

In studying his opinion, one is struck by what some legal
experts would term the weakest part of the opinion, particularly in regard to the monopoly questions. The opinion
virtually glossed over prior circuit court opinions that
found the NFL in violation of antitrust law: James McCoy
"Yazoo" Smith against Pro Football and the now-famous
John Mackey case. In the first case, Smith won, and the
victory invalidated rules for the NFL draft. In the second
case, John Mackey, a free agent, won and wiped out the
so-called Rozelle rule, which required compensation for a
free agent. In both cases, the antitrust question was key. In
the USFL case, the antitrust violations were, in a sense,
pushed aside as irrelevant. Anomalies were allowed to
stand.

Being an attorney allows one to understand legalese, but
there are some things about this case I will never understand. How can a duly adjudicated illegal monopoly celebrate a court victory, one that affirms it as a monopoly?
How can a monopoly win any case on appeal? Some things
boggle the mind!

My day on the stand in the USFL vs. NFL trial was June
25, 1986.

Harvey Myerson, a dynamic and flamboyant attorney, an
able trial lawyer, was the USFL attorney, and Frank Rothman, an old friend and formerly my lawyer in a case
involving a Philadelphia sportswriter and me, was the
attorney for the NFL.

To lead off, Myerson established the fact that I was
employed by Cap Cities/ABC Radio Networks. For some
people, mine would have been an awkward position, since
my testimony would contradict that of Cap Cities executives
Roone Arledge and Jim Spence. For me, it was neither
awkward nor uncomfortable, because I have always told the
truth as I know it, no matter whom it may contradict. I have

lived by the truth all my life, and on June 25, 1986, I was not about to change. Let the chips fall where they may. I never played the game, and you can put that on my tombstone.

Myerson established the fact that I was notes editor of the Law Review at New York University. He then set about to establish, for the court record, my awards and honors.

Much to the discomfort of Mr. Rothman and the NFL crowd, and to the amusement of Judge Leisure, Harvey went through my long career with ABC (at the time thirty-three years) and my long list of awards. He mentioned the Emmys, the Pointer Fellowship, the Mark Hellinger–Bob Considine Award, my American Bar Association awards, the Ronald Reagan media award, the Order of the Leather Helmet, the Jackie Robinson award, and he recounted my eight years of teaching courses at Yale.

Rothman didn't appreciate my testimony. I had him in the palm of my hand and everyone in the courtroom knew it. At times, I had the courtroom roaring with laughter.

William Nack, writing in *Sports Illustrated,* said:

> On cross-examination, the NFL co-counsel, Frank Rothman, had just asked Cosell if he knew Tex Schramm, the president of the Dallas Cowboys, and NFL owners Wellington Mara of the New York Giants, Arthur Modell of the Cleveland Browns, Alex Spanos of the San Diego Chargers, and Leon Hess of the New York Jets. Cosell said he did. In fact, all except Hess were present in the courtroom. Now Rothman asked him, "Do you find each to be men of high integrity?"
>
> After gazing disbelievingly at Rothman, Cosell finally said, "Men of high integrity? . . . I don't think they are villains, sir. I do think they have been misled and their actions have not been in the public interest."
>
> Having led once with his chin, Rothman led with it again. "Do you find them to be truthful men, sir?" he asked. Now Cosell did not hesitate. "Not in recent cases involving actions of the National Football League, sir," Cosell said.
>
> What Rothman had done before the jury was elicit testimony that challenged the actions of five NFL leaders and raised questions about their truthfulness. A

cardinal rule in trial interrogation is that you never ask a witness, particularly a hostile one, a question to which you do not already know the answer.

Not that any of Cosell's answers were foreseeable. In four hours of testimony laced with humor, sarcasm, anger, and bombast, and delivered with all the famous Cosellian voices, ranging from sedate storyteller to wounded bull, he transformed room 318 from a courtroom to a stage, and he needled Rothman at every turn.

"I'm not as smart as you are," Rothman, who once represented Cosell, said at one point.

"Well," said Cosell, "we had learned that long ago."

At another point, Rothman told Cosell, "If I ask you a question you don't understand, you stop me," to which Cosell fired back, "If you ask a question that I don't understand, you will have the biggest story of the century."

You don't have to be a genius to recognize that Pete Rozelle and the entire NFL were very upset with ABC for giving the USFL a television contract during its first three spring seasons. Yet Arledge denied that Rozelle or anyone else from the NFL ever expressed a negative reaction to the network's decision.

Who's kidding whom?

I testified that during a lunch conversation in 1984, Arledge told me, "You have to understand, Pete's all over me on the grounds that I am sustaining the USFL for their spring contract."

In other testimony, I revealed that, a few years earlier, Pete Rozelle had expressed concern to Roone Arledge that I was going to testify before a Senate subcommittee regarding a bill that would make it easier for the NFL to switch franchises from city to city. During my long career, I must have testified before congressional committees at least two dozen times, and until that point, Roone Arledge had never questioned the propriety in my doing so. As detailed in my last book, despite Rozelle's anxiety, I did testify before Sen. Arlen Specter's committee.

The NFL was never shy in trying to censor my

"Sportsbeat" show, which was the strongest investigative sports program ever shown on television.

Normally the censorship attempts would be made through Jim Spence, whom Arledge charged with running the day-to-day TV sports operation. Then Cap Cities took over ABC and blew Spence to oblivion.

Every time Spence attempted a dose of censorship or suppression, I would tell him to go to hell and issue a strong protest to Arledge.

I must say that in my thirty-eight years of doing radio for ABC, I have never encountered attempts at censorship from executives. Shelby Whitfield and all other executives have never made an attempt to interfere with my opinions or the editorial content of my commentaries. There have been plenty of times when they didn't agree with me, but I have always enjoyed total freedom. I'm sure that the NFL knew that if it couldn't control me on television, there's no way they could control me on radio.

In reality, however, the NFL attempts at censorship ultimately had nothing to do with the USFL's "losing" its case. There is no doubt in my mind that Donald Trump is the man responsible for the "loss."

The jury simply didn't believe Donald Trump, who—in case anyone has forgotten—was owner of one of the USFL franchises. He was not a good witness, and Judge Leisure could not hide his disdain for the tycoon. The jury felt Trump was simply using the USFL to force an NFL franchise for himself.

Trump testified that Pete Rozelle actually promised him a franchise: "Pete stated that the NFL was going to be around for a long time, and that [I] would have a very good chance for an NFL franchise, whether it be the New Jersey Generals or some other team; and that what he wanted in return was . . . staying for the spring in the USFL and not bringing a lawsuit . . . the thing that Mr. Rozelle specifically did not want was a lawsuit on antitrust grounds."

Rozelle denied ever offering Trump a franchise.

Later, it appeared that in spite of Rozelle's denials, Trump would wind up in the NFL. The Sullivan family, longtime friends of mine, were desperate to sell the New

England Patriots. No sooner were the Generals uniforms packed away in mothballs than Trump was showing interest in the Pats. A couple of things worried Donald, however. The Patriots were hip deep in debt, and it dawned on him that the NFL might be setting him up. Remember that Trump was an important player in bringing the USFL suit against the NFL. The USFL's appeal was very much alive, and had Trump joined the NFL club of owners, he would become both plaintiff and defendant in the same case. With these factors in mind, the man who was to write *The Art of the Deal* realized that buying the Patriots under those circumstances didn't look like such a good move.

Now that the USFL is only a memory, it's a safe bet that Donald Trump will never again be encouraged to buy an NFL franchise. The truth is, the league views him with distaste.

Trump had also made a number of efforts to secure a major league baseball franchise when Peter Ueberroth was commissioner. Peter said, "I'll never allow you in baseball. You're in gambling. You run casinos. You'll never get into baseball."

Since that time, Trump's name has been mentioned in connection with a new baseball league, and he has been mentioned as a possible owner for the New York Yankees. Don't hold your breath.

Had Donald Trump been a better witness against the NFL, he might have had great impact on the history of pro football. As you know, gambling involvement does not bar ownership in pro football. Trump had his chance at being a football oligarch and he blew it.

CHAPTER ELEVEN

Scabs and Court Fights

The National Football League always tried to make it appear that the USFL was a "Mickey Mouse" league, that USFL players couldn't make it in the great, holy NFL. But once the United States Football League suspended operations, the NFL went after the "Mickey Mouse" players, like sharks after fresh meat.

No less than 192 USFL players were signed by the NFL, including such superstars as Herschel Walker, Reggie White, Jim Kelly, and Anthony Carter. At one point, the New Orleans Saints had fifteen ex-USFLers on their forty-five-man roster, and seven of those were starters. And who was the head coach of the Saints? Ex-USFL coach Jim Mora.

What did ex-USFL players Sean Landeta, Bart Oates, Chris Godfrey, and Maurice Carthon mean to the New Jersey Giants? A Super Bowl victory, that's what.

Then there was ex-USFL quarterback Doug Williams, who led the Washington Redskins to a Super Bowl victory with his phenomenal performance against the Denver Broncos. Additionally, ex-USFLers Kevin Bryant, Gary Clark, and Ricky Sanders had some memorable years with the Redskins.

One could go on and on with these examples. Certainly there was a combination of irony and poetic justice when the ex-USFL players not only brought new blood to the NFL, but added life and excitement to the tired old league. Some of the lesser-known players in the USFL were able to become starters in the NFL, and some players, such as Keith Millard with the Vikings, developed into superstars. Millard was the NFL's Defensive Player of the Year in 1989, but missed the 1990 season with an injury.

No one appreciates the impact made by USFL players in the NFL more than Carl Peterson, the general manager of the Kansas City Chiefs. Peterson, one of the better football brains of our time, built a championship team with the Philadelphia Stars, who later became the Baltimore Stars.

Former USFL coach Jack Pardee, now head coach of the Houston Oilers, a man who beat melanoma cancer, and the only person to be named Coach of the Year in the National Football League (Chicago Bears), the World Football League (Florida Blazers), and the United States Football League (Houston Gamblers), was one of the biggest boosters of the USFL. Pardee says his best team ever would have been the merger team of the New Jersey Generals and the Houston Gamblers. Ironically, that team never got to play a game, since the league suspended operations. Much to the displeasure of most NFL personnel, Pardee firmly states that his old Houston Gamblers club, with Jim Kelly triggering the run-and-shoot offense, would have been competitive in the NFL.

Not only did the NFL load up with USFL players, it adopted the fledgling league's instant replay. The last USFL commissioner, Harry Usher, who was Peter Ueberroth's right-hand man on the Los Angeles Olympics, and who succeeded former television executive Chet Simmons as commissioner, said, "We were the innovators of instant replay to assist game officials, and now the NFL is using it to enhance their product."

That just proves my earlier point—competition breeds a better product. Instant replay has been a controversial device, and the NFL regularly threatens to ditch the rule. When it comes to a vote, however, the league keeps it. I must admit that instant replay is something that I have no strong feeling about, one way or the other.

There is no substitute for competition in creating excellence, whether in football or in any other business. The best years of pro football were the years when the old AFL went head-to-head with the NFL, creating competition, bidding wars, new markets for football, not just for the fans but for the players, too. Competition is better for everyone, but until a higher court, perhaps the Supreme Court, deems otherwise, the NFL, the illegal monopoly, will keep a lock on pro football.

Once the NFL killed off the USFL, it set its sights on defeating the NFL Players Association. The National Football League simply has a hard time recognizing the rights of the players to organize themselves as a union to negotiate with management. Oh, management has recognized the sports union to a degree, but there have been more attempts at union-busting than at good-faith bargaining. It is plain that unions are no longer very popular in this country, but they were key in making this country great. Men and women have lost jobs, and in some cases, their lives, fighting for unionization.

Maybe you don't see a connection between those men and women who risked everything they had to ask for minimum wage, overtime, and safe working conditions, and football players, basketball players, and baseball players, especially given the rather substantial wages some of them receive. The connection is there, however, and it is as real as the Super Bowl, the NBA Finals, and the World Series. And I'm telling you, it's every bit as important, because what is at stake when professional athletes strike is a principle, and a protection for every working man and woman, a protection once fought for in the streets of our nation, with fists and guns, and lynchings and mass arrests.

Everyone needs to remember that unions didn't spring up overnight to harass the bosses and stifle productivity. They grew slowly out of desperate need, but the way people talk about unions today, you'd think poor Sam Gompers sat up every night trying to think of ways to ruin the economy and let Japan corner our markets.

We forget about history. There's no perspective anymore when it comes to unions, no historical context. But the context does exist, the history is there, and sports unions are legitimate heirs to it.

Unionization came late to professional sports, and in some ways it may seem alien to the sporting world, but it's not. Athletes have to fight for the same control over their wages and working conditions and pensions and compensation that everyone else does. Certainly in this respect they're just like those who work on a Ford assembly line, or who work for the postal service. The salary range may differ vastly, but the principles do not.

The baseball players union was started in 1954, about the same time the NBA players organized. The NFL and AFL players didn't organize until 1968. The football unions merged in 1970, when Ed Garvey, the brash, young, liberal attorney from Minnesota, came onto the scene as executive director.

In recent years, the sports unions, like all unions, have felt the consequences of Ronald Reagan's tough stand on unions. The President's method of handling a strike by the air traffic controllers union was to kill off the union and hire inexperienced personnel to replace the union personnel. The NFL owners would later do the same thing in the 1987 NFL strike, when they hired scabs at $1,000 per game to replace the regular players. Since the public apparently didn't care enough about its own safety in the air to raise an outcry about the destruction of the PATCO union, the NFL owners figured the public wouldn't care too much if it was Herschel Walker or Herschel Smith on the field, as long as there was a game. In many ways, the owners turned out to be correct. The anti-union climate in the country certainly worked in the owners' favor, as they set out to destroy the NFLPA.

Let me be clear about this. Unions are not perfect. Like many organizations, they have had problems with corruption. Maybe we've seen one too many labor leaders hauled off to serve time for having broken the law. And maybe unions have sometimes demanded too much, and given too little in return, for the public to feel much sympathy for their cause.

Remember, however, that it is not just some union leaders who go to jail, but bosses as well. Remember that in spite of huge salaries for athletes, the team owners, like all bosses, want to keep as much of the profits as they can, while they criticize the players for being greedy. And if the unions weren't doing the players some good, the owners wouldn't be so dedicated to busting them.

Remember that just as football, basketball, and baseball are a part of our country's history and a part of our culture, so are unions. In fact, perhaps there is nothing quite so solidly American, nothing that is a more perfect blending, than the mix of sports and unions. Only in America would baseball, basketball, and football players unionize and strike. It is my feeling that Americans should be proud of them.

On September 22, 1987, the NFL players went on strike. I supported Gene Upshaw, who succeeded Ed Garvey as NFLPA executive director, and the players.

To my way of thinking, the owners' hidden agenda in the strike was union-busting—the NFL wanted to destroy the Players Association once and for all, and the owners felt the time was right to get away with it. These twenty-eight wealthy men and women wanted unfettered control of every aspect of their business, including control of the players via the college draft, free agency, salaries, compensation, and pensions. The bottom line for such control would be union destruction.

The announced main issue was free agency. Men who play for the NFL want to be able to choose their employer, a right nearly all of us enjoy. Oh, yes, I've heard the argument that in certain specialized fields employees do not have that right. The diplomatic corps was cited as one such example. Obviously, it's absurd to try to make an analogy between the two. If you're a member of the diplomatic corps and an expert in French, Arabic, and Portuguese, you might wish for a posting to France, but instead be sent to Brazil. But there are valid reasons for lack of choice, the same way the military has valid reasons for assigning soldiers to certain places, without the soldier's having a choice.

But if you can block and tackle in Detroit, you can block and tackle in Dallas or Green Bay just as well. There is no need to have a system whereby twenty-eight people dictate where you live and work and raise a family, just because it suits them financially.

The NFL is a private business, not the State Department,

not a branch of the United States government. How can anyone seriously compare the business of conducting U.S. foreign policy with the business of playing pro football?

A key point is the way in which the NFL has managed to be treated by the majority of the media, and by the public, as if it were some special branch of government, providing some hugely important service to the American people. The NFL is never on the defensive. The poor owners have to cope with the angry Gene Upshaw and the greedy, greedy football players. How did this happen? How did it happen that a handful of rich men and women running a private business at enormous profit to themselves get depicted as the ones getting the bad deal? The ones being exploited?

If you resent the players' salaries, look at the net worth of the owners in the league. The players will suddenly look poverty-stricken in comparison. The players are the ones who suffer the risk of physical injury, actually suffer many injuries, and undergo numerous operations, and what is the average length of a player's career in the National Football League? Less than four years.

However, when it comes to labor negotiations, the owners are the ones to whom the public gives the benefit of the doubt. The owners are the ones who won't bend. They are the ones who won't compromise. They are the ones who look to reject all forms of free agency.

Another point that comes up when football players go on strike is the fans' claim that they have a right to professional football. That is not the case. It is nowhere written in the Constitution that Americans have the right to watch the NFL on Sundays, Monday night, or any other night. I know this may be a big shock to those who talk about the "rights of the fans," but those rights do not exist, not by law or judicial opinion.

Those were my feelings at the start of the strike in 1987, and they remain my feelings now. When the NFL owners trotted out the scabs in an effort to break the strike and bust the union, I wrote the following open letter to the strike-breakers, the scab laborers:

Dear Sirs:

I am not so sure you are worthy of so polite an initial greeting, but I extend it anyway, before I ask you this simple question. Why? Why would you consider committing such a dishonorable act? Why would you willingly offer yourselves as sacrifices to what is one of America's ugliest historical traditions? Why would you want to become a blot in history books, villains of the peace instead of men of character?

"Strikebreaker" is a disgusting term. "Scab" is even worse. Webster's defines a scab as "a dirty, paltry fellow; a scoundrel" and as "a workman who works for lower wages than, or under conditions contrary to, those prescribed by the trade union; also, one who takes the place of a workman on a strike." It's a label as shameful as Nathaniel Hawthorne's scarlet letter once was. Yet it would seem that you are all willing, perhaps even proud, to wear it.

You want the money, any money, any amount the owners will pay you, you say. In other words, there is a public price tag on your soul. It's said that every man has his price. I don't know if that is true. But it appears true of all of you. That in itself is sad. What is even sadder is that your price is so cheap. Your venality so surfaced that any or all of you didn't think twice but jumped at the chance to play again after you'd been cut. Or to play for the first time in the NFL, when no one wanted you there in the first place, because no one deemed you qualified to be there. You all positively leaped at the chance to do other men public harm. To steal their jobs from them. To encourage the owners to destroy the union, and to encourage the public to side against your fellow athletes, who risk much to go on strike. You all just hung there on the ready-to-wear rack, polyester leisure suits all of you, for the owners to pick up and try on for size. Really, gentlemen, you should be ashamed of yourselves.

There are issues more important than money. There are some things that do not come with price tags hanging from their sleeves. Those things are such apparently outmoded concepts as honor, courage, morality, and the character to say no to a cheap payday. To stand firm on a principle. You, who dare talk of yourselves as role models, you who dare to present yourselves to the children and the adults of this nation as athlete-heroes, now present yourselves as athlete-scabs. Strikebreakers. Job stealers. Men who'll sell out, do anything for a dime, ignore principle, for your own temporary personal benefit and greed. The values—or rather, the lack of values—you are willing to impart to the public may not concern you. But it concerns me deeply. You are branding yourselves scabs for the rest of your lives. Not just publicly, but among the fraternity of professional football players. Nobody likes a scab. If character is in short supply these days, recriminations and retribution still exist aplenty. No, I do not think I would want to be Mark Gastineau these days. [Gastineau crossed the picket line.] Gastineau already had enough trouble with his professional life and his personal life. Now he will have union troubles, too. NFL veterans who had little to gain from striking were willing to walk out. They don't like people such as you, Mr. Gastineau. They don't like you at all.

And can you blame them, you and the others? You sent a signal to twenty-eight enormously rich men and women with enormous power to shape and control public opinion, and you told them they are right, not the men who play the game every week. You told them loud and clear where you stood. And then you put yourselves on display for the media, dangled yourselves as proof that the union was wrong, or the union was split, and some of you even said you were too well paid to strike, when you know full well that money is not, and never was, the only issue; when you know full well that the right to have a viable union and to expect the owners to bargain in good faith, and the right to free agency, were always the basic issues. When you know full well that, while very well paid, most football players do not earn the supersalaries we all read and hear about.

But then again, judging from your conduct, money is obviously the only issue in your eyes. If you are willing to accept scab dollars, don an NFL uniform, and walk out onto a field while the men who really belong there walk picket lines outside, your eyesight extends no further than your bank balance. Your judgment doesn't even go that far.

To some, the sorriest sight is watching the players walk the picket line. To me, the sorriest sight is watching you guys show up to toss a pigskin, and talk into those microphones about your big chance to play, or keep playing, in the NFL. Moral bankruptcy is never pretty.

I find it particularly distasteful when it's clad in shoulder pads and wearing a jersey that has "scab" written above its number.

And perhaps I find it a particularly unattractive sight because I remember one young athlete, once upon a time, who refused to take a step forward and be inducted into the Army. His name was Muhammad Ali. In so refusing to join the Army, which was against his religious beliefs, he was stripped of his right to fight, and lost the best years of his career and his life, fighting for his rights. He didn't even have a union to back him up. He stood alone. Whatever Muhammad Ali became later on, his act of courage marked him for life, made him a legitimate athlete-hero, and earned him a permanent place in our history, and in our ongoing battle to protect and secure our liberties.

The NFL union battle lacks that kind of drama. Right now America is politically a different place from what it was in 1967. But the underlying principles, the things that count, do not, have not, changed. You could all learn a lesson from the courage of Muhammad Ali. You could apply it to the union, to the strike, to your lives.

Instead you choose to line up with those who are called scabs. Rivers of blood and years of violence have been spilled so that Americans have the right to unionize and strike. Every scab act diminishes those rights. If they eventually disappear, you'll have yourselves to thank for your contributions to the diminution of freedom. You're a sorry bunch of men.

[Signed]
Howard Cosell

As it turned out, the NFL Players Association lost its battle. The TV networks carried the scab games, and they made their rights payments to the owners on schedule (even if they did demand some rebates later on). The public, at least to some degree, accepted the lousy scab football, and the real players lost about $80 million in salaries for missing a quarter of the season. Actually, the players would recoup about one quarter of that, because the National Labor Relations Board ruled that the owners unfairly prevented the players from returning to work for game four of the season. Each owner was saving anywhere from $500,000 to $800,000 in salaries every week the strike went on, so they clearly wanted the strike to last as long as possible.

The NFLPA didn't have a strike fund, a fact that contributed to unrest, hardships, and dissatisfaction among the union membership. As a result, the NFL players were forced to return to work without a collective bargaining agreement, something they still don't have to this day. The union was left in shambles. The owners had stopped the automatic dues checkoff from the players' salaries, and it remains that way to this date.

In a great miscarriage of justice, Gene Upshaw was declared the big villain in the strike. The NFL management, most of the media, and some of the players were quick to award the goat horns to Upshaw. It was all so unfair; Gene Upshaw is a fine man, with the best interest of the players at heart.

Upshaw is memorable as one of the most formidable, if not *the* most formidable, offensive guards in the history of pro football. Upshaw had been a tackle out of little Texas A&I when Al Davis drafted him to play for the Raiders. The first thing Davis did was convert Upshaw from a tackle to a guard and place him next to Art Shell. For the next decade, they were the finest guard-tackle tandem in football.

In a word, Upshaw was tough. Huge, unbelievably quick, indefatigable, and intense. He was the finest lead-run blocker in the game, and equally great on pass blocks. He was also a born leader. His spirit picked up where Jim Otto's had left off. And he was solid, playing in 217 games—more than any other in Raiders history—starting in 207 consecutive games, and missing only one game in fifteen seasons.

He inspired his teammates, became team captain, the player rep for the union, and he would tell people, "I'm the best, baby, and don't you forget it."

That was Upshaw, gruff on the outside; if you knew him, however, you knew he was soft as jelly on the inside. He knew where he wanted to go, what he wanted to do when the cheering stopped, and now for several years, he's been doing it as head of the National Football League Players Association.

Upshaw inherited his post from Ed Garvey, and Upshaw says Garvey taught him a lot: "I learned from Ed that you've got to face the challenge. You've got to take the risk. When you take on the NFL, you take on the most powerful sports league in the country, and a formidable political power. They have a huge public relations machine, and they crank it up all over America. Relatively speaking, I run a small office with a handful of people. The NFL runs a large office. Plus they have twenty-eight 'satellites,' I call them, the twenty-eight teams and twenty-eight cities, who also crank up their machines. They turn public opinion against us overnight. They may have twenty-eight satellites, but we have sixteen hundred players."

In 1987, during the strike, when Upshaw said "the players are the game," he was called "militant," a label he dislikes because he sees it as negative, as focusing on the fact that he is black. He argues that no one labels Southern senators Strom Thurmond or Jesse Helms "militant" for holding strong views and speaking their minds.

I see his point, although I disagree. I see "militant" as a compliment, as proof of Gene's willingness to take on the owners and the commissioner at no small risk to himself. Some had thought that Upshaw's position as head of the players union might keep him out of the Pro Football Hall of Fame at Canton, Ohio. That was not the case, and he entered the Hall in 1987.

Losing the strike that same year, however, was a crushing

blow, probably the low point in Upshaw's career. I felt sorry for the man and I expressed my sentiments in an open letter to him:

Dear Gene:

I recently wrote an open letter to those men—scabs—who crossed the picket lines to play football. Now, as the strike collapses and the union-busting triumphs, it is time to write you, and the men in your rank and file who have stood firmly by the union and you.

First, let me say that you have just cause to be proud. You were not afraid to battle for your principles, not afraid to stage a strike, not afraid to take on powerful owners, the greedy TV networks, and even the fans, in an attempt to win the rights that most other working people in this country take for granted. And most important of all, as much as you wanted to win, and you deserved to win, you were not afraid to risk a possible loss. That takes enormous character and courage. And you are to be applauded for both.

The NFLPA faced two formidable foes. The first was the NFL. The twenty-eight convicted monopolist owners have, literally, no scruples, no conscience, no honor. Their illegal, unrestricted monopoly practices, and the lack of competition in the business of football, have created a power base so enormous and corrupt that it is almost untouchable. Operating in collusion with the networks, it is virtually unbeatable.

The owners would put animals in uniform, toss them on a field, and call it the NFL. They would be certain the public would attend and bet lavishly on the outcome, and certain that the networks would carry them. They would not be wrong in their assessment of the public or TV. They are men without conscience, but they are not stupid. They hauled in their scabs. Enough fans responded to make it worthwhile for them and TV.

As you know, the owners could never have managed so well without the cooperation of TV and most of the print media. Except for a handful of us, the NFL owns the communications industry in this country. That fact alone was an insurmountable barrier for the union. To win public support for a strike is key. When you cannot fairly make your case before the public, the public will turn against you. Then perhaps the only thing that can save your cause is solidarity. The only thing that will eventually bring the public around is sticking to your guns, no matter what the odds.

And that did not happen. The other foe the union faced was betrayal from within.

You were betrayed by your rank and file, Gene. Too many of them never understood the purpose of the strike and the need to hold out, no matter what happened. This has always been a problem for the NFL union; it has never been a problem for the baseball union. I have thought long and hard as to why. I have no answers. I only have the evidence before my eyes and yours: quislings in your ranks.

Remember Quisling, Gene? He was the Norwegian who collaborated with the Nazis during World War II, turned over his country to them. His name became synonymous with betrayal and traitor. The NFLPA is lousy with quislings. What the owners couldn't accomplish with their monopolies and with TV, the quislings accomplished for them. The quislings allowed their union to be busted, broken by a handful of men who cloak themselves and their sport in piety and purity and the American flag, while everything they truly stand for is un-American. Anti-American. Anti-competition. Anti–free market. Anti-labor. Anti–freedom of speech, anti–freedom of choice, even anti–equal protection under the law. You understand this. John Spagnola understands this. So do Gary Fencik and Harry Carson and many, many of your rank and file. But not enough. Not in the end. The quislings won out. Collaborators, too many, consorting with the enemy.

Thomas Paine drew a cartoon more than two hundred years ago. It was a snake in sections. Each section represented one of the thirteen colonies. The caption underneath read, "Join or die." I've thought of that cartoon often these past few weeks. Everyone had to join, or die. It was the only way to win.

Now, the recriminations have begun. You are going to be blamed. You are going to be told your strategy was wrong, your demands were wrong, it wasn't the right time, a strike was a mistake. The Monday-morning quarterbacks will be out in force, second-guessing ad nauseam. I can't tell you you did everything right. I can't tell you there might not have been other ways to go, other remedies to pursue. But I think you did well, Gene. And no, you are not to blame. No individual can be held responsible for 1,600 others over time. I wonder what Eugene Debs would have done with your rank and file? Probably sobbed into a pillow every night.

The NFL aim was always to bust the union. You know it. I know it. In truth, those owners have not negotiated in good faith. The union did. The union was willing to compromise. The owners didn't give the compromises the time of day. The owners didn't give the union the time of day. Union-busters don't agree to binding arbitration. The convicted illegal monopoly, the NFL, does not want to have to answer to an arbitrator and the law. You know it would lose. I know it would lose. The NFL knows it would lose.

And therein lies the saddest part of all this. When one party in a strike won't negotiate in good faith, everyone involved becomes a victim, and a loser. The players, the union, the public, and one day, yes, even the holier-than-thou NFL. For there is no greater evidence of the NFL's arrogant contempt for the law than the way in which it has conducted itself during this strike. This is still America. And somehow, some way, the law will prevail.

So keep your chin up, Gene, and the rest of you who held fast and stood firm.

There are other remedies at law. And you have done a very interesting thing in that regard by filing your broad-based lawsuit against the NFL, a lawsuit that is reminiscent of John Mackey's lawsuit against the league that was successful. You have right on your side. And that's the most important weapon of all.

Sincerely,
Howard Cosell

After losing the 1987 strike in devastating fashion, it was plain to Gene Upshaw and the union that the players would have to take another approach. The NFLPA has never had what might realistically be termed a "successful" strike, but this twenty-four-day walkout was a disaster for the players and left them with little recourse but the court system.

Marvin Powell, the articulate offensive lineman who played for the New Jersey Jets, and eight other players on behalf of the members of the NFLPA, and other players in the league, filed litigation against the NFL. The eight others were Brian Holloway of the Patriots, Michael Kenn and Mick Luckhurst of the Falcons, Mike Davis of the Chargers, James Lofton then of the Packers, Dan Marino of the Dolphins, George Martin of the Giants, and Steve Jordan of the Vikings. The Minneapolis suit attacked the first right of refusal and compensation system that bars any free agency in the NFL. Besides challenging the NFL's player restraints, the NFLPA accused the owners of numerous unfair labor practices, including charges of trying to bribe players to cross picket lines and threatening to trade or cut player reps to the union.

The suits asked for an immediate injunction that would make more than three hundred veteran players free agents before the start of the 1988 season.

To the disappointment of the union, U.S. federal judge David Doty refused the injunction and ruled that the players should go back to the bargaining table. However, he did order a jury trial and predicted that the players would probably win the court case. That prediction by Judge Doty scared the owners, and they appealed his decision to the Eighth Circuit Court of Appeals.

The Powell suit specifically accused the owners of violating antitrust law by enforcing the first refusal—compensation system after the expiration of the 1982 collective bargaining agreement between the players and the owners. That contract, which the players stupidly agreed to in exchange for benefit concessions, contained provisions that restricted free agency, giving a player's original team the right to match a competing club's offer.

If the club declines to match the offer, then the player's new team must compensate the other team with draft choices.

Under this arrangement, over a twelve-year period only two players, Wilber Marshall and Norm Thompson, have changed teams. Thompson, a defensive tackle, went from the Cards to the Colts in 1977, and Marshall, a linebacker, went from the Bears to the Redskins in 1986. And that is the sum total of the league's record of voluntary player movement in a twelve-year period.

After the NFLPA filed its suit in 1987, the NFL tried to take the heat off by implementing what is known as a Plan B system, in which teams protect thirty-seven players and permit the rest to become free agents. This was the league's answer to the union's charges that the owners were violating antitrust law by enforcing the first refusal–compensation system.

The owners claimed they were exempt from antitrust law because the old collective bargaining agreement was still valid. They said the players were trying to win in court what they could not win at the bargaining table.

Actually, that part is true, but as already outlined, the players never had much chance at the table.

The owners staged their biggest celebration since their victory over the USFL when the Eighth Circuit Court of Appeals overturned Judge Doty's decision in November of 1989. The three-man panel of judges, in a 2–1 ruling, said the owners were exempt from antitrust law because of the previously negotiated union contract. That's right, the one that was negotiated seven years earlier, and the one that had expired three years earlier.

In his dissenting opinion, Judge Gerald W. Haney said the Appeals Court ruling "permits the owners to violate antitrust law indefinitely."

The court gave the players the choice of striking or returning to the negotiating table. Some choice! The owners hailed the decision as a victory that would send the players back to the table. Wrong.

I'm happy to say that Gene Upshaw has retained the services of one of the great antitrust lawyers in America, Jim Quinn, a member of the renowned New York law firm of Weil, Gotshal and Manges. This brilliant Notre Damer was trained by, worked with, and later represented the late great Larry Fleischer, who had so much to do with shaping the destiny of professional sports in this country.

From his office on the thirty-second floor of the General Motors Building, overlooking the great Manhattan skyline, the Central Park reservoir, and the Wollman Skating Rink, Jim Quinn was to develop a plan that would give the NFL owners headaches and sleepless nights.

The union would decertify, disband, and reorganize as a trade association. This meant the organization was no longer the official collective bargaining agent for the players, and that every player, under decertification, became a free agent and could file a lawsuit.

On December 5, 1989, Gene Upshaw announced the decertification, saying, "It's become clear that the owners are seeking to use the union, or the former union status of the NFLPA, against the players. We do not intend to be an organization whose reason for its being is to help the owners annihilate its players. We will continue our fight in court, before the Supreme Court and other courts, and try to insure through antitrust laws the players' right to free agency."

Jim Quinn told me, "The players will effectively become independent contractors. They're going to have the rights, under antitrust laws, to make significant damage claims as to the restraints that the NFL continues to impose on the players."

On this issue, it's likely that the owners will fight until the bitter end. It may take the players several trials in front of several juries before it is settled and justice is done.

To the surprise of no one, the owners immediately tried to counter the players' new offense. The league went to court, again in its favorite locale of Minnesota, asking federal court judge David Doty to declare that the NFL Players Association was still acting as a union. The owners' claim was that regardless of the union's efforts to decertify, it is still a union and not just a trade association as it claims.

Judge Doty scheduled a hearing on the matter. If the judge rules the NFLPA still to be a union, and therefore the legal collective bargaining agent for the players, individual players would be prohibited from pursuing lawsuits concerning free agency. Such a ruling would be a severe blow to the players.

Despite all the roadblocks and efforts of sabotage by the NFL, I feel it is fair to say that Gene Upshaw and Jim Quinn will turn out to be quite a team. There are those who will be surprised at the success of this combination. Jim Brown, in his book, *Out of Bounds,* wrote that Upshaw simply wasn't equipped to fight the owners. He pointed out that these are powerful people who can pick up the phone and call the president—the president of the United States—and get action in a moment.

To that argument, Jim Quinn responds, "Well, I think that's simply not true. Gene is bright, and he's well respected by most of the players. He recognizes what the critical issues are and what's in the best interest of the association members. I think the key in these circumstances is to ensure that the leader is somebody that the followers respect, and I think Gene fits that bill one hundred percent. I think Gene is just fine."

Once the determination was made to appeal the Marvin Powell case to the Supreme Court, Quinn and his staff, working with the NFLPA legal staff, developed a brilliant idea. They went to the state attorneys general across the nation, asking for their support, asking for briefs to the Supreme Court in support of the players' position, and asking the Supreme Court to hear the appeal on full argument.

Initially, Quinn and the union forces were able to muster the support of attorneys general from twenty-five states, but by the time the powerful and wealthy NFL lobby was through exerting its pressure, the number of states supporting the players union had dwindled to eight. It was another example of the enormous strength of the owners' lobby.

On June 1, 1990, at the fiftieth reunion of my NYU law class, class of '40, I encountered NFL commissioner Paul "I'm Too Tall" Tagliabue, class of '65. We met and talked genially at that affair, but surprisingly, he all but disclaimed knowledge that, in three days, eight state attorneys general were submitting briefs to the Supreme Court in support of the Powell case. I found his warmth curious because this was the same man who had refused to attend the Maxwell Club dinner because of my presence. Some things in life are difficult to decipher.

The eight states that held firm were New York, Texas, Michigan, Utah, Louisiana, Hawaii, Wyoming, and Arizona; each state presented a brief to the Supreme Court. After hearing from the eight states, the Court decided it would ask the federal government for its opinion before rendering a decision.

On June 4, 1990, the Court asked the U.S. solicitor general, Kenneth W. Starr, "to express the views of the U.S. government." It meant that the Court would not even decide if it would hear the case until the fall of 1990.

Starr's deputy solicitor general, Lawrence Wallace, said that the agency would contact a number of federal agencies and would require several months before filing a brief with the Supreme Court.

Union attorney Jim Quinn is optimistic. Jim says, "I think we have an excellent chance of getting the Supreme Court to hear this. We think the lower court's decision was plainly wrong. It was directly in conflict with a number of prior Supreme Court decisions and other lower-court decisions holding that union members in general, and players on sports teams in particular, don't give up their rights, under the antitrust laws, simply because they join a union."

Appearing on one of my ABC Radio programs, Quinn said, "We believe the ruling that the Eighth Circuit Court made that the so-called labor extension to the antitrust law exists beyond the term of the collective bargaining agreement has no basis in law. We think it's in direct conflict with established principle, and we are confident that once the Supreme Court agrees to take the case and review the precedent that is applicable, it will reverse the decision."

One thing that baffles me is the need for the Supreme Court to ask the government for advice about whether it should get involved in the NFL's lengthy labor dispute. Of course it should.

The delay of course permits the NFL and its gigantic

lobby to swing into action. Never underestimate the power of the NFL lobby, no matter which of our agencies or institutions may be involved. They can be expected to bring out their heavyweight lobbying weapons for this fight. Stifling free agency is that important to the owners. The owners will call on numerous legal firms, several public relations firms, their friends on Capitol Hill, plus others, to turn up the heat and tighten the screws on those who will be making recommendations to the Supreme Court.

Gene Upshaw, however, shares Quinn's optimistic view of the court's request for advice from the government: "This is a very encouraging sign, that the Supreme Court thinks this issue is important enough to get the government's input. We are optimistic that the U.S. government, like the eight states whose attorneys general submitted briefs on the players' behalf, will support the players."

Predictably, the NFL Management Council, an arm of the owners, said it couldn't understand why Quinn and Upshaw were so optimistic.

"To view the events as anything but procedural business is a misstatement of the working process of the Supreme Court," Jack Donlan, the Management Council's executive director, said. He continued, "There is no basis for elation or optimism. There is no credible basis for forecasting how the High Court will act."

The U.S. Solicitor General finally recommended that the Supreme Court hear the case, but by a vote of 7 to 2, the high court said "no." Unbelievable. The power of the NFL is staggering. It was another blow to the players.

But the NFLPA did not put all its hopes into the Supreme Court appeal. In April of 1990, eight players, with the support of Quinn, Upshaw, and the Players Association, filed an antitrust suit in New Jersey against all of the teams in the NFL, and the NFL itself, attacking the NFL's so-called Plan B restrictions on the ability of veteran players in the NFL to seek fair wages and to seek competitive wages in an open marketplace.

The players who joined in the suit were Freeman McNeil of the Jets, Mark Collins and Lee Rouson of the Giants, Don Majkowski of the Packers, Niko Noga of the Lions, David

Richards of the Chargers, Irv Eatman of the Chiefs, and Tim McDonald of the Cardinals.

Quinn gave his reasons for selecting New Jersey as the site of the suit: "The courthouse in New Jersey has excellent judges. The Third Circuit, which is the appeals court to which one would go based on whatever happens at the trial level, is a good appeals court in the antitrust parlance, a favorable one from a plaintiff's standpoint. And in light of the fact that there has been a prior decision in Minnesota, and in the Eighth Circuit of Appeals, that had gone unfavorably to the football players union, we felt that New Jersey was a good site. In addition, three of the eight players filing the suit play their home football games in New Jersey at Giants Stadium."

The NFL recognized the truth of this and filed a motion asking that the case be moved to Minneapolis. On June 11, 1990, in response to their motion, it was ruled that the case would be tried in Minnesota.

The league had argued that the Freeman McNeil lawsuit is not unlike the Marvin Powell case, which was tried in Minnesota. The fact that the ruling on the union status of the NFLPA was set for Minnesota played a significant role in Bissell's decision.

After Judge John Bissell's ruling for the league, Quinn admitted to me that it was a defeat. There's no doubt he would have been more comfortable with a case in New Jersey, but he said, "Judge Doty is a fair judge. We will win in Minnesota."

Earlier in June of 1990, a remarkable thing happened. The New Jersey Jets admitted that they still considered Freeman McNeil a valuable property by signing him to a series of one-year contracts. This despite the fact that the Jets did not protect him and made him available to the league as a Plan B player. In signing McNeil, the Jets urged him to drop out of the suit that he and seven other players had filed against the NFL and its teams. Freeman stood firm. He remained a part of the suit because he felt strongly that it is a system that makes no sense. It's one that has hurt him over the years, and he knows the importance of fighting for free agency.

One night at a Jackie Robinson dinner, Freeman McNeil came up to me and said, "Please keep telling the truth, Howard, we need you."

Jim Quinn was incensed that most of the media conveniently neglected to mention McNeil's lawsuit when they covered his signing. Irresponsible journalism to say the least, but regrettably, par for the course. How could *The New York Times*, a great newspaper, allow this type of reporting? It's simply another example of how much influence the enormously powerful NFL has over the media.

Jim Quinn said, "The players can't fight the owners head-to-head in that context. And that's one of the reasons why we feel that we can even the playing field in the courtroom. That's why there's going to be six or eight or twelve people, everyday people, who can look at the regulations that the NFL is imposing on these players and decide whether they are fair, whether they make any sense. And I'm convinced to a certainty that any jury looking at these rules and these restrictions will say that they're patently illegal. So I'm perfectly comfortable being in a Minnesota courtroom in front of a jury explaining to the jury why these rules make no sense and are unfair." If the players don't win the Powell case on appeal before the Supreme Court, there's an excellent chance they will win the Freeman McNeil case.

The NFL has had some limited success in the courtroom, primarily in getting delays. Every time a case has gone to trial in front of a jury or a judge, however, the NFL has lost. You can go back as far as 1957 to document when the courts started ruling against the NFL in antitrust cases. Bill Radovich, a former University of Southern California star, played three years for the Detroit Lions and then jumped to the L.A. Dons of the All-American Football League. When Radovich tried to rejoin the NFL, the owners said no and suspended him for five years for violating the reserve clause in the standard NFL contract.

Radovich, however, didn't accept the NFL ruling. He filed an antitrust suit, which he won when the U.S. Supreme Court ruled that football was an interstate business in violation of antitrust law. Thus thirty-three years ago the Supreme Court established an antitrust precedent against the NFL.

In 1974, Vikings quarterback Joe Kapp also beat the NFL in the courts, and Rams running back Cullen Bryant did the same thing in 1975. Then came the famous John Mackey case involving fifteen other players—a big antitrust victory for the players. The next player to score a victory over the NFL in court was Ron Alexander. That case was followed by the James McCoy "Yazoo" Smith case, another big win for the players.

In all, there have been six antitrust court cases that have gone against the NFL. With regard to issues covered, the courts found the league guilty of antitrust counts involving the college draft, options, free agency, and standard contracts.

Thus the players had enjoyed a long winning streak in court before the Marvin Powell setback in the appellate court. Based on the earlier precedents, how can the Supreme Court not reverse the Powell ruling?

What the NFL is really good at is stalling in the courts, and trying to force the players to give up their rights.

It's very interesting that every time the NFL has faced competition in an open market, the NFL has factually lost. The examples are plentiful: the old All-American Football Conference; above all the old American Football League, where Sonny Werblin and Al Davis combined to absolutely shatter the NFL and force a merger that should never, in my opinion, have taken place; and the United States Football League, where once again, the National Football League has been found to be a duly adjudicated illegal monopoly.

The NFL simply doesn't like competition in any form, other than perhaps on the playing field. Certainly in the economic marketplace as it affects players' services, the NFL has striven for two decades to make sure that there is no competition, and that's what the players are trying to overcome.

Given all their victories in court, the players should certainly have free agency by now. It's a shame that they gave back their court gains to the owners when they granted numerous labor exemptions in the course of negotiating collective bargaining agreements. Former NFLPA executive director Ed Garvey has to take some of the responsibility for that period. Garvey, who left his post to enter politics in

Wisconsin, may have made tactical mistakes, but he was a man who was not afraid to stand up to the owners.

I have always had great empathy for the pro football player. Baseball and basketball players have it better in many ways. Their salaries are much higher, their careers last much longer, and their sports, generally speaking, are safer. Who but football players constantly risk serious injury? Pro football players are forced to play on artificial turf, conducive to serious toe, foot, ankle, and knee damage, not to mention body burns. And why? So the owners can save money on upkeep and maintenance of the playing surface. The average length of an NFL player's career, 3.2 years, speaks for itself, and many players leave the game having undergone numerous surgeries, no longer able to walk properly or even to bend over and pick up their small children.

The football players get the short end in many areas. A very small percentage of football contracts are guaranteed, and when a football player does get a long-term contract, it's usually a series of one-year contracts, directly benefiting the owner, who has an easier time cutting the player should something go wrong.

Now that the players are playing without a current collective bargaining agreement, the owners do not pay severance when a player is cut. The owners do, however, carry health insurance; it's doubtful they could field a team, even with scab players, without paying insurance for such a dangerous sport.

In my opinion, the owners have never relented in their efforts to ruin the union. In its early years, the union was forced to obtain major loans. Once the NFLPA raised its dues to about $2,500 per year and negotiated an automatic dues checkoff with the league, its financial situation improved. However, as mentioned earlier, the owners thought they would kill off the union by stopping the dues checkoff after the last strike. That left it up to Gene Upshaw and his staff to collect dues on their own, no easy task. It's believed that currently only about half of the players are paying dues to the NFLPA.

Despite this situation, and much to the displeasure of the NFL oligarchy, the Players Association is in the best financial shape of its lifetime. Several years ago, the NFLPA discovered the magic of licensing, and of the royalties it can provide. There's money in NFL shirts, caps, key chains, and a million other things. NFL Properties, the owners' "country store," found that out many years ago.

Now, the players' "country store" is booming. The union's marketing division took in $6 million gross in 1989, and that netted down to $4.1 million in profit. That plus players' dues leaves a lot of money for legal fees to conduct the good fight against the owners.

The NFL owners, however, are a clever bunch. When they see the players and their union do something smart, they try to destroy it. The owners are now trying to buy off the bigger names in the league for exclusive marketing rights. The league is mailing substantial checks to name players as payment for exclusive marketing rights for clothing, souvenirs, etc. The owners understand if they sign the bigger names away from the union's marketing efforts, that annual gross of $6 million will shrink in a hurry.

The NFLPA is urging its players to return the checks to the owners, but when a football player gets a check in the mail for as much as $100,000, he's tempted to pocket the money. Of course not all checks are that large; some checks were for $50,000, $40,000, $30,000, $20,000, and even $10,000. Obviously, lesser-known players received checks for smaller amounts.

This maneuver by the owners is the type of thing that Gene Upshaw and his association must combat. I know the tactics of the NFL, and I'm always at the ready to assist Upshaw and the players whenever possible.

At the behest of Upshaw, I was the keynote speaker at the NFL Players Association dinner in Daytona Beach, Florida, on May 4, 1990. There was a huge turnout, including many retired players, as well as many active players.

I made it clear to the group that I would never relent in my efforts to diminish the power of the National Football League as a monopoly, and the players stood and cheered. They were thrilled that I was there, and I was happy to be there. They were so enthusiastic and appreciative I went through the whole explanation of the power of the National Football League, the power of its lobby, and how difficult they were. I assured them, however, that Jim Quinn was the best in the business and that they could count on him. And I told them that I thought they would win in the courts.

The group at the dinner represented a mixture of many football eras. Some great people came by to visit, people such as Bill Radovich, Alex Wojciechowicz, and Dick "Night Train" Lane, plus many others. Some of them had previously been critical of the union; some had criticized the plan to decertify the union. I must say, however, there was solidarity among the group that night, in fact, greater unanimity than I'd ever seen before. Men whom I had known for so many years were there to express that unanimity.

One who was not in attendance at the NFLPA dinner was Larry Csonka, and there was a very good reason. Twelve days later, it was revealed that the former Miami Dolphin running back great was going to attempt to form a new union under his leadership.

My association with Larry Csonka goes back many years. I will never forget when he telephoned me at my apartment to give me the scoop that he, Paul Warfield, and Jim Kiick were jumping from the NFL to the new World Football League. He said, "We're entitled to change leagues, and I want you to break the story."

At the time, I had my weekly magazine show, "The ABC Sports Magazine." I immediately called my producer, young Terry Jastrow, told him the story, and asked him to arrange facilities. Then I called Roone Arledge and filled him in. Arledge said, "Good Lord, what a story!" Arledge agreed with me when he said, "This is what television is all about. Are you sure they're going to talk?"

"I'm positive," I replied. "I got the call. I think we have to alert Pete Rozelle for reaction."

I called Pete, filled him in on what was happening, and he said, "Good luck to them. They'll have a devil of a time making it work. I'll watch the show."

My guests on the program were Csonka, Kiick, and Warfield, along with John Bassett, the man who was paying big money for the players to jump leagues. (Bassett later was a leader in the USFL; he has since died of cancer.) I made it clear that I agreed with them, that they had every right in the world to make a move.

It was a great show. Roone was in heaven and so was I. We went to his apartment for a drink, and he kept saying, "This is what television is really all about." They don't do sports journalism shows like that anymore.

And then, on the same day I testified in the USFL trial, I had my annual charity dinner in memory of the Munich 11, the eleven Israeli athletes who were slaughtered at the Munich Olympics. Former secretary of the treasury Bill Simon was honored that night, and Arledge, a good friend of his, was there. Larry Csonka was also present, and he said about my testimony concerning the NFL, "Boy, did you give it to them today. It was the greatest thing ever. You just destroyed 'em."

That was the Larry Csonka I knew and loved from his great days with the Dolphins.

In 1989, I went to Florida to a dinner honoring Larry Little, the former Dolphins great. Larry Csonka was not there, and no one could explain why he wasn't in attendance.

So finally it became clear why Csonka had been boycotting dinners and why he had been out of contact with me.

The great Zonk had joined forces with the NFL owners. Sold out. Deserted his old friends.

It was a joke that Csonka would seek to start his own union and in his own way denounce the leadership of Gene Upshaw. With the Powell case and the McNeil case in the courts, the timing of Csonka's announcement was even more remarkable.

Csonka claims to be financing his efforts, but he admits to having consulted with Jack Donlan, the head of the owner's Management Council.

The last job in professional football for Csonka was the general managership of the Jacksonville Bulls of the USFL. He has made a living in recent years doing commercials and speaking engagements for Miller Lite beer.

Don't expect Csonka to be successful with his union efforts. He mailed out a letter and organization cards to over 1,500 active players. He needs 751 signatures to force a preference vote and claims to have about 300 returned signature cards.

It's not likely that Gene Upshaw will lose out to someone like Larry Csonka. Gene feels his organization is close to seeing the fruits of its labor. Like a true labor leader, Upshaw said, "I won't let anyone stand in the way of our progress, including Larry Csonka. I will crush him." Echoes of John L. Lewis and George Meany.

When Csonka was telling reporters such as Dave Klein of the *Newark Star-Ledger* that he had the signatures of about 300 players, Upshaw scoffed, "It's closer to three than three hundred." It seems to me that Klein has been a longtime open and notorious supporter of the NFL owners, and isn't it curious that Klein wrote the Csonka claim the day before the court hearing involving the NFL's change-of-venue request? It was another shrewd NFL move. They don't miss a trick. Judge John Bissell did read the article; as a matter of fact, he mentioned the Csonka union effort during the course of the hearing.

Gene Upshaw made clear his feelings about Larry Csonka in the following letter:

May 30, 1990
Larry Csonka

Dear Larry:

I have read with interest, amusement, and finally, sadness, your letter to the NFL players soliciting them to sign cards to authorize *you* to represent them in collective bargaining with the NFL.

I find it strange, indeed, that someone like yourself, who benefited so much by having the opportunity to join a club in the World Football League, and, then to return to the NFL as a free agent, would let himself be used by the NFL to undermine the efforts of today's players to offer their services in a competitive market. I suppose your most recent involvement in professional football as General Manager of the Jacksonville Bulls explains why you are now so interested in helping NFL management find a way to stop the unprecedented gains in salaries and bonuses that NFL players have enjoyed the past three years *without* a collective bargaining agreement. (Players' salaries have gone up 43 percent in the last two years alone, and they'll go up even higher with the new TV money that's now available.) These increases have come in the face of a highly restrictive system imposed by the owners. Imagine how players would do with the real free agency they are entitled to under the law?

If you are truly interested in helping today's players, why haven't you stopped and asked yourself why NFL management is so anxious to get an agreement? Do you think that the owners suddenly—after decades of screwing players in every imaginable way—have gotten religion and that they are going to open up their bank account and freely spread their money around because they now realize that players are worth more than they are getting? *The league is desperate to make a deal because it wants a salary cap and a wage scale and it can't implement one without a union to sign on the dotted line.*

You criticize me and my advisers for letting Management implement Plan B. Well, even a little competition beats none at all. I'll bet the Plan B players who have gotten $50,000 to $200,000 signing bonuses and contracts with base pay as high as $700,000 and average of $315,000 wonder where you've been. You don't seem to realize that Plan B backfired on the owners—they actually competed for players and drove base salaries up, not only for Plan B players, but, for veterans as well. Ask Jim Kelly! Ask Chris Doleman! Ask Max Montoya! See if they're "confused." None of this would have been possible if the *players* had not decided that we should not sign the proposal management had on the table in October 1987. Would you have signed that deal? Or agreed to Plan A a year later?

Sure, there's a lot of money out there! And even in the highly restrictive system imposed by the owners, the players are getting a higher percentage of it than the Clubs want to pay. Whatever the players get will always be too much for the owners.

The simple fact is that our strategy is working and

Management knows it. The *Powell* case is in the Supreme Court, and Management is scared to death that ultimately they'll be on the hook for hundreds of millions of dollars in antitrust damages. But even apart from *Powell* and the steady escalation of player salaries over the past two years, the Clubs still face countless millions of dollars of legal liability in the *Freeman McNeil* case, at least $25 million in back pay in the NLRB case, $30 million in the Developmental Squad case, and $25 million in money that sits in federal court in Baltimore to be paid into the Pension Plan.

The undeniable fact is that the NFL players are far better off today without a collective bargaining agreement or a union than they would be with them. Sure, everyone would like higher per diem and meal money. But that's "chump change" when compared to the signing bonuses, reporting bonuses, work-out bonuses, other incentives, and the base pay the players have been able to get without an agreement containing a wage scale and salary cap.

You say that you "respect and admire" me, that you would hire me as a "consultant." You say I've gotten some "bad advice," and you can do better. Well, I played in the League for sixteen years and was involved with the NFLPA from the very beginning. I was there in the negotiations of 1968, 1974, 1977, 1982, and 1987! Where were you? What's your experience in labor negotiations on the players' side, not the owners'?

I'm proud of my advisers. Dick Bertelsen is one of the most experienced attorneys in professional sports. And it was in part through his efforts and Lindquist and Vennum's that you were able to return to the NFL in 1976, and sign with the Giants as an unrestricted free agent. Doug Allen has been active in organized labor for sixteen years, and he did more than pass out donuts; he was involved in NFL negotiations in 1982, and, *representing players* as Executive Director of the USFLPA, sat across the table from the USFL *owners*, who you represented. Ed Glennon and his partners have represented NFL players in antitrust litigation for more than fifteen years. Jim Quinn and Jeff Kessler have represented the players associations in professional baseball and basketball for nearly two decades. Since the early 1980s, Chip Yablonski has successfully represented the NFLPA in every conceivable type of litigation. Who are your advisers? What are their credentials? No self-respecting labor leader or laborside lawyer I know would be a party to the fraud you're trying to put over on the NFL players. Neither I nor any of the NFLPA's advisers would lend their names to, or reputations to, your misguided efforts.

NFLPA finances are a matter of public record. We are not in the "red." We had to write off some dues we didn't collect when the owners cut off dues checkoff, but we are strong and getting stronger. We are committed to making certain that the players have the same freedom of contract as other professionals. We get our revenues from the players, through licensing and membership fees. Who's financing you? Larry, I would hope that you would take the time to study what has really happened in the NFL since 1987 and not just buy wholesale the line of Jack Donlan and Paul Tagliabue. They get paid to protect the owners' profits, not to help the players.

> Sincerely,
> [signed]
> Gene Upshaw
> Executive Director
> National Football League Players Association

Upshaw used to block for Csonka in the Pro Bowl, and they were inducted together into the Pro Football Hall of Fame. But since Csonka's effort to undercut Upshaw, it's a good idea not to invite them to the same party.

When one runs for office or tries to start a union, one had better be ready to have one's dirty linen scrutinized. And so Larry Csonka is learning.

Chuck Mortensen, writing in *The National,* said, "He [Csonka] has some skeletons, off-field mistakes—including an investigation into alleged marijuana smuggling—he has acknowledged that he wants to put behind him."

Back in July of 1981, United Press International reported

an investigation by federal agents involving the possible link of former Dolphins stars Larry Csonka and Jim Kiick to a multimillion-dollar marijuana organization. The wire service reported, from the *Fort Lauderdale News and Sun-Sentinel,* that a smuggling operation termed Operation Grouper operating in the states of Louisiana, Georgia, and Florida grossed about $300 million a year. The inquiry started back in 1978 and involved the use of undercover agents who offered drug smugglers secure harbors to dock their marijuana-laden ships, and work crews to unload the illegal marijuana.

The newspaper account went as follows: "In November 1980, Csonka and Kiick were in New Orleans. Undercover agents posing as offshore loaders said they received a telephone call from the two players requesting their services. A few days later, the agents met with Kiick and Csonka, who tried to arrange a large marijuana deal that would be unloaded at an old plantation called the Snake Farm."

UPI said that according to the agents, the players were not part of Operation Grouper, but were using some members of the group to set up their own independent deal. The agents said that the deal fell through and that Csonka and Kiick were told to return when it was all set up. According to the *Fort Lauderdale News and Sun-Sentinel,* the telephone call and the meetings were taped by the agents.

Reached at his Ohio farm, Csonka said: "I wasn't aware there was ever a case. I talked to the U.S. attorney in New Orleans, they sent me a subpoena to appear before the grand jury, and I made that appearance. That's all the contact I've had with them. It would be silly for me to comment on such a one-sided story."

The Associated Press reported on April 16, 1981, citing a New Orleans television station, WVUE, that Csonka did appear before the federal grand jury, but refused to answer questions on the constitutional grounds that answering them might tend to incriminate him.

Larry Csonka was never indicted on the marijuana smuggling charge and has denied involvement in drug smuggling activity, but to put it mildly, the adverse publicity does present an image problem. If, however, Csonka can get the necessary 751 signatures, which seems highly unlikely, the NFL might be happy to help him launder his image.

Csonka is the third person to make a run at forming a new union. Art Wilkinson, a former agent, and Tom Gatewood, a former fringe player, failed miserably in their efforts, and Csonka is odds-on to suffer the same fate. It is my opinion that Larry Csonka will be better off tending to his farm in Lisbon, Ohio.

<u>CHAPTER</u> TWELVE

Millionaires in Short Pants

The contract called for $3.5 million a year for five years plus a $10-million bonus. A very good deal for any corporation's chief executive officer, right? Maybe the head of General Motors or General Electric? No, it's the deal the NBA owners gave their commissioner, David Stern.

The commissioner's new contract was announced at the 1990 NBA All Star Game in Miami. Exact terms were not revealed, but the media followed the lead of the Associated Press and reported a figure of $27 million, including a bonus of $15 million, as the total worth of the contract.

David Stern is a close friend, and Emmy and I had traveled to the All Star Game as his guests. When I kidded David about the $15-million bonus, he said, "That's just newspaper talk, Howard. The bonus is not nearly that big."

I later learned that the bonus was indeed $5 million lower than the reported figure, but the annual salary, $3.5 million, was higher. The entire package of $27.5 million was $500,000 higher than originally thought.

A salary deal of this proportion for a commissioner was unprecedented in sports. Never in their wildest dreams did Pete Rozelle, Bowie Kuhn, or Peter Ueberroth envision this type of a sweetheart deal. Stern had parlayed his success in formulating a six-year labor truce and a huge TV and cable contract into the richest commissioner's contract of all time. His new deal easily quadrupled the annual monetary value of any salary package for any previous commissioner—in all sports.

The master of marketing had promoted himself into fat city. It's understandable that the NBA owners were very appreciative of Stern for elevating the NBA from a shaky, drug-ridden sports organization into unprecedented national and international acceptance. This sport, with tall men wearing short pants—some of the men tall enough to qualify for a sideshow at the circus—was now the fastest growing of all sports in terms of popularity, and the best paying of them all. A league with 80 percent black players in a country with a 12 percent black population had captured the nation's imagination. Perhaps the NBA has done more for black acceptance than any other sports entity.

And perhaps it is fitting that the NBA commissioner has by far the richest contract of any commissioner. After all, the NBA average player's salary is light years ahead of players in other sports. My personal reaction to Stern's $27.5-million deal? I told David that he should give half of it to Vicki Fleisher, the widow of Larry Fleisher. And I was not joking!

Larry Fleisher was a great man. He was the best sports labor leader of all time. I'll go further than that—Larry Fleisher was the most honest man I ever met in all of sports, and he contributed more to sports than anyone I've ever known.

He conceived the idea of the NBA Players Union and was its general counsel and executive director for twenty-seven years. At the same time, Larry was the personal agent for many of the game's great players.

Larry's contributions, both in professional basketball in a firsthand sense, and in professional sports generally, were enormous. He was a visionary in seeing, first of all, back in the sixties, that the only real way to improve the players' lot was to inject into the overall system some form of competition among clubs. This establishment of competition enabled the players to have better negotiating positions.

He was the first one to file an antitrust lawsuit against

sports club owners. Ultimately he guided the NBA Players Association to the strongest position of all sports unions.

Fleisher left his job with the union in October of 1988 to take a vice presidency overseeing basketball operations for the International Management Group, the worldwide organization that represents athletes in many sports.

Larry had been planning to leave the union in 1986, at the completion of twenty-five years, but it took him two years longer than expected to hammer out the new, six-year collective bargaining agreement with David Stern and the NBA owners. When he founded the union, the average salary of the NBA player was $9,400. Under the last deal negotiated by Fleisher, the NBA's average annual salary for players has reached the magic million-dollar mark.

Under the 1988 agreement, the players and the owners are practically partners. The players are guaranteed 53 percent of the league's revenues in either salary or benefits.

Larry's life came to a tragic end in May of 1989, when he suffered a heart attack. After playing squash at the New York Athletic Club on Central Park South, he collapsed in the shower room and was pronounced dead at Roosevelt Hospital a few blocks away. It was a sad day for basketball, pro sports, and for humanity.

Over the years, Larry Fleisher became my closest friend in sports. He was a brilliant man; Bronx-born and educated at NYU and the Harvard School of Law. Over a period of many years, we would lunch together at least once a week at the Hampshire House bar on Central Park South. We had a very close relationship and kept no secrets between us.

Despite his job as a labor leader, I really didn't know anyone who didn't like Larry. He was such a warm and loving and loved human being.

I never saw such an outpouring of love as was displayed at his funeral and burial. I was one of those who eulogized Larry at the service in the Community Church of New York on East Thirty-fifth Street. And the manner in which I was chosen to speak is something that I will always cherish. Larry's son Eric came to me and said, "My father told me that if anything ever happened to him and I needed anything, that I should call on you. He admired you so much. He told me that you were the smartest man he knew in sports, that you were the most knowledgeable and had sports in its proper perspective. So I am coming to you to request that you speak at the service for Dad."

I was honored to join a list of speakers that included Sen. Bill Bradley, Oscar Robertson, Paul Silas, John Havlicek, David Stern, Donald Fehr, and three of Larry's children, Nancy, Eric, and Mark.

I recalled Larry as a close, personal, and caring friend. Smart, honest, up-front, and a very funny man with a great sense of humor.

Bill Bradley eulogized Larry as "the most successful labor leader of the twentieth century."

David Stern said Larry was "a remarkable man and a personal friend, an effective union leader who always worked for the good of the sport of basketball."

Larry was a rare breed among agents. When many agents were taking 20 percent and more from players for services rendered, he was taking only 2.5 percent.

Oscar Robertson said, "He was honest, a genuinely honest man."

Another basketball great, Earl "the Pearl" Monroe, said, "Larry was like a brother, a father, a lawyer, and a friend, all in one."

One couldn't forget the scene at Larry's burial in the Kensico Hills Cemetery, a nondenominational cemetery in Valhalla, New York. The love that poured out at the Community Church was evident at the burial site. I remember the way Bill Bradley and Dave DeBusschere, both former New York Knicks greats, kissed the casket. Larry had represented DeBusschere in a lot of different capacities, as a player, as a coach, as a general manager, and as a commissioner of the ABA. My heart ached for Nancy Fleisher, who screamed uncontrollably in grief for her father.

Emmy and I stood there with David Stern and his wife, Diane. David was crying like a baby.

After the burial, many of Larry's closest friends went to Jim Quinn's house. However, Emmy was fatigued after a long, uphill walk to the burial site, so we went directly to our apartment to grieve alone.

Fleisher left behind a union that had never been more

solid. Why? Because Fleisher never bit off more than his union could chew, never maintained an unnecessarily adversarial position with management, and never counted upon union support from the media or the public. His wisdom paid off for everyone concerned with the NBA.

Four past presidents of the NBAPA, Oscar Robertson, Bob Lanier, Junior Bridgeman, and Paul Silas, formed the committee that selected a replacement for Fleisher. They chose Charles Grantham, who is no Fleisher, but a man who learned from Larry, worked with him in the union for ten years, and a man who will reap the benefits of Larry's past wisdom and work.

There were major differences between Fleisher and the other labor leaders in sport, and this is where Fleisher understood that the union does indeed have an underlying common bond with the owners. He watched the league grow from a time when its place in the American sports scene was virtually nil, to a point where there is unparalleled prosperity, and franchises can be sold for more than $100 million. Not too many years ago, NBA attendance was down, TV ratings were poor, league sponsors were sparse, and some clubs were in serious financial trouble.

Larry saw his sport imperiled by the drug scene, and he worked in concert with Stern to produce what is unquestionably the best drug program in sports, with a real concern for the individual rights of the players, but also for the owners and the integrity of the sport itself.

Like football—and unlike baseball, which has an antitrust exemption—basketball is subject to antitrust law, and Fleisher went after those laws in the Oscar Robertson case, which began in 1971 and was settled by agreement in 1976. Stern was deeply involved in that settlement as well.

During that period of time, two things happened in the NBA: first, the players made impressive gains in compensation and in other areas, thanks to the union; and second, the league made impressive gains in marketing and merchandising its products and in building the prestige, stability, and prosperity of its franchises.

Larry Fleisher would not be happy, however, until he achieved more freedom for the NBA players, and a bigger piece of the monetary pie, money he knew the players deserved. So it was Fleisher who came up with the idea of decertifying the union and going after the league with antitrust suits.

When the 1983 collective bargaining agreement expired in 1987, Fleisher maintained that labor exemptions granted to the league under that agreement had expired as well, and the union filed a sweeping federal antitrust suit in New Jersey. The NBAPA always named its legal actions after the president of the union at the time, so this suit was to be known as the Junior Bridgeman suit.

Fleisher and the players claimed that the NBA was in violation of antitrust law in terms of the draft, the salary cap, and the right of first refusal. The NBA argued that even though the old collective bargaining agreement had expired, the owners and the players were still collectively bargaining, and so the owners were still entitled to the labor exemptions and were not in violation of federal antitrust law. (It's exactly the same claim that the NFL is currently making against the NFLPA.)

The federal judge in New Jersey, Judge Dickinson R. Debevoise, ruled right down the middle and said that the collective bargaining relationship did not protect the owners from antitrust prosecution. At the same time, however, he ruled that the mere expiration of the agreement did not mean an automatic violation, that a certain amount of time had to pass. Debevoise left that time period open and called for a jury trial to determine the outcome of the case.

As already stated, Larry Fleisher was a brilliant man and had anticipated that such a ruling might be handed down. Back in 1987, he had begun toying with the idea of decertifying the NBA Players Association, and by the time of the 1988 All Star Game, he felt the time was right for such a move.

Larry explained the option to the players at the union meeting during the break, saying that his plan would work because the courts solidly upheld the antitrust rulings of the past. Take away the union, take away the collective bargaining procedure, and you leave the owners wide open for successful antitrust prosecutions.

"If we remove ourselves as the bargaining agent, then the owners are in a terrible position," Fleisher said. "But for us, all we give up really is the benefits package, and the players can buy their own benefits and protections. They don't have to have the NBA to do that. Without the union, and without a collective bargaining agreement, each player is free to negotiate for himself. Furthermore, every single player in the NBA, and every single college kid signing in the NBA, will be able to sue the NBA under antitrust law, to get rid of the draft, the first-refusal rights, and the salary cap. This is my opinion and is the opinion of all the antitrust experts I've consulted."

The plan was ingenious, outrageous, brilliant, and not even risky. Fleisher said, "It's the one sure way to go. Give up the union. Let the antitrust laws apply."

The plan did work for the NBAPA. Within a short period of time, it brought David Stern and the owners to their knees and resulted in the best collective bargaining agreement ever given any sports union. Stern and his lawyers were sharp enough to know that they wanted no part of decertification.

Larry Fleisher felt that the decertification plan could work for the NFL as well; despite the fact that the two cases were not exactly the same, Larry felt there were enough similarities, and that the same federal laws would apply. Larry knew the football union was in desperate shape, having nearly been destroyed by the strike, and Larry advised Gene Upshaw that decertification was his best hope.

Fleisher told me that the NFL owners' negotiator, Jack Donlan, was accused of being a union-buster, and Donlan replied, "Oh, no, we don't want to bust the union. Bust the union and we lose our antitrust protection."

For someone like me, who deeply believes in the need for unions, it was a bit difficult at first to swallow Fleisher's arguments and reasoning. Initially, his proposal came across as the antithesis of everything I stood for—and everything Fleisher stood for. Imagine a union man advocating the disbanding of a union.

But the mere threat of decertification worked for Larry, and only time will tell if decertification will work for Gene Upshaw and the NFLPA.

The momentous agreement molded and agreed to by

Larry Fleisher and David Stern in April of 1988 boggled the mind. The players received a large percentage (53%) of the gross, reduced the draft of college players and foreign players to two rounds, and best of all, received a projected annual salary of $900,000 per player by 1992, despite a salary cap. As already stated, the salary projection proved conservative. The staggering TV and cable agreement pushed the annual player's salary to $1 million by the start of 1991. Larry Fleisher didn't live to see it happen, but all the players know all these things happened because of him.

Fleisher also did more. Some of the greatest players in the history of the game, whose careers ended prior to 1965, had never been a part of the NBA pension fund. Fleisher got the owners to agree to work out a plan to take care of such players as Bill Sharman, Dolph Schayes, Sweetwater Clifton, Bob Pettit, Cliff Hagan, Paul Arizin, George Mikan, and many more.

In a nutshell, Larry Fleisher was the ultimate pragmatist in a field where few pragmatists are found. Perhaps most important of all was Fleisher's understanding of the public attitude toward sports unions. More than any other sports union leader, Fleisher comprehended the suspicion and hostility of the fans toward unionization, and he never counted on public support for his cause. Knowing that anti-union attitude so well, Fleisher moved carefully all along, standing up for his players, but in a manner designed to alienate the public as little as possible. He never fooled himself for a minute that he was living in a climate that was favorable toward labor.

Larry never made the mistake of thinking too romantically about labor and management. He kept the romance out, and so did David Stern. (Owners and commissioners, too, often get caught up in the romance of labor disputes and envision themselves as the last remaining bulwark against total union control of business and industry.)

Stern always respected Fleisher, and Larry always respected David. Stern has the capacity to forget all about adversarial positions in the court against Fleisher and to turn most of his attention to marketing and promoting the league.

A quiet, shy man who doesn't demand to be in the public

eye, Stern has emerged as a kind of a miracle worker. Indeed he and Fleisher in reality worked some miracles together.

A decade ago, the NBA was so drug-infested that the future of the league was in doubt. Larry Fleisher and David Stern were aware of the situation and knew something had to be done. Actually it was Fleisher and the players who came up with the drug plan that is now the most successful program of its kind in professional sports.

One thing that confronted Larry during much of his career was the charge of conflict of interest, usually leveled by NBA owners. He was representing and leading the union on one hand, and at the same time, he was individually acting as agent for dozens of players. From a legal standpoint, there was no conflict because the players and the union didn't have conflicting positions, weren't adversaries as a pure legal matter.

Even beyond that, however, as a purely moral or ethical matter, the charge was totally ridiculous. All the players knew Larry was also representing certain individual players; yet every year when he was up for reelection as union head, he was rehired by the players. They could have thrown Larry out at any time, yet they chose to stick with him for twenty-seven years, when he left on his own to go with IMG. They knew Fleisher was terrific, and to suggest a conflict of interest was pure silliness.

Larry could take the heat from owners and agents alike, however. He cared about how the players felt, and for good reason: they loved him. He was a fair and honest person.

Fleisher and Stern actually made a good team. Both men were visionaries enough to recognize the international possibilities for pro basketball, which has already become one of the most popular sports on an international basis; witness the way European teams are paying American players big money, such as over a million dollars to Danny Ferry in 1989.

David Stern in particular should receive much credit for recognizing the international appeal of pro basketball. Before too many years, the NBA will have a European division. Pro basketball is better positioned for international involvement in the nineties than football and baseball. The fact that basketball is an Olympic sport, already played around the world for the past five or six decades, gives it an enormous step up in terms of exporting American basketball to Europe, Asia, and other parts of the world. Despite claims of the NFL, I think the dawning of American football as a major international sport may not come in this century, if ever.

The working relationship between Fleisher and Stern was a thing of beauty. And you have to give Stern credit for having a personality that permitted that type of relationship. Most commissioners have huge egos. Most are high profile. Not Stern. He sits in a fancy office that is the size of half a basketball court, on the fifteenth floor of the prestigious Olympic Tower overlooking Fifth Avenue, but he does his marketing and promotion wheeling and dealing from behind the scenes.

David became the fourth commissioner of the NBA in 1984. In seven short years, he has become the most successful commissioner in the history of the NBA, and despite the media campaign and support of Pete Rozelle, Stern has become the most successful commissioner of any sport in my time.

It did not happen overnight for David Stern. As a lawyer, he has worked with or for the NBA since 1967. In 1978, he was named general counsel for the organization, in 1983 he was elevated to executive vice president for business and legal affairs, and the following year, he succeeded Larry O'Brien as commissioner.

One of the smartest things Stern did was to rid the league of shaky owners, those with financial difficulties, and those with unsound business practices. About half of the NBA franchises have changed hands in the last six years.

One example of how the worth of pro basketball teams has escalated is Portland. Larry Weinberg bought the expansion Trailblazers in 1971 for $3.5 million. In 1988, he sold the team to computer millionaire Paul Allen for a record $70 million.

If the Portland Trailblazers were worth $70 million in 1988, what is the value of the Los Angeles Lakers, the Boston Celtics, Chicago Bulls, New York Knickerbockers, or Detroit Pistons?

In 1987, four new expansion clubs, Miami, Charlotte,

Orlando, and Minnesota, each agreed to pay $32.5 million for the right to enter the league. The new clubs rarely win, but they are sensationally successful, with profits that are unprecedented for expansion franchises. Charlotte, with an arena seating 23,388, has a waiting list for season tickets, and as an expansion team, it led the league in attendance in 1989, its first season. Unbelievable! And the other clubs were on the upswing as well. NBA attendance jumped 31.3 percent and set a new record every year from 1983 to 1988.

However, it was the television turnaround that was the key to the pro basketball miracle. In 1982, public interest in the NBA and TV ratings had dipped so low, the final game of the championship series between the Los Angeles Lakers and Philadelphia 76ers was shown via tape delay instead of live prime time. From that sorry state, the league went to impressive ratings and as already mentioned, almost $1 billion a year in TV and cable revenues. The NBA claimed that its Nielsen ratings soared 46 percent from 1979 through 1986. The marketing of superstars such as Michael Jordan, Larry Bird, Magic Johnson, and Julius Erving had a lot to do with it. The NBA's ratings boom was even more impressive when one considers that the other sports ratings were down during the same time period.

The popularity of its superstars likely did more for the game than the promotion and marketing, which sometimes reached levels of absurdity. With due respect to Stern, the master of promotion, ad nauseam, in the NBA is Pat Williams, the general manager of the Orlando Magic. Williams, who previously held positions with the Atlanta Hawks, Bulls, and 76ers, is the P. T. Barnum of the NBA. Some of his not-so-classy promotions have included hot dog eating contests, pig racing, wrestling bears, Big Feet Night, Skyscraper Night, Weightlifter Night, and coat throwing. A couple of these need explanations. Anyone with size 13 or bigger got in free on Big Feet Night. Any man over 6'4" and any woman over 6' received a pass on Skyscraper Night. Anyone weighing over 250 pounds got in free on Weightlifter Night, and as a sideshow, four of the heavies were placed on a table at halftime and weight lifter Paul Anderson tried to get the table off the floor. It didn't work. The table broke.

Williams is the same man who says of Stern, "We have had people in this league who would have trouble selling Blue Cross to Humpty-Dumpty. David Stern can sell an anvil to a drowning man. He can sell a pogo stick to a kangaroo. David Stern could sell a stethoscope to a tree surgeon. He won't be happy until he walks down the streets of Peking and sees every kid wearing an NBA hat."

I love David Stern, but I would like to think that the Michael Jordans, Larry Birds, Patrick Ewings, and Magic Johnsons have more to do with the success of the NBA than some of the inane promotions.

David deserves the accolades for being the most impressive commissioner of the eighties, but his league does have some warts. There is too much violence, too much fighting, and the fines seem an ineffective deterrent. The season is too long, and the regular season means too little. And too frequently, the home court means an automatic win. And David has had to throw a half dozen players out of the game for drug use. The Chris Washburns and the Micheal Ray Richardsons leave a bad taste in the mouths of fans.

David Stern has some work remaining, but the NBA is secure in the knowledge that the league is in the best possible hands.

<u>CHAPTER</u> THIRTEEN

Community Rape; Franchise Chess Revisited

No sooner had Jose Canseco become the highest-paid player in a team sport in America, with a $23.5-million, five-year contract that calls for $5 million for the last year, than Darryl Strawberry proclaimed he was worth more.

Canseco is the muscular slugger who denied the charge of Tom Boswell of *The Washington Post* that he was a steroid user. While some continue to question his body bulk and muscle development, there can be no doubt about Jose's ability to hit a baseball. Nor can there be any doubt about his ability to be, as Will Clark of the San Francisco Giants says, "a jerk." Canseco has spent a goodly amount of time breaking California speed and gun laws, and he has been sued for failing to fulfill card-signing obligations. But then, such are the heroes of American sport today.

Strawberry, who has spent several years disappointing those who labeled him a superstar, who has gone through alcohol rehabilitation, and who was involved in a highly publicized wife-beating episode, thinks he should now be a $5-million-per-season player. After the All-Star break in 1990, when Strawberry was in the midst of a terrific hitting tear, the Mets offered Darryl a new contract calling for more than $3 million for each of the next three years; Strawberry's reply: "It was an insulting offer." Where is the sanity in sports? Here is a player with great potential, but at this stage of his career, to pay him money worthy of the greats of the game is ridiculous. With today's sports salaries being what they are, maybe Ted Williams, Joe DiMaggio, Willie Mays, Hank Aaron, or Mickey Mantle would be deserving of this kind of remuneration, but a Canseco or a Strawberry at $5 million? Preposterous!

Free agent Strawberry was signed by the Dodgers, who paid him almost as much as Canseco. Then the Red Sox made pitcher Roger Clemens the highest paid player at $5 million per season. If the owners and general managers are dumb enough to pay these outrageous sums, then more power to the players. After all, I made some huge money as a broadcaster during my salad days. I do know, however, that the American Broadcasting Company got a fair return for my services. People such as Leonard Goldenson, the late Elton Rule, and Roone Arledge recognized that.

People frequently ask me if the players of today are deserving of the astronomical salaries. Realistically, they aren't, but in our society, a person deserves what he can command. With pay television on the horizon, it's very likely that some of you will live to see the heavyweight champion of the world make upward of $100 million for one fight.

In an individual sport such as golf, players such as Jack Nicklaus, Arnold Palmer, and Greg Norman, mostly through endorsements, already make about $8 million a year. And the Lendls, Beckers, and Grafs of the tennis world approach that figure as well.

Then there's the 5'6" Diego Maradona of Argentina, who makes $8 million a year in salary and endorsements for playing soccer. He demonstrated in the '90 World Cup that he's washed up at thirty, yet here's an athlete who demands a minimum of $10,000 for a brief interview with anyone from the media. Unbelievable!

World Cup soccer is a farce. The '90 Cup in Italy was a sleep inducer. There was no offense at all. Take away the fouls and penalty shots and you had nothing. America will have an easy act to follow in 1994 when it hosts the match, but don't hold your breath. My old friend Henry Kissinger may love it, but to most Americans, the vast majority of Americans, soccer will always be a colossal bore.

Getting back to the outrageous money in sports, sure it's out of whack, but it's our system. The NBA's average per-player salary is about five times that of President Bush. And if Tom Cruise can negotiate $30 million for a movie, and if Jack Nicholson can demand $40 million for making *Batman*, who's to say that it's absurd for an athlete to make $3 million or $5 million a year? In reality, we know they're not worth it, but if the marketplace allows it, so be it.

As I said on Louis Rukeyser's "Wall Street Week" television program on January 19, 1990, "If Darryl Strawberry can get paid $4 or 5 million a year, which is possible, then I think baseball deserves whatever it gets."

The sad thing about the big-money contracts is that the fan, the consumer, winds up getting screwed. If the Lakers pay Magic Johnson $3 million a year, they claim they have to charge $350 per game for a front-row seat. That's right, that's the actual price. If the Miami Heat or Minnesota Timberwolves or any other NBA team comes to the Forum to play the Lakers, a single front-row seat costs $350. Other clubs have some cheap seats. Front-row seats for the Detroit Pistons and Portland Trailblazers go for a modest $150 per game.

Portland, a team without a true superstar—Clyde "the Glide" Drexler is a fine player, not a superstar—surprised everyone by making it to the NBA Finals in 1990. The Trailblazers split the first two games with the Pistons, but then, inexplicably, lost three straight on their friendly home court.

The Blazers capitalized on their bittersweet fortune by doubling ticket prices for their front-row seats. After Portland raised courtside seats from $75 to $150, Bob Barnett, a Blazers VP, told the AP, "Last year's league average for a courtside seat was $100. The Lakers charged $350. We're just trying to catch up."

The Blazers gave a break to fans who sit in the second row. Those seats only went up from $60 to $100.

Can you imagine paying $150 for a Portland Trailblazers–Orlando Magic game?

And who do you think gets hurt when the networks charge

$700,000 to sponsors for a thirty-second Super Bowl commercial, as was the case in 1990 in New Orleans? The consumer, the viewer, of course. When the NFL commands $3.6 billion in its TV-cable contract, the price of commercials goes up, and the sponsor ends up passing the cost along to the consumer. And the football fan as well as the non–football fan gets shafted again.

It's just a matter of time before some network will be charging $1 million for a thirty-second Super Bowl commercial.

The Super Bowl ticket is one of the better examples of how sports dollars have skyrocketed. For the first three years, tickets ranged from eight dollars to twelve dollars, and there were many empty seats (about 30,000) at Super Bowl I between Green Bay and Kansas City. Since that first game, all have been sellouts, and now, Super Bowl tickets are priced at $150; and it's not unusual for scalpers to sell premium tickets for $2,000 each. The $150 is for all seats; even if you are nosebleed high in the end zone of a 90,000-seat stadium, it is still $150. In addition, it is extremely hard for average fans to obtain a Super Bowl ticket, since corporations and the wealthy control most of the seats. It's truly a corporate spectacle for the rich and the connected.

Baseball has long been the best buy among professional sports, but even the price of America's pastime is escalating. A family of four can't go to a regular-season baseball game these days without spending $80–100. That's based on four good seats, parking, and some concessions items such as hot dogs, soda, beer, etc. It's not like the good old times, which used to feature Ladies' Day, and a liberal amount of doubleheaders.

Now, you rarely get doubleheaders unless they are rain induced. Of course, the Boston Red Sox have long been famous for the day-night double dips. Fill up Fenway for game one, then empty the park and make 'em all pay again for the night game. What an awful way to rip off the fans.

Whom would you expect to have the highest prices in the National Football League? Maybe someone like the San Francisco 49ers with all their Super Bowl wins and the highest payroll in football? Wrong. It's the Phoenix Cardinals, and there's a story behind it, one that concerns "franchise relocation"—to me, one of the nastiest phrases in sports.

The Bidwill family has owned the Chicago–St. Louis–Phoenix Cardinals ever since 1932. The team jumped from Chicago to St. Louis in 1960, and from St. Louis to Phoenix in 1988.

Nothing infuriates me more than franchise relocation. I devoted much space in my last book to the Raiders' move from Oakland to Los Angeles, the Rams' move from Los Angeles to Anaheim, the Colts' move from Baltimore to Indianapolis, and the Jets' move from Queens, New York, to East Rutherford, New Jersey. The latest moves in the National Football League have been equally appalling.

The Bidwills began their St. Louis community blackmail in 1985, when they met with officials from Phoenix. Bidwill had been holding out for a $170-million domed stadium in St. Louis. The good citizens of St. Louis were not ready for that expenditure, and Bidwill didn't appreciate the downscaled offer of an outdoor stadium that would cost a paltry $117 million. It was clear that the football Cardinals would move to the city offering the highest bid. Besides Phoenix, other cities to take part in the vulgar process would be Memphis, Baltimore, Jacksonville, and Columbus. Meanwhile, St. Louis was bidding against the five locales in what was to be a futile effort to retain the Cardinals.

The negotiating process dragged on, and the cities kept sweetening the pot. Bidwill had to let the league know by January 15, 1988, whether he planned to move to another city. St. Louis officials agreed to improve their proposal, to give Bidwill a $5-million practice facility and office complex, and reduce his rent at Busch Stadium to practically nothing until a new domed stadium could be constructed. It would be a 70,000-seat-plus stadium, with at least sixty-five sky boxes to be sold for a minimum of $40,000 each. Bidwill could keep that money and would receive a bigger percentage of the concessions.

But William "Give Me a Bid" Bidwill was looking for a better offer. If the price was right, he would leave St. Louis in a New York minute.

Football-starved Phoenix wound up giving the best offer.

Bidwill had made it known that he wanted a cash franchise fee of $7 million for starters. The Arizona bidders exceeded that figure with an offer of $10 million, and before the deal was put to bed, the package was worth well in excess of $20 million.

The Cardinals would play their games in the 70,491-seat Arizona State University stadium. Bidwill would keep 90 percent of most ticket revenues, but would keep all the revenues from five hundred special seats, priced at $500 each, and sixty air-conditioned luxury boxes priced at $40,000 each. Bidwill and Arizona State would split the concessions and parking money, and the Arizonans matched the St. Louis offer of a $5-million practice facility.

Baltimore, Columbus, Jacksonville, and Memphis were all well short of the Phoenix offer, so Arizona it would be.

Alvin Pete Rozelle, fresh from his court losses to Al Davis on franchise relocation, did nothing to save the franchise for St. Louis, not even lip service. Davis and Robert Irsay had successfully moved clubs without league approval, and no owner was about to oppose Bidwill's shift. The vote was 26–0, with abstentions from Al Davis and Joe Robbie. Davis's lawyers wouldn't allow him to vote because of ongoing litigation, and Robbie abstained because he favored another Arizona group, headed by his close friend Joe Foss.

One ridiculous aspect of the Cardinals' move to Phoenix involved the club's lease agreement in St. Louis. The Cards' lease contract ran through 1990, but Bidwill simply ran out on the lease. When it comes time to franchise hop, the oligarchs simply break the contract. It's a simple case of twenty-eight greedy and wealthy people wanting to be richer and more powerful.

It didn't take long for Bill Bidwill to alienate the people of Arizona. For starters, he implemented the highest ticket prices in the NFL. On top of the outrageous ego-seat prices, the special loge and luxury boxes, he priced the stadium seats at $40, $30, and $25—a move that represented a price gouge of the highest magnitude. Cardinal seats in St. Louis had sold for $22. Unfortunately, the transported Cardinals' caliber of play didn't improve with the price hike. The combination of high-price tickets and mediocre play resulted in the Cardinals' struggling to draw 40,000 people per game. That meant an average of about 30,000 empty seats per game in a prime football area, one where even an expansion team should have flourished. There were grumblings around the league, and many of the NFL owners were blaming Bidwill for screwing up a dynamite football market.

Public sentiment against Bidwill seemed to peak in 1989, when late in the season, he fired popular head coach Gene Stallings, who was not blamed by the fans, at least, for the spotty performance by the Cardinals. The dismissal of Stallings came after the coach stated that he did not want to return as head coach in 1990, and although he didn't say it, the implication was that Stallings was fed up with working for Bill Bidwill. Gene's decision so angered Bidwill that through his general manager, Larry Wilson, he denied Stallings a chance to have a final meeting with his players.

Stallings, a gentleman and an excellent football coach, landed on his feet in a nice manner. He accepted the head coaching job at the University of Alabama, his alma mater. The pressure to win at Alabama is tough, and Stallings felt the heat after losing his first three games in 1990. But fortunately, he didn't have a Bill Bidwill to contend with.

Maybe St. Louis mayor Vincent Schoemehl, Jr., said it best. His city is still aiming for a new stadium, as a lure for an NFL expansion team. "My worst nightmare," said the mayor, "is that we'll get the new stadium built and that Bidwill will want to come back to St. Louis. The thought keeps me awake at night."

One franchise move pains me as much as the Cardinals' switch. As I detailed in *I Never Played the Game*—and it bears reemphasis—when Wellington Mara deserted New York City and moved his team to New Jersey, he incurred the displeasure of many people, among them Norman Redlich, one of the nation's outstanding legal scholars. At the time of Mara's move, Redlich, once dean of the New York University School of Law and then corporate counsel for New York City, was negotiating with Mara to prevent the move, and he insists that Mara misled him. Redlich protested, and was joined by the late Red Smith in denouncing the move, but it was to no avail.

In reality, Bill Bidwill and Wellington Mara were novices at franchise free agency when compared to my old friend Al

Davis, the managing partner of the Los Angeles Raiders. Many thought his moving days were over when Davis made his celebrated court-approved move from Oakland to Los Angeles. Wrong!

First, let me say that I like Al Davis. We have had a close friendship for much of our lives. I have always recognized his legal right to move his franchise, his personal property, but as Al wrote in the foreword to this book, I have on moral grounds always opposed his franchise moves.

There will always be critics who claim that Al and I are self-serving close friends who stick together. It's true that we're both Jews who grew up in Brooklyn. Al went to Erasmus High School; I went to Hamilton High. It's true that we share many things. We're both controversial, we're renegades in the eyes of our peers, we get bad press, take a lot of heat, and at times, we're prime targets for cheap headlines and commentary.

Al Davis, however, is a winner, and he's afraid of nothing. Who else would accuse Commissioner Alvin Pete Rozelle and the owner of the Los Angeles Rams, Georgia Frontiere, of scalping Super Bowl tickets in 1980? Rozelle wriggled off the hook, but Georgia's husband went to jail in the case that followed Davis's charges.

My good friend Alex Spanos, owner of the San Diego Chargers, describes Davis as "probably the smartest man in professional football, if not in all of sports."

As an excuse for seeking greener pastures, Davis used the fact that Oakland officials wouldn't make stadium improvements. He couldn't use attendance as a reason, because the Raiders played to a packed house.

After Al hightailed it to the California southland, he discovered that Tinseltown was not Utopia. His blue-collar villains were not accepted in the trendy environs of L.A., and his Raiders played to many empty seats. Moreover, Al discovered that in many ways the Los Angeles Coliseum was antiquated, and it lacked the most-cherished owner's dream, luxury boxes.

The first indication that Al was serious about moving the Raiders again came when he initiated talks with officials in Irwindale, a Los Angeles suburb, located twenty miles east of downtown L.A.

To let Davis know they meant business, the Irwindale officials gave Al $10 million up front, all nonrefundable money. That's right, a cool $10 million just to talk. His total cash inducement, "mover's fee" if you will, was to be $30.5 million. In addition, the Raiders would get a new stadium, valued at $125 million, and a $50-million commitment from the city to purchase land for the stadium, prepare the stadium site, and provide parking for the stadium. The entire offer to Davis was valued at more than $200 million.

Meanwhile, the Los Angeles Coliseum managers slapped Davis with a $58-million breach-of-contract suit because of his plans to move. Court fights had never bothered Al. He knew he could always buy his way out of the lease, make a settlement. His thinking was no different from Bill Bidwill's.

And like Bidwill, Davis recognized that the more bidders in the franchise free-agency game, the better it would be for him. Sacramento would become a serious player in the game, Oakland saw a chance to get their Raiders back, and Los Angeles would make the obligatory move to sweeten the pot in an effort to save its franchise.

The Sacramento offer was very impressive. The Raiders would receive a package worth $335 million, including a 72,000-seat privately financed stadium, and a cash fee of $50 million to be financed through public funds.

Sacramento was so eager to obtain an NFL franchise that within ten days, the city council approved the plan to offer Davis a $50-million franchise fee. Amazingly enough, the plan did not require a public vote. The city would issue a $50-million bond to pay Davis, guaranteeing repayment by imposing a 5-percent ticket tax on all live performances in the city and raising the Sacramento hotel tax to 11 percent from 10 percent. Apparently there's no limit to what city administrations will do to fatten the coffers of NFL owners.

The Irwindale and Sacramento offers would pale in comparison to the one put together by the city of Oakland. On March 12, 1990, Al Davis broke a long silence on his plans for the Raiders by accepting from Oakland a proposed fifteen-year, $602-million package.

Dressed in white rather than his usual Raiders black,

Davis announced his decision at the NFL owners meeting in Orlando, Florida. Perhaps it might have been more appropriate had he dressed in gold. None of the owners opposed his move this time. It's likely they all viewed the $602-million deal with envy.

In making the announcement, Davis quoted advice that former Dodger owner Walter O'Malley had given him: "The city that gets you doesn't win you, the city that has you loses you." That was advice from the man who started franchise chess when he took my beloved Dodgers away from Brooklyn and located them in Los Angeles.

Paul Tagliabue was still new as the league's commissioner and couldn't pass up the chance to chide Davis: "A lot of people had doubts that the Raiders would do well in Los Angeles."

Oakland mayor Lionel Wilson, who was personally involved in the fourteen-month negotiations with Davis and his limited partner, Jack Brooks, called the announcement "an eventful day in history for Oakland." Wearing a Raiders black-and-silver jacket, Wilson proclaimed that Oakland "will become the sports capital of the world." The mayor said it was a done deal, and that the paperwork would be completed within a week. Not true.

Not all the good citizens of Oakland agreed with a deal that would guarantee Al Davis $602 million, including a cash franchise fee of $54.9 million, $53.5 million to renovate the Oakland Coliseum, and a $67.5-million "loan," which the Raiders did not have to repay.

This offer was made despite the fact that the city of Oakland at the time was in sad financial condition, and the Oakland public school system was officially broke. Unbelievable!

Mayor Wilson and the City Council had underestimated the opposition to the sweetheart of all sweetheart sports deals. Oakland might love football, but some people retained their sanity.

The deal was quickly coming unglued. Within days after Davis's announcement, opponents of the offer delivered more than 33,000 names on petitions to the city clerk, demanding that the football issue be put to a public vote in

November of 1990. The petition represented, by more than 13,000 names, the number needed to put the measure on the ballot.

Davis quickly told Mayor Wilson that he would pull out of the deal if it went to a public vote, explaining that he couldn't wait that long to decide where he was moving.

It was apparent to all that the $602-million guarantee was not going to fly. Oakland officials and representatives of Davis quickly revised the guarantee from $602 million down to $428 million. Though a sharp reduction, it was still the sweetest deal ever offered any club owner in professional sports, but the $428-million offer did not hold up, and the guarantee dropped so low that neither side would publicly disclose the figure.

To complicate matters, the Oakland voters swept Mayor Wilson out of office in June 1990, and many felt the football issue was the main reason for his defeat.

On June 14, 1990, Al telephoned my office to say that he was in New York and wanted to have lunch. I had always had the feeling that Davis wanted to stay in Los Angeles. I came away from our lunch at the Regency Hotel, however, with a clear understanding that Al would be moving the Raiders back to the Oakland Coliseum. Even with the problems, it was clear that the Oakland offer was by far the strongest of all the bidders'.

It was equally clear that it was not going to be as easy as initially thought. The Oakland A's were not happy about sharing stadium dates with a football tenant again; the A's were even making noises about seeking another stadium.

Meanwhile, Los Angeles was making a last-ditch effort to save the Raiders. L.A. mayor Tom Bradley met with Davis at Al's home and came away saying that he "didn't consider the matter over until it's over." Two days later, the L.A. Coliseum commission voted to sign an agreement with MCA-Spectacor to perform a $145-million renovation of the Coliseum. However, the deal hinges on either retaining the Raiders or attracting another NFL team to the Coliseum.

The city had already offered the Raiders a onetime cash inducement of $30 million to stay in L.A., and it agreed to drop its $57-million breach-of-contract suit against the

Raiders in exchange for a long-term commitment from the team.

During the 1990 season, Davis flip-flopped again, jilted Oakland for the second time, and promised to sign a new twenty-year lease with the Los Angeles Coliseum, making my original prediction correct. But keep in mind that with Al, the future is always uncertain. The man is a football business genius; without a doubt, the smartest operator in sports.

What Davis and all other club owners would like to do is own the stadium, or at least control the concessions. Stadium or arena operations is now the name of the game.

There's gold in parking, concessions, and souvenirs at sporting events. Consequently, owners now maneuver to own or control the arena or stadium. Walter O'Malley was the one to start it all when he privately built Dodger Stadium in Chavez Ravine.

The idea is to get public officials to give the club owner the land for the arena or give sweetheart leases, and naturally, city, county, and state tax breaks are appreciated.

Working behind the scenes with Davis in the area of stadium operations are Ed Snider, owner of the Philadelphia Flyers and the Philadelphia Spectrum Arena, and the famed Pritzker family of Chicago.

The Pritzker family is one of the wealthiest in America. *Forbes* magazine issues a conservative estimate of the family's net worth at $3.5 billion. The family owns the Hyatt Hotel chain, Braniff Airlines, and many, many other companies. It's impossible to gauge accurately the family's worth because so many of their assets are hidden in a complex maze of privately held companies, joint ventures, and partnerships that do not release financial information of any type.

It is known that the Pritzkers are becoming more and more involved in sports. They own Ticketmaster, the country's largest computerized ticketing service, which in 1989 sold $300 million of tickets to sporting events.

The Pritzkers also manage the New Orleans Superdome, the Nassau Coliseum on Long Island, New York, and other sports arenas.

If sports operators and owners are looking for money,

they often find it from people looking to become involved in stadium or arena operations. The Jacobs brothers, who own the Emprise Corporation, have long been famous for giving huge, interest-free loans in exchange for a percentage of concessions. They were the foremost partners of stadium, arena, and racetrack operators until the corporation was convicted, along with two Mafia members, of felony charges —criminally conspiring to obtain secret ownership of the Frontier Casino in Las Vegas back in April of 1972. At that time, Emprise, under the name Sportservice, controlled concessions of seven major league baseball clubs, eight NFL teams, five NBA clubs, and fifty-six horse and dog tracks in the U.S. and Canada. They are still very active in the industry, but tend to be more low-key than in past years.

Abe Pollin, a nice man who owns the Washington Bullets and the Washington Capitals, was one of the pioneers in arena operations. In 1974, he built the Capital Centre in Landover, Maryland, and over 300 million people have paid their way in to watch basketball, hockey, concerts, ice shows, boxing, wrestling, rodeos, and tractor pulls. And talk about sweetheart deals. How about a ninety-nine-year lease for one dollar? Yes, one dollar, plus access roads to the arena, and all kinds of tax breaks. The Washington, D.C., area didn't have a suitable sports arena, so officials were eager to make an operator such as Pollin an offer that he couldn't refuse.

It's easy to see why the trend is for more privately owned arenas. Surprisingly enough, fourteen arenas in the NBA are now privately owned. They are: Madison Square Garden, the Boston Garden, the Omni in Atlanta, Chicago Stadium, Cleveland's Richfield Coliseum, the Palace at Auburn Hills (Mich.), the Summit in Houston, the Market Square Arena in Indianapolis, the Forum in Los Angeles, the Bradley Center in Milwaukee, the Spectrum in Philadelphia, the ARCO Arena (Sacramento), the Capital Centre, and the Minnesota Arena. What a joy for those arena owners and/or operators to keep the parking, hot dog, and beer money, and not have to share it with city, county, and state officials.

In baseball, Fenway Park, Tiger Stadium, Wrigley Field, Busch Stadium, and Dodger Stadium are privately owned. In football, Joe Robbie Stadium in Miami is privately owned, and Washington, D.C., officials have offered to give the Redskins land next to Kennedy Stadium so that Jack Kent Cooke can build himself a 72,000-seat, football-only stadium that would bear his name.

Perhaps the best example of what arena operation means to a club is the Detroit Pistons. Bill Davidson's club drew huge crowds, sometimes 40,000–50,000 people, as they set season attendance records in the huge Pontiac Silverdome. As a tenant, the Pistons drew 908,242 fans in the '86–87 season, and 1,066,505 in '87–88. But Davidson couldn't wait to get into his new, but smaller arena, the Palace at Auburn Hills. He paid $70 million to build the arena, but he takes in $12 million annually from ego suites alone. The Palace has 180 luxury suites, which sell from $30,000 to $120,000 per year. The corporations snap them up, and the owners grin from ear to ear. The Palace seats 21,454, and in the first two years of operation, Davidson has never failed to sell out any event. The profits are enormous.

Owners in all sports are always crying poor mouth, but every time a franchise sells, it sells for a tremendous profit. Here are some figures from franchise sales that have not previously been mentioned in the book: the Denver Nuggets, which sold for $19 million in 1985, were resold in 1989 for about $54 million. That sale was historic, because the buyers, Bertram Lee and Peter Bynoe, were the first black owners in professional sports.

George Argyros, worth about $500 million, bought the Seattle Mariners for $12 million in 1981. After one losing season after another, George, in 1989, sold the franchise for $80 million to Jeffrey Smulyan and Michael Browning. Who says you have to win to make money?

In 1990, the San Diego Padres were sold by Mrs. Ray Kroc, the owner of the McDonald's chain, to a group headed by Tom Werner for $75 million. The late Ray Kroc had paid $10 million for the club in 1974.

It's the same story in the NFL. Victor Kiam is a man I respect as a merchandiser of shaving products, a man who lives on Wire Mill Road in Stamford, Connecticut, which is where Walter "Red" Smith, a revered sportswriter of the past, used to live. In 1988, he bought the struggling New England Patriots from my old friend Billy Sullivan for $90 million. Billy had paid just $25,000 for the rights to the team in 1959.

In 1989, an Arkansas oilman named Jerry Jones bought America's team, the Dallas Cowboys, for a cool $150 million. (He would proceed to make most of the state of Texas unhappy by firing Tex Schramm, Gil Brandt, and Tom Landry, all institutions in the state, but the fans warmed up to the new owner the following year when the team started winning.) Bum Bright, who sold the club to Jones, had bought it for $85 million in 1984. Clint Murchison, in 1960, had paid only $6,000 to the NFL for the expansion club.

The NFL owners keep crying and crying about economic conditions, but they keep buying and/or selling for record prices. The NFLPA may have a point when it claims the owners don't care that much about winning. It's nice to win but not necessary. Why? Each NFL club starts the season with $50 million in the bank before the first kickoff. Every NFL franchise receives $32.6 million annually as its share of the national TV-cable package, and in 1989, each club received $18 million as its share of profits from sales by NFL Properties. The NFLPA souvenirs do nicely and keep the association going, but the owners' merchandising is about one hundred times as large.

Have no pity for the professional sports club owners in America. They gouge the fans and the taxpayers in a systematic manner. It's enough to make one nauseous!

CHAPTER FOURTEEN

Limburger Smells Better

What do Craig Bodzianowski, with an artificial right foot, Benny Harjoe, with a pacemaker in his chest, and Aaron Pryor, blind in the left eye, all have in common? They are licensed prizefighters in America. Unthinkable! Shameful!

Bodzianowski, who has been billed as "the amputee from Chicago," lost his right foot and part of his leg as the result of a motorcycle accident in 1984. Prior to the surgery, Craig had established a 13–0 professional record. Give Bodzianowski credit for courage, but give boxing authorities credit for stupidity. How insane, allowing a man with a prosthesis to box. Realistically, what boxer in his right mind wants to beat a man with an artificial foot, and what boxer in his right mind wants to risk losing to a one-legged fighter?

The opportunistic handlers of Bodzianowski, working with equally opportunistic, bloodsucking promoters, matched Craig with a string of stiffs, enabling him to compile a postsurgery fight record of 11–3–1. However, when Bodzianowski was matched with a fighter of merit, former cruiserweight champ Alonzo Ratliff stopped him—twice. Then an unknown fighter by the name of James Waring beat him in November of 1989.

Despite those three losses, the WBA (World Boxing

Association), one of the many outrageous alphabet boxing organizations, still ranked him number nine in the world. That was good enough for a promoter named Mike Acri to match Bodzianowski against undefeated Robert Daniel, on July 19, 1990, in a twelve-round WBA cruiserweight world championship match. The challenger managed to plod awkwardly through twelve rounds on his artificial foot, only to lose a decision.

The promoter admitted that he could have signed a better boxer, but he liked the appeal of a white, one-footed fighter doing battle with a black champion.

How sick! Boxing has never been sicker. The mere thought of officials allowing a man with an artificial foot in the ring, and the fact that such a man can last twelve rounds in a title fight, are a double indictment of this alleged sport.

And how crazy of the State of Oklahoma to give Benny Harjoe a license to box despite the pacemaker in his chest. It's equally crazy for the state of Wisconsin to allow Aaron Pryor to box, after a doctor in Nevada proclaimed him to be "legally blind" in the left eye. In May of 1990, Pryor beat thirty-six-year-old Darryl "Pea Man" Jones, an "opponent" with a 13–13 record. Such garbage!

And some people still wonder why I walked away from the boxing cesspool. There are those who accuse me of being a hypocrite for having made millions of dollars from working boxing and then walking away from it. Absurd! I quit boxing in 1982 at the zenith of my career. I gave up millions when I became fed up with the danger, the corruption, and the crime.

All of this was done years ago and explained in detail in my last book. Nonetheless, people still think of me when they think of boxing.

A couple of years back, I got a call from a professor of law at Harvard named Arthur Miller, a man with whom you may be familiar due to his appearances on network television where he talks in a Socratic manner about the legal issues of the day. Professor Miller did a show about boxing, and he asked me to participate. I thanked him for the invitation, but I told him, "No more."

I told him he was bound, and understandably so, to

include all viewpoints on the question of boxing and whether it should be regulated or banned. I told him he was bound to include the likes of Don King, Bob Arum, and boxing writers, and this, too, was understandable. But the days when Howard Cosell appears with those people to contest their every word, to puncture their self-serving statements, to bombard them with evidence and more evidence about the danger of boxing, are over. No more.

But he is an old friend, so I did talk with the professor at length. I told him about testifying before many congressional committees, starting in 1972. I told him that in some cases the memory of the committee sessions is sharp and strong, but sometimes they blend together in memory becoming one huge room, with an immense table of witnesses and a dais of elected officials stretching endlessly to the horizon. And each time I sit testifying to senators, congressmen, and/or judicial officers, reiterating over and over and over again the horrible tales of danger done to young men and older boxers as well.

I tell them about Ray Seales, and how he was totally blinded in the ring; how Ray Leonard was licensed to fight again after undergoing surgery for a detached retina; and how Muhammad Ali, a once glorious man, is now brain damaged and punch-drunk from boxing. I talk about the connection between the media and boxing, and the seemingly insatiable appetite for fights that reigns supreme in every network-television sports division, and now at places such as HBO and ESPN. How they'll put anyone into a ring and hype it as a major event and turn on the cameras and let young men be destroyed and damaged for life.

I talk of danger, of corruption, and of possible crime. I tell of FBI agents who visit my office, looking for information on a man named Robert Lee from New Jersey, a man who has been investigated time and time again for alleged criminal activities. This same man is the founder of the IBF. What is the IBF? you ask. It's the International Boxing Federation. In boxing, you can get up one morning, proclaim a federation or a council, line up fighters, get on TV, and you are "legitimate." That's the kind of sport boxing has become, with no enforceable standards of eligibility or safety, no controls, no credible unified body running the sport, protecting the boxers, and protecting the public.

For almost two decades I have talked and talked and talked on these issues. I have sought federal standards, a federal boxing commission, enforceable safety standards, and uniform state licensing standards. I have even advocated the abolition of professional boxing in its present form. If it can't be cleaned up and regulated, then it shouldn't be permitted.

Sometimes I feel as if I'm crying into a well, but no matter, the right to cry "No more" is mine. I'm out of that arena now, and it would take a lot more than a TV talk show to lure me back.

I must admit, there are times when I feel that pro boxing is such a disgrace that it's not deserving of comment. However, it's impossible to close one's eyes and seal one's ears, and I do have some strong opinions about what I've seen happen in boxing over the past five or six years. Additionally, since I'm doing an overview book on sports, then I'm obligated to express my views.

From the very beginning, I felt Mike Tyson was an overrated fighter. When most of the media were hyping Tyson, falsely presenting him as one of the all-time great fighters, on my daily radio programs I was persistent in adamantly stating his vulnerabilities and weaknesses.

First of all, it is impossible for me to take Mike Tyson seriously as a person. He is so utterly ignorant, so uncultured, and has been a criminal for most of his life. There is nothing very complex about Mike Tyson. He has certain basic, barbaric instincts and seemingly uncontrollable emotions.

This opinion is supported by José Torres, former world light-heavyweight champ, as well as former chairman of the New York State Athletic Commission, in his book *Fire and Fear: The Inside Story of Mike Tyson*. It is my feeling that Torres quoted Tyson accurately when Tyson said the best punch he ever landed was against his then-wife, Robin Givens. And I think Tyson was serious when he said he would like to break an opponent's nose and push the bones back into his brain. Nice guy.

I think Tyson needs professional help from persons expert in the field of mental health, but I don't think he'll get that help, or achieve any development as a person, as long as he's in the hands of Don King.

I first met Mike Tyson at the '84 Olympic trials, where he was beaten twice by Henry Tillman—deservedly beaten. His trainer, my old friend Cus D'Amato, argued otherwise at the time, but Cus had trained Tyson to be a professional fighter, not an amateur. There's a big difference in the rules and the scoring in the two arenas.

During the Olympics, Mike was still with his team, although not a member of it, and would sit next to me on many occasions, cheering wildly for the American boxers. After the competition was finished, he joined with the American team, led by Mark Breland and Evander Holyfield, as they carried me on their shoulders around the arena.

In regard to his former teammates, it was clear that Tyson handled himself with good sportsmanship, so there are traces of goodness in him. I'm not disposed to forget that. I found that very interesting.

There was never any doubt about Tyson's brute strength, and comanagers Jimmy Jacobs and Bill Cayton brought him along correctly. Most of his early opponents were stiffs, and Tyson looked like a world-beater against them.

His trainer, Cus D'Amato, had taken Tyson out of a life of street crime and made him a boxer. Earlier Cus had been trainer and manager of Floyd Patterson and José Torres, both world champs. D'Amato was a wise and good man, a rarity in boxing, an honest man who could survive in the business.

Back in the fifties and the mid-sixties, boxing was controlled by the IBC (International Boxing Club), headed by Jim Norris, Truman Gibson, and a man known simply as Mr. Gray, who was really gangster Frankie Carbo.

Cus broke with the IBC and refused to do business with them. Together, he and I fought a long battle with the IBC, eventually winning in federal court when Judge Sylvester Ryan issued a decision that broke up the IBC and its corrupt stranglehold on the sport.

During all those years, a man named Jim Jacobs was at D'Amato's side. He, too, was a clean man, a man of character, and he learned much from Cus D'Amato.

Jacobs, along with his business partner, Bill Cayton, became a comanager of Mike Tyson. Jacobs and Cayton, who together had the world's largest collection of fight film, a collection worth millions, were managers of other fighters in addition to Tyson, among them Edwin Rosario and Wilfred Benitez, both of whom became world champions. Jacobs and Cayton knew the business, and they were good for Tyson.

When D'Amato died, Jacobs replaced him in his role as father figure to Tyson. In March of 1988, however, the fifty-eight-year-old Jacobs, who had battled leukemia for nine years, died after contracting pneumonia.

The deaths of both these men, especially coming so close together, left Tyson in a very vulnerable position. Mike had never been close to Bill Cayton, who was himself over seventy years old and in poor health.

Promoter Don King smelled an opportunity for what he does best: splitting a boxer from his manager and stealing the fighter. King, with the full backing of Donald Trump, who also wanted a piece of Tyson, slipped the knife into Bill Cayton's back and gained control of Tyson. Cayton went to court and legally retained the title of manager, but it was clear that Tyson had become a puppet of King, who would make all the decisions in the future.

At the same time, Tyson was undergoing a breakup in his disastrous marriage to actress Robin Givens. Iron Mike was having more fights with his wife than he was with boxers. After a celebrated court battle with Robin Givens and mother-in-law Ruth Roper, Tyson obtained the divorce in the Dominican Republic. He then went on his merry way, with several car accidents, a three A.M. street fight with beleaguered journeyman boxer Mitch "Blood" Green, and a number of psychiatric examinations. Givens and Roper proclaimed that Mike was a manic-depressive; others feared a chemical imbalance in the brain of the youngest heavyweight champ of all time.

Whatever it is, it's not a pretty picture. It's plain that Tyson is a confused, vicious, and mean-spirited young man.

After knocking out former Olympic gold medalist Tyrell Biggs in the seventh round, Tyson said he "could have knocked him out in the third round, but I chose to do it slowly so that Biggs would remember it for a long time. I wanted to hurt him real bad."

Viciousness and meanness, however, do not make Mike Tyson a great fighter. In fact, I think he was the most overrated fighter of my time. Tyson has never come close to achieving the skills of a Muhammad Ali. Ali was much quicker and smarter; he was a master boxer who would have made Tyson look like a novice.

Tyson's shortcomings were apparent when James "Bonecrusher" Smith took him to a twelve-round decision. He looked equally bad against an out-of-condition Tony Tubbs, was so-so against poor Frank Bruno, and was destroyed by journeyman James "Buster" Douglas. His wins over a puffed-up Michael Spinks and a thirty-eight-year-old Larry Holmes were not impressive, at least not to me.

I have publicly stated these views all along, and I was among the few who were not surprised in February of 1990 when Tyson lost his title in a tenth-round knockout. Buster Douglas, of all people, an up-and-down fighter from Columbus, Ohio, stood up to Tyson and dominated him. They called it the biggest boxing upset of all time. It wasn't. The sportswriters have made Mike Tyson the most overrated fighter of all time.

I was in Florida the week of the Tyson-Douglas fight. As I pointed out to local Miami TV reporters the night before the fight, Iron Mike is not a great fighter. He may become one, if he fully develops his skills, but only time will tell.

One of the powder puffs among the list of Tyson's wins was a victory over young Marvis Frazier back in July of 1986.

Marvis was a mere fourteen years old when I met him in 1975, a child who accompanied his father, Joe, to the Ed Sullivan Theatre in New York City. Joe, fresh from his loss to Ali in the Thrilla in Manila, was to be a guest on my show "Saturday Night Live." They took their seats in the first row, reserved for celebrities.

During the telecast, I stepped down off the stage and into the audience to interview Joe briefly. The bout had been an exceptional one, another great chapter in the Ali-Frazier battles, where both men fought like gladiators, and Manila was as great a fight as I've ever seen.

"I hit him with blows that would have crushed walls, Howard, and he wouldn't go down," Joe told me.

When I finished talking with him, I turned to Marvis. "How do you feel about your father boxing?" I asked.

He hesitated momentarily, his manner shy and self-effacing. "I hate it," he replied quietly.

"Why?"

"I worry every time he goes into the ring. I worry he'll get hurt, hurt bad."

"Would you like to see him quit boxing?"

"Yes."

I looked at Marvis, who so obviously didn't want to hurt his father's feelings, yet could not stop himself from answering honestly, and I asked, "Despite your fear, do you want to be a boxer? Do you ever think of following in your father's footsteps?"

"No, I don't want to be a boxer. I don't want to grow up and fight."

It was a touching scene, the boy and his father standing side by side, Joe so massive, Marvis tall, but still so young and physically undeveloped. It was a scene I replayed in my mind eleven years later when I saw an obviously scared Marvis Frazier get into the ring with Mike Tyson. Marvis was demolished in the first round.

Joe Frazier and I go back a long way together. I am very fond of him, and I know he loves his son. I also know that he fell prey to a common parental ailment—he wanted to make his son an extension of himself. It can't be done, not by Joe, not by any parent. Marvis's disastrous performance against Tyson was proof of what is already a truism for every parent. Fortunately, young Frazier was not seriously injured.

Many other fighters have been less fortunate, and not much is heard about it. Such was the case with James Morris Jones, who, on May 2, 1987, made his professional debut in a scheduled six-rounder on a card at the Prince Georges Community College in Maryland, just outside Washington, D.C. His opponent was Charles Ingram, who had fought only one previous bout. In the fourth round, Ingram hit Jones with an overhead right, a perfect punch to the chin. That blow would mark the end of a normal life for Morris Jones. The twenty-three-year-old Jones was taken to nearby Prince Georges Hospital Center, where he underwent three hours of brain surgery.

A Washington neurologist, Dr. Michael Dennis, was quoted by *The Washington Post* as saying, "What can happen with a sudden blow is an acceleration of the skull backward, the brain is in a fluid-filled medium, and doesn't accelerate initially. Under these circumstances, a shearing effect can occur, tearing veins that bridge the gap between the brain and the lining of the skull."

Jones woke from a coma a couple of days after the surgery, but underwent a long hospitalization. He has been unable to pay a $500,000 medical bill, receives a $269 monthly social security disability check, and lives with his mother. Jones made $350 for his one pro fight.

He has recovered some memory and most of the movement on his left side. His sister, Bertha Wright, says, "Some things Morris can understand, most complicated things he can't. He speaks very well, but sometimes he'll repeat something four or five times without realizing he's already said it."

For every success story in pro boxing, there are hundreds of stories like Morris's. There are hundreds of pro boxers who are nothing more than human punching bags, and these fighters are called "opponents." Their fighting records are ridiculous, with loss after loss, getting knocked out in one state one week, then fighting in another state the next week. The physical exams given fighters in many states are jokes, plus some boxers use several different names to avoid detection. The system is a disgrace.

Roy Jones, Jr., the American Olympic boxer who was robbed of a decision in the Seoul Olympics, was involved in a strange professional bout in Pensacola, Florida, in June of 1990. Jones scored a first-round knockout over a fighter who was billed as Derwin Richards, the Texas junior middleweight champ. There was one problem. The real Richards was in Texas when the bout took place. What a sham. Professional boxing at its best.

One sad, but at the same time laughable, pro boxing practice is the licensing of over-the-hill fighters who want to pick up one last paycheck. The best example of this unfortunate practice is George Foreman, an old friend of mine. I was with him for his Olympic gold medal victory in Mexico City, when they stuck the American flag in his hand; I was beside him throughout his brilliant pro career. But his comeback is sad. Foreman is a nice, funny man who jokes about his eating habits and lifeless opponents, but at forty-two years and about forty-five pounds overweight, he's a boxing sideshow at its worst. Jimmy Young, who upset George and touched off religious hallucinations in Foreman after their bout in San Juan, himself went on to be a human punching bag after he was forty years of age. And how about Jerry Quarry fighting at forty, and Larry Holmes wanting to make a comeback at forty? Ludicrous! How can this go on in a civilized country?

After Buster Douglas KO'd Mike Tyson, Don King tried to pull off the biggest robbery since Brinks. Or maybe the Great Train Robbery in England. King couldn't stand by and see his new meal ticket dethroned. Millions of dollars would go down the sewer. King—boxing's number-one convicted felon—claimed that the referee should have counted Douglas out at the end of the eighth round. The whole world knew Douglas was the fair and rightful winner, but that didn't stop Don from leaning on people, such as his old pal José Sulaiman, head of the WBC, demanding that the win be taken away from Buster Douglas.

As it turned out, the massive public outcry around the world against the efforts of King caused him to back away from his robbery attempt.

One of those who recognizes the need for a federal commission to oversee the boxing mess is Gov. Jim Florio of New Jersey. We discussed the sordid situation and then agreed to dispatch a joint letter to Tom Foley, the Speaker of the House of Representatives in Washington, urging that a federal regulatory board establish controls and standards to provide stability and uniformity in the boxing profession.

Need for a federal commission was further demonstrated in the months following the Douglas-Tyson bout, when Don King and Buster Douglas became involved in litigation.

After the promotor tried to steal the boxer's title, Douglas was in no mood to allow King to promote his next match, as stipulated in their Pre-Tyson agreement. King wanted to promote a Tyson-Douglas rematch at an Atlantic City casino owned by his ally Don Trump, but Douglas said, "No thank you," and signed to make his first title defense against top-ranked contender Evander Holyfield at Steve Wynn's new Mirage Hotel in Las Vegas. King attempted to block that fight by filing, in a U.S. District Court in Manhattan, a breach-of-contract suit against Douglas.

The case went on for a couple of weeks, with King and his buddies, Bob Arum and Donald Trump, joining in on the testimony against Douglas. King and Arum have been longtime bitter enemies, but with the chance to make some money on co-promotions, they embraced each other like blood brothers. Both belong in the Hypocrites Hall of Fame.

Just as the Douglas side started its testimony, King became afraid that he was losing the case, and that prompted the two sides to negotiate an out-of-court settlement. King got $4 million, the beleaguered Trump received $2 million, and Douglas was free to fight Evander Holyfield in his first defense. But if Douglas won that fight, then King would be allowed to promote a rematch between Douglas and Tyson. Both sides claimed victory. Some mess. Boxing smells to high heaven.

Incidentally, the highlight of the court case was an admission by Don King that he is a liar. The con man with papers to prove it—he was inmate No. 125734 at the Marion (Ohio) Correctional Institute where he served three years and eleven months for killing a man—admitted that he lies to, of all people, the press. Boxing writers may figure that lying to most people is a misdemeanor, but to the press, that's a felony. How could anyone have been surprised at King's confession?

One thing the trial accomplished, before the out-of-court settlement, was to expose further the scandalous procedures of boxing promoters and matchmakers. It was just another demonstration of how much we need a federal boxing commission to regulate, mediate, and eradicate the injustices and clandestine actions that exist in the foulest of professions.

A former chairman of the New York State Athletic Commission, John Branca, an old friend of mine, agrees with me about the serious need for a single regulatory body to govern the sport. John knows that exclusive promotional contracts should not be executed between boxers and promoters, agreements that serve to circumvent the original manager-boxer contract, giving the promoter exclusive rights to the services of the boxer, while leaving the manager and boxer powerless. In these personal services contracts, the conditions state that the boxer fights for the promoter or he doesn't fight for anyone.

These one-sided agreements are simply a license for the promoter to steal. This contract is not only the promoter's way of circumventing the boxer-manager relationship, it overrides the manager's responsibility to his or her fighter. The effect of such deals ultimately is chaos and confusion in the profession, and in many cases, the state boxing commissions are rendered powerless.

A favorite trick of King's is to sign a fighter to a contract, assign his son Carl as that fighter's manager, and give the fighter a third of his share of the purse, after expenses. Tim Witherspoon, a heavyweight, once sued King, claiming that he received only $115,000 of the $1.7 million that had been allocated to him.

The King-Douglas-Wynn fiasco clearly demonstrated how a promoter can control the destiny of a fighter and insidiously, the fight game itself. Shockingly enough, it's not uncommon to see the promoter have exclusive promotional contracts for both fighters in the same fight. And in the case of King, he might have additional contracts with both managers in the same fight. Talk about conflict of interest!

John Branca points out that the state commissions, or better yet, a national commission, should not allow or recognize promoter options on a fighter for future bouts. The way it works now, in order to obtain a title fight, the boxer sometimes has to give the promoter a number of options—perhaps as many as six—on his future fights. In this manner, having options and exclusive promotion rights on both fighters, one promoter can maintain control of a championship battle for many years.

Not only should promoters not coerce or force a fighter to

sign a boxing contract with options, it should be against the law for promoters and boxers to agree on written or verbal options for fights. To enforce this law, a state or federal commission should review and approve all boxing contracts. It's a fact that options and exclusive-promotion contracts make a boxer a virtual slave, in essence taking away the boxer's human rights. Moreover, such contracts give the promoter a monopoly.

What a smelly scene. It's just as Rod Serling wrote years ago in *Requiem for a Heavyweight:* "Boxing—if there were headroom, they'd hold it in a sewer."

Perhaps surprisingly, the only time I have been sued for slander or libel in my thirty-eight years of telling it like it is came when the World Boxing Council sued me, claiming that a passage in my last book, *I Never Played the Game*, was libelous.

Naturally, I won the case. When you deal in truth, you don't have to worry about slander or libel. Many of those who are criticized do threaten to sue, of course, but it's always the guilty who threaten the loudest.

In dismissing the WBC suit against me, Judge William C. Conner, U.S. District Court, Southern District of New York, concluded, "Acting as the third man in the ring, the court rules that low or not, Cosell's blow was struck in good faith, and raises his arm in victory. Cosell's motion for summary judgment is granted, and the case is dismissed."

But did the press record my victory? Of course not. Since I won the case, the newspapers gave it little to no play. Unsurprising.

Earlier in this book, I revealed my strong negative feelings about Sugar Ray Leonard's latest comeback. He's such a competitor, loves the spotlight, and therefore, he doesn't seem to be able to walk away from the ring. I opposed his risking his damaged eye in the bout with Marvin Hagler, and I saw no reason for him to fight Donny Lalonde, and then Tommy Hearns and Roberto Duran in rematches. I told Leonard of my strong view when he came to my home in the Hamptons on the day that he signed to fight Hagler. His response, "Howard, I've got him at the right time. He's finished. I'll kill him."

He didn't kill Hagler, but he did win a close decision.

Lalonde was nothing, and against Hearns and Duran in the rematches, Ray showed how badly his skills have eroded. I'll be disappointed in Mike Trainer if he allows Leonard to box again. If he does, it'll be against an opponent with whom he knows he's totally safe. And if the public buys it, they're crazy.

Sugar Ray is headstrong, and maybe Trainer can't keep him from boxing. Leonard should be thankful to Trainer. He's been with him since the beginning of his professional career, and Trainer and the original group of Leonard backers have been good to Sugar Ray. They protected him monetarily and in other ways. Despite an expensive divorce, Leonard is in good shape financially.

Even though he didn't need the money, Leonard did fight again and my fears were confirmed. A young fighter named Terry Norris knocked Leonard down twice and gave him a terrible beating. After the fight, a puffy Sugar Ray Leonard retired for good, another case of a boxer who took one beating too many. Even though he said it was his last fight, he said that before, so who really knows with this man.

In the past few years, Sugar Ray has come in for much criticism for dumping his old friends. It was a shame to see his trainer, Angelo Dundee, the best in the business, thrown aside. The same with handlers Janks Morton and Dave Jacobs, who were with Ray from the very beginning. I'm afraid that Leonard has undergone a kind of heart transplant, and that it appears he now has a safe deposit box where his heart used to be. The situation saddens me, because I've always had a deep affection for Sugar Ray Leonard.

A situation that sickens me is the spectacle of a rich man who buys his way into the locker room. Donald Trump is a jock-sniffer. He is a tycoon who enjoys the spotlight that comes with associating with sports celebrities. You've seen him on television during boxing matches, at ringside, sitting next to Sugar Ray Leonard. He enjoyed being chummy with Herschel Walker and Doug Flutie when he owned the New Jersey Generals, and he now enjoys associating with Mike Tyson.

This obsession with sports figures is not an uncommon disease. It afflicts a lot of millionaires and frustrated jocks.

It is apparent as well in tycoons such as Ross Johnson of Nabisco and Herb Siegel of Chris-Craft in their shameless affection for Frank Gifford. To me, it's always been a sickening display, but some of these powerful men actually freak out over jocks.

For Donald Trump, however, it's more involved than mere jock worship. He wanted to own a USFL team for the excitement and money-making possibilities. He wanted to own a franchise in the NFL for the same reasons. His name has been mentioned as a possible baseball owner, either in a new league or even with the Yankees.

He has been involved in professional boxing for the excitement, the publicity, but mostly for the high rollers that it brings to his casinos. Big gamblers love the excitement of a world championship boxing match. Trump offers a high roller two complimentary $1,500 tickets, plus complimentary transportation, free hotel accommodations and food, and the sucker gambler invariably will make the trip and lose $500,000 or a million dollars at the tables. Such is the mentality of the high roller.

A year or so ago, Donald Trump was riding high. He had been on the cover of national newsmagazines. He was mentioned as a possible candidate for president. He loved the spotlight of the National Republican Convention. He docked his $30-million yacht in the Miami harbor for a week of partying in connection with Super Bowl XXIII. He was regaled as a billionaire, one of the world's richest men.

What a fall in 1990. His financial empire and reputation trembled, and his marriage and political possibilities crashed and burned. Donald Trump, the king of the egos, had reached his midlife crisis at forty-four. Donald had tried to buy or build more than reasonably possible.

It was a classic case of greed. Donald simply bit off more than he could chew. He was on such a power binge that it seemed as though nothing could stop him. He was a billionaire steamroller bent on owning the world and placing his name on most of it.

I should state that I have always had a good relationship with Donald Trump. He wanted me to buy into his New Jersey Generals. He is always urging me to attend his boxing promotions, offering me ringside seats and rides in his aircraft. I have always refused. I have never had any problems with Donald Trump, but I recognize him for what he is. You can be sure that what he does is in the best interest of Donald Trump, not the public. He builds and buys places for celebrities and the rich to live and play. He claims to give huge amounts to charities, but I've never seen him build a shelter for the homeless and the underprivileged. And very little stands in the way of Donald Trump. His ritzy apartment building on Third Avenue in New York, the Trump Palace, stands where a Catholic foundling home stood for decades. I'm sure the Catholic Church got a good price for the property, and that all the orphans were relocated, but there's a message there somewhere. For a while, it seemed that anything Trump wanted, he got.

But 1990 was to be a disastrous and revealing year for Trump. Things were not as they seemed. Trump wasn't the billionaire he was proclaimed to be. He owed banks billions of dollars and couldn't pay the interest on his loans. He became the butt of jokes by comedians all over the world. Additionally, there was the embarrassment of firms clamoring for about $30 million owed them for work done on Trump's gaudy and disgustingly flashy Taj Mahal.

At one time, it seemed that Trump would win all his skirmishes with state and gaming officials. No more. After the lovely tennis player Gabriela Sabatini of Argentina was knocked out of the U.S. Open Tennis Tournament in 1989, she was flown to Atlantic City as Trump's guest and despite being underage, a violation of state gaming laws, was given a tour of his casino. Donald was called on the carpet. Just as he was when his new Taj Mahal was found guilty of allowing hundreds of illegal aliens to work for the casino.

Trump keeps up a strong front with his PR forces doing overtime on damage control, but despite his smug smile, it would seem that Donald has seen his better days. Any political hopes he had died faster than Gary Hart's. And even though he remains active in boxing promotions, his days as a dominant sports entrepreneur seem to be behind him.

The man who brought boxing the $1,500 ringside seat has had difficulty landing the big fights in recent years. Steve Wynn stole the third Leonard-Duran "fight" from his grasp, then Wynn outmaneuvered Trump for the Douglas-Holyfield fight. Incidentally, Trump wanted to charge $2,000 for ringside seats for Tyson-Spinks back in '88, but advisers talked him into going with a modest $1,500, still a record.

One person whom Donald Trump always tries to get for his ringside prefight show is Muhammad Ali. The forty-eight-year-old three-time heavyweight champ is still loved by the people. The fight crowd chants "Ali, Ali, Ali" as he makes his way to the ring. Even the fat-cat high rollers and the movie stars strain for a glimpse of the greatest boxer of all time. The crowd explodes in a roar for Ali, but for me, it's a sad scene.

The man who took punches for twenty-seven years, twenty-one as a pro, is punch-drunk and brain damaged. I loved the man so, and it hurts me to see him in that condition. It hurts me more than words can express.

Ali and I haven't seen much of each other over the past decade. Surprisingly enough, on Saturday, May 5, 1990, I saw Ali for the first time in more than four years. I agreed to be the presenter on the sports segment of the "Night of 100 Stars," which was held at Radio City Music Hall in New York and later shown on national TV. On most occasions, Ali, because of his physical condition, has extreme difficulty speaking, and I agreed to be the presenter to Ali only if he didn't have to say anything. I didn't want him to embarrass himself.

Muhammad was happy to see me, and he threw his arms around me. He knows that I have been a lifelong supporter, even at times when few people gave him support. I was equally happy to see Ali, but at the same time, I was sad.

Muhammad talked in a whisper. "Let's go on tour, Cosell," he mouthed in soft, barely audible words. "They still love us."

We were in the greenroom at Radio City waiting to go on.

The saddest scene of the night came when Ali was being fed by Howard Bingham, for thirty years a photographer and close friend of Muhammad. Oscar Robertson, the basketball great, was seated next to Ali. The Big O said to me, "What have they done to this man?"

Joe DiMaggio was equally astounded. Ali was a superstar

in a room full of stars, but because of the ex-champ's condition the entire room was saddened. Don't let anyone such as Vic Ziegel of the New York *Daily News* try to tell you that Ali is in good shape. At least some of the time, the great man's condition is pitiful.

Leaving Radio City Music Hall that night, I had mixed feelings. It had been good to see Ali, but disappointing to see him not well. I can still remember his reaching down with his left hand to grab the fingers of his right hand to stop the tremors.

About six months earlier, I was supposed to see Ali in Detroit, helping to induct him into the National Afrikan Sports Hall of Fame. Mainly out of my respect for Ali, I had agreed to be the master of ceremonies for the event, which was held at the Cobo Hall Exhibition Center.

In addition to Ali, Olympic track star Wilma Rudolph and a couple of lesser-known sports figures were to be inducted. And the mayor of Detroit, the Honorable Coleman A. Young, was to be the featured speaker.

Imagine how I felt when I flew to Detroit and learned the following. First, no one met me at the airport as promised. Then I arrived at the hotel and learned that Ali, Rudolph, and Mayor Young would be no-shows at the dinner. I was furious! There was a sellout crowd for the dinner and the people of Detroit bought the tickets under the assumption that Ali, Rudolph, and Mayor Young would be in attendance. It smacked of a rip-off. I was told that Ali was delayed in London on a return trip from Pakistan, and there was no way he could get back in time. No one could give me a reasonable explanation for why Wilma and the mayor couldn't make it.

I expressed myself to the organizers in no uncertain terms. I told them I felt the people who had bought tickets were being cheated, and it seemed as though I had been lured to Detroit under false pretenses. However, I agreed to go through with the dinner and gave the audience a show for their money. Jerry Green in the *Detroit Free Press* wrote that I had saved the event. But the wire services ran a story indicating that I had been rude and abusive to the organizers. Typical. Some things never change.

The questions I am most frequently asked about Ali are:

How is his health? How do you rank him as a fighter? Does he have any money left? I will address all these issues.

As I already indicated, I feel that Ali's physical problems are a result of taking too many punches. That's my honest assessment and it's realistic. In 1984, Ali was diagnosed as having Parkinson's disease, which seemed a logical diagnosis because of his often slow, slurred speech, halting walk, and short attention span. These symptoms are painful for someone such as I, who remembers Ali as a rapid-talking superathlete, with the quick reflexes of a cat.

If he does suffer from Parkinson's, I feel there is no doubt that it was brought on by damage sustained in the ring. Muhammad fought several years longer than prudent. He was just a shell of himself in 1980 when Larry Holmes could have used him as a punching bag in their Las Vegas match at Caesars Palace. (Actually, Holmes was reluctant to hurt his old idol, pulled his punches throughout the fight, but still inflicted terrible punishment on an Ali who had lost his ability.)

Howard Bingham, who has been close to Ali since 1962, says, "It's not Parkinson's at all," but then Bingham destroys his credibility by saying, "Ali's just aging naturally. He'll live a long, healthy life."

That's simply not the truth.

The doctor who first diagnosed Ali as having Parkinson's, Dr. Dennis Cope of UCLA, says that "household pesticides, brain trauma, or tiny strokes could be the cause of Ali's problem." In 1984, Dr. Cope said there was no reason to expect Ali's condition to deteriorate, but in 1989, he told Reuters he would not discuss Ali's present condition, but "the disease is usually thought of as progressive in the majority of patients."

Ali received some unusual and controversial medical treatment in 1988. A Yugoslavian immigrant, Dr. Rajko Medenica of Hilton Head, South Carolina, stated that Ali had no brain damage and did not have Parkinson's. He told David Kindred, then of the *Atlantic Journal-Constitution,* "Ali suffers from a pesticide poisoning which causes an unsteady gait, a masklike expression, and slurred speech."

Dr. Medenica's theory was that the pesticides in Ali's blood had been used for termite treatment in homes and in gyms where Ali trained, and that Ali absorbed the chemicals through the skin. A normal level of the discovered pesticides (dieldrin, oxchlodane, and heptachlor) is .04 parts per billion. Ali's levels were 30 parts per billion, 750 times the normal.

Ali's doctors treated him with immuno-metabolic medication on July 5, 1988. He returned to South Carolina on August 24, 1988, for plasmapheresis, a blood-purging treatment. Over four quarts of blood were removed from Ali's body and replaced with blood that Dr. Medenica "customized" for Ali.

The doctor points out that risks are involved because the blood is outside the patient's body. The plasma goes through a "blood cleansing" type treatment, in which it's fortified with vitamins, then readministered to the patient.

For the procedure, Ali was attached to cardiac and blood-pressure monitors. The Yugoslav doctor is said to have treated Yugoslavia's late leader Marshal Tito, the late Shah of Iran, and the late Billy Carter. The doctor and three technicians were assisted by as many as seventeen people when they performed the procedure on Ali in Room 231 at the Hilton Head Hospital. The plasmapheresis, which took five hours, was repeated on Ali at a later date. Some people who know Ali consider Dr. Medenica to be unorthodox and don't believe the treatment helped.

My old friend Floyd Patterson, the ex–heavyweight champion and former chairman of the New York State Athletic Commission, scoffs at Dr. Medenica's diagnosis and treatment of Ali. "No brain damage? Pesticides? Next you'll be hearing he was bitten by a cockroach," said Patterson. "I wasn't born yesterday. Of all the heavyweights ever, he was the best at taking a punch, and he took shots for a long time. When he lost his legs, he lost his defense. He's been hit in the ring for twenty years, my God. The brain slaps up against the skull and it causes scar tissue. That scar tissue makes your brain not work. Common sense tells you it's obvious what's wrong with [him]."

Patterson is one of the few who knew when to get out. He can be thankful that he listened to advisers such as myself.

Incidentally, Patterson is right on the money. That was clearly demonstrated on one of the greatest "Sportsbeat" shows I ever did when Dr. Dominic Purpura, the dean of the Albert Einstein College of Medicine and former dean of the Stanford University School of Medicine used a skull to show how Ali's brain had been damaged by punches.

Muhammad spends most of his time on his eighty-eight-acre farm in Berrien Springs, Michigan, located on Lake Michigan in the southwestern part of the state. It's a two-hour drive from Chicago, and Ali sometimes drives that distance himself. He spends much of the day taking long walks, but is known to drive to college towns and pass out literature about the Islamic religion. Ali lives with his fourth wife, Lonnie, who is thirty-two. He has eight grown children from his earlier marriages and is close to all of them. Each child has been taken care of by Ali with a $1-million trust fund.

Ali, without a doubt one of the world's most recognizable people, does a substantial amount of travel. His first-class travel is always paid for by someone else, usually someone who wants to take advantage of his name and celebrity. It's still too early to tell if Ali will end up like Joe Louis, whose tax problems were well publicized. Louis died broke and in his final years was reduced to shilling for a Las Vegas casino.

At the moment, Ali is in decent shape moneywise, but he's always vulnerable to a schemer or a con man. He has little left from the $72 million that he made in the ring. He's fortunate that in 1988, he could start drawing on a $2-million trust fund that was built in 1978 and '79. Ali made $4 million in those two years, when he was marketed by IMG (International Management Group). IMG executive Barry Frank said Ali could have made much more, "but his decision to rejoin his old manager Herbert Muhammad for a $6-million fight against Larry Holmes ended any chance to market him intelligently. Ali's problem is that he can't say no to people. He allows himself to be surrounded by leeches. They suck him dry."

Of the $72 million earned by Ali, most of it went to the Muslims in "donations," to the IRS, to alimony for three wives, and to managers, agents, and lawyers in fees. The $8 million in trust funds for his offspring did come out of the $72 million in earnings.

Ali's decision to refuse induction into the Army during

the Vietnam War cost him millions in endorsements. Many years later, the public accepted him, but the stigma of being a "draft dodger" forever haunted him with most advertisers. In recent years, he has been able to endorse such products as cologne, cookies, and shoe polish. But he never made the list of America's fifty most marketable athletic personalities. Despite his familiar face, there is not much demand for punch-drunk boxers.

I've already indicated that I thought Ali—in his prime— would have beaten Mike Tyson. I think Muhammad would have beaten all the great fighters—Joe Louis, Rocky Marciano, Jack Dempsey, and Jack Johnson. He was the quickest, he was ring smart, he could take a punch, and even though he wasn't known as a devastating puncher, his punches were sharp, and he had the knack of twisting the punch at the moment of impact to make it more effective.

Muhammad is concerned with the way the public ranks him as a boxer. The morning after Buster Douglas KO'd Tyson, Ali telephoned Tom Hauser, who is writing a biography of Muhammad, and asked, "Now, who will the public say is better, Tyson or me?"

The Hauser book, expected to be eight hundred pages, will be the most lengthy account of Ali's life. Hauser has frequently contacted me, often reading to me passages of the book. My theory is that Hauser has gotten too close to his subject and is too enamored of Ali to write a completely honest and objective book.

Of Lonnie Ali, Hauser says, "If she were Catholic, she would be a saint." And Tom refuses to recognize the full extent of Ali's health problems. When Hauser was told about Ali's needing assistance to eat food, he said, "Oh, it would be a mistake to say that."

Well, I have seen it.

To which Hauser replies, "Well, he has awful table manners, not as bad as Tyson, and the food sometimes dribbles down his chin, but remember, he is frequently extremely exhausted after travel."

Enough, Tom. Tell it like it is.

One of the more bizarre episodes in Ali's life occurred in 1988, when the *Atlanta Journal-Constitution,* in a copyrighted story, claimed that an Ali impostor perpetrated a hoax on a number of U.S. senators. David Kindred suspected that Ali's lawyer, Richard M. Hirschfeld of Charlottesville, Virginia, and/or his associates, impersonated Ali in calls to Senator Orrin G. Hatch (R-Utah), Sam Nunn (D-Georgia), Arlen Specter (R-Pennsylvania), Edward M. (Ted) Kennedy (D-Massachusetts), J. Strom Thurmond (R-South Carolina), as well as then-attorney general Edwin Meese III. The alleged phony calls in an Ali-like voice dealt with these issues:

1. an investigation of a federal prosecutor in Norfolk, Virginia
2. the appointment of a law professor to a job in the Justice Department
3. legislation that could have been worth $50 million to Ali

The numerous calls were followed up by personal visits by Ali and Hirschfeld. The lawmakers and their staffers became suspicious because Ali in person was so different from the Ali on the phone. In person, he had trouble talking, but the impostor always talked rapidly, like the Ali of old.

In the end, Hirschfeld's friend Stephen Saltzburg got the Justice Department appointment; the Norfolk prosecutor, an enemy of Hirschfeld's, was cleared after an investigation; and the proposed legislation, which would have permitted Ali to sue the government for up to $50 million for monies lost when he was illegally barred from boxing for three and a half years following his refusal to be inducted into the Army, died. It's a shame Ali never received compensation for the illegal draft-dodger conviction.

Ali remained loyal to his lawyer friend Hirschfeld and publicly confirmed making the alleged bogus calls. Regardless, Kindred's series had the effect of stopping the alleged con game on Capitol Hill. However, at a news conference on the steps of the Capitol, Ali said he wouldn't discuss the matter further, because all he'd do was "make David Kindred famous, like I did Howard Cosell."

Muhammad, sometimes you're still a very funny person. And I still love you.

In December of 1990, the government filed a $2.1-million

tax cheating case against Hirschfeld. As of this writing, it isn't known if Ali will be involved in the trial.

The same month, Ali made a trip to Baghdad, kissed Saddam Hussein on the cheek, and returned with a dozen hostages. Ali was in sad physical shape, unable to talk, and forced to communicate through sign language. How sad to see Ali exploited by the madman Hussein.

Here are two stories that reflect more insight into the type of person Ali really is:

A Las Vegas casino executive and a former member of the Ali entourage, Gene Kilroy, said, "We went to this old folks' home. There was an old guy in diapers. He didn't have any teeth. They brought Ali to him and said, 'You know who this is?' The old man said, 'That's Joe Louis,' Ali said, 'That's right,' sat down and signed 'Joe Louis.' Afterward, Ali said to me, 'His whole life, he wanted to meet Joe Louis. We all look alike, so let him think he met Joe Louis.'"

Fight publicist and writer Harold Conrad, who used to work Ali's camp, told this story over lunch at the Friars Club. "We went to a women's prison. All the prisoners lined up and Ali went down the row. He was kissing every fourth or fifth one. Ali only kissed the ugliest ones. Some were cute, but Ali passed them and only kissed the ugly ones. When asked why only the ugly ones, he said 'For the rest of their lives, they can say, "Muhammad Ali kissed me."'"

Long live Ali.

CHAPTER FIFTEEN

Winfield Cleansed; Dowd and Fay Botch Boss's Execution

There were no winners in the George Steinbrenner fiasco. Not Steinbrenner. Not Fay Vincent. Not John Dowd. Not Dave Winfield. Not Howard Spira. Not the fans. Certainly not baseball. There were other losers in this chapter of a murky morass known as sports.

George Steinbrenner was a fool to pay a known gambler named Howard Spira $40,000. For that, he deserved punishment. He can't justify dealing with Spira, and it did appear that George paid him to provide damaging information about Dave Winfield.

And admittedly, George made one hell of a mess of the New York Yankees. His trades, his free agents, his managerial selections, his meddling, and his firings were atrocious. His signing neurotic, drug-rehabilitated, and injury-prone pitcher Pascual Perez to a three-year, $5.7-million contract was the last straw. However, for that, under baseball law, he did not deserve punishment. If the commissioner disciplined every owner in baseball for mismanagement, it would take all his time.

Strangely enough, the minority stockholders of the Yankees will tell you that George did a great job. He was taking in about $100 million per year in cash flow, $55 million of that coming from local cable and radio. Even with a losing team, the Yankees were easily the biggest money-making machine in baseball, with annual profit estimates ranging from $30 million up to $50 million. He's been offered over $200 million for the team, and some analysts claim it's worth at least $250 million.

For forcing George Steinbrenner to give up day-to-day operation and his senior partnership of the Yankees, Francis T. "Fay" Vincent was hailed by some as a new Judge Kenesaw Mountain Landis, generally considered to be the Rolls-Royce of baseball commissioners. Absurd! For someone as responsive to the media as is Vincent, his actions were cut-and-dried, a foregone conclusion.

Vincent's reaction to the media must be making Bart Giamatti roll over in his grave. Bart kept an even, open-minded relationship with the media. If necessary, he could be adversarial with the press, evidenced by his speech at the National Press Club. In contrast, Vincent appears to be totally subservient to the media.

Don't get me wrong. Fay Vincent is a nice man. He is smart and well educated, a graduate of Williams (ironically, Steinbrenner's alma mater) and the Yale School of Law. This 6' 3", 240 lb., owlish-looking man uses a cane because of arthritis resulting from a college accident. He fell from a fourth-floor dormitory window ledge while trying to exit a locked room. As a prank, his friends had locked him inside.

His résumé is impressive: former president of Columbia Pictures; a vice president with Coca-Cola; a high official with the Securities and Exchange Commission; an impressive private law practice, first in D.C. then in New York; and deputy commissioner of baseball before succeeding the late Bart Giamatti. As impressive as his record may be, I feel Fay made serious errors of judgment in the Steinbrenner case.

My first meeting with Vincent took place at his favorite breakfast spot, the Rendezvous Room in the Berkshire Omni Hotel. It's also a favorite eatery for David Stern and Bill White.

Over breakfast, Vincent said, "I know Bart talked with you frequently, and I want to do the same." He filled me in on a lot of details from his last day with Bart Giamatti, and that information appears earlier in this book. He expressed dismay over Mike Lupica's clubbed-fingers story and emphasized that Toni Giamatti fell to pieces after the publication of that erroneous article. It prompted me to write Toni a consoling note. Vincent also encouraged me to continue reporting the truth about all of sports and indicated that he felt I was the only one with the guts to do so.

Later, in different conversations, Vincent urged me to continue my attack on players such as David Winfield and David Cone for being paid spokesmen for the New York *Daily News,* and he complimented me for being the only reporter with the fortitude to stand up to the National Football League. And I'll give you odds that as soon as Fay reads this, he'll call Paul "I'm Too Tall" Tagliabue and say that he was misquoted or didn't say it. In the world of sports, that's the way commissioners play the game.

In all of my subsequent conversations with Fay, and there were many, I came away with a troubled feeling that he was overreactive to the media. During the baseball lockout, he was upset about a series of negative articles written by Mike Lupica in *The National.*

"My God, Fay, nobody ever reads that paper, its national circulation can't be over two hundred thousand," I said. "Why are you worried?"

Lupica had told Vincent at the earthquake-stricken World Series that he thought Fay was doing a good job, but Fay seemed concerned later when Lupica, a close friend of baseball-union lawyer Gene Orza, berated him in a phone conversation. Included was a Lupica complaint that Vincent hadn't properly thanked him for a complimentary article. Outrageous! Vincent should have told him to butt out.

Fay tends to hang on every word that is written. In an article in *The New York Times Magazine,* he talked about how much of his time is devoted to the media, giving an illustration of a call from me during the baseball lockout.

"What do you mean, what are we going to do, Howard? We'll keep at it until we get this thing settled."

And there was the time when Fay Vincent called to congratulate me on a piece written by Sally Jenkins in *The Washington Post.* Don't get me wrong, it was nice of him to call. But I was actually surprised when Fay called to discuss an article written by Michael Goodwin in *The National.* The piece was critical of Tony Kubek and other jock announcers and praised me for my longstanding position on jockocracy. It seems the man must read and be concerned with everything that is printed.

When a man is that beholden to and preoccupied with the media, the decision in the Steinbrenner case was very predictable. Just about every broadcaster and writer in New York and in the entire nation has portrayed George Steinbrenner as a bully and a liar. The headline on *Newsweek*'s cover photo of Steinbrenner, "Baseball's Most Hated Man," says it all.

In that atmosphere, Vincent was going to go easy on Steinbrenner? Fat chance. Judge Landis–type courage would have been to go the other way, the unpopular way. Landis was tough, but unswayed by the media or public opinion. All this discussion doesn't mean that I'm defending Steinbrenner. Admittedly he has been a friend of mine for many of the past eighteen years, but I acknowledge that George screwed up. His action was indefensible and reprehensible. And as the ex–football player and my old friend Paul Hornung says, "It doesn't matter if it's Pete Rose or George Steinbrenner, if you're going to dance, you have to pay the fiddler."

I agreed with Commissioner Vincent that George's attempt to defend his behavior in relation to the long association with Spira was truly feeble and "bizarre." Under the baseball system, given almost unlimited freedom by the courts, the commissioner is a dictator. But when Steinbrenner and his lawyers were screaming that Vincent and his hot-shot "investigator" John Dowd were biased, Fay made one statement that troubled me. He was quoted in *The New York Times,* defending his investigation, as saying, "It seems to me that people who have something to say publicly ought to speak to the merits and not to the techniques of the investigation." That statement smacks of the philosophy of a certain senator named Joe who came out of Wisconsin (McCarthy). Please, Fay, don't shoot from the lip. I'll give you the benefit of the doubt and blame it on "imprecise language."

Incidentally, Fay Vincent once told me that he considered

The New York Times to be "the most powerful pulpit in the world." It's okay to have respect for *The New York Times,* but don't quake in your boots when the secretary says the *Times* is on the phone. There were so many leaks to the *Times* during the Steinbrenner investigation—one day to Claire Smith and the next day to Murray Chass—the readers must have thought they changed the name of the paper to *The Leak City Times.*

As earlier indicated, I was a supporter of John Dowd in his investigation of Pete Rose. Bart Giamatti kept me advised about every step of that investigation. However, I am deeply troubled by the manner in which Dowd went after Steinbrenner. Some may say that my thinking is inconsistent, that I am biased because of my relationship with Steinbrenner. Nonsense! I owe George nothing, and I've disagreed with him on many occasions. But facts are facts. The Rose and Steinbrenner investigations were totally different.

It was my view that Dowd's mission was to get George Steinbrenner and to cleanse Honest Dave "I've Been Truly Vindicated" Winfield.

In this four-year play of immorality, Steinbrenner was dirty, Winfield was dirty. Neither distinguished himself as a paragon of virtue. And if his personal contact with me is a barometer, John Dowd certainly failed to distinguish himself or his legal profession in the investigation of George.

I had written a column in the New York *Daily News* in April of 1988 concerning the Steinbrenner-Winfield feud. I was told that Dowd had concluded that for that story, Steinbrenner had fed me information damaging to Winfield. And he made that determination without talking to me. Preposterous! Dowd was wearing blinders. I believe that he was not acting as a responsible prosecutor.

Steinbrenner's closest sidekick, self-proclaimed best friend Billy Fugazy, made a frantic ten-thirty P.M. visit to my Manhattan apartment. Fugazy was the messenger for George, and both were afraid the commissioner would nail George for going after Dave Winfield through Howard Cosell. Additionally, Fugazy was looking to extricate himself from the mess. Admittedly, Steinbrenner and Fugazy frequently bad-mouthed Winfield, but both were aware that my primary source was someone else. It happened to be the man whom I consider to be the most credible person in sports, Larry Fleisher. Larry despised Winfield's agent, Al Frohman, a man who he felt had tried to run his basketball union. Fleisher never hesitated to give me any damaging information he had regarding Winfield, Frohman, and the Winfield Foundation. When I learned that Dowd—without consulting me—was making judgments about my column, I became alarmed. I called Fay Vincent and asked him what was going on. Dowd had finished his report and obviously wasn't too happy that Vincent was asking him to call me. John requested a meeting with me the next morning, and I agreed that he should come to my apartment. Before I deal with that meeting, here is the column in question:

New York, New York—The Dave Winfield–George Steinbrenner situation has turned from a nasty limited engagement into a full-scale war. It's one of the ugliest stories in the history of baseball. It is bound to get uglier as the weeks progress. What began as a common-place feud over a tattletale book by Winfield is now scheduled to become a court battle, where Winfield and Steinbrenner will attempt to savage each other in testimony in Bronx Supreme Court, while the Yankees will attempt to hold together and play baseball with the storm swirling around them.

Frankly, at this point in time, I don't know what to make of any of it. It's so distasteful, so unfortunate, so ugly, so confused. And coming on top of all the continued scandals in New York City government, and coming in the wake of all the scandals in government—North, Poindexter, Secord, Hakim, plus Deaver, Nofziger, and now the resignations of Attorney General Edwin Meese's two top deputies in the light of Meese and Wedtech—it all becomes too much for even the most jaded of observers, such as myself. After all, I am the one who continually warns the public that sports is not fun and games, but big business. I'm the voice continually crying out in support of professional athletes' unions, and the right of athletes to strike, no matter how high some of their salaries may be. And I'm the one continually harping on constitutional rights, and due process, and illegal monopoly, and the corruption of big-time college sports. And I'm the one who quotes from *U.S.* vs. *Ali,* and *Kuhn* vs. *Flood.* In short, you'd think I'd be the one to say, *"Yankees* vs. *Winfield?* So what? Nothing new in sports and lawsuits. Just business as usual." But I can't. Not this time. I learned several days ago, and so reported, that the Yankees are intending to file suit this week against the David Winfield Foundation and David Winfield. The suit will charge both with misappropriation and misuse of Foundation funds. Since 1980, when Winfield signed with the Yankees, George Steinbrenner and the Yankees had been contributing half a million dollars a year to the Foundation, as part of Winfield's deal. (For the past two years, the Yankees have withheld the money; a total of $3 million has been paid rather than $4 million.)

Rumors of trouble and alleged corruption in the Foundation have surfaced before. They have always gone away. This time it appears they will not. Although the New York State attorney general's office claimed no knowledge of any investigation into the Foundation, my sources (who have asked to remain confidential) say that such an investigation will soon be under way.

And my sources have told me of FBI investigations dating back to the 1981 World Series. Not investigations pertaining to the Foundation; let's be clear about that. But related to a former associate of Winfield's. Yankee sources tell me that such testimony in court would be devastating to Winfield's character.

(Reached Friday afternoon by the New York *Daily News,* Winfield stated, "No comment." Steinbrenner told the *Daily News* he would neither confirm nor deny the story.)

Investigations are not indictments. Investigations are not proof of wrongdoing or guilt. But any way you look at it, it is ugly, indeed, is it not? Investigations,

FBI, character damage. The kind of stuff that, if associated with a sport, is usually associated with boxing in all its glory, not baseball.

The Steinbrenner-Winfield feud began years ago. It had been seething and twisting below the surface to a depth unfathomed by the public. It began in 1981, during the World Series, when Steinbrenner felt that Winfield, who went 1 for 22, did not give his all. It grew steadily from then on. . . . I don't know what's going to happen to Dave Winfield. I don't know what's going to happen to George Steinbrenner. But I do know this: a little honor in the right places would have spared us all one more ugly, personal scene in a country that has endured too many privacies in public forums for too long.

Dowd and Kevin Hallinan, director of security for Major League Baseball, arrived at my apartment at nine-thirty A.M. We sat in my study, surrounded by my awards, photos, and memorabilia from my thirty-eight-year association with sports.

It soon became apparent, however, that Dowd was in no way interested in discussing my credibility as a journalist. His main concern was slaughtering Steinbrenner and cleansing Winfield.

"Oh, no, Dave's clean. He's clear of the whole mess, he's as pure as the driven snow," said Dowd.

In thirty-eight years of sports journalism, I have never seen anything like it. This man seemed to have little interest in the truth. He only wanted to cleanse Dave Winfield, to "truly exonerate" him.

It was unbelievable. He didn't care about the man's record, which spoke for itself. Or about the man's mistakes in life that gave a compelling index for his total character, or absence thereof. No, he just wanted to purify that man and convict George Steinbrenner. Getting George was an easy matter. All you had to do was use the facts. Steinbrenner paid money, under what Commissioner Vincent properly characterized as "bizarre circumstances," to a known gambler. And that's that. The commissioner had every right to act and to penalize George Steinbrenner for his misdeed.

But they didn't stop there. Having cleansed Winfield, John Dowd then proceeded to set Steinbrenner up for the slaughter.

It was the most disgusting experience I've ever had in all my years in sports journalism, perpetrated by a man who Bart Giamatti had believed in, and whom I had come to believe in during the Rose investigation. I no longer believe in John Dowd. I don't ever want to see the man again. And I honestly believe Bart Giamatti would roll over in his grave if he knew what John Dowd had done in the whole series of "investigations" involving George Steinbrenner and Dave Winfield.

How sickening.

And Hallinan, the obligatory witness, sat through the meeting in my study like a bump on a log, saying nothing. He had for years known about the Winfield mess, and the Spira mess, but had done nothing. You can't convince me that Commissioner Peter Ueberroth, to whom Steinbrenner gave briefings on Winfield and Spira, kept all the information to himself. The truth was that Peter simply didn't want any involvement with the Winfield Foundation, which generated more smells than the Fulton Fish Market.

Dowd wasn't happy when I confirmed that my primary source for the article was Larry Fleisher, not Steinbrenner or Fugazy. John said my report of an FBI investigation was inaccurate. I'm still not sure that he's correct about that.

If there wasn't an FBI investigation, there should have been. At his hearing, Steinbrenner testified that—according to an Al Frohman employee—Howard Spira, the Winfield associate, had wagered and won $150,000 on the 1981 World Series involving Winfield and the Yankees. That's the series in which Winfield couldn't buy a base hit. His pathetic .045 batting average in the Series was considered the primary reason the Yankees lost to the Dodgers, four games to two. Later, Spira was to charge that Al Frohman had written a phony death threat to Winfield to be used as an excuse for the slugger's awful performance. Questions remain about where Spira got all that money to bet on the World Series. *Sports Illustrated* answered some of the questions in its August 13, 1990, issue, when the magazine revealed that Joseph Caridi, a reputed associate of the

Colombo crime family, had lent Spira $57,000 to bet on the
'81 World Series. And it became known that Spira often bet
money that he didn't have.

So it's obvious there was something going on back in 1981
that warranted attention from the FBI.

In an effort to confirm that there was an FBI investigation, Shelby Whitfield, under the Freedom of Information
Act, queried the New York City and Newark FBI office. The
result was inconclusive.

The Newark office had something regarding the New York
Yankees, Inc., but refused to release the information. In a
letter dated July 10, 1990, the FBI replied, "A search of the
indices to the central records system reveals one reference
responsive to your FOIA request.

"This reference consists of one page which is being
withheld in its entirety."

One reason the FBI gave for refusing to release the
information was that the release "could reasonably be
expected to disclose the identity of a confidential source,
including a state, local or foreign agency or authority or any
private institution which furnished information on a confidential basis, and in the case of a record or information
compiled by a criminal law enforcement authority in the
course of a criminal investigation, or by any agency conducting a lawful, national security intelligence investigation,
information furnished by a confidential source."

The New York office replied that it had two instances, a
total of three pages, where the New York Yankees were
cross-referenced to files. A cross-reference is defined as "a
mention of this subject on a file on another individual,
organization, event, activity, or the like." The FBI refused
to release anything.

Maybe they should rename it the "Freedom of Non-
information Act."

So maybe Larry Fleisher was correct about the FBI
investigation; maybe he wasn't. Although Larry Fleisher
was my most reliable source about Winfield and the Winfield Foundation, I did pursue certain information passed
along by Steinbrenner and Fugazy. As a reporter, I would
have been remiss had I not done so.

I said to Fugazy, "Show me some proof of these investigations." After that, Steinbrenner had his lawyer, William Dowling, call me, as well as his Tampa troubleshooter, Phil McNiff, the ex–FBI man who is a vice president for George's shipping firm. McNiff warned me that the witnesses in the investigation, including Howard Spira, were not too reliable.

Dowling sent another Yankee attorney, a young man named John Ertmann, to my apartment with copies of Steinbrenner's investigation into Winfield and the Winfield Foundation. I looked over the material, which seemed to confirm much of what Larry Fleisher had told me. (Not surprisingly, Winfield has denied allegations of wrongdoing.) Ertmann, who took all the material with him when he left my apartment, later was to depart the Yankee organization on unfriendly terms and appeared as a hostile witness against Steinbrenner in his interview with Dowd.

I'll be the first to admit that George Steinbrenner has many faults, and he admits to this as well. He does dumb things. He makes mistakes. Most of his trades were rotten (he does not admit that all of these were his doing).

All of Steinbrenner's mistakes and faults, however, don't justify the incredibly irrelevant, unnecessary, and erroneous attempt to purify Dave Winfield. Of course, they were convenient and helpful in baseball's efforts to push George off the end of the plank, but in no way do they effectively cleanse Winfield.

In fact, as John Keats wrote in "Ode on a Grecian Urn," " 'beauty is truth, truth beauty,'—that is all ye know on earth, and all ye need to know." The career of "Honest Dave" Winfield hardly exemplifies the work of Mr. Keats, and in his case the truth is hardly beautiful.

Dave Winfield has had a bittersweet career. He was a triple sports star at the University of Minnesota, excelling in baseball, football, and basketball. His outstanding athletic career in college was marred, however, by a shoplifting incident. His professional career really took off in 1980 when he left the San Diego Padres and was signed by the Yankees to a ten-year contract that called for a salary in excess of $20 million. Steinbrenner was enamored of superstar types and thought he had in Winfield someone to replace Reggie Jackson as the "straw that stirs the drink."

And George didn't pay much heed when Ballard Smith, who ran the Padres, warned that he would have trouble with Winfield, his agent, Al Frohman, and the Winfield Foundation, which he would move to the New York City area. Smith hinted that there had been some problems with game tickets for the Foundation in San Diego. Ballard Smith would prove to be a true prophet.

In the eyes of Steinbrenner, Winfield never completely recovered from his putrid '81 World Series performance. Meanwhile, Frohman was a constant thorn in George's side until Al died in 1987. During the years, Winfield put up some decent numbers, but George's claim that he was Mr. May, not a clutch performer in the stretch, stuck in Dave's craw.

However, many of Winfield's problems were of his own making. There were charges that Winfield's foundation was rife with graft and corruption. Bookkeeping was sloppy, records were lost or destroyed, money was misappropriated and spent indiscriminately, and an audit showed that for every dollar taken in, only twenty cents went to the kids for whom the money was intended. Winfield and Steinbrenner traded lawsuits—three each.

Whether he admits it or not, Dave Winfield, not George Steinbrenner, can take credit for bringing Howie Spira into baseball circles. And it was Winfield who loaned Spira $15,000 to pay a gambling debt. At first, Dave denied it, but owned up when Spira produced a copy of the check from Winfield, although he denies knowledge that the loan would help Spira pay a gambling debt. And, according to Spira, it was Winfield who charged Spira usury rates, 11 percent interest per week, for that loan. Spira claimed that Winfield threatened to kill him if he didn't repay. Winfield denies these allegations. Spira did repay—$18,500—and that, to my thinking, made Dave Winfield a legitimate loan shark. As a gambler, Spira had it made. He had access to inside information from Winfield, and he had access to the clubhouse as a result of being a radio stringer for NBC and WCBS. That information may have helped bookmakers or bettors with whom Spira shared it, but it didn't appear to help him. Aside from the '81 World Series, when he allegedly made big money, all indications are that Spira lost hundreds of thousands of dollars. Indications are this guy couldn't pick a winner if you held a gun on him.

Spira has been depicted by the media, and in the Steinbrenner hearing itself, as being a con artist, a cheat, a liar, a creep, a blackmailer, an extortionist, a slime, and an all-around bad actor. Not many people have come to his defense. Rightly so.

Howard gave a pretty good indication of his character when he bragged—and you always have to consider the possibility that he's lying—that due to his Winfield connections he had hundreds of thousands of dollars' worth of credit with bookmakers. He has been quoted as saying that he owes over $2 million to bookies. It's difficult to believe that he could run up that big a deficit with people who normally insist on payment, but remember that Art Schlichter and Pete Rose were able to lose some big dollars, so there may be some truth to it.

Either way, it's obvious Winfield and Steinbrenner both showed poor judgment when they elected to associate with Spira.

Winfield, however, had plenty of troubles in addition to his association with Spira, and George finally nailed him on Foundation irregularities.

Years earlier, both Tommy John and Tom Seaver had told me that they personally knew of extensive misuse of Winfield Foundation funds on indiscriminate limousine usage. Sure enough, in 1989, Steinbrenner filed suit against Winfield, charging "fraud, wrongdoing, and misappropriation of funds." Among other things, George charged that $40,000 had been spent by the Foundation on "wasteful limousine services," and that Foundation board meetings were conducted in various resorts, and that in 1987, $88,079 had been spent to raise only $35,285.

The settlement and agreement, signed by both parties, stated, "Certain allegations made by Steinbrenner and the Yankees were accurate." Moreover, Winfield agreed to pay the Foundation "$30,000 in reimbursement for certain monies inappropriately expended by the Foundation." No other explanation was given.

Don't tell me about Winfield being clean.

David had other problems as well. His former common-law wife, Sandra Renfro of Houston, the mother of his nine-year-old daughter, Lauren Shanel, won a huge palimony suit. In March of 1990, a Houston judge ordered Winfield to pay $1.6 million to Renfro, and $3,500 a month in child support. Winfield is appealing the ruling.

Then there was a suit brought by Ruth Roper, Robin Givens's mother, charging Winfield with giving Roper venereal disease.

Maybe the great writer Pete Hamill said it best and most succinctly when he told me, "Winfield is a sleaze."

To make matters worse for Winfield, he missed the entire '89 season because of back surgery. I honestly didn't think he would come back, but he showed courage in returning and has enjoyed limited success since then, hitting twenty home runs in 1990. And realistically, his better than $9-million contract, which will enable him to close out his career in Anaheim, will take care of a lot of palimony.

But vindicated? Vindicated from what? Neither John Dowd nor Fay Vincent can cleanse Dave Winfield. They can nail Steinbrenner, but they can't convince me that all of Winfield's actions have been "in the best interest of baseball."

How sad. I can still see John Dowd sitting in my study, his face flushed with triumph: "Oh, Dave's clean. I'm sure of that."

Let me be clear about Winfield. I' hold no personal animosity toward the man. I wish him the best. I last saw him in 1990 at a Friars Club roast for Bruce Willis in New York.

I said, "Dave, how are you doing? A lot of things have happened to you."

He replied, "I'm doing fine."

A photographer approached and asked if he could take our picture together. We both declined. But I still wish the man well.

One final thing about Dave Winfield. For a number of years he was the commercial spokesman for the New York *Daily News.* The Steinbrenner-hearing testimony indicated that Winfield's salary from the *News* was at least $100,000 per year. How in the world can a paper be objective in writing about a player to whom it pays money? The *News* does the same thing with Met players such as David Cone and John Franco. Even Jim Quinn, the fine antitrust lawyer whose office represents the Winfield Foundation and Winfield himself, admitted on my radio program that the practice is questionable. Quinn, however, blames the newspaper, not his client. Additionally Quinn acknowledged irregularities by the Winfield Foundation and confirmed that Winfield had written a check for $12–15,000 to cover a certain misuse of funds.

The whole mess with Winfield, and with Steinbrenner as well, is so sickening. It's obvious that all sports are inextricably interwoven with immorality. It's an insult to the intelligence of the public.

It was clear that George was trying to use me as part of his defense. There is no doubt that George dispatched Fugazy to my apartment the night before Dowd was to interview me. They are an amazing pair. They are scheming buddies, but they betray each other like clockwork.

Back in 1988, George warned me, "Don't believe anything Fugazy tells you. You can't trust him."

And during his panic-stricken late-night visit to my apartment, Fugazy told me, "Howard, you know George lies. He's a manipulator. He gets bad advice."

One is more unbelievable than the other.

Fugazy is a character who prides himself in associating with the famous and the near-famous. He is close to the powerful, such as Cardinal O'Connor, Donald Trump, and Manhattan DA Bob Morgenthau.

The Fugazys and the Steinbrenners are as thick as thieves. Fug's son, John, is director of broadcasting for the Yankees. Bill Fugazy wears a Yankee World Series ring that he claims belongs to his son. If George wanted to defy Fay Vincent and covertly direct the Yankees operation, he would likely do it through the Fugazys.

Bill Fugazy had big problems in 1990. He lost a court fight to John Kluge, one of the world's wealthiest men and a former friend of Bill's. The judge ruled that Fugazy misrepresented the value of his limousine corporation, which he sold to Kluge, and ordered Fugazy to pay $46 million in

HOWARD COSELL/WHAT'S WRONG WITH SPORTS

damages. That prompted Fugazy to file Chapter Eleven bankruptcy. He listed among his liabilities a $250,000 personal loan from Donald Trump.

For years, I have been involved with Fugazy in charitable work centering around golf. With Arnold Palmer and Frank Sinatra back in 1966, we developed a College Golf All-America program. Fugazy is chairman of the foundation. From that grew the Howard Cosell day with the All-American Golf Tournament, which precedes the Bob Hope Desert Classic at Palm Springs. My tournament draws the top celebrity golfers in the country and is unquestionably the best of its kind. And recently, we developed a whole new program for black golfers. Rachel Robinson, Jackie's widow, and pro golfer Lee Elder are involved in the program.

So Fugazy had been involved in some good work. He may be a slippery wheeler-dealer, but he has some good qualities and is a likable type. And 1990 was a terrible year for the Fugaroo. In addition to his loss to John Kluge and witnessing his friend Steinbrenner's downfall, he had a bout with prostate cancer. He's undergone surgery and is hopeful of complete recovery.

Fay Vincent and Fugazy are not compatible. The commissioner told me, "I see Fugazy every morning at the New York Athletic Club. He's always bad-mouthing me to people in the club, telling them I was fired from Columbia Pictures and he'd like to see me out of the club." Fay can't stand the guy.

Fugazy is not the only person who speaks unkindly of Vincent. Gene Orza, the outspoken lawyer, says, "Vincent is lucky he was a friend of Bart Giamatti's. He's fortunate to be where he is. Some people think he's a hack. After he left Columbia Pictures, Vincent went to Ted Turner and Bob Wussler of TBS for a job, and they turned him down." And Leo Jaffe, a former president of Columbia Pictures, says, "Fay Vincent is a fraud. Baseball will discover that." It should be noted that Jaffe later saw fit to modify this statement, noting that many people like and are impressed with Fay Vincent.

The day of my Dowd interview, I received a phone call from George Steinbrenner. For a number of years, my normal routine has been to arise at six A.M. I read the

284

newspapers, do my ABC Radio sportscast from my study, have breakfast with Emmy, and take a taxi to my ABC office on the West Side of Manhattan. I then visit the ABC Radio newsroom to see what's going on in the world, and I normally spend a few minutes in the office of news VP Bob Benson.

This particular morning, because of my interview with Dowd, my schedule was pushed back a couple of hours. I was sitting in Benson's office when a telephone call was switched from my office. It was Steinbrenner. In reference to the investigation of him and the upcoming hearing, George said, "Howard, I know you have to protect yourself, but I just want you to know, that whatever happens, I will always be the best of friends with you and Emmy."

I replied, "Fine, George," and we terminated the call.

To Benson I said, "Fasten your seat belt and put on the bulletproof vest. George is panicking. All hell is going to break loose. I know the man. He'll go down fighting."

With the help of his personal publicist, Howard Rubin-stein, Steinbrenner then started a massive PR campaign, going on all the radio and TV shows, and talking to every sportswriter who would listen. The problem was, he wasn't saying anything new; I thought the campaign was crazy.

George knew I was friendly with the commissioner, and it was apparent that the Fugazy visit to my home and the Steinbrenner call were aimed at soliciting my support. It didn't work. I never spoke to Dowd, Vincent, or anyone else on Steinbrenner's behalf.

The day of my Dowd interview and the Steinbrenner phone call, Shelby Whitfield and I had lunch at the Friars Club.

I said, "I can't believe all these people—Winfield, Steinbrenner, NBC radio, and WCBS Radio—would deal with Howie Spira. How on earth can they get that involved with someone like that? I must be the only person in the world who doesn't know the guy or who has never talked with him."

"Oh, I know him," Shelby said. "He tried to work for me at the AP and later at ABC. I never gave him the time of day. I know he did a little work for AP Radio after I left for ABC. My successor there, a friend who had worked for me for many years, Dave Lubeski, told me how Spira had attempted to ingratiate himself by sending a stretch limo to take Lubeski from the Summit Hotel in Manhattan to the National Tennis Center in Queens during the U.S. Open. That was 1981. Could it have been a Dave Winfield Foundation limo? Very likely."

Also over lunch, Shelby explained that later in 1981, he needed to purchase World Series tickets for ABC Radio Sales to use in entertaining clients. He instructed his New York beat reporter at the time, an energetic young man named Mike Leventhal, to try to secure tickets. Leventhal came back and said he could buy tickets from Howie Spira of the Winfield Foundation, but that he wanted scalper's prices, $200 per ticket. Upon hearing this, Whitfield went through the roof and threatened to expose the Winfield Foundation, a charitable organization, for scalping World Series tickets. He didn't, but he did instruct Leventhal to tell Spira to take his tickets and go to hell.

The day after our lunch, I called John Dowd and told him that if he really wanted some evidence about the Winfield Foundation, he should call Shelby Whitfield. It's no surprise to me that Dowd never called.

Meanwhile, George was after me to attend his sixtieth birthday celebration in Ocala, Florida. However, I was still irritated at the attempts of George and Fugazy to use me in Steinbrenner's defense, so there was no way I was going to attend the party.

Fugazy later told me, "It was a great celebration."

The guest list included Chrysler's Lee Iacocca, former ambassador to Italy Maxwell Rabb, Houston Astros and New Jersey Devils owner John McMullen, Meadowlands Sports Authority chief Jon Hanson, singer Robert Merrill, Senators Ted Kennedy (D-Massachusetts) and Dan Inouye (D-Hawaii), a few congressmen, and some local politicians.

The Yankee owner had to experience mixed feelings. He enjoys a good party, especially when he's the center of attention, but he couldn't have been looking forward to his hearing before Vincent, which was to start the day after his birthday.

In the weeks before the hearing, Fugazy called me almost

daily, saying that George wanted me to come to a game at Yankee Stadium. Many times I have been his guest at the Stadium but the last time I was there was Opening Day of 1990. Normally, I would attend several games during a season, including Oldtimers' Day. My refusal to attend was not a case of running out on an old friend. I simply was not about to let George use me as a pawn in his fight to survive his indiscretions with Howard Spira.

Nor was I about to be used by Vincent and Dowd in their efforts to cleanse Winfield.

Fay and I had talked frequently during the first two months of the 1990 season, and he told me he wanted me to help him write a speech that he was to give before the Associated Press sports editors' meeting in Boston.

Then, all of a sudden, communication between Fay Vincent and myself stopped. He never got back to me about the speech, and Fugazy was calling daily to say that Steinbrenner's lawyers were receiving information from Dowd that was unfavorable to me.

Finally, I called Fay Vincent to find out what the hell was going on. I was agitated at some of the things I was hearing, and I wanted an explanation. Saturday, June 23, was the forty-sixth wedding anniversary for Emmy and me. We were receiving many congratulatory phone calls, and we had planned for a big day. I was determined to make a call to Vincent, however; I wanted to clear the air so that nothing would spoil our anniversary day.

I called Vincent's home in Greenwich, Connecticut. No answer. To determine Fay's whereabouts, I called the apartment of Rich Levin, his director of public relations, and a man for whom I have respect and admiration. Our relationship goes back to the Los Angeles Olympics, when he worked for Peter Ueberroth.

Rich said Fay was in Montreal, where ironically enough, he and his wife were celebrating their wedding anniversary. After listening to me, Levin gave me the number of the Four Seasons Hotel and suggested I call Vincent.

I reached Fay and we exchanged pleasantries, including anniversary congratulations. I was frank and direct. "Fay, I am hearing some upsetting things about the Dowd report.

You don't owe me a damn thing, but I would appreciate an explanation."

He responded, "Howard, the only thing about you in the Dowd report is a denial that there was an FBI investigation of Winfield or the Winfield Foundation. That's all."

I continued to Vincent, "What happened, Fay? You said you wanted me to help you with the Boston speech."

"Oh, it turned out to be a brief speech. They only gave me ten minutes, but I do owe you an apology. I should have called you."

"You don't owe me anything, Fay. Have a good time in Quebec."

The conversation ended on a pleasant note.

The next time I heard anything from Fay Vincent was about two and a half months later through an indirect message from Bud Selig, owner of the Milwaukee Brewers. Bud and I were speakers at a sports symposium on August 10 in Madison, Wisconsin. The organizer of that symposium was Ed Garvey, former executive director of the NFL Players Association.

It was good to see my old friend Selig. He said, "I spoke with Fay yesterday, and I told him I would be seeing you today. The commissioner said, 'Tell Howard hello. I like him so. I miss him.'"

I replied to Selig, "I'm worried about Vincent. He's no Bart Giamatti. He's too responsive to the media, and how in the world can he attempt to cleanse Dave Winfield?"

Incidentally, I told it like it is at the symposium, and as usual, the crowd loved it.

It was during the Steinbrenner investigation and hearing that Joe Garagiola came on my "Speaking of Everything" program. Joe, who is fighting an uphill battle trying to revive the faltering "Today" show, is a Steinbrenner fan. However, Garagiola also happens to be a friend of Fay Vincent's. As noted earlier, Fay asked him to emcee the memorial service for Bart Giamatti, and he did a remarkable job.

I knew Joe was fond of Steinbrenner, and I mentioned this to Fay in one of our earlier conversations, indicating that George was helpful to Joe on a project for retired ballplayers called BAT (Baseball Assistance Team).

Joe didn't think Vincent would do more than slap

Steinbrenner on the wrist. He said, "The man has done so much for the game and for people, Howard."

Garagiola told the following story on my program: "I know George Steinbrenner is coming in for a lot of heat. But there are twenty-six club owners, and only one club owner has really come forward and offered to help BAT. I talked to Steinbrenner and said, 'George, if you could just give us a quarter or a tenth of a game to help us out.' He said, 'I'll do you better. I'll give you the net proceeds of a game.' It was a game against Kansas City, after the All-Star Game, and we got a lousy break. It rained and ABC had switched it to a night game, meaning a smaller crowd. That hurt us and I thought we'd get maybe $10,000 or $12,000. Howard George wrote us a check for $150,000. I mean, that's putting it where your mouth is."

One could say that $150,000 is not all that much money for someone who takes in $100 million a year. But the point is he didn't have to do it, and the other owners didn't contribute.

There really is a good side to George Steinbrenner—my family has grown up knowing George, and he has been nice to them—but that doesn't mean that George doesn't have some faults. For example, he does have a terrible temper. He fired a secretary on the spot for booking him on the wrong plane, and he is said to have fired a low-level employee for ordering him the wrong sandwich. As indicated earlier, he makes many mistakes, but measured against the bigger things, I'm not sure he is the ogre he is portrayed to be.

He called me up when there was a big furor over my last book. George said, "What the hell is all the fuss about? We all know what Frank Gifford is. I like Frank. He was a hell of a football player. He's a nice guy, but he's not a journalist. You're the journalist."

So I have mixed feelings about George.

Much of the hatred for the man is generated by the sportswriters, but at the same time, much of his negative press is deserved. He plays ball with sportswriters, seeks to use them, manipulates them. The primary beneficiary of his leaks used to be New York *Daily News* writer Bill Madden. Madden has since turned on Steinbrenner and coauthored a negative book about Georgy Porgy. At the Giamatti news conference to announce Pete Rose's banishment, I said to Madden, "Bill, you are still working Georgy Porgy, aren't you?" He replied, "None of your damn business."

I needled him, "Bill, I don't know, are you sure what you're doing? Maybe the time has come for you to tell that goddamn newspaper that you've had enough. It's ugly."

"Let me tell you something," Madden retorted. "You're finished. Mike Lupica is going to get you."

"What arm of the law does he represent?" I replied.

Lupica is one of those who for years has savaged Steinbrenner. He'd like nothing better than to dance on George's grave.

But no man is all good and no man is all bad. Here's one more example of some of the goodness in Steinbrenner. Football great Otto Graham, the ex–Cleveland Brown All-Pro and Hall of Famer, probably wouldn't be alive today if it weren't for George. Otto survived cancer, and the operation, the hospitalization, and the treatment were all paid for by George Steinbrenner. That matters to me a great deal. I've seen George do other things like that. So don't tell me that everything about George Steinbrenner is bad.

Some claim that George has destroyed the Yankee tradition. That's baloney. He may have the organization in baseball disarray, but it's impossible to destroy the Yankee franchise or the club's tradition. That's because the society has implanted in its mind—the society will never change—that the Yankees are something special. There is a tradition there that no other team has, and nothing will destroy that. Nothing. Wins and losses can't change it. It's the New York Yankees. Despite their record, the Yankees are consistently a strong draw on the road. It's the main reason the Yankees command the top television money, make the most profit, and it's the main reason the club would sell for over $200 million were it placed on the market today.

When Joe Garagiola was by the ABC Radio studios to guest on my program, we made a dinner date for the next week at Sweets in Manhattan's South Street Seaport, one of the world's great restaurants. With our wives, Audrey and Emmy, we had a great meal, over which we discussed the impending Steinbrenner penalty.

Joe said, "I still think he'll get off lightly."

A week later, Emmy and I went into the Isle of Capri for dinner and bumped into Joe and Audrey.

Joe was still saying, "I think George will get a slap on the wrist."

"I don't think so, Joe," I replied. "Vincent is too reactive to the press. He'll throw the book at George."

The same week at the Friars Club, I had a discussion with a brilliant prosecutor, Rudolph Giuliani, the former Manhattan district attorney who narrowly lost to David Dinkins in the New York City mayoral race. I asked for his opinion about the Steinbrenner case. Giuliani replied, "Vincent had better not try to take away Steinbrenner's property. Such a move won't stand up in court."

Finally the hearing came, presided over by Vincent; it lasted a day and a half. The session was supposed to be hush-hush, but a complete transcript was leaked or sold to *The National*. It really made no sense for either side to leak the 372-page transcript, but little in this entire affair has made much sense.

Murray Chass of the *The New York Times* went on WFAN, the all-sports radio station in New York, and said flatly, "The transcript was not leaked. *The National* paid big money for it."

Steve Hershey of *USA Today* told friends that his sources indicated *The National* paid $11,000 for it.

An associate editor of the paper said he wasn't aware of any payment, but admitted that the paper had doubts about the authenticity of the transcript. However, the editors finally convinced themselves of its legitimacy and printed excerpts.

Once *The National* printed excerpts, the commissioner's office then sold complete copies to the media for the $75 printing cost.

The hearing was lawyer dominated, but Vincent was tough on Steinbrenner all the way. He hit George hardest for paying the $40,000 to Spira in 1990 during Vincent's administration and for not telling him about the payment. Fay banged away at George for conducting his own investigations, and for not informing the commissioner's office that two officials of the Yankees—the stadium manager and the chief financial officer of the club—were fired for selling

Yankee property for their own personal gain, items that were left over from promotional giveaways.

George was a dead duck. At one time, Steinbrenner and his own lawyer disagreed over whether George had known that Howie Spira was going to use the $40,000 to pay off gambling debts. George's lawyer said George hadn't been aware of it, but George interrupted and said that he had known.

It was obvious that Steinbrenner was grasping at straws during the hearings. He thought that by bringing up past baseball dirt, he might justify some of his own. He dredged up a story about a major league baseball star's having paid someone to murder his wife; the commissioner in that case had replied that the misdeed had been done in the off-season, indicating that it wasn't a baseball matter. No names were mentioned, but the transcript indicated that a judge was paid $30,000 in that case. When is Fay Vincent or a past commissioner going to explain that one?

At another point in the hearing, when Vincent was asking Steinbrenner why he didn't report to the IRS the two employees who were making money from the sale of stolen merchandise, George replied, "You know all of us in baseball have been aware that many major league players have been beating the IRS at card-signing shows by accepting cash payments." Following the Pete Rose case, baseball had warned its players about not reporting earnings. Once again Vincent offered no explanation to George's point.

But two wrongs don't make a right, and George didn't help his case by pointing out the misdeeds of others.

Vincent made a big deal about going to his home on the Cape to ponder his decision. Who's kidding whom? A child could tell from the tenor of Vincent's questions in the hearing transcript that he was going to clobber Steinbrenner. Fay's period of meditation simply gave both sides a chance to work the media.

Long before George was called to the baseball palace to hear his punishment, the word was out that it would be a two-year suspension. To the surprise of everyone, however, George asked that in lieu of the two-year suspension, he be permitted to step down as operational head of the Yankees for life, as long as the words "suspension" or "banned" weren't used, and he could name one of his sons as new general partner.

It sounded like a tough sentence, and most of the world cheered Vincent. Word of Fay's announcement spread throughout Yankee Stadium during a game, and the Yankee announcers and the crowd rejoiced together. None of them really knew what the hell the decision meant, but lynch-mob mentality was on the loose. The same people who for years had called for George's neck were celebrating his misfortune.

Over the next few weeks, there would be a sickening scenario, with the Steinbrenner and Vincent sides trying to outtrash each other.

George was accused of plying the FBI with personal favors and attempting to use it as his personal police force. Vincent accused Steinbrenner of not living up to the deal. George countered with the same charge. Fay accused George of trying to renegotiate his deal, and Vincent said he would sever George from baseball if he violated the agreement in any way, including going to court.

The repulsive circus went on. George's son Hank decided he didn't want any part of the Yankees, and Steinbrenner's second choice to succeed him as general partner, Leonard Kleinman, was rejected by Vincent. The commissioner set a hearing for Kleinman so that he could answer charges of irregularities in the Howie Spira case, but Kleinman answered the notice of the hearing by announcing his intention of taking Vincent to court. Meanwhile, two of George's buddies, limited partners Dan McCarthy and Harold Bowman, filed suit in Cleveland on behalf of all the limited partners. The suit, which Steinbrenner claimed he did not initiate or support, was an attempt to get a temporary restraining order blocking Vincent's order that Steinbrenner resign as general partner by midnight August 20. The judge ruled against George, and his resignation became effective as scheduled.

The commissioner's office threatened the limited partners when Steve Greenberg, the deputy commissioner, made the asinine statement, "This is war." It was a poor choice of words by Steve, rendered especially inappropriate by the fact that it was made on the same day that three thousand

Americans were taken hostage in an act of war in the Middle East.

About the only person to come to George's defense after Vincent's ban, excluding George's family, of course, and some players and ex-players, was Gabe Paul, the ex–general manager of the Yankees. Gabe's an old friend of mine who for many years lived in my Manhattan apartment building.

The night of Vincent's decision, Gabe called from Tampa where he now lives and said, "My God! It's so unfair. Vincent caved in to the media. It's unbelievable."

Paul, who has always been sympathetic to George, added, "It's crazy. He should never have been suspended the first time by Kuhn." Gabe has admitted to having maintained a close relationship with Steinbrenner during his first suspension, breakfasting with George almost daily, and discussing the daily operations of the Yankees. Bowie Kuhn has since said that he would have kicked George out of baseball for life had he known of his contact and involvement with Gabe Paul during his suspension.

When I called Gabe to see what he knew about Bob Nederlander, Steinbrenner's eventual choice to become senior partner, Gabe said, "He's low-key. He'll do a good job." Paul also said he didn't understand why the other owners should have to approve Nederlander. He added, "After all, they are all competitors. How can they tell a competitor how to run his business?"

Meanwhile, at long last, someone finally picked up on what I had been saying for months on my radio shows. *Sports Illustrated* did a piece in which questions were asked about Winfield, Spira, Dowd, and Vincent. And the *New York Post* referred to a Dowd-Spira conspiracy that brought Steinbrenner down. And in an admission that amazes me, Dowd admitted to making changes in the transcripts of testimony. Dowd defended these changes as routine.

The sad thing is, Fay Vincent didn't have to condone all this. George was guilty of paying Spira the money. That was enough. Vincent could have booted Steinbrenner cleanly. There didn't have to be a kangaroo court and a whitewash of Winfield.

The commissioner's office botched it. They just gave

Steinbrenner more ammunition to go down kicking and screaming.

Had Fay carried out the execution neatly, George's lawyers would have had no legitimate request to the baseball owners that an investigation be made of the practices of Fay Vincent and John Dowd. Nothing came of the request, however.

On August 22, Steinbrenner suffered another setback when the USOC asked him to become inactive as a VP on the Olympic Committee until further notice. Many felt it was a way of easing George out the door gracefully. Always the fighter, however, George said he hoped to return to active status on the Olympic Committee after his baseball situation cleared—whatever that meant. It didn't take long. In January 1991, Steinbrenner was back in good standing with the USOC.

Do you think the Yankee fans won when George Steinbrenner was canned? No way. The day before Georgy Porgy officially gave up his reign, he extended the contract of field manager Stump Merrill through the 1992 season. Merrill is a legitimate minor league manager if I have ever seen one. On his final day, George gave an old favorite, Gene "Stick" Michael, the general manager's job for the next three years.

The Yankees may have produced some exciting youngsters during the second half of 1990. Kevin Maas, for one, looks to be a legitimate home run hitter. But remember, the kids were playing on a last-place club with no pressure. The Yankees have a lot of holes, and under the misdirection of Stump Merrill, they have a long way to go, and it won't be an easy trip. If there is any consolation, it is the lack of strength in the American League East—one club is as bad as the next.

One thing appears certain. Unless Fay Vincent goes ahead and boots Steinbrenner out of baseball entirely, chances are that George, one way or another, will continue to call the shots. On the night of August 19, 1990, he went on WFAN and repeatedly stated that the Steinbrenner family will continue to control the Yankees. It's like Dallas Green said the day after George's resignation: "George thinks he's above the law, and his presence will still be felt with the Yankees."

And if Vincent tries to force George to sell all of his Yankee stock, Steinbrenner would have a hell of a chance of winning in court. As Marvin Miller, the former baseball union boss, told ABC's Barbara Walters, "This is America. Even the baseball commissioner is unable to be a total dictator." It's like I said at the beginning: there were no winners in L'Affaire Steinbrenner.

CHAPTER SIXTEEN

Two Shocks on Christmas Day

The position of baseball commissioner is a cushy job. One's salary starts at $650,000 per year, and there are many big-time perks.

Running a $1.1-billion-a-year business is demanding, but it can also be fun. One gets to attend the games free, and the red carpet is always out. For the most part, the commissioner is treated like a king. My old friend Bowie Kuhn used to refer shamelessly to himself as "the baseball czar."

Ideally, the baseball owners want a charismatic person who exudes style and class. Ford Frick had dignity. Bowie Kuhn was aristocratic and stuffy. Peter Ueberroth was classy and aloof. Bart Giamatti was scholarly, but eloquent and charismatic.

When Bart died, I thought the owners might select someone who was flamboyant and high profile. Bowie actually thought they might ask him to come back, and he was ready to take the job. "I'm prepared for it if they ask me," Bowie said.

Kuhn is an old, dear friend of my family—like a family member to my daughters—and I didn't have the heart to tell him that the owners would never consider inviting him back. When I discussed it with Brewers owner Bud Selig, Bud said, "It's crazy that Bowie would even think of such a thing. He's insane. Everyone gets upset when he goes on shows, giving all types of opinions on baseball matters. His Pete Rose comments are a good example. The man had a long run, but he's history."

Actually, the owners wasted little time in naming the fifty-two-year-old Fay Vincent to succeed Bart. Since Fay was Bart's choice as deputy commissioner, drab or not, to most of the owners he seemed like the logical choice. Only a few owners expressed concern over personality.

Fay's a wealthy one. His stock in Coca-Cola alone is worth more than $20 million. Baseball union leader Donald Fehr, a smart and perceptive man, will tell you that the commissioner normally is a stooge for the owners anyway, so it's fitting that he be wealthy like the owners.

A black cloud seemed to follow Vincent in his first year, and he must have wondered if the job was worth the trouble. Soon after he took office, the San Francisco earthquake spoiled the World Series, which was a one-sided bore. That was followed by a thirty-two-day lockout of the major league players in a bitter labor dispute. Wet weather threatened to wipe out his first All-Star Game (there actually was a long rain delay in the game, which must have been the dullest game of baseball ever played). Then the Cooperstown Hall of Fame Game was rained out and the induction ceremonies had to be moved inside the next day. And finally, Vincent's disciplining of George Steinbrenner was messier than mud wrestling.

But still, the man loves the job, and by mid-August of 1990, Fay had attended games in all twenty-six major league parks.

Vincent's first hot potato was the World Series, interrupted after two games by a major earthquake, and the commissioner handled it in a predictable way.

The correct and sensible thing to have done out of respect to the victims, the scores who died, and the hundreds who were injured, would have been to cancel the last two games of the Series. That wasn't about to happen, however. There was no way the owners and the players were going to lose any money on the Fall Classic. Vincent did play it smart. He delayed the resumption of the Series for a few days and made all the correct PR moves. He involved the local officials and ABC Television, along with the owners and players.

As it turned out, the Giants could have mailed in the last two games. The Athletics won both in lopsided fashion to sweep the Series, and the TV ratings were so poor that Dennis Swanson, the head of ABC Sports and the man who discovered Oprah Winfrey, didn't even want to discuss them.

The big labor dispute before the 1990 season—it seems baseball has one every four years—had been predicted far in advance. The owners' game plan, a successful one as it turned out, was to lock the players out of spring training camps.

Fay Vincent made a smart move when he replaced Barry Rona with Chuck O'Connor as head of the Player Relations Committee. Rona had the stigma of representing the owners during the days of collusion, and the owners lost every collusion case that went to arbitration.

Negotiations between the owners and players started November 28 and lasted until March 18, when a settlement was announced. The lockout became official on February 15, and the next day, Donald Fehr told me he felt "the owners were finally serious about wanting a contract."

Throughout the negotiations, I was talking with both sides, Vincent and Fehr. Both were candid in keeping me advised.

When March 1 rolled around and there was no agreement, the lawmakers decided to get into the act. This always makes baseball nervous, because as previously stated, the owners enjoy antitrust exemptions at the pleasure of Congress. So when the U.S. Senate passed a resolution by a vote of 82–15 urging both sides to "settle their differences promptly and begin a complete spring training and a regular season as soon as possible," it got some attention.

In a refreshing change, Vincent was a hands-on commissioner during the negotiations. In past negotiations, commissioners too frequently took the hands-off approach, shying away from the talks. People such as Donald Fehr and even Marvin Miller were admitting that Vincent's approach was refreshing.

Finally on March 18, agreement was reached on a four-year contract, calling for 17 percent of two-to-three-year players to be eligible for salary arbitration. The players had extracted their pound of flesh from the owners' $1.5 billion, four-year national TV contract.

The owners and players lost little during the lockout, but the big losers were the states of Florida and Arizona, which lost scores of millions in spring training revenue.

The settlement of the labor dispute may have been the high point of Vincent's reign as commissioner. The man may have made points with the writers in sacking Steinbrenner, but to me, he hasn't shown much greatness as a commissioner. He's certainly no Giamatti, and I'm not sure he's even equal to Ueberroth or Kuhn. He may prove to be the worst commissioner since General William Eckert, the "unknown soldier" who was commissioner before Kuhn. Don't be surprised if his tenure is short.

Vincent showed little courage in failing to defend National League president Bill White in a dispute with the umpires union. White almost resigned, and it's my strong feeling that any further showing of nonsupport by Vincent will result in Bill's resignation.

Vincent further irritated me by lobbying for the abolishment of the designated hitter rule in the American League, a rule that has added excitement to a game that needs all the excitement it can muster. It appears that should two writers from *The New York Times* come out against something in baseball, Vincent will immediately join the cause.

Vincent, like most commissioners, is quick to throw his support to franchise relocation. He lobbied for passage of a tax law that would have provided funds for the construction of a stadium in Santa Clara, permitting the Giants to move from San Francisco's Candlestick Park. No luck. The citizens voted no, and now Vincent and the Giants' owners will elicit support from the highest bidders so that the Giants can conduct another relocation sweepstakes.

On Christmas Day of 1989, I was to receive two shocks, both baseball related. Emmy and I, along with our daughters and grandchildren, have long enjoyed a tradition of Christmas dinner at the Andy Robustellis. This Christmas, the Robustellis had thirty-six people for dinner, including fourteen of their grandchildren. We were at our daughter Jill's home on Christmas morning when I got a surprise call from Bowie Kuhn, who was spending the morning with his daughter-in-law, who happened to live nearby.

I told Bowie we would be at the Robustellis for most of the day and that he and Luisa should drop by.

"Do you think it'll be all right?" Bowie said.

"I'm sure it'll be fine," I said. "They have thirty-six people and two more won't matter at all." It was obvious that Bowie had something he wanted to tell me, and he said he would be there.

When he arrived, he hit me with a shocker: "We put our houses up for sale, and we've moved to Florida." The Kuhns had an expensive home in Ridgewood, New Jersey, and a family estate in Quogue, Long Island, near our place in the Hamptons.

I said, "Bowie, it's no time to sell property. The market's so soft."

"You're absolutely right," he replied. "But I have to do it."

My God, I thought, Bowie must be in terrible shape financially. I knew that the law firm he formed with Harvey Myerson had gone under, leaving them with huge liabilities, but I had no idea that it was this bad.

Later Christmas Day, after a wonderful meal at the Robustellis, we returned to our Manhattan apartment, still worried about the Kuhns.

Those thoughts, however, were soon replaced by the horrible news that Billy Martin had been killed in an accident near his upstate New York home. Predictably, Billy's life ended after a drinking bout with a longtime friend, George Reedy. Billy's pickup truck, driven by Reedy, skidded off an icy road and went down an embankment.

I was shocked! I had known Billy for most of my career, and I had always liked him. The man had many faults, but he possessed many good qualities as well.

I agreed to deliver a eulogy for Billy at his wake at the Campbell Funeral Home the night before his services at St. Patrick's Cathedral.

I've given so many eulogies for sports figures, it seems as though I'm the official sports eulogist. There was Roger

Maris, Larry Fleisher, Carroll Rosenbloom, Mike Burke—
the list goes on and on. None, however, is more vivid in my
memory than the one I delivered for Alfred Manuel "Billy"
Martin.

I stood next to the casket, with the widow, Jill Martin,
with Billy's Yankee cap and Yankee jacket bearing #1
hanging between us.

I didn't mince words:

> I know that alcohol was a lifelong problem for Billy
> Martin, but I have known Billy Martin for thirty-four
> years. And for thirty-four years, Billy Martin was my
> friend. He returned from military service in 1955 and
> came by the ABC Radio studios in Manhattan. That's
> when we became friends. Billy had actually started
> with the Yankees in 1950, a year before Mickey Mantle.
> Mickey, I see you sitting there.
>
> And having had that thirty-four-year friendship with
> Billy, I'm in a position to tell you things about Billy
> Martin that you won't hear anywhere else, not any-
> where. And that's what I'm going to do tonight, give
> you an insight into the true values of the man, and what
> made him tick.
>
> One day I got a call from His Eminence Francis
> Cardinal Spellman. He said, "Howard, you know I'm a
> Yankee fan, and Mickey Mantle is my hero. And my
> birthday is coming up four days from now. Could you
> bring Mickey to the residence for a visit with me? That
> would be a great birthday present!"
>
> I contacted Mike Burke, who was running the Yan-
> kees. He said, "Good Lord, of course, Mickey will be
> there."
>
> But Mickey was frightened. He was a green country
> kid from little Commerce, Oklahoma.
>
> However, Mickey came to the residence and met me
> there. But he did not come alone. He brought Billy,
> because Billy was telling him how to act, what to say.
> Billy was preparing him for the whole meeting, which
> went swimmingly. When we came out, Mickey was
> elated. The cardinal had been so gracious to him,
> asking him questions about the Yankees and his per-

sonal life. Mickey credited Billy for the success of the meeting.

When Mickey tells you that Billy was a blood brother to him, believe him. He's telling it like it was. There were so many incidents, but one of the greatest nights in the entire history of baseball was in Scottsdale, Arizona. It was a dinner honoring Kenny Boyer, who was dying of cancer at the time. He was in Tijuana using laetrile in the hope that it would cleanse his body and somehow rid him of the cancer. But he had come back to Scottsdale for the dinner, which was presided over by Joe Garagiola, Bob Uecker, and me. They came from everywhere, east and west, north and south. There were owners, managers, coaches, and players. Billy Martin was in attendance. And Reggie Jackson was there. And in spite of all the past problems between Reggie and Billy, Reggie was happy to see Billy.

Mickey, you gave me an interview that night with Billy. And you said, "Howard, this is Billy Martin. He's my blood brother. He cares about people. He's always helping. People just don't understand him." I'll never forget those comments, made by Mickey in total sincerity.

At that time I started recognizing some people in the audience at Billy's wake, people who knew him well, many of whom had been helped in some way by Billy, people such as Dick Williams and Dick Tidrow and Jim Spencer and Bucky Dent. And Tommy John.

You, Tommy John, and your wife, Sally. I don't have to tell you about Billy, as a manager or as a player. He was a journeyman player, but like the old man Casey Stengel used to say, he could produce under crisis conditions, and thus the incredible performance of the '53 World Series. Managing? Name the team. Detroit. Minnesota. Texas. How about Oakland? He could turn a team around overnight. So his baseball credentials don't have to be spelled out, back and forth, by me.

No, I'll just tell you about the real Billy Martin. Billy was standing next to the batting cage in

Scottsdale on a hot spring-training afternoon. The kid in the cage was lunging, honing, working, and Billy, speaking so the kid could hear every word, said, "He has the capacity to be the greatest player of all time. All he has to do is believe it. You have to let him know it. Tell him how you believe in him. Tell him what he means to everyone else around him."

The kid smiled and he kept hitting away and hitting away. Finally, he was out of the cage, and he came over to Billy. "You're my man," said Billy. The kid who was in the batting cage? Rickey Henderson.

And that was the real Billy Martin.

The crowd was transfixed as I said:

Now perhaps the greatest Billy Martin story of all. It was at my pro-am golf tournament in Palm Springs. I tell you, Billy loved that tournament. He loved golf. He won the tournament twice.

This particular day, one of the great leaders in the history of American sports, maybe the greatest leader, made his last public appearance at that golf tournament. He was Colonel Earl "Red" Blaik, the former Army football coach.

We reminisced. We reminisced about his favorite player whom he ever coached. It was the all-America end Don Holleder. And how he converted that all-America end to a T-formation quarterback. And they were calling Holleder "Blaik's Folly." But the day of the famed Army-Navy rivalry, an underdog Army team, which had lost three games, crushed a Navy team led by great all-America quarterback George Welsh, now the coach at Virginia. Suddenly "Blaik's Folly" was Blaik's hero. Later, Major Don Holleder was to die on duty in Vietnam, and Colonel Blaik told me on national television, yes, he meant more to him than any man who ever played for him.

The colonel and I reminisced through all of that, and at the end of it, Billy Martin, sitting there, quietly, silently, with Joe DiMaggio, said to me, "Howard, please introduce me to this man. There's nobody in this world I've ever looked up to more." And Joe DiMaggio said essentially the same thing.

So I took Colonel Blaik over to Billy Martin, and I said, "Colonel, this is Billy Martin; you know, he's managed the Yankees a few times. Of course, you know the Yankee Clipper, Joe DiMaggio."

He said, "Yes." And he looked at Billy Martin with a wry smile, and he said, "Yes, I know you, young man. You know how to lead men. You can produce winners." And Martin's face lit up. He was all aglow, praise from Colonel Blaik. Suddenly, he was being symbolized as everything that Billy dreamed of being, a great leader of men. "But," Colonel Blaik said, "you've got to remember one thing, young man." This was three years ago and Billy was on the verge of sixty. "Always remember," he said, using the title of his great book, "You have to pay the price."

And now, Billy lies here, and he's paid the ultimate price. But for that day at least, he had received communion from the man who looked for all the world like MacArthur, who indeed got permission from General MacArthur to play two-platoon football. This great man had given the ultimate accolade to Billy Martin, and Billy never forgot it. The last time I was with Billy, he said, "Colonel Blaik thought I was a leader."

So Billy, you lie there now, and you've paid the price. But I want the people here to know, and I want you to know, George Steinbrenner, that the happiness you brought to Roger Maris, you also brought to Billy Martin. And when Billy was placed in the monument area of Yankee Stadium, it was heaven for him to smell the flowers while the scent was still there.

And as Joe DiMaggio says, Billy doesn't belong in the Hall of Fame as a player—forget the '53 World Series—but he belongs there as a manager. He could strategize like nobody else. He was a great manager.

That was the Billy Martin I knew. God bless your soul. May you rest in peace.

There wasn't a dry eye in the house. Mickey Mantle, with tears streaming down his face, came over to me, hugged me, kissed me, and said, "Howard, I can't tell you. I've got to get out of here."

Over three thousand mourners said good-bye to Billy the next day at St. Pat's. Steinbrenner critics accused him of orchestrating the funeral for publicity purposes. George and Bill Fugazy sat next to Mickey Mantle and Richard Nixon.

Before his body was cold, many sportswriters were ripping Billy for his drinking and his fighting and for the way he had treated them. They didn't know the Billy Martin I knew.

Martin's death capped off a horrible year for baseball. There had been the Pete Rose scandal; then Bart Giamatti's death; the earthquake during the World Series; and now Billy's death on Christmas Day.

And on top of that, baseball was worried that it might have an indigent ex–baseball commissioner.

I had met with Fay Vincent two days before Christmas, and he told me he was hearing awful stories about Bowie Kuhn's financial situation. There had been all kinds of stories following the collapse of the Myerson & Kuhn law firm, but little did I realize the true impact of the situation until Bowie talked with me on Christmas Day.

At Billy Martin's funeral, I sat with Bill White, the new president of the National League. Bill said, "Fay is very worried about Bowie. We can't have an indigent commissioner, baseball can't allow that."

I agreed with Bill.

White stated, "I don't understand it. Bowie should have a good pension." Bill said he would take it up with Fay on January 2, when the baseball offices reopened following the holidays.

The next week, I spoke with Vincent. "Howard, I expect Bowie's debts are absolutely huge. We're gonna have to take care of him. I'll reach him somehow, I'm gonna help him."

Fay explained that Bowie wasn't receiving a pension, that he had elected to take a lump cash settlement of almost $1.5 million in lieu of a pension.

Vincent asked, "What is he going to do in Florida?"

"On Christmas Day," I replied, "he said he would open a consulting firm and would deal with mergers and arbitrations."

"What does he mean, 'mergers and arbitrations'?"

"I don't know, Fay; it's a sad thing. The man is trying to create a business somehow. He asked me if I knew anyone in Florida who might give him leads."

The case of Bowie Kuhn is indeed very sad, and also very curious. After he left baseball, he missed the commissionership in a serious way. For fifteen years, from 1969 through 1984, he had enjoyed the good life, the chauffeured limousines, the extravagant expense account, and most of all, the royal treatment that baseball and society extend to the commissioner.

After Bowie left office, he and his wife, Luisa, found it hard to adjust. When he would go to functions such as the Tennis Hall of Fame inductions at Newport, Rhode Island, something they normally attend every year, he still acted like the baseball czar, and Luisa still referred to him as the commissioner.

And Bowie ruffled the feathers of official baseball when he showed up at the Baseball Hall of Fame ceremonies in Cooperstown holding court with the media and giving his opinion on issues involving Pete Rose and George Steinbrenner.

When Bowie left baseball, he went back to his old law firm in New York, Wilkie, Farr, Gallagher. His salary was reported to be $175,000, quite a comedown from the commissioner's job, and some legal experts claimed that Bowie never regained his stride as an effective lawyer.

Besides, his heart was elsewhere. His well-known dream was to own a major league baseball team in his native Washington, D.C. Bowie frequently talked with me about buying into such a club, but nothing ever developed, and truthfully, I was never interested.

Kuhn made a major change in his life when he joined flamboyant trial lawyer Harvey Myerson, our old friend from the USFL case, in a New York law firm to be named, appropriately enough, Myerson & Kuhn.

Harvey set his annual draw at an attractive $1.4 million; Bowie was to receive a substantial $500,000 annually; scores of other lawyers were also signed up at inflated salaries. The firm's prospects looked great, but it was too good to be true.

Even had the legal firm made it big, Bowie's heart was still in baseball. That fact was obvious when he came on a radio program with me in August of 1989 and, strangely, began saying nice things about an old enemy, George Argyros, then the owner of the Seattle Mariners.

Off the air, I said, "Bowie, what gives with Argyros? You have always been so outspoken about the man. Good Lord, he was one of the men who got you fired as commissioner."

"Howard, I'm trying to make up with Argyros. I'm trying to encourage him to drop the sale of the Mariners to Jeff Smulyan and the Indianapolis group. I want him to sell the Mariners to me so that I can move the club to Washington, D.C."

What a wild scenario. Fay Vincent told me, "How crazy. The man's insane." This was a classic case of a former baseball commissioner trying to manipulate the sale of a ball club for his own personal gain.

Argyros went ahead and sold the club to Smulyan.

In November of 1989, *The American Lawyer* published a shocking story of total failure of the Myerson & Kuhn firm. It included numerous charges of illegal appropriation of funds by Myerson for his personal use. There was the purchase of an $89,000 gift from Cartier. Before the end of the year, the firm went belly-up, with liabilities of $11 million. The firm's assets wiped out much of that, but in the end, Harvey and Bowie were still held personally accountable for over $3 million. Myerson came up with $800,000, but Bowie's creditors accused him of skipping town. Newspaper headlines screamed, "Kuhn Reported to Be in Hiding From Debts." It was the worst kind of publicity for Bowie and Luisa, and my heart ached for them.

Here's what made it look so bad for Bowie. In January of 1990, he sold their home in New Jersey and bought a house in Florida. The Florida home, at Marsh Landing on Ponte Vedra Beach, cost $1 million and under Florida law, cannot be touched by creditors. For days, a Florida deputy sheriff searched for Bowie to serve him with papers from creditors in New York. Little did it matter. It turned out that Bowie was pretty well protected.

Not only could creditors not touch his new million-dollar home, he put his $1.5-million baseball settlement into an

IRA, which creditors could also not touch, and the $1.3-million estate in the Hamptons was in Luisa's name and therefore protected from those seeking payment from Myerson & Kuhn. Bowie may be many things, but he's not indigent.

After all the adverse publicity, Bowie was moved to put out a combination press release/letter to the media and friends in which he explained his move to Florida and defended his position in regard to creditors of the law firm.

In essence, Bowie said he didn't feel responsible to the creditors, although his lawyer said Bowie had come forward with $250,000.

Kuhn told the press that in spite of being hounded by creditors, he had no plans to file for personal bankruptcy and was in good financial shape. The former commissioner said he was not concealing his whereabouts and was not hiding his property.

Bowie made a trip back to New York in the middle of May, having called in advance to find out if he could stay at our apartment. We took good-natured kidding from our friends about harboring a fugitive. Bowie looked good and we enjoyed his visit, but as earlier stated, he made me nauseous by telling me that Pete Rose belongs in the Hall of Fame.

On August 20, 1990, the Kuhns were at their summer place in Quogue and Bowie dropped by for a cocktail. The ex-commissioner was blasting Fay Vincent for the job he was doing. Bowie was correct when he said, "Fay has butchered the Steinbrenner case. All of baseball is being run by *The New York Times.*"

The ex-commissioner also feels that he has been constantly criticized unfairly since he left office. Bowie said, "You have to look at the facts, Howard. In a recent phone conversation with Peter Ueberroth, I told him, 'Peter, you know I disagreed with your decision to pardon Willie Mays and Mickey Mantle and to allow them back into baseball despite their PR jobs with gambling casinos.' I told him that I felt his decision would open the door to wrongdoing."

And somehow, Bowie rationalized that the Rose problem and the Steinbrenner-Spira problem supported his argument.

Additionally, Bowie defended his outspokenness about the Rose case this way. He said, "Rose's attorney, Reuven Katz, asked me if I would be willing to be an arbitrator in the Rose-Giamatti dispute. I indicated I would be willing to help in any way I could."

Kuhn explains that his hostility to Vincent developed after "Fay told Giamatti that he shouldn't trust me and questioned my veracity."

Bowie added, "Baseball didn't fare too poorly during my reign of rigid gambling policies and old-fashioned values."

However, there is now a postscript to the story. I had lunch with Bowie on Tuesday, November 6, 1990, at the Friars Club. Suddenly Bowie was saying to me, "I haven't made up my mind yet about Fay Vincent."

This is my own surmise: I have to believe that Bowie is seeking some favor from Fay Vincent for his own purposes, and this adds to my disappointment in Bowie Kuhn.

Le Grand Boo is something. Many times I have disagreed with him, but in spite of my disappointments, I still like the man. He can stay at my place anytime.

CHAPTER SEVENTEEN

Sex, Lies, and Videotape

This is a different chapter for me to write. It deals with AIDS in sports, homosexuality in sports, sexual promiscuity in sports, and gang rape in sports. These are not very dignified subjects, but all are part of the sports scene, and in doing a book of this nature, I feel compelled to address them.

The American public seems to hold its sports heroes in such high esteem, puts them on pedestals, that the public becomes shocked or incensed when the heroes demonstrate that they are mere mortals who share the weaknesses of others.

Our sports heroes are expected to live the exemplary life of the traditional "American hero," heterosexual, monogamous, and virtuous—high goals, and difficult for some to attain. We seem to expect our athletes to be as we would have politicians be—puritan clean.

The same American public is more liberal when it comes to TV, movie, and music stars, whose personal lives are constantly scrutinized and generally held to a standard of "the more flamboyant and outrageous the better." We would need many pages to list all the gays in the entertainment field, and if a male movie star or singer sleeps with another man, the reaction by some seems to be "how artistic." When a pro football player does it, it's an outrage. And when a pro basketball player such as James Worthy of the L.A. Lakers orders up two hookers to his Houston hotel room and gets caught in a police sting, it's headline news, just as when Olympic star Edwin Moses picks up an undercover "hooker" in Hollywood.

I should point out that motion picture studios and gay stars themselves go to great lengths to protect their sexual identities. We've all heard of convenience dating and convenience marriages to deceive the public regarding the sexual preference of gay stars. Among the stars who took great care to stay in the closet were Rock Hudson, Liberace, and Montgomery Clift. It remains a fear that America is not ready to accept homosexuality among its entertainment heroes. It appears that the feeling is the same in regard to sports stars.

If you're going to make the millions of dollars in sports and be the role model for America's youth, you'd better conform to the "hero standard" or pay the consequences.

This may seem ironic, as fans welcomed back with open arms players who have disgraced themselves and their profession through shameful behavior. Keith Hernandez, a self-admitted cocaine abuser, was one example, and womanizer extraordinaire Wade Boggs was another.

Where unpopular behavior has hit athletes is in the pocketbook in regard to endorsements. Commercial sponsors and advertising agencies shy away from jocks who have involved themselves with scandal or controversy.

Sports has always been full of hell-raisers, hard drinkers, and womanizers. Babe Ruth was one of the worst. But only in recent years has the media started to publicize the indiscretions of sports figures. This parallels the changes in the way the media covers political figures. Is this part of a trend toward tabloid journalism or sensationalism? Whether it is or not, it is now accepted procedure by practically all electronic and print journalism outfits.

Right or wrong, most sports fans in America expect their sports heroes to be as pure as the driven snow. I can't quarrel with this, as I do not condone permissive behavioral patterns, and I don't hesitate to detail indiscretions in this chapter. The accounts, most sad and some humorous, are factual, and the names have not been changed to protect anyone.

One of the most hideous problems facing America and the world is AIDS. And sports is not immune.

In the boxing ring corners of many states, it is now mandatory that cornermen wear rubber gloves in an effort to prevent the transmission of the AIDS virus.

Many people seem to automatically associate AIDS with homosexual and intravenous drug abusers, but it's becoming more apparent that AIDS is a threat to all Americans.

As of this writing, four outstanding professional athletes have died of AIDS; two contracted the virus through sexual activity and the other two through intravenous drug use.

First, there was ex–Washington Redskin All-Pro tight end Jerry Smith, followed by former world lightweight boxing champ Esteban DeJesus, the automobile racing star Tim Richmond, who drove Indy cars and NASCARs, and ex–major league player Allen Wiggins.

Smith was a Californian who played college football at Arizona State under Frank Kush, a coach who had his priorities out of whack. Kush had a drill sergeant mentality and was perhaps the most outrageously demanding of all college coaches.

In 1964, Jerry Smith was a Redskins ninth-round draft choice with a reputation of being an overachiever. He became a 210-pound undersized tight end in his rookie season under Redskins head coach Bill McPeak. He later played for Otto Graham, Vince Lombardi, Bill Austin, and George Allen. In all, Jerry played with the Redskins for thirteen seasons and still ranks among the team's leading pass receivers with 421 catches, 60 of them for touchdowns. He was an All-Pro for two seasons and helped the Redskins reach the Super Bowl in 1972.

Vince Lombardi said of Jerry, "I wish I had a whole team of Jerry Smiths."

During his football career, it wasn't well-known that Jerry Smith was gay. Actually, he struggled with his sexuality in his early years with the Redskins and was bisexual. Finally, women lost out, and Jerry became an open homosexual.

Smith wasn't the only gay on the Redskins. Another was Dave Kopay, a running back who also played for the San

Francisco 49ers, the Detroit Lions, the New Orleans Saints, and the Green Bay Packers.

Kopay and Smith were lovers in 1969 when both played for Vince Lombardi. Jerry actually introduced Kopay to gay bars in Washington and other places such as Fort Lauderdale and Acapulco.

Other times, Smith would make trips to Fort Lauderdale, Fire Island, Santa Monica, and Cleveland, where he frequently visited gay bars and, using an assumed name, would pick up male lovers.

Smith met and became friends with Roy Cohn, the famous New York lawyer, at Fire Island. He later shared Mardi Gras dinners with Cohn in New Orleans. Cohn, too, was a homosexual who died of AIDS.

According to *Washingtonian* magazine, Smith often used the name Lance, but dropped that name after Lance Rentzel of the Dallas Cowboys was arrested for exposing himself to a young girl.

Yes, all of this in the National Football League. Maybe it really is the National Fantasy League. So much for the macho image of the NFL.

There have been a number of gay or bisexual football players in the NFL over the years. But Kopay, at the urging of Smith, was the first to come out of the closet. He wrote a best-selling book, *The David Kopay Story,* about his homosexuality.

Most of the Redskins knew about Smith's sexual preference, but since he didn't bother most of his teammates, nobody seemed to mind. As long as he performed well on the field, that was what mattered.

One exception was Jon Jaqua. Smith took a liking to Jaqua from the very beginning, worked with the handsome Jaqua after practice, found him an apartment not far from where Smith lived in Georgetown, and finally got into bed with him under false pretenses.

In the May 1987 issue of *Washingtonian,* Perry Deane Young, coauthor of the Kopay book, wrote:

> One night after a preseason game on the road, Kopay and Smith went out to a gay disco, where they both got drunk. When they returned to the team's hotel, Kopay

went to sleep and assumed Smith had done the same. But the next morning, in the hotel coffee shop, Kopay was approached by a nervous Jaqua, who asked if he could speak to him alone in the lobby. Then he told Kopay that the night before, Jerry had come to his room and asked if he could sleep there because he'd been locked out of his own.

Jaqua obliged, but after they had lain down, Smith put his arms around him and tried to make love to him. Jaqua was shocked and said he dragged Smith into the bathroom so they wouldn't wake up his roommate. With the bathroom light in his eyes, Smith crossed himself and sobbed, "God, forgive me; I don't know what I was doing, I must be crazy."

Kopay, in an awkward position because of his homosexuality, told Jaqua that Smith was just drunk and didn't know what he was doing. Kopay would eventually confess to Jaqua that he, like Smith, was homosexual.

After leaving football, without officially coming out of the closet, Smith lived openly as a homosexual, actually owning and operating a gay bar called The Boat House in Austin, Texas. A local gay newspaper, *This Week in Texas,* listed the former NFL All-Pro as the owner of The Boat House and noted his past association with the Washington Redskins.

The straight press took no notice that the once-famous football player was running a gay bar.

It was while in Austin that Smith contracted AIDS.

In 1985, Smith returned to Washington and moved in with Joe Blair, the former public relations director for the Redskins. Years before, Jerry had lived with Blair.

Smith was hospitalized in December of 1985 and was in and out of hospitals until he died on October 15, 1986, at the age of forty-three. Having dwindled down to one hundred pounds, he was skin and bones and died a horrible death.

Two weeks after his death, at a Redskins home game before another sellout crowd of 55,671, Smith was inducted posthumously into the Redskins Hall of Stars at RFK Stadium.

Thus concluded the sad story of the NFL's first victim of AIDS. For the most part, the NFL was able to suppress the real story of Jerry Smith's life and death.

There was a third gay player on that Lombardi-coached Redskins team. Vince told me, "I've got a big gay player who sure as hell can't play football. He had good statistics in school, but he was a wasted draft choice."

In May of 1989, former world lightweight boxing champ Esteban DeJesus died of AIDS at the age of thirty-seven. Esteban first gained prominence when he floored Roberto Duran in the first round and went on to win a ten-round decision in a nontitle fight at Madison Square Garden. It was Duran's only loss in the first thirteen years of his career. Duran avenged the defeat with an eleventh-round knockout of DeJesus in Panama in 1974, and Roberto won their third fight, a twelve-round knockout of Esteban in Las Vegas in 1978.

From having worked his fights, I can personally attest that Esteban DeJesus was a great fighter. But sadly, he started using cocaine and heroin early in his career.

On Thanksgiving Day of 1980, after having injected himself with cocaine, DeJesus became involved in a traffic dispute and with a pistol, fatally shot another driver, a twenty-one-year-old man, in the head. He was sentenced to life in prison.

In 1985, Esteban learned that his brother, with whom he had shared needles, had died of AIDS. Shortly thereafter, the ex-champ—he was WBC lightweight champ from 1976 to 1978—tested positive for the AIDS virus, and was released from prison and assigned to an AIDS clinic in the Río Piedras district of San Juan, Puerto Rico.

DeJesus wasted away to ninety pounds before he died.

Another tragic story. From lightweight champ of the world to marijuana, to cocaine, to heroin, to cocaine-heroin speedballs, to first-degree murder, to a terrible death from AIDS.

The third prominent sports figure to die from AIDS was flamboyant race car driver Tim Richmond.

This hard-charging driver with movie-star good looks was the Rookie of the Year in the 1980 Indy 500. But he proved undisciplined as an Indy car driver and crashed in a number of races in 1980 and 1981. His family finally took him out of the Indy car, forcing him to switch to NASCAR racing. Despite being a Midwesterner, he was a natural on the good old boy circuit. Richmond never won the NASCAR national championship, but one year, he won more NASCAR races than any other driver.

Tim was always confronted with drug rumors. NASCAR initiated a drug-testing program for drivers, and many thought it was aimed at Richmond. In 1987, he tested positive and was barred from the Daytona 500. NASCAR officials refused to reveal the identity of the drug for which Richmond tested positive.

A week later, Richmond was retested, and the result was again positive. This time, NASCAR officials revealed that the drug in Richmond's body was ibuprofen, a drug found in over-the-counter preparations under the brand names of Advil, Motrin, Nuprin, and Rufen. It is normally taken to relive pain, stiffness, and inflammation caused by a number of disorders, including arthritis and gout.

A couple of years later, Richmond was hospitalized because of double pneumonia. He came back from the illness and won two major races, at Pocono and Watkins Glen, but those were his last two races. He was rehospitalized with what was again described as double pneumonia.

In August of 1989, Richmond died at the age of thirty-three. His family released a statement revealing that Tim had died of AIDS, contracted from a heterosexual relationship.

The highly touted Tom Cruise movie *Days of Thunder* was based on the life of Tim Richmond.

In January of 1991, baseball suffered its first death from AIDS when Allen Wiggins died at the age of thirty-two. Wiggins, an infielder, came up through the Los Angeles Dodger minor league organization, but spent his major league career with the San Diego Padres and Baltimore Orioles.

He helped lead the Padres to the World Series in 1984, the only World Series appearance for the Padres in the 22-year history of the club. Wiggins was treated for cocaine dependency in 1985 and was suspended from baseball indefinitely in 1987 when he failed a drug test.

AIDS is the scariest problem to come along in years. America must become better educated to the danger of AIDS, and more resources must be devoted to developing a cure for this heinous monster.

The Jerry Smith story raises the question of the level of homosexuality in sports. There appears to be more than most people realize. Last year, Dave Pallone, a National League umpire from 1979 until 1988, when he was fired for "unprofessional behavior," wrote a best-selling book called *Behind the Mask.*

In the book, Pallone reveals that he is a homosexual and has made love with a couple of major league players and a movie star. He didn't reveal names, but on Phil Donahue's show, Pallone said there were enough gays in baseball to field a complete team and a front office.

Pallone had a controversial ten-year career, getting his break into the majors as a scab during the umpires' strike. He had a hot temper and was involved in the Pete Rose confrontation when the then Reds manager was suspended for thirty days and fined $10,000 for shoving Pallone.

The umpire became more daring about his homosexuality in the mid-1980s. He frequented many gay bars and left himself vulnerable to straights in baseball, who set him up twice with "sexual encounters" and then reported him to baseball officials. Eventually, Pallone was fired by Bart Giamatti after Pallone was allegedly involved in an upstate New York homosexual incident involving young males. He admitted to having been on the scene of the crime in Saratoga, New York, but proclaimed his innocence.

Pallone didn't blame Giamatti for his dismissal, but cited pressure from National League owners.

In his book, Dave Pallone defends sodomy, a disgusting subject for most of society, and against the law in many states and the military.

Normally, I'm a liberal, and I'm well-known for respecting the rights of minorities and all individuals. But in the case of homosexuality, let's just say that I don't condone it, and you won't find me marching in any gay rights parade. Like Bowie Kuhn, in some ways, I'm old-fashioned.

However, it's common knowledge that there have been many talented gay professionals. And in my thirty-eight years in the electronic media, I have worked with some bisexuals who were excellent professionals and some who weren't.

There have always been questions about the sexual preferences of athletes in women's tennis and women's golf.

Billie Jean King lost a lot of money from endorsements and other opportunities after an old female lover named her in a palimony suit. King refuses to discuss the issue. When a reporter for the old *Washington Star* tried to contact Billie Jean for a comment for a series on sports homosexuality, the former tennis great slammed the phone down.

Tennis great Martina Navratilova handled her bisexuality differently. Navratilova, in her best-selling book, *Martina*, coauthored by George Vecsey, the excellent writer of *The New York Times,* openly discussed her bisexuality.

Martina wanted to go public earlier, but her managers prevented her from doing so because they feared such a disclosure might have a negative effect on her application for naturalized citizenship (her book was not published until after she became an American citizen). Martina's relationships with prominent author Rita Mae Brown and current gal pal Judy Nelson, the Texas beauty queen, are well documented.

Surprisingly enough, Martina's coming out of the closet didn't seem to have much effect on her career. But after she won her record ninth Wimbledon singles championship in 1990, the Australian ex–tennis great Margaret Court gave her some stinging criticism that was played heavily around the world.

In newspaper and radio interviews, Court, a winner of twenty-five Grand Slam events, including all four in one year, blasted Martina for being "a bad example for younger players because of her admitted homosexuality."

Margaret said that some tennis players have been led into homosexuality by older players. She also said that she believes Martina was influenced into a lesbian lifestyle during her early years on the pro tour. "If I had a daughter on the circuit, I'd want to be there," Court said. "I'd want to protect her against the advances of Martina and others like her."

On the advice of her manager, Peter Johnson of International Management Group in Cleveland, Navratilova would not comment on Court's quotes.

Tennis authorities must hold their breath about "unfavorable publicity" resulting from their switch-hitters.

One tennis star they never had to worry about was Chris Evert. She was a great player and a great representative. Chrissy had a torrid love affair with Jimmy Connors, a fling with movie star Burt Reynolds, followed by a failed marriage to British tennis player John Lloyd, and now a storybook marriage to the handsome former ski star Andy Mill.

Baseball players have long been famous for sexual encounters, and there have been some strange cases. Players Jim Bouton and Dave Winfield wrote books detailing the sexual appetites of the players and the baseball groupies or Annies.

And who can forget the Yankee pitchers Mike Kekich and Fritz Peterson, who swapped not only wives, but kids as well? Even more shocking was the girl who was obsessed with Phillie first baseman Eddie Waitkus and invited him to her hotel room, and seriously wounded the player by shooting him in the chest with a rifle.

That incident made the sexual high jinks of Wade Boggs and Steve Garvey in the eighties seem like child's play.

Boggs, the major league's best percentage hitter in the eighties, took sex on the road to a higher level—maybe *lower* level is more appropriate—by traveling with his mistress.

The now-legendary California mortgage banker Margo Adams, a brunette in her thirties, traveled with Boggs for four seasons. Boggs lived a double life—one with his wife and family at home, and one with Ms. Adams on the road.

When it got too heavy for Wade, and he attempted to drop

Margo, the designated road performer went to court and tried to win a $12-million suit. Boggs was relieved when the judge threw most of the suit out of court, and Wade settled with Margo for a small sum.

But proper old New England was rocked when Margo wrote an article for *Penthouse* and exposed many of the sexual habits of Wade's teammates.

Boggs made his situation tougher by going on national television and saying that he was "addicted to sex." He had to face many T-shirts and bumper stickers that read "I Slept with Wade Boggs." Others were far too raunchy for a family book.

Somehow, Wade managed to save his marriage, avoided a trade to another city, and avoided a beating or worse from his teammates.

Boggs was lucky. He didn't have to wait too long until Steve Garvey came along and made people forget him.

During his brilliant eighteen-year career with the Los Angeles Dodgers and San Diego Padres, which included ten All-Star Game appearances, Garvey was known as squeaky clean, enjoyed a Boy Scout image, and openly coveted a career in politics.

But it emerged that Steve Garvey was a phony. He was not the model husband and father he seemed to be. Steve had a long affair with his secretary. His teammates saw through him. They would often be delighted when he failed; an example was their cheering when he was unsuccessful in laying down a bunt.

Los Angeles pitcher Don Sutton once had a clubhouse fight with Garvey, allegedly over Steve's phoniness.

To fans across the nation, but not to his teammates, it was a shock when he and his blond wife, Cyndy, separated in 1981. Their bitter divorce, which featured a custody fight over their two lovely daughters, wasn't final until 1985.

During the separation, Cyndy had eyes for composer Marvin Hamlisch and claimed that when Garvey and Hamlisch finally talked, Steve simply gave her away.

Ms. Garvey was a local talk show host in Los Angeles and later in New York, but blew her New York job when she insisted that her pay match that of her cohost, Regis Philbin, a veteran and highly talented performer. With that miscalculation, Cyndy essentially ended her TV career. Garvey didn't hit his stride as a womanizer until the late eighties.

Steve retired from baseball after the Padres refused to sign him for the '88 season. He then made a failed attempt to become president of the team, but the Padres did give him a retirement day, showering him with gifts, including a $50,000 Mercedes.

During 1988 and 1989, it appeared that Steve Garvey was trying to impregnate the entire country. He was still maintaining a romance with his old secretary, Judy Ross. That affair dated back to 1981. Garvey lived with Ross, and Steve frequently talked with her about marriage.

At the same time, Garvey was carrying on a cross-country romance with Cable News Network assignment editor Rebecka Mendenhall of Atlanta. He was juggling the two girls.

In July of 1988, Steve found out that a San Diego medical sales representative, Cheryl Ann Moulton, was pregnant with his child. Later, a DNA test proved that Garvey was the father of the baby, and a San Diego Superior court ordered him to make support payments.

On November 25 of 1988, Garvey asked Mendenhall to marry him. They set April 1 as the wedding date. Ironically, Mendenhall would give birth to Garvey's son on October 13 of 1989.

Meanwhile, Cyndy was hounding Steve for being behind by $25,000 in alimony and child support, and Steve told Rebecka that Cheryl had informed him that she was pregnant with his child. Garvey then told Rebecka that the wedding was off. "Marriage isn't for me," he said.

At about the same time, Judy Ross was becoming skeptical that Steve was going to marry her.

Surprise, surprise. Garvey went to his annual ski classic in Deer Valley, Utah, and fell in love with a former high school cheerleader, Candace Thomas. After a whirlwind romance, which included dancing at the Bush inauguration and attending the Super Bowl (they became engaged the night of the game), Garvey married Thomas.

Meanwhile, Steve said he would support his offspring from Moulton and Mendenhall. Ross was shut out completely and said, "I don't know how he dealt with us all in the course of a year. The man's got great stamina."

Garvey's shenanigans had alienated his daughters, who refused to see their father, and Steve had the audacity to say that Cyndy was poisoning them against him.

Garvey was having financial problems and was making a living doing the morning radio program on XTRA in San Diego, shades of Denny McLain. Garvey was receiving $12,000 per month for the show, but claimed he was in debt to half the world.

It's no surprise that Steve's political ambitions had gone *pffft*. By comparison, Gary Hart's looked great.

Across the country, comedians and cartoonists were dumping on Steve Garvey. He was the butt of many jokes on the Academy Awards show.

His image didn't improve when Margo Adams wrote in *Penthouse* that Garvey was a nicer guy and better lover than Wade Boggs. What praise.

T-shirts and bumper stickers read:

"Steve Garvey: Father of My Country"

"Honk If You're Carrying Steve Garvey's Baby"

"Steve Garvey Is Not My Padre"

Steve had led the Padres to their only divisional pennant, but his new exploits had practically wiped away his previous accomplishments.

Until Steve Garvey came along, my favorite bumper sticker was:

"Honk If You've Been Married to Georgia"

The Rams owner, Georgia Frontiere, had been married seven times.

So much for baseball's most solid citizen, Steve Garvey. It speaks well of the role models for America's youth.

There are many examples of jock paragons of morality.

Luis Polonia of the '89 Yankees is a prime example. After a game in Milwaukee, Luis took a fifteen-year-old girl to bed in his hotel room, and the girl's parents filed charges. Polonia could have received ten years in prison and a $10,000 fine, but after the Yankee lawyers went to bat for him, he served a sixty-day jail term and paid a $1,500 fine.

Baseball does not have a monopoly on sexual misconduct. Houston Oilers running back Mike Rozier, the former

Heisman Trophy winner, was named in a paternity suit twice in a month by women who each claimed he was the father of their unborn child. The second suit was filed by Rita Baldwin, twenty-five, according to lawyer Glen Lilly, who also represents Pamela Gobert, twenty-three, who filed suit against Rozier earlier in the month. Both women sought medical costs and child support for their children.

In 1990, New York Giants running back Dave Meggett was arrested for attempting to solicit sexual favors from an undercover female officer in Baltimore. Giants general manager George Young said, "It saddens me whenever I hear about this kind of thing." That's more than he said when Lawrence Taylor went into cocaine rehab. (Meggett was later acquitted of this charge.)

I have been a one-woman man for forty-six and a half years, and to me, womanizing is revolting. It was one of the reasons why I tired of "Monday Night Football." Emmy and I were constantly exposed to the mistresses.

We saw the television industry get excited about Shoal Creek in golf, and it should have. But why hasn't anything been done about the bias and discrimination against women in tennis? The U.S. Tennis Association pays an equal amount to women and men for its championship, but none of the other majors do this. The Australian Open pays over $23,000 more to the male winner, Wimbledon pays over $11,000 more to the male winner, and The French Open pays $77,000 more to the male winner. How do the women's lib groups allow the television networks to get away with this?

One of the ugliest problems confronting sports in the nineties is gang rape. There have been a number of sickening cases.

In May of 1990, four Washington Capitals hockey players were in the back of a limousine parked behind a Georgetown bar named Champions with a seventeen-year-old girl.

Charges were filed against the NHL players, but were later dropped. However, the Capitals quickly unloaded to other teams three of the players involved.

Other sexual assault incidents involving athletes have

been reported at the University of California-Berkeley, Oklahoma University, St. John's University (New York), the University of Minnesota, the University of Wyoming, Kentucky State University, and a Glen Ridge, New Jersey, high school.

Two Oklahoma Sooner football players, Bernard Hall and Nigel Clay, were convicted of felony rape and went to jail.

Experts in the field have tried to analyze the problem. Athletes are, for the most part, macho, and they stick together in group situations.

Dr. Claire Walsh, the director of the University of Florida's Sexual Assault Recovery Service, says there's a great deal of peer pressure to conform, and that can turn rape into a team activity. "The male bonding is one of the dynamics of gang rape," Walsh said. "It's the desire for inclusion within the group. Not participating can result in the rejection of one of the group."

On November 27, 1990, NFL commissioner Paul Tagliabue ruled that three New England Patriot players— Zeke Mowatt, Robert Perryman, and Michael Timson— were guilty of sexually harassing reporter Lisa Olson in the Patriots locker room on September 17. Mowatt's fine was $12,500; the other players were fined $5,000 each. The New England Patriots were fined $50,000 for their failure to respond properly to the incident.

There was a horrible effort by some, including NBC's Will McDonough, to exonerate the players for their behavior, actions that would have meant sure arrest and prosecution for most Americans not protected by the sports establishment. Many rightfully described the players' actions as "verbal rape."

Tagliabue had Special Counsel Philip B. Heymann conduct a thorough investigation. His report concluded that the players' actions were "degrading and humiliating to Ms. Olson." The commissioner called the actions of the players "completely uncalled for and improper." The report concluded that the naked players confronted Olson, and that Mowatt smiled and purposely displayed himself to her in a suggestive way. The actions of the Patriots players and the club were disgraceful, and the fact that some media members and fans attempted to shift the blame to Olson was equally disgraceful. This incident is a typical example of sexual behavior all too prevalent in the sports world.

Myra Hindus, a sexual harassment counselor at Princeton University, said, "The whole phenomenon of male bonding in this culture and the way that men are socialized to be sexual aggressors could play out in any all-male group or institution, from athletic teams to fraternities, in this way [rape]."

"It's a major problem for higher education," said David Cawood, the assistant executive director of the NCAA. "But it's a concern the NCAA has no jurisdiction over. It's understandable that athletes bring focus to the problem that doesn't get noticed otherwise."

How typical. Cover for the jocks. It's not an NCAA matter.

The former hockey great Don Dryden, a lawyer out of Cornell University, hits it on the head. The ex–Montreal Canadien star and Hall of Famer said the problem is really "a sense of power that comes from specialness, reputation, money, whether it's an athlete, businessman, or entertainer —anyone who finds himself at the center of the world therein has a sense of impunity."

In other words, many jocks and famous people feel they can participate in sexual assault without punishment. They feel there should be one type of justice and one set of laws for them, and another type of justice and another set of laws for others.

Gang rape by jocks is fast becoming an epidemic problem that demands the immediate attention of school and professional administrators, as well as law enforcement officials across the country.

It's time the sports community recognizes that being athletic and macho does not give one liberty to rape and assault.

CHAPTER EIGHTEEN

Cocaine, Steroids, and Bible Belt Urine

Drugs are the most serious domestic problem facing our nation today. There's a vicious epidemic raging through our society, and this problem requires the strongest possible measures to combat it.

In 1990, for the first time, it appeared that the government might be making some headway in its war against drugs. Crackdowns on the drug lords in Central and South America are reported to have resulted in smaller amounts of cocaine on American streets; the fight is not over, however, and drugs remain a gigantic menace.

Dr. Robert O. Voy, the former medical chief of the United States Olympic Committee and member of the President's Commission on Drugs, contends that most people still don't recognize the dangers of cocaine. He points out that statistics show that 50 percent of all cocaine users will eventually lose their jobs and destroy their careers; worse yet, he notes that 50 percent of all cocaine users will at some time attempt suicide.

What many people don't realize is that because cocaine is not just a narcotic but also one of the best stimulants known to man, it has replaced amphetamines as the preferred stimulant of jocks. Once amphetamines were so popular, so common, that they used to pass out greenies or uppers in the NFL as if they were candy.

"I lived through the day with professional football when we actually gave the athletes, particularly with the NFL, amphetamines to use, which gave them this kind of aggression which you see on Sunday afternoons," said Voy.

"Because cocaine is such a great stimulant, it is being used by athletes in preference to amphetamines," said Voy. "What I hear from them is that it's smoother acting, more controllable in the up-and-down effects than the amphetamines."

Dr. Voy, a remarkably candid man, said, "I remember traveling with the NBA in my early days, when the pushers would actually stuff cocaine into the gym bags of the NBA players as they walked through the airport."

He continued, "The same thing happens with Olympic athletes who suddenly become visible on the front pages as potential gold medal winners who are going to have a few million bucks to spend. Of course, the pushers come out of the woodwork to give them the drug to use for recreational purposes, ultimately to get them addicted and become a very important customer."

Cocaine is so addictive that experts claim many are addicted after two hits. And because of the unbelievable money involved, there's a tremendous con job that's going on in society to get our young people addicted.

Dr. Voy claims that "in spite of what you read, there is no cure for cocaine addiction. You can talk to all the detox centers and all the rehab programs, and they are revolving doors. The treatment works for a certain amount of time, but in my opinion, cocaine addiction so far is an incurable disease."

The old snortable cocaine was a problem, but nothing compared to the crack or smokable cocaine, which is 90–95 percent pure cocaine. When used in a pipe or a bong, it reaches the brain in ten seconds, just as quickly as if one injected it into the bloodstream.

Dr. Voy does an excellent job of describing what happens when cocaine hits the central nervous system and the brain:

It fires off all the neural transmitters, neuroepinephrine and dopamine, in one fell swoop. It's like the Fourth of July. Everything goes off, which is what gives that tremendous high for about ten to twenty minutes, then one of the counteractions of cocaine is to block the re-uptake of neuroepinephrine and dopamine, and what that does is to cause the system to be in a deficit situation for the normal hormonal stimulation, and because of that, there's a tremendous crashing that follows. It's this tremendous high and this tremendous down that leads the individual to find more cocaine to get rid of that terrible feeling, or to turn to pot, alcohol, or some other drug that they need to allay that terrible feeling.

Athletes as a whole are a curious lot, and many are reactive to trends. Many sports fans and hangers-on attempt to curry favor by actually giving drugs to jocks, and of course, most professional athletes make big money and can afford to purchase drugs.

Nothing demonstrated the dangers of drugs more than the tragic and senseless death of Len Bias, the University of Maryland basketball star who signed with, but never played for, the Boston Celtics. He died of a cocaine overdose. Other athletes have been killed by drugs. Cleveland Browns All-Pro defensive back Don Rogers was a cocaine victim. The death of John Matuszak, who played for the Kansas City Chiefs, Washington Redskins, and Oakland Raiders, was drug induced, and Los Angeles Raiders defensive starter Stacy Toran was drunk when he died of injuries sustained in an automobile accident.

Sadly enough, the deaths of these players don't seem to have served as a warning to others. The problem of drug abuse in sports continues.

We even came close to losing some coaches because of players in drug stupors. Tom "Hollywood" Henderson, the former Dallas Cowboys linebacker, admitted that while under the influence of drugs he once laid in wait with a loaded rifle, debating whether to kill his head coach, Tom Landry. And Spencer Haywood has a similar story, admitting that when he was on drugs, he almost killed Paul

Westhead, then his head coach with the Los Angeles Lakers and the current head coach of the Denver Nuggets.

Dr. Voy agrees with my old friend Ed Koch, who advocated using the Army and Navy to shoot down airplanes and torpedo the boats that bring cocaine into New York's airports and harbors. Both also favored capital punishment for pushers. There can be no doubt that we have a major drug problem in Western society. and that the battle against cocaine is a long way from being won.

This may come as a shock to some people, but I feel the only way to control the drug problem in athletics and sports is through random testing under rigid conditions. I admit this is an invasion of privacy, but the problem is so epidemic that under the circumstances, I think it is justified.

To those in the overall society who feel that the legalization of drugs is the answer to our problems, I say nonsense. Some claim that it works in certain European countries, but I don't believe it.

I've already stated in this book that the NBA has the best drug policy in sports. That's to the credit of the late Larry Fleisher, David Stern, and the players themselves. Oh, the NBA still has problems. Players such as John Lucas and Roy Tarpley have been in and out of rehab, and the Michael Ray Richardsons and Chris Washburns have been booted for life.

On the baseball front, Peter Ueberroth did a good job of cleaning up that sport's drug epidemic in the eighties.

Plea bargaining was the name of the game for Dale Berra, Enos Cabell, Keith Hernandez, Jeffrey Leonard, John Milner, Dave Parker, and Lonnie Smith, all major leaguers who testified against two cocaine pushers in a Pittsburgh courtroom. All admitted the use of the drug, and while most people go to jail when they admit cocaine use, none of these ballplayers did. Ueberroth did take disciplinary action against this group, plus other players—Joaquin Andujar, Al Holland, Lee Lacy, Larry Sorensen, and Claudell Washington. Most were fined and required to perform community service.

Ueberroth initiated a drug-testing program, despite the players union fighting him every step of the way. Baseball is confident that its worst drug days are behind it. Nonetheless, America's favorite pastime must still live with the fact that Vida Blue, Willie Wilson, Jerry Martin, and Willie Aikens, all former Kansas City Royals, went to jail for drug offenses, and Steve Howe of the Los Angeles Dodgers and Texas Rangers was suspended for life because of repeated drug use.

Due to heavy pressure from Don Fehr and the union, baseball has dropped the idea of random drug testing. Currently, the only major league players tested are those with a past history of drug usage and players who are reported by law enforcement authorities to have involvement with drugs. As constituted, this is not a strong program, and Fay Vincent should act to strengthen it.

One of the saddest and most interesting cases of drug abuse is Donn Clendenon, the ex–major leaguer whom I have known since he came to the Miracle Mets of '69 and helped lead them to the World Championship.

Donn recalls, "Howard, I remember you saying when I first walked into the Mets clubhouse, 'This could put the Mets into the championship.' You were the only one who ever thought that and said it."

Clendenon is a smart man, an attorney who practiced law after his baseball career, became a VP with Scripto Pens, and later worked with General Electric and the Mead Corporation. But at age forty-seven, Clendenon started doing cocaine, and it almost ruined his life. He says:

I was addicted to cocaine after I freebased it one time. I was a heavy user and was sinking fast when I picked up the phone one day, called my secretary, Yetta, and asked her to get me a list of the top ten rehab centers in America. I decided on St. Benedict's in Ogden, Utah, and flew there two days later.

While undergoing drug treatment there in '87, they discovered through a bone marrow test that I had leukemia. After it was determined that the leukemia is in remission and I finished my drug rehabilitation, I went to South Dakota to become commissioner of the North American Baseball Association, but the league never got off the ground.

Then I became chairman/director of the South Da-

kota State Centennial Games and was practicing law on
the side. It was in August of '88 that I was representing
some guys who had been relocated to South Dakota
with new identities in a federal witness-protection
program. One of them, out of Chicago, had been a drug
addict since '65. I had talked him into entering the
Keystone Rehab Center, which is twenty-seven miles
from Bismarck.

It was then that Clendenon made a horrible mistake. The
federal witness leaned on Donn to help purchase a half gram
of cocaine for his girlfriend and threatened to leave Keystone if he didn't do so.

"At first I refused," Clendenon said, "but later agreed to
ask my former housekeeper, Robin, to secure the cocaine."

It developed that Robin was working for the police, and
Donn Clendenon wound up pleading guilty to intent to
distribute cocaine. "It was a classic case of entrapment, but
I pleaded guilty in a plea bargain. It cost me my six-figure
job with the State."

In January of 1989, Clendenon enrolled at the University
of South Dakota for twenty-seven semester hours of alcohol
and drug studies. After that, Donn took a job as a technician
at the Keystone Rehabilitation Center and has advanced to
the position of drug counselor.

Donn Clendenon says he's fearful that the leukemia will
come out of remission and his future will depend on
whether chemotherapy is successful. Meanwhile, he claims
to be happy and content working as a drug counselor
outside of Bismarck, North Dakota.

He's aware that in all likelihood his involvement with
drugs destroyed his chances of administrative or managing
jobs in baseball.

I began this discussion of drugs in sports with football.
There is a reason. Football has had the most shameful drug
history of all sports. During the seventies the players popped
uppers like clockwork, and during the eighties, anabolic
steroids were in vogue. The NFL waited until 1990 before it
implemented a steroid test with some teeth, one that called
for year-round random testing. Time will tell whether the

league carries out the program with credibility. Meanwhile, at least one player, Steve Courson, the ex–Pittsburgh Steeler, is struggling for his life because of damage from anabolic steroids.

In his book, *Living on the Edge,* Lawrence Taylor of the New Jersey Giants openly bragged about substituting clean urine in place of his "dirty urine" for drug tests. And I think it's safe to assume that Taylor is not the only player to have used this trick. To be frank, in order to be sure of a test's validity someone has to observe the player urinating into the bottle.

Dr. Voy said, "It's no problem to get clean urine. You can buy drug-free urine from a person in Austin, Texas, for thirty-five dollars a bag. There's a guy in Cleveland who advertises that he'll go do a test for anybody for expenses and a hundred bucks."

Prof. Alan Dershowitz of the Harvard Law School once said on a program of mine, "You can buy Bible Belt urine, which comes from someplace in Tennessee where people go to church every day."

So, the end result is clear. Someone must witness the test.

It's not commonly known, but Lawrence Taylor was treated as an outpatient at a drug rehab center in New York a year before I broke the story of his drug rehab in Texas in 1986. During his treatment in 1985, LT is alleged to have used someone else's clean urine when he was tested by the rehab center. Taylor had it down to a fine science and would squeeze the clean urine out of a small plastic container.

When Lawrence Taylor went into drug rehab in Houston in early February of 1986, I had given a lot of thought to going with the story before I actually broke it.

One day during the '86 season, Shelby Whitfield was being driven to the Newark International Airport when he and the limo driver started talking football.

"What's with the Giants?" the driver asked.

"I think Lawrence Taylor has some problems," Whitfield said.

"I know he does," replied the driver.

"How do you know?"

"I was driving George Young [the Giants general manager] and another man, and I heard them talking about Taylor's cocaine problem and that the league and law enforcement officers knew about it."

Of course, when I broke the story, Young knew nothing.

I knew that breaking a story as big as Lawrence Taylor doing drugs would be dynamite. I had to be sure of the facts. I knew that supporters of the Giants and the National Football League would attack the story, maybe attempt to distort the facts.

Then came a conclusive bit of proof. Bill Parcells was in Haglers in his hometown of Oradell, New Jersey, when someone overheard him popping off. "LT is in rehab and I'm the one who put him there."

I phoned my good friend Al Davis and told him that LT was in rehab and that I was going to break the story. Al and Parcells are very close, and Al called Parcells and told him that I had the story. I suspect that Al also told him he might want to talk with me.

Parcells telephoned my office, but since I wasn't there, they switched him to Shelby. "Howard's in Washington but I know what you're calling about," said Whitfield. "And Howard's breaking the story tomorrow morning." Bill was panicking. He talked to Whitfield for about twenty minutes and said that he wanted to talk to me before I went on the air. Parcells gave Whitfield a private number where he could be reached at Giants Stadium at six A.M. the next morning. Whitfield came into his office early, called Parcells at six A.M., and Bill picked up on the first ring. Shelby then connected him with me at my apartment.

"Howard, I'm trying to save the sonuvabitch."

"I don't disagree with that, Bill. I hope he recovers, but I have a responsibility to break this story."

"Howard, I want people to know that I have tried to clean up the Giants' problem." He went on about the almost twenty-five cocaine users on the Giants team when he arrived, and that now he had gotten it down to a very few.

I promised Parcells that I would handle him gently.

Here is the text of my statement on Lawrence Taylor that I aired on my morning sportscast, February 14, 1986:

This, on a personal level, is one of the saddest, most difficult programs I have ever had to do. I have a duty to disclose to the public another drug case in the National Football League. It involves a young man I got to know very well when I did a "Superstars" show some years back when I was still doing "Monday Night Football." It involves a young man who is one of the authentically great football players I have ever seen, and this young man has been portrayed to be that. And rightfully so, in New York City and its environs. He is a member of the now New Jersey Giants, and his name is Lawrence Taylor. And he is presently in a drug rehabilitation center. Drugs are not a new thing to the Giants, or to any football team, at the professional level and—too often—at the college level in this country. And one gets tired of talking about it, except that one must. And so, over the past three years I've watched the Giants, they've had a drug problem in profusion. And that drug problem has been well handled and carefully delimited. Lawrence Taylor is a sick man in this regard, and one can feel compassion for him. But one can no longer hide what was happening. And now, on a team where much of the drug problem has been eliminated, the hope is that it will be eliminated, too, in the case of Lawrence Taylor. That's basically the story, so hard for me to tell. I don't know, now that this story is disclosed, what the position of the Giants' management will be. I don't know what it can be, except for that management to continue working very hard, and hopefully, to help Lawrence Taylor.

For details on the Lawrence Taylor case, let either the Giants' management, or the commissioner's office, speak to it.

Within the next day, we had confirmed that Lawrence Taylor was in Houston. At first we thought he was in a treatment center in The Woodlands, north of Houston, but we quickly learned that he was in Methodist Hospital in Houston.

We knew LT was staying with Ken Burroughs and Ivery

Black, and we had a contact in Houston who was aware of Lawrence's whereabouts practically all of the time. Taylor only stayed in Methodist Hospital for a few days, then started his famous outpatient treatment of playing golf.

In my daily broadcasts, I kept the heat on the Giants, eventually forcing them to admit Taylor's drug problem, and to admit to his treatment.

On February 20, the Giants released a statement in Taylor's name, admitting to the drug problem and the treatment. The statement, for the most part, was written by Bill Parcells.

Until the release of that statement, some sportswriters had questioned the credibility of my story, had done so for six days.

Giants GM George Young was telling the media that if Taylor were being treated, he'd know about it, and he didn't know about it. Incredible!

Steve Rosner, Taylor's business manager, called me and said Taylor had never used drugs in his life, and that I would be sued for a huge amount of money. Unbelievable!

Vic Ziegel, New York *Daily News* sports editor, called Shelby Whitfield and questioned the accuracy of the story. How dare the man. He insulted my credibility, yet the next day he printed the entire transcript of my broadcast.

Bill Parcells visited Emmy and me not long after I broke the Lawrence Taylor story. He came to our apartment for cocktails, then he and I had dinner at the Isle of Capri and returned to our apartment where we visited some more. Parcells and I go back a number of years. In 1983, he asked me about the ownership of the Memphis Southmen of the USFL, who had made him an attractive offer to jump leagues.

Parcells and the Giants have had a rocky relationship. There was at one time no love lost between Parcells and General Manager George Young. Parcells admitted that in his book, and those close to the Giants claim that the relationship is even more strained than either will admit. The Giants refused to give Parcells the raise he wanted after he won the Super Bowl, and for a period he was very unhappy, threatening to leave the club.

Parcells is a good guy who is close friends with Bob

Knight and Al Davis, and make no mistake about it, he's a great football coach.

But Bill is overprotective of players, especially in regard to drug abuse. It's okay to rehabilitate them, but don't overprotect them and try to cleanse them in the eyes of the public.

The fact that Lawrence Taylor came back and helped the Giants to a Super Bowl victory is a credit to Taylor and to Bill Parcells. But on the other hand, where is the morality of the National Football League and the Giants? How many games did Taylor play when the man was doing cocaine? In his book, he admitted that he had done the drug for years, and he knew that the Giants and the commissioner's office were aware of it.

I saw LT at a Tommy John charity dinner in August of 1990. Lawrence was cordial and seemed happy to see me. I like the man, but he hasn't been a model citizen, or a role model for anyone. In addition to his problems with drugs, he has elected to associate closely with some very "wise guys," including a convicted felon. One of LT's closest friends is Vincent Ravo, who served ten months in a New Jersey prison for a gun conviction. While Ravo was awaiting his sentence, LT, on Giants stationery, wrote a letter to the judge requesting leniency for his close friend, with whom he has taken vacations. Yes, LT is, as he likes to say, a "wild and reckless dude." In many ways, he's similar to Mike Tyson. On NBC's "NFL Live," Taylor told O. J. Simpson that he's happy on the field when he "hits a person and sees him shaking and quivering and the bubbles are coming out of his nose—that's a great hit." That's also a demented philosophy and a dangerous one. It's my hope that neither Taylor nor Tyson comes to a violent or tragic end.

Taylor slipped a second time and was suspended for drug abuse, missing the first four games of the 1988 season. Overall, he did not have a good year on the field and later was arrested for DWI, but was acquitted. The Giants management must quake in fear of a possible third, career-ending violation by LT of the NFL's drug policy.

On November 1, 1990, Shelby and I lunched at the Hampshire House on Central Park South, one of my favorite luncheon spots. It was there about seven years ago that I had lunch with Roone Arledge, at which time I advised him to hire Brent Musburger away from CBS. He tried but failed, and as you know, Musburger later joined ABC after he was fired by CBS Sports.

After lunch, Shelby and I, looking for a taxi, walked about a block, passing Mickey Mantle's Restaurant. A local New York sportscaster, Bill Mazer, was originating a radio talk show next to the front window of the restaurant, and he waved for me to come inside. Mazer begged me to come on the air. I agreed and he pushed back his scheduled guest, running great Eamon Coghlan, for fifteen minutes.

In the course of the conversation with Mazer, I made a remark about LT's using "Bible Belt urine" in his drug tests. It touched off a furor. Sportswriters rushed to the defense of LT and goaded him for a reaction. His friends and associates quickly came to his aid, saying LT had turned over a new leaf, that he was now a model citizen. I hope this is so. Taylor himself called me a "silly old fool who is senile." He demanded a public apology and threatened legal action.

I was dumbfounded.

In no way did I attempt to defame Lawrence Taylor. It was a tempest in a teapot, or to use another cliché, the writers made a mountain out of a molehill. Taylor had indicated that he wanted to let the matter die, but his writer friends and hero worshipers wanted some Cosell blood.

A few days later at the Plaza Hotel, I joined Lesley Visser of CBS, Dick Schaap of ESPN, and Robert Lipsyte of public television in conducting a sports symposium. There were other members of the media in attendance when I made the following statement:

When I made my recent remarks about Lawrence Taylor, they were directed primarily at the National Football League, which, as you know, I hold in low esteem. I wanted to use the illustration of LT's use of drugs and the manner in which he evaded detection—as he so frankly and graphically described in his own words in his book—as an example of what is wrong with the NFL. His problems were symptomatic of the ills that grip the sport. Indeed nearly all sports. The

NFL was part and parcel of what happened to Taylor and others. It was not a pretty picture and not one which should be condoned or forgotten.

For LT's sake, I do hope he has straightened out his life, and more power to him. I hold him no ill will. If my remarks were misinterpreted, I am sorry. And I do apologize.

By the same token, do not expect me to treat him as some sort of hero. What he did to himself, his team-mates, the sport, and those who admired him caused irreparable damage. We have seen it happen time and again—all too frequently.

I recall the day Keith Hernandez returned to the Mets' lineup to the cheers of the crowd—some kind of hero! Heroes must be made of sterner stuff.

Every day we are reminded of the pervasive influence of drugs in our society and in sports. It is all too easy to forget the mistakes of the past—if we do, we are doomed to relive them. And that is the true essence of my recent comments.

Three players who are three-time drug losers are Tony Collins of the New England Patriots, Stanley Wilson of the Cincinnati Bengals, and Dexter Manley of the Washington Redskins. All were banned from the NFL for life.

As with the NBA, however, a lifetime ban in the NFL doesn't really mean a lifetime ban. When training camp rolled around for the 1990 season, there was Tony Collins, reinstated, trying to find a spot with the Miami Dolphins. Dexter was reinstated, dropped by the Redskins, and signed by the Phoenix Cardinals.

I feel empathy for Dexter. He's made so much personal progress in improving himself in the area of reading, but the man must overcome a bigger challenge—demon cocaine.

I remember talking with Manley's agent, Bob Woolf, who said, "Howard, I don't know what to do. Dexter swears to me that he's clean, that he's being railroaded by the NFL. We may go to court."

Shortly thereafter, Manley confessed that he had been lying to Bob Woolf. He had indeed used cocaine again.

The Stanley Wilson case is so typical. A product of the suspect University of Oklahoma football program, he started doing cocaine in college and, the night before Super Bowl XXIII, blew a lucrative career by going on a coke binge. He was barred from the Super Bowl game, and later from the league. Wilson implicated three other Bengals, claiming that Daryl Smith and Rickey Dixon were also doing cocaine supplied to them by teammate Eddie Brown the week of the game, something the Bengals and the players denied.

The following year at Super Bowl XXIV in New Orleans, new commissioner Paul "I'm Too Tall" Tagliabue was busy denying the claim of WJLA-TV in Washington that the NFL had engaged in racism by failing to discipline three white quarterback stars who had tested positive for drugs.

It's common knowledge that drugs are used by a wide spectrum of athletes.

The Mets sent Dwight Gooden to Smithers Alcoholism and Treatment Center for cocaine abuse. They sent Darryl Strawberry to the same place for alcohol abuse. (That came after he allegedly threatened his wife, Lisa, with a gun.)

Kevin Mack, fullback of the Cleveland Browns, went to drug rehab for thirty days and then to prison for thirty days on drug charges. He came back during the 1990 season to play for the Browns in the playoffs. Jail is nothing new for NFL stars. Remember the legal troubles of Mercury Morris of the Dolphins and Bob Hayes of the Cowboys.

In the 1990 season, placekicker Donald Igwebuike of the Minnesota Vikings was indicted for participating in smuggling heroin from his native Nigeria. Another embarrassment for the NFL.

Earl Ferrell, the leading rusher for the Cardinals in the '88 and '89 seasons, missed the entire 1990 Phoenix Cardinal season because of drug use. He was in rehab in '85 and reportedly tested positive for cocaine three times during the '88 season, but was not punished at the time because the traces were small and he was already under treatment. How absurd! What a program!

Former Chicago Bears running back Calvin Thomas, who

sat out thirty days of a season for drug abuse, claimed that he saw four teammates doing drugs just days before a scheduled test in August of 1987. Thomas said they were not suspended.

No sport is immune from drug problems. As mentioned earlier in the book, Bob Probert of the NHL's Red Wings spent three months in jail in 1989 for drug charges. The aforementioned Derek Sanderson had a severe problem, and Edmonton's All-Star goalie Grant Fuhr revealed that he had used cocaine for seven years before undergoing rehab treatment in 1989. When Fuhr was asked why he lied to Oilers management when confronted directly, he said, "It's not the kind of thing you tell your boss." He was barred from hockey for the '90–'91 season.

Jockeys, perhaps the greatest athletes of all, also have had problems with drugs. Pat Valenzuela, Chris Antley, Pat Day, and Ron Franklin are just some who have acknowledged bouts with cocaine.

The problems go on and on ad nauseam, involving colleges, high schools, junior high schools.

Reggie Cobb, the great running back at the University of Tennessee, was booted off the team in midseason of 1989 for cocaine use. Later, it was revealed that the school had spent $10,000 to put Cobb through a drug rehabilitation program before the season had started.

Syracuse University basketball officials were shocked when they learned that Derek Brower, a substitute player whose career at Syracuse ended in 1988, had pleaded guilty to drug trafficking in a case that included cocaine and weapons charges. The 6'9" Brower admitted that he was an enforcer in a cocaine ring.

Steroids, which I have already touched on briefly, are now a major problem at all levels. *The Journal of the American Medical Association*, in a 1989 article by Dr. Kenneth Kashkin of the Yale University School of Medicine and Dr. Herbert Kleber, a Yale psychiatry professor, claimed that one million Americans illicitly use anabolic steroids to promote muscle growth and enhanced athletic performance.

One study estimated that 250,000 high school seniors use anabolic steroids despite the known health dangers. Dr. Charles Yesalis, professor of health policy and sports science at Penn State University, said, "There are some hard-core kid steroid users out there. They don't care if their body parts fall off, they're going to use the stuff." Drs. Kashkin and Kleber claim that recent studies prove that users of steroids may become addicted and crave the hormones much in the way a cocaine addict craves cocaine.

The worst abusers of steroids are thought to be professional wrestlers; football players, however, are close behind. In fact, steroid use is so widespread among college players that to be competitive, many coaches feel they have to turn their heads and allow players to use the drug.

Cases such as Brian Bosworth at Oklahoma and Tony Mandarich at Michigan State are eye-openers to the public. And there have been many published reports about steroid use at Michigan State. And even Notre Dame, which has the reputation of being one of the cleanest programs, in the face of charges of widespread anabolic use, admits to five cases where players tested positive.

Golf is a professional sport that has been able to avoid scandal by not testing for drugs. The PGA and the USGA simply don't test.

The tennis pros started a testing program a few years back; however, it's a program strictly geared to protect the player. If a tennis player tests positive, he receives treatment and there is no public disclosure. ATP officials say any disclosure is up to the player. Fat chance.

An obscure satellite doubles tennis player went into drug rehab a few years back in Florida and came close to publicly revealing some big-name drug users, but the story was suppressed.

Ex–tennis star Vitas Gerulaitis, a close friend of John McEnroe's, was the subject of a major cocaine investigation a few years back and narrowly escaped indictment. McEnroe and Bjorn Borg have been publicly linked with cocaine usage, but both have denied it, and in the case of McEnroe, his lawyer/father, John senior, demanded a retraction from an Irish tabloid and received it. The elder McEnroe claims that John has pushed for testing by the Players Council, and John senior thinks that's enough to prove his son's innocence.

Realistically, one would be naive to think that there has

not been drug abuse in the rich, glitzy fast lanes of professional tennis and golf. Both sports are very clubby, however, and any report pursuing drug stories in either sport would probably be ending his or her career or at least damaging relationships with a lot of players. Do they dare ask the question about what Andre Agassi, supposedly a religious man, with some erratic behavior and a weird entourage, is doing growing what looks like a "coke nail" on tour? While Agassi has never been linked to drug use, you'd think someone would be curious enough to ask.

In the world of Olympians, track and field athletes, weight lifters, and many others have used steroids over the past decade. Drug abuse in the Olympics may be the nastiest mess of all.

It took an incident such as the disqualification of Canada's Ben Johnson and the stripping of his records and medals before the world really became aware of drug abuse in the Olympics. But it's nothing new.

At a seminar in Colorado Springs, Colorado, prior to the Seoul Olympics, Dr. Robert Voy revealed some remarkable information about the role of drugs in the Olympics.

Since the ancient Olympics, athletes have used drugs to enhance performance. Strychnine and wine was the favorite concoction of the ancient Greeks.

There have been eighteen recorded deaths in the history of Olympic sport from the abuse of amphetamines in various concoctions. Some people will take any risk to win a medal, even a risk that may prove fatal.

In an effort to ensure fair competition, the IOC has been conducting some form of testing for the past twenty-two years. The testing didn't really become sophisticated, however, until the Pan American Games in Caracas, Venezuela, in 1983, when it became apparent that drug users would be detected and many Americans left the games before their competitions.

After that, many athletes started using blocking agents that would render the test invalid. Dr. Voy described how some Eastern Europeans—the Soviets in particular—would void themselves of urine and replace it with clean urine through a catheter shortly before the test. He claimed the coaches would carry the catheter with them prior to the procedure, and that the trick could be performed in about ten minutes. Dr. Voy said that in his case "it would probably take me ten hours to get up enough nerve to insert the catheter through the penis into the bladder."

Like I said, some people will do anything to win a medal.

Then there's blood doping, reportedly a common practice among Olympic cheaters, and for which there is no test. Blood doping, or blood packing as it is also known, is the practice of removing two units of blood from the athlete, freezing it, then thawing it and returning it to the athlete's body shortly before competition. The extra two pints of blood added to the system boost the number of red blood cells, increasing the oxygen-carrying capacity of the blood and thereby improving the athlete's endurance. There's enough medical documentation to prove that blood doping can improve endurance somewhere from 12 percent to 30 percent. That's a fantastic thing. Testing at the University of New Mexico has shown that you can knock as much as sixty-seven seconds off a ten-kilometer race by using blood doping.

The IOC has asked all Olympic countries to conform to random, year-round testing for drugs, and the USOC adopted the program late in '89. The USOC said it would spend $1 million on drug testing in 1990, testing 4,400 athletes in 37 sports at 197 sites. The use of blocking agents remains a problem, however, and Dr. Voy, in his book *Drugs, Sports & Politics,* says that some federations are tipping off the athletes about the dates of the tests. Incredible!

It appears that the only foolproof way of testing for drugs would be through blood tests, but most countries disapprove of the pinprick or needle as an excessive procedure. Other countries reject the blood test on religious grounds.

So what it boils down to is this: as long as athletes feel they can get an edge—whether it's to build muscle strength, increase weight, increase speed, decrease weight, slow heart rate, steady the nerves, allay pain, or increase courage—many will take drugs.

In the case of the Olympians, athletes, coaches, trainers, administrators of national and international federations, doctors, and pushers will stick together in an unholy alliance to beat the system.

With professional sports, college and high school sports, the story is much the same.

The urge for fame, glory, victory, and money is too great. Unfortunately, sports priorities around the world are out of whack.

CHAPTER NINETEEN

Footprints Cast in Stone

I know it's immodest of me to say so, but I don't think there will ever be another Howard Cosell. I don't think the industry will allow it. Undoubtedly my critics are saying, "Thank God!"

Agent Art Kaminsky hit it on the head when he said, "I'm glad Howard is doing another book. He's the only one who can tell the truth and get away with it."

There's no question that I was lucky to have Roone Arledge, a genius at his trade, a man who was smart enough to give my career full backing. Give the man full credit. Without Arledge, there would have been no Howard Cosell as the world knows me. Additionally, he has made ABC News number one, just as he did ABC Sports.

Earlier in this book, I devoted much space to the ills of the journalistic sports media, electronic and print. From a journalistic standpoint, sports on TV are at an absolute nadir. I know that Terry O'Neil claims to have initiated an in-depth program of sports journalism at NBC, but who's kidding whom? The fact is I'm still the only one who will dare to take on the entire media.

How can a man at a newspaper—_USA Today_—be permitted to program sports for the entire TV industry? Do give him his due, however. Rudy Martzke is read by 6 million readers a day, including every sports programmer in the business. Certain producers, directors, executives, and sportscasters call him daily, hoping for a mention in his TV column. They hope and pray for a high mark in his inane grading system of programs and performances. I have never really recognized Rudy Martzke, but a lot of people do.

People such as Stan Isaacs, a TV writer with *Newsday*, a New York/Long Island newspaper, have copied Martzke in handing out grades.

In 1988, Roone Arledge came on a TV program of mine, "Speaking of Everything," and commented that among TV critics sports critics are the worst. He agreed that it is ridiculous when writers with few or no qualifications attempt to award grades for broadcasts and performances.

Rudy Martzke claims to have discovered Bob Costas, and when he's not on the phone with that NBC sportscaster, he's on the phone with Dick Vitale or Al Michaels of ABC. And how can Rudy Martzke ride cross-country with John Madden of CBS on the Maddencruiser, a customized Greyhound bus, and still be objective about John Madden? One man who doesn't appreciate Rudy Martzke is Curt Smith, a speechwriter for President Bush. Smith was angered by Rudy's support of CBS and Major League Baseball in their cutting out the "Saturday Game of the Week." Here are excerpts from a letter of protest that Mr. Smith wrote Mr. Martzke:

I hope the Commissioner's office appreciates what a faithful mouthpiece you are (I will eschew more appropriate terms not because they are inaccurate, but because they would be pejorative). . . .

I believe crow is not edible in public places. Nor do I expect you or your newspaper to condemn a CBS package that has become the *Exxon Valdez* of sports network pacts. I also recognize that you have attended CBS production meetings and are a valued spokesman for CBS President Neal Pilson. I am sure his network appreciates your continued support.

* * *

After I had expressed my views of Mr. Martzke in an article in *The Washington Post,* Curt Smith wrote me a warm note, saying that he was happy someone else agreed with him about Rudy Martzke.

Earlier, I wrote that *The National,* the sports daily that started at the beginning of 1990, originally published in three cities—New York, Los Angeles, and Chicago—hopes to become competitive with *USA Today.* By the end of 1990, *The National* had expanded distribution to San Diego, San Francisco, Detroit, Boston, Miami, and Baltimore-Washington. It was scheduled to expand to Philadelphia and Atlanta in 1991.

The editor of *The National* is Frank Deford, probably the most talented painter with words in the business. He's a man of uncommon intelligence, intellect, and dimension. He knows what he's talking about. He has magnificent perspective.

I had Deford on my radio program to discuss his new project. He is backed by a wealthy Mexican, a man named Emilio Azcarraga, the major financial source of Televisa, which is 90 percent of Mexican television. Mr. Azcarraga not only owns television networks in Mexico, but he also produces a considerable number of television programs that are seen not only in the Spanish-speaking world, but are dubbed for viewing in other parts of the world as well. He's been very much involved in American television, but always in the context of the Spanish language. He was the original owner of the Spanish-language network Univision, which he sold to Hallmark for several hundred million dollars. Mr. Azcarraga is prepared to invest up to $100 million in *The National.*

Peter O. Price, former publisher of the *New York Post,* like Deford a Princeton graduate, is the president and publisher of *The National.* However, after less than a year, Price had his wings clipped by owner Azcarraga. He was allowed to keep his title as president and publisher, but Jaime Davila, an executive with Univisa, another Azcarraga enterprise, took over Price's office and usurped most of his duties. In January of 1991, Price left *The National.* Additionally, Price's assistant publisher and the directors of circulation and finance were dismissed. Perhaps even more significant, the paper stopped publishing its Sunday edition, and a spokesman said that the Sunday circulation had been running about 225,000, well below the weekday average of 275,000. The changes touched off speculation about the future of the paper.

Deford hired some very talented writers, men such as David Kindred, Mike Lupica, and Norman Chad. It may prove, however, that the quality of writers is not important. It may prove that the real question is whether there is a market for the paper. It remains to be seen if you can sell a sports paper five days a week, even if you have bureaus in many places across the country. My personal fear and firm belief is that Deford has a terrible Achilles' heel in his determination to be involved with the networks and television in general.

Frank did NBC-TV work when he was with *Sports Illustrated,* and he permits his staffers to do television, even on a regular basis. I've always maintained that it's a terrible conflict of interest.

I also wasn't surprised to see Deford anchoring a TV show with two of his writers, a syndicated show called *"The National's* Top Ten Moments in Sports." It was obviously geared toward promoting *The National,* with various shorts of *The National's* offices throughout the program. And the producer of the show was none other than Donald Dell, whose production company, ProServ, syndicated the program. Now Don Dell is a man who knows something about conflict of interest. He has announced many tennis tournaments involving players his company represents.

And what about the pro wrestling column in *The National?* How ugly. How insane. Is that column meant to appease NBC, which airs pro wrestling? Is it to make Dick Ebersol happy? He sold pro wrestling to his neighbor Brandon Tartikoff for millions of dollars. And if it's correct as said that Frank Deford rewrites the wrestling column (without his by-line), then that's like Hemingway writing classified ads.

So time will tell about *The National.* The owner has deep pockets and optimism, as evidenced by the five-year contracts given to the writers. But the paper faces huge distribution and printing problems. And just because sports dailies click in Europe doesn't mean they will in America. As I said, only time will tell.

The jockocracy is as strong as ever in the broadcast booths, but I covered that issue in my last book. However, as way of an update, I agree with *The National's* Norman Chad. Tim McCarver is unbearable. He's got that whiny voice. He talks incessantly about totally irrelevant things. I feel for Jack Buck on CBS. He's a fine announcer, but McCarver drags him down.

McCarver's as bad as Tony Kubek, now a Yankee cable broadcaster. They belong together. Tony's basically a cheese salesman; that's what he did when he quit playing baseball. He should go back to selling cheese. Kubek always called Georgy Porgy "Mr. Steinbrenner," and Tony loved to appeal to sportswriters by knocking George.

Vin Scully knows how to broadcast baseball. Some say he's tough to work with, but he's a real pro. Sure, he can talk too much, like everybody else. In my time, I was guilty of that. But Scully's great with words and anecdotes.

The jockocracy continues strong in football. Dan Dierdorf must think he's paid by the word. He was a good football player, but as a sportscaster he makes Frank Gifford look good.

And thank God my old friend Bobby Beathard is back in football where Bill Walsh belongs. Walsh is a football coach, a great football man, but not an exceptional broadcaster. It's simple. The jocks are not journalists or broadcasters.

When Walsh came by the ABC studios for an interview in the fall of 1990, it seemed to me as though he missed coaching. You don't have to be too smart to figure out that Walsh and the 49ers' controversial owner Eddie DeBartolo were not close. To be truthful, the main reason Walsh left the 49ers was DeBartolo. The 49ers were fined $500,000 by commissioner Paul Tagliabue when DeBartolo, the son of Ed DeBartolo, Sr., one of the wealthiest men in the country and one who is frequently connected to the underworld by rumors, transferred the ownership of the 49ers to his father's corporation without the approval of the league. The other owners in the National Football League despise DeBartolo for overspending and heaping lavish bonuses on his ballplayers. The bottom line for DeBartolo is that it has paid off in four Super Bowl championships.

One thing I found very interesting in my conversation with Walsh is that he regretted he never tried the single-wing formation with the 49ers. He felt that Steve Young could have run the formation to perfection, and that the league's defenses would have had a difficult time stopping the old formation, which was once common in the college ranks. It may sound outrageous, but remember, in many circles, Walsh is known as a football genius.

Even though Walsh wanted to try Steve Young at directing the single wing, Joe Montana was the coach's meal ticket over the years. Many consider Montana the greatest quarterback of all time, but I don't agree. If I had one game to win, I would select Terry Bradshaw, Sid Luckman, Otto Graham, John Unitas, Bob Waterfield, Norm Van Brocklin, and Sammy Baugh over Joe Montana.

Back to jocks in the booth: my only conflict with my collaborator on this book, Shelby Whitfield, is his willingness to hire jocks. Over the past years, he's hired Dick Vitale, Jim Valvano, Lute Olson, Ken Norton, Angelo Dundee, Paul Hornung, Marv Levy, Dick Butkus, Craig Morton, Oscar Robertson, Earl Monroe, and Phil Esposito, just to name a few. Shelby says they add marquee value and help commercial sales and program clearance. Nonsense. They're still jocks, not journalists or broadcasters.

At least Whitfield hasn't started hiring sportswriters. That's the new fad in television. Who can hire the most writers? Conflict of interest is rampant; these people can't have two masters. At least Lesley Visser had the gumption to quit her *Boston Globe* job once she started with CBS. Bud Collins, who works for NBC, eventually resigned as a *Globe* staffer.

Maybe Mark Mulvoy, the managing editor of *Sports Illustrated,* heard my cry of many years. In May of 1990, Mulvoy issued a new policy prohibiting writers covering a specific sport for the magazine to cover the same sport for television. It remains to be seen if he holds to his mandate. He indicated that writers who wanted to continue with TV and write for the magazine would have to resign from *SI* as staffers and submit articles as free-lancers. Writers Peter Gammons and Ralph Wiley said they would resign, but Curry Kirkpatrick was undecided.

The Boston Globe, the paper that withheld drug stories in the interests of the Patriots and the NFL during Super Bowl XX in 1986, is a huge conflict-of-interest offender. Will McDonough leads the way, with Bob Ryan and John Power other *Globe* staff writers who appear on TV.

To be fair, the *Globe's* Jack Craig, a longtime critic of mine, was the first person to write about *SI's* new policy.

Stick with it, Mark Mulvoy; it's the right thing to do. The writers may be journalists, but they sure as hell aren't broadcasters, and they can't serve two masters.

I will admit that I did a column for two years for Tribune Features, but I had given up television by that time. To be completely honest, I probably shouldn't have done the column while I was still doing radio.

I must admit that I took some personal delight in seeing Mulvoy adopt a policy that I had been advocating, just as I was amused to see the NFL lean on the networks to have them stop using point spreads and making predictions against the betting line. I had opposed this practice for years. I confess to some satisfaction at seeing the NFL change the policy, even though, deep down, I know the league wants gambling on its games.

Perhaps the biggest change in the industry since my last book has been the growth and success of ESPN. Cap Cities/ABC owns 80 percent of the Bristol, Connecticut, cable network, and it comes under the wing of my dear friend Herbie Granath, the president of video enterprises and a trustee of my will. ESPN is now the most profitable entity of Cap Cities broadcasting, and despite an expected loss of about $40 million in its 1990 baseball coverage, ESPN expected to make about $125 million profit overall. Herb named a new president of ESPN in 1990, selecting Steve Bornstein to succeed Roger Werner. I'm proud of Herb Granath, a fine man and a good friend who deserves every success. He recognized my contributions to the company and monitored my success all the way.

A couple of years back, I agreed to give a comment to a

TV crew about Harry Caray's selection to the Baseball Hall of Fame. The crew came by my summer home in the Hamptons. I said, "Sure, it's great Harry's going into the Hall of Fame. He tells some great stories, plays each year in my golf tournament, and drinks vodka like Bowie Kuhn. I think it's great he's going into Cooperstown." Then the producer said, "Mr. Cosell, we're embarrassed. We've been ordered to ask this question. If you answer it, it will be great. If you don't, we'll understand." So they put the question to me. Tim McCarver had given them a statement that "Harry Caray was telling it like it is before anyone ever heard of Howard Cosell, and Cosell never batted in Harry's league."

We were on my sun deck. I broke out in a loud guffaw.

"You've been ordered to ask me that question? I'll be delighted to answer it. Timmy is now a big man in baseball. I interviewed Timmy throughout his career. I really felt that Timmy was a good soul of great overachievement, of vaulting ambition, and in the context of the broadcasting industry as it presently is, he is achieving. But his remark is ridiculous. And I would like for him to tell me when he, Tim McCarver, or anybody else, fought for Muhammad Ali's constitutional rights, or fought for Curt Flood in his suit against baseball. Those are matters that affect a whole society, not a baseball game. Does this deprecate Mr. Caray? In no way. Mr. Caray has taken by storm the local population in Chicago. He owns them. And he can sing 'Take Me Out to the Ball Game' in a very enthusiastic way. I think he absolutely belongs in the Hall of Fame."

They called me back and said McCarver was livid, pissed off at my remarks. I almost died laughing, haven't laughed harder since I heard McCarver try to quote something on the air. He analyzes a simple ground ball into something complicated. What overkill. An insult to the listener's intelligence. He's banal and verbose.

One of the biggest conflict-of-interest awards goes to Larry King of CNN for anchoring the "Goodwill Games," the personal athletic competition of his boss, Ted Turner. King is a man who beat a nasty gambling habit, and he's an excellent interviewer, but I cringe when he does something

such as the Goodwill Games debacle or goes to Atlantic City
to interview Donald Trump when he opens a new gambling
casino. The man's involved in all types of conflict. He writes
a column in *USA Today* and has done Oriole broadcasts and
halftime reports on the NFL. Come, Larry, be a journalist.
You can't have that many masters.

There were those who criticized me for anchoring the
"Battle of the Network Stars" and the "Superstars" competition. Trash sport they called it. But we never made any
excuses or false pretenses about it. It was simple athletic
competition between some stars who were having fun.
There were no conflicts of interest or ulterior motives.

One doesn't have to look hard to find apparent conflict of
interest. Here in the New York area, there are two
sportswriting brothers, Dave and Moss Klein, who cover the
Giants and the Yankees for the *Newark Star-Ledger*, the
largest newspaper in New Jersey. At one time some members of the Klein family had an interest in a travel or tour
agency that hosted parties arranged by Dave Klein and
attended by Giants players. How can a writer be involved in
these activities and not let it affect his or her objectivity in
covering the club? The answer is simple: it can't be done. As
noted earlier, Dave Klein is one of the country's most
friendly writers in regard to the NFL and the New Jersey
Giants.
Even more questionable is the fact that the Klein family
publishes a Giants weekly newspaper, and Dave is the
featured writer. It's a paper aimed at the most rabid fan, and
its contents are predominantly favorable to the Giants
organization and its coaches and players. It is similar to
other fan-oriented publications throughout NFL cities, and
other so-called publishers and reporters are equally guilty.
There are some papers which as a matter of policy refuse to
allow their writers to write for NFL club programs and other
publications, but you can name those on the fingers of two
hands.
It takes courage to criticize the press. The print medium is
a powerful force in this country, and sportswriters are

normally a close fraternity who rarely criticize one another. Many of them have been unified in their criticism of me, many resented the fame and fortune that I have achieved. In a rare moment of candor, Mike Lupica of *The National* wrote that in my heyday I had the aura of a rock star. Some resented that fact.

However, the massive criticism never killed the fire in my belly. Nor has it served to diminish the high regard in which I hold myself. A couple of years back at the U.S. Open Tennis Championship, I was having lunch with Bowie Kuhn and Bill Simon, former secretary of the treasury and ex–U.S. Olympic Committee president, in the U.S. Open Club. Simon remarked that the threesome might realistically be labeled three "has-beens." My instant retort was, "Bill, you are two-thirds correct."

Emmy has always been by my side to cut me down to size when my ego got too big, or to pump me up when I needed it. When one is a living legend, and at the same time a human lightning rod, one can catch a lot of flak. But all in all, I think I have done an excellent job of coping with fame. I'm confident that any amount of scorn and abuse from critics and enemies can't alter my contributions to the sports and broadcasting worlds.

It was just over a year ago when the late ABC president Elton Rule said to me, "Howard, you have been a true giant in your field, a fearless journalist, a pioneer of journalism in the electronic sports medium. You belong in the Television Hall of Fame, and I am going to nominate you and push for your election." Cancer cut short Elton's life; it may well be that I'll never be elected to the Hall. If that's the case, it's not the end of the world.

With the sports halls of fame, where sportswriters and broadcasters vote, it is likely that I have alienated too many people to receive any plurality. That doesn't bother me one bit—but I must admit that I do appreciate it when people such as Jack Buck, Dick Enberg, and Curt Gowdy publicly state their feelings about my contribution. Moreover, when the beleaguered Chet Forte, a brilliant director, publicly stated in 1990 that I "made 'Monday Night Football,'" that I *was* "Monday Night Football," it made me feel good.

I've always considered it my duty to speak out in this country. There's got to be a voice such as mine somewhere, and I enjoy poking my stick at every issue and passerby.

I cherish a quote Gene Upshaw gave to *The Washington Post:* "Howard is honest. If he was anything else, he would not be Howard. His footprints are in the sand. People will know he walked through here."

Gene probably misspoke. My footprints are probably cast in stone.

<u>CHAPTER</u> TWENTY

No One's Lived a Better Life

I have lived a wonderful life. You can't have the life I've had and not be grateful.

There are few regrets. I have had a great career, and I have authored four sports books, including this one, of which I am proud.

Perhaps there is a tiny regret, a regret that I never received the opportunity to commentate on straight news, something I know I could have done well, and I sometimes wonder what would have happened had I entered the world of politics. I could probably have accomplished a great deal in the areas of sports and education. Leaving those things undone, however, has not really bothered me. The fact is, I declined to run for the U.S. Senate in 1976 out of deference to my family. They have always been the number-one priority in my life, and my family members didn't want me in the political arena.

There has been a great deal of personal satisfaction in being able to tell the truth about sports in this country and trying to keep everyone honest, and exposing the ills in the world of sports has been fun.

One of the nicest things ever said about me was written in the book *Inside ABC,* authored by former ABC vice president Sterling Quinlan. He stated, "Howard Cosell has become the most versatile on-air star of all three networks, is the most highly paid, and has become the most sought-after spokesman of any network in history."

Believe it or not, I'm human, and that type of recognition is gratifying.

Likewise, I find it disturbing when I hear or read that some poor, misguided soul has accused me of being a bitter old man, a venomous old man, a sad caricature of myself.

What bull!

Just because I've continued to be truthful and critical, some have said that I should have retired and assumed the role of an elder statesman, fading quietly into the background. Do my critics think I'm not an elder statesman? What do they want me to do, wear slippers and smoke a pipe? I am an elder statesman, and will continue to be one, but don't expect me to be quiet or dishonest.

No, there's no need to call people imbeciles, incompetents, and ignoramuses all the time, but there is a need to be heard. Someone has to speak out! Even my harshest critics should admit that.

I'm thankful for the good health that has blessed not only myself, but my lovely wife of forty-six and a half years, my two daughters, and my five grandchildren. We had a scare when Emmy developed lung cancer in 1988, but she sailed through surgery and has made a fine recovery. Emmy was a heavy smoker until the cancer came along, but she stopped completely when the doctor said, "It's the grave if you don't give up the smokes."

She's a real trouper and she enjoys life. Not too many months after Emmy's surgery, we spent two weeks' vacation at The Breakers in West Palm, my favorite hotel and a place where my photo hangs on the wall. Then in 1990, she made vacation trips with me to Palm Springs and later to Florida.

As for my health, it's as good as can be expected for seventy-three. When you've been around that long, there's a little wear and tear, but I'm in fine health. My doctors are happy with my condition. A couple of years back, I had a nosebleed problem that required surgery, but that's fine now. I also have no weight problem. I gave up cigarettes when Emmy stopped, watch my diet, and rarely have a cocktail. At one time, I enjoyed a martini as much as the next person, but now, if I order a cocktail, I'm just as likely not to finish it. The truth of this fact, of course, flies in the face of those who would label me a two-fisted drinker. One other thing: for most of my adult life, I have had a trembling of the hands, a familial condition that people have frequently mistaken for Parkinson's disease. I have never had Parkinson's; instead, an insignificant disorder inherited from my mother's side of the family.

Now, I'll make an effort to answer some questions that I've heard asked about me down through the years. Yes, I was once considered a hypochondriac, but I've long overcome that complaint; I require no more medicine than the average person.

Insecurities? Sure, I have some. Being Jewish and brought up in Brooklyn during the Depression, in the time of Hitler, I have all the Jewish insecurities attached to such a person. But I keep them well under control.

Do I miss doing television? Basically, no. Not "Monday Night Football." Not boxing. If there's anything I miss, it's horse racing. I loved covering the Kentucky Derby and the Preakness. These are great events, and Thoroughbred racing people are great people. The Penny Tweedys, Eddie Arcaros, and William Hartacks are unforgettable. Racing is an honest sport.

The greatest athlete of my time? With all due respect to Muhammad Ali, Jimmy Brown, Michael Jordan, Bo Jackson, and Wayne Gretzky, the greatest athlete of my time was a horse, Secretariat. His performance in the Belmont, an unbelievable 31½-length win in world record time, measured against all individual performances in the world of sport, is the greatest feat of all time. Nobody topped Big Red.

Have I been wrong on occasion? Absolutely. When you're in this business for thirty-eight years, and you're not afraid to take stands, you're going to miss a few. I never thought the Olympic Games would be held in Seoul, and they shouldn't have been. It was a terrible risk of lives. I also thought the USFL, on appeal, would win a realistic amount of money in its case against the NFL. And it should have. I admit that I underestimated Boris Becker when he first came on the tennis scene, but in his prime, before he married into the fast lane of Malibu and Hollywood, John McEnroe was the greatest tennis player ever to swing a racket. When I first laid eyes on Wayne Gretzky, I said he would become the greatest hockey player of all time. And he has.

One of the highs in this business is making predictions on the air and having them prove true. This was the case in 1990 when I predicted victory for the Cincinnati Reds over the prohibitively favored Oakland A's and their overrated manager, Tony LaRussa, in the World Series. I know Tony well. I have been in his little law office in Sarasota, Florida. He's a nice man, but he's not the baseball genius the media has made him out to be. The experts were premature in using such words as "genius" and "dynasty" in describing LaRussa and the Oakland A's. And I said all of this on the air before the World Series.

Another of the recent predictions that flushed me with pride was my position that Evander Holyfield would become heavyweight champion of the world. I have been on the Holyfield bandwagon since I called his fights during the '84 Olympics. He was by far the best boxer in the L.A. Games. I accepted an invitation from the Friars Club to make prefight comments before the Holyfield-Douglas fight, which was shown on closed-circuit TV before another packed house of about five hundred people spread over the three levels of the club. Just as I had done with the Leonard-Duran fight, I scored another bull's-eye with my prefight prediction: that Holyfield would win by knockout. For days, I was accepting congratulations from members, and before my critics start saying that I am a hypocrite for calling for a ban on boxing and then taking part in the Friars Club's showing of the fight, let me point out that I again called for the ban of the sport for medical reasons before I made my prefight prediction.

I feel that Holyfield is a great fighter. Despite criticism that he's an overstuffed light heavyweight with skinny legs, he's the best heavyweight since Ali. Evander has remarkable hand speed, throws sharp combinations, and beats his opponent to the punch. He reminds me of former heavyweight champion Ezzard Charles. I don't think he'll have any trouble beating Mike Tyson or any of the heavyweight contenders.

Two of the happiest days of my life occurred in 1990. While attending the dedication of a new gravestone for Jackie Robinson with Rachel Robinson, Bill White, and other friends, Wyatt Walker, one of Dr. Martin Luther King's top aides, said, "Howard, we are going to plan a national human rights day in Howard Cosell's name." The fact that Wyatt Walker would even consider such a thing overwhelms me. It's evidence that my lifetime of fighting for the rights of blacks and other minorities has not gone unnoticed.

The Museum of Broadcasting gave me one of my happiest moments when they honored me on September 24 with a dinner called "An Evening with Howard Cosell." The Museum had given similar honors to Walter Cronkite and Edward R. Murrow. At the dinner, the Museum showed a wonderful film retrospective that featured many memorable events of my career. This honor moved me to tears, and I deeply appreciated the attendance of scores of greats in the broadcasting industry.

One of the real joys of my life is my involvement with the Howard and Mary Edith Cosell Center for Physical Education at the Hebrew University in Jerusalem. The Center has an endowment of over a million dollars, and great work is being done there. I'm pleased that I've been able to make substantial contributions, and I hope others will continue to do so.

I'm equally pleased that I've been able to work with Bob Pearlman and the American Friends of the Hebrew University. It's been a great experience to help develop the Hebrew University Annual Sports Torch of Learning Dinner into one of the top affairs of the country. I'm always ready to travel anywhere to emcee an affair or speak for the American Friends of the Hebrew University.

One of the greatest times of my life came in 1985, when my family and I visited Jerusalem. And one of the great surprises of my life came when Emmy and I were visiting the Wailing Wall and someone tapped me on the shoulder and asked what I was doing there. I turned to find Don Shula, Bob Griese, and Earl Morrall. Ever with the correct word for the moment, I replied, "The logical question is, 'What are you doing here?' At least I'm Jewish."

"We're just tourists," Shula replied. It's a small world.

Another shock in Israel came in the bathroom of the Henry Kissinger Suite of the King David Hotel. The bathtub was so damn deep, I couldn't get out without Emmy's help. The great Cosell was as helpless as a baby.

One thing I've never had to worry about is driving in traffic—in Jerusalem or New York. I've never learned to drive a car. That's not unusual for someone who has spent his entire life in New York. My old friend Barbara Walters never learned.

Perhaps the funniest story in sports about people not driving involved Joe DiMaggio. Like DiMaggio, Frank Crosetti lived in northern California. Crosetti bought a new car to drive to spring training in Florida and asked DiMag if he wanted to ride with him. Joe quickly accepted. Crosetti drove until someplace in Arizona, then said to DiMaggio, "Okay, you take the wheel for a while, Joe," to which DiMaggio responded, "Frank, I can't drive."

Driving is something I've never missed. I've ridden in a jillion New York taxis, and over the past thirteen years, my family and I have been fortunate to have a great limo driver in a gentleman named Murray Landis. He's driven many stars and celebrities over the years, and my ego is always massaged when Murray tells strangers that Muhammad Ali and I are the two most recognizable people he's ever driven. Murray delights in telling people that when Kirk Douglas and I walked out of Yankee Stadium together after a game, fans were yelling to me and failed even to recognize Kirk, a huge movie star at the time. New Yorkers have their priorities in order!

And I don't deny it. I feel good when I walk down the streets of New York or any other city and the people recognize me. Taxi drivers and truck drivers honk and holler. People stop and shake hands; ask for autographs. "How are you?" they say. "We miss you. Please come back. What do you think of Tyson? How is Ali?"

It's amazing. Want me to be egotistical again? Okay, I'll say it. That's a recognizability that Bob Costas and Al Michaels, two very good announcers, will never enjoy.

I've been all over the world. I've been regaled in every country, including behind the Iron Curtain. In Egypt, they gave me a plaque.

Another source of great satisfaction for me is the mail. Now that I'm off TV, the hate mail doesn't come anymore, but after a TV guest appearance, or after a newspaper or wire service story, I'll get letters and calls from old friends, many of whom are important people.

A favorite example is this letter from a senior vice president of Feed the Children:

Feed the Children
Washington Office
P.O. Box 8001
Alexandria, Virginia 22306

May 1, 1990

Dear Howard:

I read Monday's piece about you in *The Washington Post*. I can attest to the fact people around the world love Howard Cosell.

Some months ago in a small village about thirty miles outside of Kinshasa, Zaire, the principal of the church school had his children all dressed and primed to sing a welcome for me. As we stood outside the ramshackle school, the principal leaned over smiling and asked me in broken English did I know Howard Cosell.

Without hesitation, I told him I certainly did and gave him a brief report—however limited—as to what you were doing. The children sang with gusto. My interpreter informed me the principal announced that I was a friend of Howard Cosell's.

I pray that your wife's health continues to improve.

Most cordially,
Harry Covert, Senior Vice President

I've met a lot of great people, and many have befriended me.

For those who haven't seen things my way, I don't give a damn. At this stage of my life, I don't have time for feuding.

My goal in writing this book was to define the issues, detail the ills, uncover the unholy alliances, and emphasize that when it comes to sports, our priorities are out of whack. The only logical conclusion is there's plenty wrong in sports, and you can only correct the evils by exposing them and discussing them.

CHAPTER TWENTY-ONE

My Lost Treasure

Postscript

On November 18, 1990, three days after I had finished the manuscript for this book, my beloved wife of forty-six and a half years died of a heart attack. It was a sudden attack at five o'clock in the morning. Regrettably, I was away in Kansas City on a speaking engagement for a charitable organization. The death of Emmy is something that I've always feared. And as fate would have it, I was away from her side at the time of death, just as I had been away from my father when he expired. Emmy was loved throughout the broadcast and sports industries. She was a great person, a great wife, companion, friend, mother, and grandmother. I've always said that I couldn't go on without her. But being the fighter that she was, she would, I know, want me to go on. I still have two wonderful daughters, five wonderful grandchildren, and a world of friends. And I have the memories of forty-six and a half wonderful years with Emmy.

A week after Emmy's death, I returned to my ABC Radio program, and in my first program after her death, I delivered the following eulogy:

> This is the most difficult broadcast I have ever had to do in my whole life. A man's grief should be a private thing, but sometimes there has to be public notice taken.

I have lost the treasure of my life. My wife and I had forty-six and a half marvelous years together. Moments never to be forgotten, people never to be forgotten.

And everybody who ever touched Emmy Cosell knew that she was special, that she was warm, compassionate, that she was not fragile. She was valiant. Everybody who ever knew her knew that she was indeed the better half of my life. It will be difficult to go on without her, but go on I must, with our two daughters, with our five grandchildren. Life has been so good to us, sometimes almost unbearably so.

And she knew my favorite poem. She knew that the most beautiful poem ever written was John Keats's "Ode to a Nightingale." "My heart aches, and a drowsy numbness pains my sense, as though of hemlock I had drunk, or tasted of flora or some sweet Provençal song." And then the poem went on because John Keats was just a boy, even though a genius. And death was waiting for him. And he understood that life is but transitory, and so is beauty. He understood all of it. Everything. He said to himself, "Forlorn! the very word is like a bell to toll me back from thee to my sole self." He knew that he was dying. But he also knew that he had tasted the beauties of life. And he wrote the most sensitive words ever written.

And so I say in memory of my glorious wife, my heart aches and a drowsy numbness pains my sense, and I thank whatever gods may be, Emmy, for your unconquerable soul.

On December 5, hundreds crammed into the All Souls Unitarian Church at Eightieth and Lexington Avenue in Manhattan to attend a memorial service for Emmy. It was a fitting service honoring a Presbyterian, a WASP who for forty-six and a half years had lived a wonderful life with a Jew. Football great Andy Robustelli, literary great Robert Lipsyte, and John Cardinal O'Connor delivered eulogies for Emmy. Singing great Robert Merrill sang Emmy's favorite songs. It was a fine tribute to a great lady.

INDEX

Aaron, Hank, 112–13
ABC television network, 7–8, 153
  college football and, 61, 62, 63
  Forte case and, 142–45
Acri, Mike, 246
Adams, Margo, 320–21, 323
Agassi, Andre, 343
Agents, 65–79
  registration of, 78–79
  state laws and, 38, 78–79
  Walters-Bloom case and, 69–77
AIDS, 313–18
Aikens, Willie, 331
Albert, Marv, 18
Alexander, Ron, 207
Ali, Lonnie, 266
Ali, Muhammad, 124–25, 193, 261–68
  financial status of, 265–66
  impersonation episode, 266–67

  physical problems of, 261–62, 263–64, 265
  racism and, 105
  ranking of, as fighter, 266
  Saddam Hussein and, 268
  Tyson compared with, 251
Allen, Doug, 214
Allen, Hank, 95
Allen, Paul, 227
Amphetamines, 327–28
Anderson, Dave, 141
Anderson, Paul, 228
Andujar, Joaquin, 330
Anti-Semitism, 93–94
Antitrust suits:
  vs. NBA, 223
  vs. NFL, 163–64, 177–84, 199–207
Antley, Chris, 341
Aponte, Angelo, 151
Arena operations, 241–43
Argyros, George, 243, 308
Arizona State University, 235
Arkansas, University of, 110

Arledge, Roone, 9, 143, 346
  on critics, 347
  Csonka-Kiick-Warfield
    interview and, 210
  USFL suit and, 182
Arum, Bob, 3, 10, 255
Ashe, Arthur, 89, 120, 122
Auburn Hills, 242, 243
Auerbach, Red, 97
Augusta National, 96, 120
Axthelm, Pete, 146
Azcarraga, Emilio, 348

Baker, Russell, 1
Baldwin, Rita, 324
Barkley, Charles, 87, 156
Barnett, Bob, 232
Bartholomay, Bill, 27
Bascom, Roberta, 19
Baseball:
  designated hitter rule in, 300
  drug policy and, 330–32
  Hall of Fame, 139–42
  labor dispute of 1990 and,
    299
  racism and, 102–13
  salaries in, 2, 230–31
  sexual misconduct and,
    320–23
Baseball Assistance Team
  (BAT), 288–89
Baseball Writers Association,
  140
Basketball. *See* College
  athletics; National
  Basketball Association.
Bassett, John, 210
Baughan, Maxie, 55
Beathard, Bobby, 175, 350
Beauchamp, William, 62, 63
Becker, Boris, 359

Bell, David, 25
Bell, Theo, 114
Benitez, Wilfred, 250
Benson, Bob, 6, 285
Bergesch, Bill, 128
Bernstein, Al, 10
Berra, Dale, 330
Berst, David, 38, 54
Bertelsen, Dick, 214
Bertovich, Ron, 86
Berwanger, Jay, 35
Betting on sports. *See*
  Gambling.
Bias, Len, 49, 329
Bickerstaff, Bernie, 97–98
Bidwill, William, 234–36
Biggs, Tyrell, 251
Bingham, Howard, 261, 263
Bissell, John, 205, 212
Blab, Uwe, 79
Black athletes, 122–25. *See
  also* Racism. Props 48 and
  42 and, 81–82, 84–86,
  88–90
Black, Ivery, 335–36
Blaik, Earl "Red," 304–05
Blair, Joe, 315
Blood doping (packing), 344
Bloom, Lloyd, 69–77
Blue, Vida, 331
Bodzianowski, Craig, 245–46
Boggs, Wade, 320–21
Borg, Bjorn, 342
Bork, Robert, 129
Bornstein, Steve, 352
Boston Globe, 351, 352
Boswell, Tom, 230
Bosworth, Brian, 55
Bowlen, Pat, 167
Bowling, Ronald G., 157
Bowman, Harold, 293

Boxing, 245–68
  disabled fighters and, 245–47
  federal commission for, 254–57
  monies involved in, 2–3
  promoter agreements in, 255–57
  racism in, 122–24
Boyer, Kenny, 303
Brademas, John, 31, 33, 34
Bradley, Bill, 41, 79
  Fleisher and, 221
Bradley, Tom, 240
Braman, Norman, 166
Branca, John, 256
Brandt, Gil, 57
Breland, Mark, 249
Bridgeman, Junior, 222, 223
Bright, Bum, 244
British, betting by, 159–60
Brokaw, Tom, 98, 99, 100
Brooks, Jack, 239
Brower, Derek, 341
Brown, Bobby, 11
Brown, Dale, 43
Brown, Jim, 6, 115, 202
Brown, Larry, 48–49
Brown, Rita Mae, 319
Browne, Joe, 172
Browner, Joey, 118
Browning, Michael, 243
Broyles, Frank, 62
Bryant, Cullen, 207
Buck, Jack, 350, 355
Buoniconti, Nick, 147
Burke, Mike, 302
Burroughs, Ken, 335
Byars, Walter, 39
Bynoe, Peter, 243

Cabell, Enos, 330
Cahan, William G., 11
Calipari, John, 86
Cambra, Joseph, 137
Campanella, Roy, 106
Campanis, Al, 102–04
Canseco, Jose, 230
Cap Cities, 180, 183, 352
Capital Centre, 242
Capitelli, Frank, 77
Caray, Harry, 131, 353
Carbo, Frankie, 249
Caridi, Joseph, 277
Carnegie-Mellon, 35
Carnesecca, Lou, 153–54
Carter, Cris, 73
Cashen, Frank, 111
Causwell, Duane, 86
Cawood, David, 326
Cayton, Bill, 122, 249, 250
CBS television network, 19
  Jimmy the Greek and, 116–18
Chaney, John, 84–87, 89, 95
Chapman, Rex, 87
Chass, Murray, 291
Cheerleaders, racism and, 102
Cher, 8
Chicago, University of, 34
Cincinnati Reds, Rose and, 128, 137, 138
Cindrich, Ralph, 68
Clancy, Gil, 10
Clark, Perry, 153
Clark, Will, 111, 230
Clay, Nigel, 325
Clements, Bill, 56
Clements, Kathe, 70–71
Clemson, 50, 51, 58, 59
Clendenon, Donn, 106, 107, 331–32

Clift, Montgomery, 312
Coaches:
  black, 97–98, 110, 114,
    118–19
  college, 44–55
Cobb, Reggie, 341
Cocaine, 327–29
Cohn, Roy, 314
College athletics, 31–90
  agents and, 67–79
  coaches in, 44–55
  economics of, 28–29
  educational failures and,
    36–37, 40–41, 81–90
  eligibility for, 63, 64
  foreign players in, 79–81
  Giamatti on, 28–30
  gambling and, 152–54,
    156–57
  NCAA and. *See* National
    Collegiate Athletic
    Association.
  Props 48 and 42 and,
    81–82, 84–85, 88–89
  recruiting for, 42–44, 51–54
  Senate hearings on, 33
  TV deals and, 61–63
  UAA and, 34–35
  win-at-all-costs theory in, 37
College Football Association,
  61, 62, 63
Collins, Bud, 351
Collins, Tony, 339
Colombo crime family, 72,
  278
Colonial League, 34
Columbia University, 64
Concessions, income, 241–42
Cone, David, 271, 283
Conflicts of interest, media
  and, 349, 352, 353–54

Conner, William C., 257
Connors, Jimmy, 320
Conrad, Harold, 268
Contracts, college coaching, 45
Cook, Marlowe, 171
Cooke, Jack Kent, 243
Cooper, Chuck, 97
Cope, Dennis, 263
Cornwell, David, 164
Cosby, Bill, 84
Cosell, Emmy, xii–xiii, 358
  death of, 365
  eulogy for, 365–66
Costas, Bob, 18, 363
Courson, Steve, 333
Court, Margaret, 319
Covert, Harry, 363
Crack, 328
Craig, Jack, 352
Creighton University, 40
Crites, D. Michael, 136
Crosetti, Frank, 362
Csonka, Larry, 210–17
Culverhouse, Hugh F., 118,
  165–66
  Rozelle's retirement and,
    165, 167, 175
  on Stanton, 101

Daily News. See New York
  Daily News.
D'Amato, Cus, 249, 250
Daniel, Robert, 246
Daniels, Aaron, 6, 175
Daniels, Lloyd, 85, 90
Davidson, Bill, 243
Davila, Jaime, 348
Davis, Al, 118–19, 207,
  236–40
  Cardinals' relocation and,
    235, 236–37

Parcells and, 334
Rozelle's relationship with, 174, 237
Upshaw and, 194
USFL suit and, 177
Davis, Willie, 114, 115, 120
Dawkins, Pete, 41
Dawson, Len, 147
Day, Pat, 341
DeBartolo, Eddie, 350–51
DeBartolo, Ed, Sr., 350
Debevoise, Dickinson R., 223
DeBusschere, Dave, 221
Deford, Frank, xiii, 348–49
DeJesus, Esteban, 316
Dell, Donald, 349
Dennis, Michael, 253
DePaso, Tom, 72, 78
Dershowitz, Alan, 333
Designated hitter rule, 300
Detroit Pistons, 243
Dierdorf, Dan, 350
DiMaggio, Joe, 304, 305, 362
Dixon, King, 156
Donahue, Phil, 118
Donaldson, Sam, 7, 8
Donlan, Jack, 204, 211, 224
Dooley, Vince, 62
Doty, David, 199, 201–02
Douglas, James "Buster," 122, 251, 254–55
Douglas, Kirk, 362
Douglass, Maurice, 71
Dowd, John, 129
  Steinbrenner case and, 272–74, 276–77, 286, 294
Dowling, William, 279
Drexler, Clyde, 232

Driesell, Charles "Lefty," 49, 53
Drugs, 327–45
  baseball and, 330–32
  NASCAR and, 317
  NFL and, 327–28, 332–39
  Olympics and, 343–45
  Operation Grouper and, 216
  Taylor story and, 333–39
  tennis and, 342
  testing for, 332–33, 342, 343–44
Dryden, Don, 326
Duffy, Kevin, 150
Duke University, 47
Dundee, Angelo, 258
Dungy, Tony, 115
Dupree, Marcus, 54
Duran, Roberto:
  DeJesus vs., 316
  Leonard vs., 2, 8–10, 257–58
Duren, John, 87
Durning, Charles, 9

Ebersol, Dick, 349
Eckert, William, 300
Economics, 1–5
  academics and, 28–29
  of coaching, college, 44–46
  franchise relocations and, 234–41
  franchise sales prices and, 227–28, 243–44
  of recruiting, 43–44, 51–54
  stadium (arena) operations and, 241–43
Edmond, Rayful, III, 88
Educational failures, 36, 40–41, 81–90
  economics and, 28–29

Edwards, Harry, 82, 99, 105
Elder, Lee, 120–21, 284
Elgin, Doug, 93
Ellenberger, Norm, 53
Emprise Corporation, 242
Enberg, Dick, xiii, 355
Erickson, Ed, 23
Ertmann, John, 279
Eskin, Howard, 86
ESPN, 352
    college football and, 61, 62
Evert, Chris, 320
Ewing, Patrick, 2

Federal Bureau of
        Investigation, Winfield
        and, 275, 277–78
Feed the Children, 363
Fehr, Donald, 298, 299, 331
Feinstein, John, 43, 49
Fenlon, Mary, 88
Ferrell, Earl, 340
Finks, Jim, 169–71, 174
Fitzgibbon, Henry, 128
Fleisher, Eric, 220
Fleisher, Larry, 68, 201,
        219–27
    Winfield story and, 274,
        278
Florida, University of, 156
Florio, Jim, 254
Foley, Tom, 254
Football. *See* College athletics;
        National Football League.
Foote, Edward, 32, 33
Ford, Danny, 58
Ford, Phil, 51
Foreign athletes, 79–81
Foreman, George, 254
Forte, Chet, 142–45, 355
Foss, Joe, 235

Foster, Bill, 32
Foster, George, 111
Fox, Gray, 1
Francesa, Mike, 145
Franchise relocation, 234–41
    baseball, 300
Franchise sales prices, 227–28,
        243–44
Franco, John, 283
Frank, Barry, 68, 265
Franklin, Ron, 341
Franzese, John "Sonny," 72
Franzese, Michael, 72, 77
Frazier, Joe, 251–52
Frazier, Marvis, 250–51
Frazier, Walt, 93
Free agency in football, 189,
        200, 204, 207
Freshman eligibility, 64
Friars Club, 8
Frieder, Bill, 154
Frohman, Al, 274, 277, 280
Frontiere, Georgia, 166, 237,
        323
Fugazy, Bill, 273, 278,
        283–84, 286, 306
Fugazy, John, 283
Fuhr, Grant, 341

Gambler's Anonymous,
        144–45
Gambling, 4, 126–61
    in foreign lands, 159–60
    Forte case and, 142–45
    NFL scandals of, 145–48
    oddsmakers and, 146–48,
        149
    point-shaving scandals and,
        152–54
    Rose case and, 126–42
    tout services and, 150–51

Gammons, Peter, 352
Garagiola, Joe, 288–89, 290–91, 303
Garber, Gene, 128
Garrett, Alvin, 95
Garvey, Cyndy, 321–22, 323
Garvey, Ed, 188, 195, 207, 288
Garvey, Steve, 321–23
Gastineau, Mark, 192
Gaston, Clarence "Cito," 109
Gatewood, Tom, 217
Gay, Everett, 71
Gaze, Andrew, 80
Georgetown University, 87–89
Gerulaitis, Vitas, 342
Giamatti, A. Bartlett, 15, 21–30, 90
    "clubbed fingers" story on, 11–13
    on college sports, 28–30
    death of, 22–26
    on media, 15–17, 20
    Pallone and, 318
    Rose case and, 22–23, 128–31, 137–38
Giamatti, Marcus, 24, 27
Giamatti, Toni, 24, 271
Gibson, Althea, 120
Gibson, Truman, 249
Gifford, Frank, 174, 289
Gilbert, Andre, 102
Giles, Bill, 128
Gillick, Pat, 109
Gimelstob, Gerry, 86
Gioiosa, Tommy, 131, 136
Giuliani, Rudolph, 291
Givens, Robin, 248, 250
Glennon, Ed, 214
Gobert, Pamela, 324
Golenbock, Peter, 46

Gooden, Dwight, 340
Goodwin, Michael, 271
Gotti, John, 142
Gowdy, Curt, 355
Graham, Otto, 290
Granath, Herbie, 352
Grantham, Charles, 222
Graziano, Rocky, 9
Green, Dallas, 295
Green, Hugh, 118
Green, Jerry, 262
Greenberg, Steve, 293
Gregory, Dick, 82
Gretzky, Wayne, 2, 359, 360
Griese, Bob, 362
Grouper, Operation, 216

Hagler, Marvin, 10, 257
Hall, Bernard, 325
Hall of Fame, Baseball, 139–42
Hallinan, Kevin, 276, 277
Hamill, Peter, 282
Hamilton, Leonard, 32
Hamlisch, Marvin, 321
Haney, Gerald W., 200
Hanson, John, 169
Harjoe, Benny, 246
Haskins, Clem, 110
Hauser, Tom, 266
Haywood, Spencer, 329
Hearns, Tommy, 257
Hebrew University, 361
Heffernan, Jim, 173
Helmsley, Leona, 136
Hemond, Roland, 108
Henderson, Tom "Hollywood," 329
Henefeld, Nadav, 79, 91–92
Hernandez, Keith, 312, 330, 339

Index

Hershey, Steve, 291
Hesburgh, Theodore, 74
Hess, Leon, 163, 175, 181
Heymann, Ira Michael, 39
Heymann, Philip B., 325
High, Tim, 156
High school betting scandal, 157
Hill, Calvin, 108
Hilliard, James, 133–34
Hindus, Myra, 326
Hirschfeld, Richard M., 267–68
Hoatling, Ed, 116
Holland, Al, 330
Holleder, Don, 304
Holmes, Larry, 263
Holtz, Lou, 63, 102
Holyfield, Evander, 249, 255, 360
Homosexuality, 318–20
    movie stars and, 311–12
    NFL players and, 314–16
Hookstratten, Ed, 68
Horford, Tito, 32–33
Houston Gamblers, 186
Howe, Steve, 331
Hudson, Rock, 312
Hunt, William E., 135
Hussein, Saddam, 268

Iacocca, Lee, 101
Ibuprofen, 317
Igwebuike, Donald, 340
Illinois, University of, 54
Inabet, B. C., 50, 51
Indiana State University, 92–93
Ingram, Charles, 252
Instant replay, 186

Intercollegiate sports. See College athletics; National Collegiate Athletic Association.
International Boxing Club, 249
International Boxing Federation, 247
International Management Group, 68, 220, 265
Irwindale, California, 237–38
Isaacs, Stan, 144, 347
Ivy League, 64–65

Jackson, Jesse, 107
Jackson, Mark, 156
Jackson, Reggie, 303
Jacobs brothers, 242
Jacobs, Dave, 258
Jacobs, Jimmy, 249, 250
Jaffe, Leo, 284
Janofsky, Michael, 166
Janszen, Paul, 131, 136
Jaqua, Jon, 314–15
Jastrow, Terry, 210
Jenkins, Sally, 271
Jewish athletes, 93–94
Jockeys, 121–22
John, Tommy, 281, 303
Johns Hopkins University, 34
Johnson, Ben, 343
Johnson, Jack, 122–23
Johnson, Jimmy, 33
Johnson, Magic, 119
Johnson, Peter, 320
Johnson, Ross, 259
Johnson, Thomas "Sarge," 9
Jones, Darryl "Pea Man," 246
Jones, James Morris, 252–53
Jones, Jerry, 244
Jones, K. C., 96–98
Jones, Roy, Jr., 253

Journalism:
 conflicts of interest in, 349,
  352, 353
 unprofessionalism in, 8–20
 women in, 96

Kahn, Roger, 131–33
Kaminsky, Art, 68, 346
Kapp, Joe, 207
Kashkin, Kenneth, 341, 342
Katz, Reuven, 129–30, 132,
  133, 310
Keating, Larry, 81
Keats, John, 279, 366
Kekich, Mike, 320
Kelly, Eamon, 153
Kelly, Jim, 186
Kemp, Jack, 169
Kentucky, University of, 48,
  52
Kessler, Jeff, 214–15
Keteyian, Armen, 153
Kiam, Victor, 96, 243
Kiick, Jim, 210, 216
Kilmer, Billy, 152
Kilroy, Gene, 268
Kindred, David, 14
 Ali stories by, 263, 267
 on Giamatti's death, 22, 26
King, Billie Jean, 319
King, Carl, 256
King, Chris, 92
King, Don, 10, 122
 contractual technique of,
  256
 Douglas litigation by,
  254–55
 Tyson and, 250, 254–55
King, Larry, 353–54
Kirk, Dana, 48
Kirkpatrick, Curry, 352

Kleber, Herbert, 341, 342
Klein, Dave, 212, 354
Klein, Moss, 354
Kleinman, Leonard, 293
Kluge, John, 283, 284
Knight, Bob, 42, 50, 79
 on gambling, 149, 153
Koch, Ed, 117, 330
Kopay, Dave, 313–15
Koppel, Ted, 102–03
Kornheiser, Tony, xiii
Kroc, Mrs. Ray, 243
Kubek, Tony, 350
Kuhn, Bowie, 106, 297, 355
 on critics, 309–10
 financial situation of, 301,
  307–09
 Giamatti and, 27
 NFL antitrust case and, 172
 Rose case and, 128, 141,
  309–10
 Steinbrenner's suspension
  by, 294
Kush, Frank, 313

Lacewell, Larry, 55
Lacy, Lee, 330
Lalonde, Donny, 257
Landini, Richard G., 93
Landis, Murray, 362
Landry, Tom, 329
Lanier, Bob, 222
LaRussa, Tony, 360
Las Vegas, 154, 155
Lee, Bertram, 243
Lee, Robert, 247
Leisure, Peter K., 178, 183
Lemon, Jim, 95
Leonard, Jeffrey, 111, 330
Leonard, Sugar Ray, 247,
  257–58

Leonard, Sugar Ray (*cont.*)
  Duran vs., 2, 8–10, 257
Leventhal, Mike, 286
Levin, Mark, 78
Levin, Rich, 287
Lewis, Tommy, 57
Liberace, 312
Lidz, Franz, 17
Lilly, Glen, 324
Lipsyte, Robert, 366
Little, Larry, 211
Lloyd, John, 320
Loans, agent-player, 67, 70
LoCasale, Al, 175
Locke, Tates, 50–51, 92–93, 154
Lombardi, Vince, 65–66, 314, 316
Los Angeles Raiders, xiii, 236–41
Louis, Joe, 123, 124
Lubeski, Dave, 286
Lucas, John, 52
Lupica, Mike, 12, 270, 271, 290
  on Cosell, 355
  Giamatti story by, 11–12
Lustberg, Lawrence, 144
Lynn, Mike, 101, 118

Maas, Kevin, 295
Mack, Kevin, 340
Mackey, John, 180
Madden, Bill, 289–90
Madden, John, 347
Maegle, Dickie, 57
Malone, Mary, 53
Malone, Moses, 52–54
Manley, Dexter, 40–41, 339
Mantle, Mickey, 141, 302–03, 305–06

Mara, Wellington, 163, 169, 181, 236
Maradona, Diego, 231
Maris, Roger, 113
Marist College, 80
Marovich, George M., 76–77
Marshall, Robert O., 149
Marshall, Wilber, 200
Martin, Billy, 301–05
Martin, Jerry, 331
Martzke, Rudy, 347
Maryland, University of, 49–50, 52
Matthews, Shane, 156
Matuszak, John, 329
Maxwell Club dinner, 173
Mays, Willie, 141
Mazer, Bill, 338
McCarthy, Dan, 293
McCarver, Tim, 350, 353
McCormack, Mark, 68
McDonough, Will, 325, 352
McEnroe, John, 342, 360
McGuire, Al, 79
McGuire, Paul, 146
McLain, Denny, 100
McLaughlin, Ed, 175
McMillen, Tom, 47, 79
McNeil, Freeman, 204, 205
McNiff, Phil, 279
Medenica, Rajko, 262–63
Media. *See also* Print media; Television.
  conflicts of interest in, 349, 352, 353
  sensationalism and, 312
  unprofessionalism in, 8–20
Meggett, Dave, 324
Mendenhall, Rebecka, 322
Merchant, Larry, 147
Merrill, Robert, 366

Merrill, Stump, 295
Metzenbaum, Howard, 33
Miami, Florida, 1989 riots in, 164–65
Miami of Florida, University of, 31–33
Michael, Gene "Stick," 295
Michaels, Al, 18, 363
Michaels, Walt, 151
Michigan, University of, 36
Michigan State University, 45–46
Miles, Leo, 164
Mill, Andy, 320
Millard, Keith, 186
Miller, Arthur, 246
Miller, Marvin, 296
Mills, Chris, 48
Milner, John, 330
Mission, Shawnee, 81
Mitchell, Bobby, 114
Modell, Art, 163, 173, 181
Moegle, Dickie, 57
Molloy, Edward, 62
Monopolistic status:
   of NBA, 223
   of NFL, 163, 177–84, 199–207
Monroe, Earl "the Pearl," 221
Montana, Joe, 351
Moral standards, 311–12
Morrall, Earl, 362
Morris, Kyle, 156
Mortensen, Chuck, 215
Morton, Janks, 258
Moulton, Cheryl Ann, 322
Mourning, Alonzo, 88, 91
Mowatt, Zeke, 325
Muhammad, Herbert, 265
Mulcahy, Robert, 169
Mulvoy, Mark, 351–52

Munson, Thurman, 173
Murchison, Clint, 244
Murphy, Isaac, 121
Musburger, Brent, 116, 338
Museum of Broadcasting, 361
Myerson, Harvey, 180, 307–09

Nack, William, 181–82
Nadel, Norbert A., 129
NASCAR, drugs and, 317
Nash, John, 90
National, The, 271, 291, 348–50
National Basketball Association (NBA), 218–29
   antitrust suits and, 222–23
   expansion clubs in, 227–28
   international involvement of, 226–27
   salaries in, 2, 220
   television and, 2, 228
National Basketball Association Players Association (NBAPA), 220
   decertification move by, 223–24
National Collegiate Athletic Association (NCAA), 30, 37–40
   agents and, 70, 79
   discipline by, 48, 54, 55–56, 58–60
   Props 48 and 42 and, 81, 84–85, 88–89
   sexual harassment and, 326
National Football League (NFL), 3
   censorship by, 172, 182–83
   commissioner selection by, 168–72
   drugs and, 327–28, 332–39

National Football League
(NFL) *(cont.)*
franchise relocations and,
234–41
free agency in, 190, 200,
204, 207
gambling scandals of,
145–48
homosexuality in, 313–16
monopolistic status of, 163,
177–82, 199–207
Plan B system of, 200, 204,
213
racism and, 113–20, 164
Rozelle's retirement and,
162–69
sexual harassment case of,
325–26
strike (1987) of, 188–94
TV deal of, 2, 173
USFL players in, 185–86
USFL suit vs., 163, 177–84
National Football League
Management Council, 204
National Football League
Players Association
(NFLPA), 78, 165,
189–210
antitrust suit by, 199–207
Csonka vs., 210–17
decertification of, 201
1987 strike by, 188–94
National Football League
Properties, 209
Navratilova, Martina, 319
NBC television network, 18,
19
Notre Dame deal with, 61,
62
Nebraska, University of, 38
Nederlander, Bob, 294

Neinas, Chuck, 62
Nelson, Judy, 319
New England Patriots,
183–84, 325–26
Newhouse, Robert, 57
New Jersey Giants, 333–37
New Mexico, University of,
52, 53
Newspapers. *See* Print media.
New York *Daily News,* 151
commercial spokesmen for,
282
Giamatti story in, 11–13
New York Mets, 111
New York Post, 151
New York University, 35
New York Yankees, 269–70,
290, 295
Norris, Jim, 249
Norris, Terry, 258
North Carolina State
University, 46–47, 51–52,
67, 68–69, 153
Notre Dame, 61–64
Nuxhall, Joe, 134

Oakland bid to Raiders,
238–42
O'Connor, Chuck, 299
O'Connor, John Cardinal, 366
Oddsmakers, 147–48, 149
Oklahoma State University, 41
Olson, Lisa, 96, 325–26
Olympics, drugs and, 343–45
O'Malley, Peter, 103
O'Malley, Walter, 239, 241
O'Neil, Terry, 19, 346
Oregon, gambling in, 160–61
O'Reilly, Bill, 23
Orza, Gene, 284
Owens, Jesse, 123

Packer, Billy, 79, 93
Paine, Thomas, 197
Palace (Auburn Hills), 242
Pallone, Dave, 318
Palmer, Arnold, 284
Palmer, Paul, 76
Parcells, Bill, 156
    drug policy and, 334–35,
        336–37
Pardee, Jack, 186
Parker, Dave, 330
Paterno, Joe, 63, 64
Patriot League, 34
Patterson, Floyd, 264
Paul, Gabe, 294
Payton, Walter, 119
Pearlman, Bob, 361
Peete, Calvin, 120
Peppler, Pat, 66
Perez, Pascual, 269
Perles, George, 45
Perryman, Robert, 325
Peters, Ron, 128, 131
Peterson, Carl, 186
Peterson, Fritz, 320
Phelps, Richard "Digger,"
        63–64, 82, 83
Philbin, Regis, 321–22
Phoenix Cardinals, 233–34
Pierce, Ted, 66
Pilson, Neal, 19–20, 116, 147
Piniella, Lou, 109, 138
Pinzka, Barbara, 134
Pitino, Rick, 48
Pitts, Elijah, 115
Plan B system in NFL, 200,
        204, 213
Point-shaving scandals,
        152–54
Point Spread Consultants, 150

Pollin, Abe, 242
Polonia, Luis, 323
Portland Trailblazers, 227, 232
Powell, Marvin, 199
Power, John, 352
Price, Mark, 93
Price, Peter O., 348
Pringle, Wes, 156
Print media:
    conflicts of interest and,
        349, 352, 353
    gambling promotion by, 149
    sensationalism and, 312
    television alliance with, 5
Pritzker family, 241
Probert, Bob, 100, 341
Propositions 48 and 42, 81,
        84–85, 88–89
Pryor, Aaron, 246
Purpura, Dominic, 265

Quinlan, Sterling, 357
Quinn, Jim, 201–06, 214, 283

Racism, 91–125
    in baseball, 102–14
    boxing and, 122
    Campanis interview and,
        102–04
    cheerleaders and, 102
    coaching and, 97–98, 110,
        114, 115, 118–19
    in football, 113–20
    jockeys and, 121–22
    management positions and,
        106–10, 114–15, 119
    New York Mets and, 111
    oversensitivity vs., 94–96
    Props 48 and 42 and, 81,
        84–85, 88–89

Racism (*cont.*)
San Francisco Giants and, 111
Stanton letter and, 98–102
Radovich, Bill, 206
Randle, Sonny, 55
Rape, 324–25
Ratliff, Alonzo, 245
Ravo, Vincent, 337
Reagan, Ronald, 188
Recruitment for college sports, 42–44, 51–55
Redlich, Norman, 236
Redshirting, 64
Reedy, George, 301
Reizner, Sonny, 4, 155, 161
Renfro, Sandra, 282
Rentzel, Lance, 314
Reporting. *See also* Print media; Television.
unprofessionalism in, 8–20
women in, 96
Reynolds, Burt, 320
Richards, Derwin, 253
Richardson, Nolan, 110
Richmond, Tim, 316–17
Rickey, Branch, 103
Ringo, Jim, 65
Ripken, Cal, Sr., 108
Ritchie, James, 159
Robbie, Joe, 235
Roberts, Cliff, 120
Roberts, Oral, 52–53
Robertson, Oscar, 222, 261
Robinson, Eddie, 84
Robinson, Frank, 107–09
Robinson, Jackie, 89, 112, 124
Campanis and, 103
Robinson, Jackie, Jr., 124
Robinson, Rachel, 124, 284
Robustelli, Andy, 300, 366

Rogers, Don, 329
Rogers, Johnny, 38
Roland, Johnny, 119
Rollins, Wayne "Tree," 51
Rona, Barry, 299
Rooney, Andy, 117
Rooney, Dan, 163
Rooney, Kevin, 122, 149
Roosevelt, Theodore, 30
Roper, Ruth, 250, 282
Rosario, Edwin, 250
Rose, Pete, 14, 126–42
Giamatti and, 22–23, 128–31, 137–38
Hall of Fame and, 139–42
Pallone and, 318
Rosen, Al, 111
Rosenbloom, Carroll, 146, 166
Rosenthal, Dick, 62
Rosner, Steve, 336
Ross, Judy, 322
Ross, Kevin, 40
Rothman, Frank, 180–81, 182
Rozelle, Alvin Pete, 102
cocktail meeting with, 174–76
on Csonka switching leagues, 210
Davis and, 237
franchise relocation and, 235
on oddsmakers, 147
racism and, 114
retirement of, 162–68
USFL suit and, 179, 182–84
Rozelle, Carrie, 165, 176
Rozier, Mike, 323–24
Rubin, Carl, 129
Rubinstein, Howard, 285
Rudolph, Wilma, 262
Rukeyeser, Louis, 232

Rule, Elton, 355
Russell, Bill, 97
Ruth, Babe, 113
Ryan, Bob, 352
Ryan, Sylvester, 249
Ryan, Tim, 10

Saam, By, 174
Sabatini, Gabriela, 260
Sacramento, California, 238
Salaries, 2, 231, 232
    baseball, 2, 230–32
    college coaching, 44–46
    NBA, 2, 220
Salem, Joe, 102
Saltzburg, Stephen, 267
Sanchez, Miriam, 178
Sanchez, Willie, 92
San Francisco Giants, 111, 300
Scab players (in 1987 strike),
    190–94
Scamdicappers, 150–51
Schembechler, Bo, 74, 174
Schlichter, Art, 145
Schmeling, Max, 123
Schoemehl, Vincent, Jr., 236
Schramm, Tex, 57, 118, 163,
    181
Schultz, Richard, 39
Scully, Vin, 350
Seales, Ray, 247
Seaver, Tom, 140, 281
Secretariat, 359
Selig, Bud, 288, 297
    Giamatti and, 24, 26
Senate hearings on college
    sports, 33
Serling, Rod, 257
Seton Hall, 80
Severine, Lou, 175
Sexual assault, 324–26

Sexual misconduct, 311–12,
    320–26
Shackleford, Charles, 67, 153
Shanahan, Mike, 118
Shell, Art, 119, 194
Shelton, Craig, 87
Sherrill, Jackie, 58
Shoal Creek Country Club, 96
Shula, Don, 362
Siegel, Herb, 174, 259
Sifford, Charlie, 120
Silas, Paul, 222
Silverdome, 243
Silverman, Ed, 143
Simmons, Chet, 186
Simmons, Edwin, 71
Simon, Bill, 211, 355
Sinatra, Frank, 284
Skiles, Scott, 100
Slaughter, John, 50, 75
Sloan, Norm, 51
Slusher, Howard, 68
Smith, Ballard, 280
Smith, Curt, 347
Smith, Dean, 33
Smith, James "Bonecrusher,"
    251
Smith, James McCoy "Yazoo,"
    180
Smith, Jerry, 313–16
Smith, Lonnie, 330
Smits, Rik, 80
Smulyan, Jeffrey, 243, 308
Snider, Ed, 241
Snyder, Jimmy "the Greek,"
    116–18, 146, 151
Soccer, 231
Sokolove, Michael, 128
Sorensen, Larry, 330
South Carolina, University of,
    156

Southeastern Louisiana State, 54

Southern Methodist University, 56

Southwestern Louisiana, University of, 54

Spanos, Alex, 181, 237

Specter, Arlen, 182

Spellman, Francis Cardinal, 302

Spence, Jim, 183

Spiegel, S. Arthur, 135

Spira, Howard, 158, 269, 277–78, 280, 285–86, 291–92

Sportservice, 242

Sports Illustrated, 351

Sports reporting, 8–20 *See also* Print media; Television.
women in, 96

Stadium operations, 241–43

Stahl, Lesley, 85

Stallings, Gene, 236

Stanton, Roger, 91, 98–102, 117

Starr, Kenneth W., 203

State laws, agents and, 38, 78

Steinberg, Leigh, 68

Steinbrenner, George, 269–70, 272–96, 306
commissioner's hearing and, 290–92
Donaldson interview with, 7–8
Fugazy and, 273–74, 283
good side of, 288–89, 290
Vincent and, 270, 272, 274, 276, 287–89, 291–96
Winfield and, 273–83

Yankees' status and, 269–70, 290, 295

Steinbrenner, Hank, 293

Stern, David, 218–19, 229
Fleisher and, 220–23, 224–27
gambling and, 147, 156
salary of, 2
Williams's (Pat) comments on, 229

Steroids, 332–33, 341, 343

Stone, Leonard, 11–12

Strauss, Bob, 171

Strawberry, Darryl, 111, 230, 231, 232, 340

Strikebreakers, 190–94

Strikes, NFLPA, 188–95

Stroud, Ed, 95

Sulaiman, José, 254

Sullivan, Billy, 101, 243

Summerall, Pat, 174

Super Bowl ticket prices, 233

Super Bowl XXIII, 164–65

Sutton, Don, 321

Sutton, Eddie, 48

Swann, Lynn, 101

Swanson, Dennis, 62, 299

Switzer, Barry, 54–55, 155

Tagliabue, Paul, 96, 202
Davis and, 239
early decisions by, 173
naming of, as commissioner, 171
racism and, 340
sexual harassment case and, 325–26

Talese, Gay, 12

Tampa Bay Bucs, 118, 165

Tarkanian, Jerry, 47–48, 85

Tartikoff, Brandon, 349

Taylor, Lawrence, 3, 333–39
Television, 2–3. *See also specific networks.*
  booth talent in, 350
  college football and, 61–63
  conflicts of interest in, 349, 352, 353
  critics' relationship with, 346–47
  gambling promotion by, 146–48, 150
  instant replay and, 186
  NBA and, 2, 228
  NFL deal with, 2, 173
  oddsmakers on, 146–48
  print media alliance with, 5
  unprofessionalism in, 8–11, 17–20
Temple University, 76, 84
Tennis:
  drug testing in, 342
  homosexuality and, 319–20
  sex discrimination in, 324
Texas, state of, 38, 56–58
Texas, University of, 156
Theokas, Charlie, 86
Thomas, Calvin, 340–41
Thomas, Candace, 322
Thompson, David, 51
Thompson, John, 86–89
  compensation of, 45, 46
  gambling and, 154–55
Thompson, Norm, 200
Thompson, Richard B., 157
Ticketmaster, 241
Ticket prices, 233, 235
Timson, Michael, 325
Toran, Stacy, 329
Torres, José, 248
Tose, Leonard, 146, 166
Tout services, 150–52

Townshend, Graeme, 92
Trainer, Mike, 258
Tremor, 359
Trump, Donald, 183–84, 258–61
  Don King and, 250, 255
Tulane University, 152–53
Turfway Park, 136
Turner, John, 88
Turner, Ted, 284
Tyson, Mike, 122, 248–51

Ueberroth, Peter, 2, 297
  drug policy and, 330
  gambling and, 184
  Giamatti and, 27–28
  Kuhn and, 310
  racial problems and, 105, 107
  Rose case and, 128, 130
  Steinbrenner and, 277
Uecker, Bob, 303
Unions, 187–89
  agents and, 78
  baseball, 299–300
  NBAPA, 220–24
  NFLPA. *See* National Football League Players Association.
Unitas, Johnny, 152
United States Football League, 163, 177–84
  players from, in NFL, 185–86
University Athletic Association, 34–35
University of Oklahoma, 46, 55, 340
Upshaw, Gene, 165, 189, 194–99, 201, 202, 204
  on Cosell, 356

Upshaw, Gene *(cont.)*
  Csonka vs., 211–12
Urine tests for drugs, 333
USA Today, 346, 348
Usher, Harry, 186

Valenzuela, Pat, 341
Valvano, Jim, 46–47, 67, 68
Vecsey, George, 141, 319
Vincent, Francis T. "Fay,"
      270–72, 284
  first year in office of,
      298–300
  gambling and, 146
  on Giamatti's death, 23–24
  Kuhn and, 306–10
  media and, 271
  Rose case and, 134
  Steinbrenner and, 270, 272,
      274, 276, 286–89, 291–96
Visser, Lesley, 351
Vitale, Dick, 53
Volk, Jan, 97
Voy, Robert O., 327–29, 333,
      343–44

Wade, Bob, 50
Wagering. *See* Gambling.
Waitkus, Eddie, 320
Walker, Wyatt, 361
Wallace, Lawrence, 203
Walsh, Bill, 350
Walsh, Claire, 325
Walters, Norby, 69–77
Walton, Joe, 175–76
Ward, Bruce, 80
Ware, Andre, 38, 101
Warfield, Paul, 114, 210
Waring, James, 245
Warren, Mike, 151
Washburn, Chris, 46–47, 81

Washington, Claudell, 330
Washington Post, The, 95
Washington University of St.
      Louis, 35
Watson, Arthur, 147
Weinberg, Larry, 227
Weiss, Don, 174
Welsh, George, 304
Werblin, Sonny, 207
Werner, Roger, 352
Werner, Tom, 243
Westhead, Paul, 329–30
Westin, Av, 23
Wexler, Anne, 171
Wexler, Arnie, 134, 144
WFAN, 144–45, 291, 295
Whisenant, John, 52
White, Bill, 21, 110, 300,
      306
White, Mark, 57
Whitfield, Shelby, 5–6, 155
  Parcells and, 324
  on racism, 95
  Spira and, 285–86
  sportscasters and, 351
Wiestart, John, 47
Wiggins, Allen, 313, 317–18
Wiley, Ralph, 352
Wilkinson, Art, 217
Williams, Doug, 99, 100, 185
Williams, Edward Bennett, 49,
      107–08, 175
Williams, Gary, 50
Williams, John "Hot Rod," 2,
      152
Williams, Pat, 228
Williams, Ted, 127
Wilpon, Fred, 111
Wilson, Larry, 236
Wilson, Lionel, 239
Wilson, Stanley, 165, 339

Wilson, Willie, 331
Winfield, Dave, 271, 273–83
Winfield Foundation, 275, 277, 280–83
Winter, Ralph, 179
Witherspoon, Tim, 256
WJLA-TV, 19, 340
Wolter, Steve, 135
Women reporters, 96
Wood, Willie, 115
Woods, Tony, 71
Woolf, Bob, 67–68, 339
World Boxing Council, 257
World Series of 1989, 298
WRC-TV, 19, 116
Wright, Bertha, 253

Wussler, Bob, 284
Wyche, Sam, 96, 173
Wynn, Steve, 255, 260

Yablonski, Chip, 215
Yesalis, Charles, 341–42
Young, Coleman A., 262
Young, George, 324, 334, 336
Young, Jimmy, 254
Young, Perry Deane, 314
Young, Steve, 351
Younger, Paul "Tank," 114

Zane, William, 25
Zucker, Steve, 70

VALVANO

Jim Valvano
with Curry Kirkpatrick

A provocative memoir by one of today's most outspoken and colorful sports figures who takes readers inside the pressure-cooker world of championship-level college basketball.

Jim Valvano became one of the best known coaches in college basketball during his long, successful career guiding the North Carolina State Wolfpack to national prominence. Now, for the first time, with his unique court-side perspective and with his flair for outspoken observations and outrageous humor, Valvano tells his story his way.

Available from Pocket Books

POCKET
B O O K S

44-02